The Vision of William concerning

PIERS THE PLOWMAN

BY

WILLIAM LANGLAND

(OR LANGLEY)

ACCORDING TO THE VERSION
REVISED AND ENLARGED BY THE AUTHOR
ABOUT A.D. 1377

Edited by the
REV. WALTER W. SKEAT
LITT.D., D.C.L., LL.D., PH.D.

Elrington and Bosworth Professor of
Anglo-Saxon in the
University of Cambridge

TENTH EDITION
REVISED

OXFORD
AT THE CLARENDON PRESS

Oxford University Press, Ely House, London W. 1

GLASGOW NEW YORK TORONTO MELBOURNE WELLINGTON
CAPE TOWN SALISBURY IBADAN NAIROBI LUSAKA ADDIS ABABA
BOMBAY CALCUTTA MADRAS KARACHI LAHORE DACCA
KUALA LUMPUR HONG KONG TOKYO

FIRST EDITION 1869
TENTH EDITION 1923
REPRINTED 1928, 1932, 1940
1944, 1948, 1950, 1953, 1958
1962, 1965, 1968

REPRINTED LITHOGRAPHICALLY IN GREAT BRITAIN
AT THE UNIVERSITY PRESS, OXFORD
BY VIVIAN RIDLER
PRINTER TO THE UNIVERSITY

CONTENTS.

INTRODUCTION.

THE title 'Piers Plowman,' or, as I prefer to write it, 'Piers the Plowman,' is one which has been frequently misconstrued and misunderstood by many authors, and concerning which many text-books have blundered inextricably. It is most important that the reader should have a clear idea of what it means, and as it is rather a difficult point to explain accurately, I must ask him to give me his best attention; and I cannot refrain from adding the hope that, if he succeeds in mastering the explanation of it, he will abstain from using the phrase in future in the old slovenly way.

The difficulty is three-fold, as originating in a three-fold error. The three mistakes commonly made are these. First, *Piers Plowman* is used as though it were the name of an *author* [a]; secondly, two poems which are quite distinct, and the respective titles of which are familiarly expressed as *The Vision of Piers Plowman* and *Pierce the Ploughman's Crede*, have been frequently confounded together; and thirdly, the name of 'The Vision of Piers Plowman' is commonly given to what is really the 'Liber de Petro Plowman,' of which the 'Vision' forms only about a third part [b]. I must ask the reader to bear in mind that, in what I am now going to say, I make no reference whatever to the *Crede*, and do not make any assertion about it till I again expressly mention it by its full title. Unless this be remembered, our chance of arriving at the truth is much lessened.

Just as Christian is not the author of Bunyan's Pilgrim's Progress, but only the subject of it, so Piers the Plowman is not the author of the Vision, but the subject of it; he is the personage

[a] This mistake occurs, for instance, in 'Chaucer's England,' vol. ii. p. 230, by Matthew Browne; who should have known better.
[b] It was Crowley who originated this error, but I do not see why it need be perpetuated.

seen in a dream, not the dreamer himself. Neither does the Book describe one continuous dream, but a succession of several; in some of which Piers is neither seen nor mentioned. Yet the whole poem is named from him, because he is the most remarkable figure in the group of allegorical personages who pass successively before the dreamer's sleeping sight. He is of more importance than either Lady Holy-church, Lady Meed, Falsehood, Conscience, Reason, Hunger, or the impersonations of the Seven Deadly Sins; for he is the type of a truly honest man [c]. But we may dismiss the consideration of his character for the present.

The true name of the dreamer, the poet, is not certainly known. The poem has been ascribed to one Langland, whose Christian name has been variously given as William, Robert, and John. Yet of the author's Christian name we are sure; for in nearly all the numerous MSS. it, is invariably given as William, not to mention that the author frequently calls himself *Wille* in various passages. The true surname is more doubtful, but in an able article in the North British Review (April, 1870), Professor C. H. Pearson has forcibly argued that the name must have been Langley rather than Langland; nevertheless, I would rather adhere, for the present, to the traditional form. We have then advanced clearly as far as this, viz. that one William Langland, during the latter part of the fourteenth century, wrote an alliterative poem describing a series of dreams, in *some* of which he beheld the person whom he calls Piers the Plowman, after whom the poem (or part of the poem, at least) was named.

Strictly speaking, only a *part* of the poem was *at first* named after Piers. The true title of the latter portion was originally *Visio ejusdem de Do-wel, Do-bet, et Do-best*, or the Vision of the same [William] concerning Do-well, Do-better, and Do-best; but the two portions were subsequently treated as constituting one long Book, and the name *Liber de Petro Plowman* was conferred upon the whole.

We must next consider the forms in which the whole poem exists. There are not less than forty-five MSS. of it still extant,

---

[c] See p. xxviii for the full meaning of the name

(nearly all of which I have carefully examined at various times,) and from a comparison of these it is evident that it takes five or six distinct shapes, of which some are due merely to confusion, or to the carelessness of the scribes; still, after all allowances for such causes of variation have been made, it is clear that *three* of the shapes are due to the author himself. It is certain that he altered, added to, and re-wrote the whole poem, not once only, but twice. It was the great work of his life, and may have occupied him, though not continuously, during nearly thirty years. Let us call the three forms of the poem, as at different times composed, the A-text, B-text, and C-text. They differ widely, and are marked by various peculiarities, and different dates may be with some accuracy assigned to them. Let us consider them separately.

The A-text, which is distinguished by peculiar freshness and vigour, and a rather greater amount of vehemence and rapidity than either of the others, was certainly composed first, about A.D. 1362. As compared with the others, it is but a first rough sketch, and extends to not more than 2567 lines. In it, the Vision of Piers the Plowman, and the Vision of Do-wel, Do-bet, and Do-best are kept quite distinct, the former consisting of a Prologue and 8 Passus (1833 lines), and the latter of a Prologue and 3 Passus (734 lines). In the Prologue to the former Vision (which contains but 109 lines) the curious fable of the rats conspiring to bell the cat is entirely omitted; and in the description of the Seven Deadly Sins, the character of Wrath was, by a curious oversight, forgotten. The best MSS. of it are the Vernon MS. at Oxford, MS. Trin. Coll. Camb. R. 3. 14, Harl. 875, Univ. Coll. (Oxford) 45, and MS. Rawl. Poet. 137 in the Bodleian Library. Long extracts from the Vernon MS. are given in 'Specimens of Early English,' Pt. II. ed. Morris and Skeat, 1872. A comparison of these with the corresponding passages of the present volume will shew more clearly than any detailed explanation what the A-text is like.

The B-text. The curious ending of the A-text shews clearly that the author's original intention was to wind up his poem and have done with it. Not foreseeing the extraordinary popularity which his work was destined to enjoy, he had recourse to the not uncommon device of killing himself off, in words which may be thus modernized—

> ' And when this work was wrought, ere Will might spy,
> Death dealt him a dint, and drove him to the earth,
> And he is enclosed under clay; now Christ have his soul[d]!'

And so the matter rested for nearly fifteen years. But the grief of the whole nation at the death of the Black Prince, the disquieting political events of 1377 (the last year of Edward III.), and the dissatisfaction of the commons with the conduct of the duke of Lancaster, roused our poet as they roused other men. Then it was that, taking his text from Ecclesiasticus x. 16, *Væ terræ ubi rex puer est,* he composed his famous version of the well-known fable of the rats wishing to bell the cat, a fable which has never elsewhere been told so well or so effectively. Then it was that, taking advantage of his now more extensive acquaintance with Scripture, and his familiarity with the daily scenes of London life, he re-wrote and added to his poem till he had trebled the extent of it, and multiplied the number of his Latin quotations by seven. The additions are, most of them, exceedingly good, and distinguished by great freedom and originality of thought; indeed, we may say that, upon the whole, the B-text is the best of the three, and the best suited for giving us a fair idea of the author's peculiar powers. It is with the B-text that the present volume is especially concerned, though only a *portion* of it is here printed. The *complete* text comprises the two Visions, viz. of Piers Plowman, and of Do-wel, Do-bet, and Do-best; the former consisting of a Prologue and 7 Passus (as here printed), and the latter of three Prologues and 10 Passus, viz. a Prologue and 6 Passus of Do-wel, a Prologue and 3 Passus of Do-bet, and a Prologue and 1 Passus of Do-best. But in many (perhaps all) of the MSS. the distinctions between the component parts are not much regarded, and in some there is no mention of Do-wel, Do-bet, and Do-best

---

[d] MS. Rawl. Poet. 137, fol. 31. But it is possible that these three lines (with four more preceding them) were added by one John Butt, whose name follows just afterwards.

whatever, but the whole is called *Liber* (but never *Visio*) *de petro plo999man*, and made to consist of a Prologue and *twenty* Passus. Not to go into further details, it is necessary to add that there are two perfect MSS. of the B-text which are of special excellence, and do not greatly vary from each other; from one of these, MS. Trin. Coll. Camb. B. 15. 17, Mr. Wright printed his well-known and convenient edition of the whole Book, and upon the other, MS. Laud 581, our text is based. The reader will now readily perceive that this volume contains the whole of the B-text of the Vision of Piers the Plowman, *properly so called*, but does *not* contain the Vision of Do-wel, Do-bet, and Do-best, which is appended to it in all the MSS. in order to complete the 'Liber.' If then, in the notes, I quote from Passus eleven, for instance, I quote from a Passus which is strictly the *third of Do-wel*, but which is commonly called Passus 11 of Piers the Plowman, as being a more convenient notation.

Concerning the C-text, I need not say much here. It was probably not composed till 1390 or even later, or, still more probably, it contains additions and revisions made at various periods later than 1380. Throughout these the working of the same mind is clearly discernible, but there is a tendency to diffuseness and to a love for theological subtleties. It is of still greater length, containing 10 Passus of Piers the Plowman, 7 Passus of Do-wel, 4 Passus of Do-bet, and 2 Passus of Do-best; or, according to the shorter notation, it contains 23 Passus, all *Prologues* being ignored in this text only. It may be remarked that the short poem of Do-best stands almost exactly the same in both the B and C versions.

Besides this extraordinary work, with its three varying editions, I have shewn (in my edition of the C-text for the Early English Text Society) that we are indebted to the same author for a remarkable poem written in 1399, which has been twice printed by Mr. Wright, the more convenient edition being that published for the Camden Society in 1838; and I have again printed it, as an Appendix to the C-text, with a few corrections. This poem has no title, and Mr. Wright named it a Poem on the Deposition of Richard II. This cannot well be accepted, because it is obvious, from internal evidence, that the poem was written in September, before Richard was deposed, and before the poet had any but the vaguest expectation that his deposition would take place. I have therefore given it, in my own reprint, the new title of 'Richard the Redeles' (i. e. Richard devoid of counsel), having adopted this expression from the first line of the first Passus. It is proper to observe that Mr. Wright has expressed a different opinion concerning the authorship of the poem, but he was misled by a marginal note in his MS. to which he attached some importance .

The printed editions. The Book concerning Piers the Plowman has been several times printed. Robert Crowley printed at least three impressions of it in one year, A.D. 1550; from a copy of one of which Owen Rogers produced his edition of 1561. Crowley used a very good MS. of the B-text[f], and his edition is of some value. Rogers's reprint abounds in errors, and is worthless. Dr. Whitaker printed a C-text MS. in 1813, from a MS. then belonging to Mr. Heber, but afterwards purchased by the late Sir T. Phillipps. This edition, though evidently brought out with much care, is nevertheless disfigured by innumerable errors of the editor, who has displayed more zeal than knowledge. But the MS. which he chose is the best of its class, and I have therefore reprinted it (with hundreds of corrections) for the Early English Text Society (1873). Mr. Wright printed his first edition, from the Trinity B-text MS., in 1842, and his second and revised edition of the same in 1856. A complete critical edition of the whole poem, in all its three forms, from a comparison of all the best MSS., with various readings in the footnotes, accompanied by a volume containing full notes with glossary and indices, has been published by the Early English Text Society, and has been edited by myself. Vol. I., containing the A-text, was published in 1866; Vol. II., containing the B-text, appeared in 1869; Vol. III., containing

---

[e] See his Edition (Camd. Soc.) p. vi, where 'liber hic' should have been printed 'liber homo,' an error which vitiates the whole argument.

[f] This MS. was probably destroyed. At any rate, it has not yet been found. It contains a line about S. Gregory in Pass. V (fol. xxiii, l. 6 of Crowley) which I cannot find elsewhere.

the C-text and 'Richard the Redeles', in 1873; and lastly Vol. IV., containing notes, glossary, &c., in 1877 and 1884. The text in this volume is taken from Vol. II. The notes will be found (in a fuller form) in Vol. IV.

This is, perhaps, the best place to say a few last words about Pierce the Ploughman's *Crede*. The facts concerning it are these, viz. that about the year 1394, when the popularity of the 'Liber' was well established, some writer of unknown name and of narrower views, wrote a short poem of 850 lines in alliterative verse, as a satire against the friars, to which he gave the name of Pierce the Ploughman's Crede, no doubt with the view of attracting attention. His conception of the Ploughman, however, is very different. In the 'Book,' the ploughman is a person seen in a dream, and is the personification of the honest and hardworking Christian; but in the 'Crede,' the ploughman is a poor man with whom the author meets in the flesh, whose merit is that he knows all the articles of the Creed, of which the friars knew nothing. The 'Crede' is written with great asperity, and is a very remarkable poem in many respects; but I cannot believe that William can have been very much pleased with the compliment paid him, as it is marked by a lack of charity totally at variance with the widely charitable views by which many passages of the Book are distinguished, notwithstanding sharp words elsewhere. The confusion between the two poems no doubt arose from their being in the same metre, and of nearly the same date, and from the fact that the title of one was borrowed from that of the other; and this confusion has been increased by the circumstance that they have been three times printed in close contact with each other, viz. by Owen Rogers in 1561, by Dr. Whitaker in 1814⁸, and by Mr. Wright. But this is not the place to enter into further details concerning it. The reader will find them fully given in my edition of the 'Crede,' published separately by the Early English Text Society in 1867. The most interesting result in connection with this poem is that the author of the

---

⁸ Dr. Whitaker's edition of the 'Crede' is not bound up in the same volume with the 'Vision,' but was published in the same form and style at nearly the same time.

'Crede' was almost certainly the author of the 'Plowman's Tale,' which appears in some editions of Chaucer, though it is certainly not his[h]. The 'Crede' may now conveniently be finally dismissed from our consideration.

THE AUTHOR'S NAME AND LIFE.

The author's Christian name was certainly William, as has been already said. The oldest evidence for his surname is an entry in one of the Dublin MSS. in a handwriting of the fifteenth century, to this effect: 'Memorandum, quod Stacy de Rokayle, pater *Willielmi de Langlond,* qui Stacius fuit generosus, et morabatur in Schiptone under Whicwode, tenens domini le Spenser in comitatu Oxon., qui prædictus Willielmus fecit librum qui vocatur Perys Ploughman.' Again, in a MS. belonging to Lord Ashburnham, is an *early* note to the effect that ' Robert, or Will*ia*m langland made pers ploughman.' But I am bound to add that I have discovered a colophon, in three MSS. of the C-text (viz. Digby 102, Douce 104, and Lord Ilchester's MS.), which runs thus— 'Explicit visio Willelmi .W. de Petro le Plowma*n.* Et hic incipit visio eiusdem de Dowel.' This is testimony that is difficult of explanation; Professor Morley thinks that W. may stand for Whicwode, whilst I myself own to a fancy that it may be merely a title, such as Wigorniensis (i. e. of Worcester). It may serve to remind us that if we adopt the name of Langland (which, as being traditional, I prefer to Langley,) we do so chiefly for convenience. Bale has a short passage concerning our author, wherein he calls him Robertus Langelande, and says that he was born at Cleobury Mortimer, in Shropshire. Shipton-under-Wychwood, mentioned above, is in Oxfordshire, four miles from Burford, and not at any very great distance from Banbury[i].

---

[h] Mr. Morley, in his 'English Writers' (vol. ii. 442), cites Mr. Black's opinion that the composer of the 'Plowman's Tale' was also author of a poem 'Against Lollardie,' a supposition which appears to me absurd, and like attributing a tract *against* reformation to Luther. The reader will observe, on the other hand, that in the *Plowman's* Tale we have a *second* instance of title-copying by William's imitator.

[i] It is somewhat curious that the poet, in the C-text, Passus III., l. 117, goes rather out of his way to mention the 'beadle of Banbury,' as if he had a grudge against him.

ll other particulars, we must trust to allusions made in
ms themselves; and if we rely upon these, and arrange
rmation they afford us, we may frame a brief sketch of
vhich is quite consistent and which I believe to be true.
herefore assume their credibility, and give the reader
ts, sometimes in the poet's own words.

time of writing the B-text of Do-wel, he was forty-five
ige, and he was therefore born about A.D. 1332, probably
iry Mortimer. His father and his friends put him to
ossibly in the monastery at Great Malvern), made a *clerk*
of him, and taught him what holy writ meant. In 1362,
of about thirty, he wrote the A-text of the poem, with-
iought of continuing or enlarging it. In this, he refers
d III. and his son the Black Prince, to the murder
II., to the great pestilences of 1348 and 1361, to the
retigny in 1360, and Edward's wars in Normandy, and
particularly to the great storm of wind which took
iaturday evening, Jan. 15, 1361–2[1]. This version of
ie describes as having been partly composed in May,
iering on the Malvern Hills, thrice mentioned in the
called the Vision of Piers the Plowman. In the In-
ir Prologue to Do-wel, he describes himself as wan-
t all the summer till he met with two Minorite Friars,
he discoursed concerning Do-wel. It was probably
r this that he went to reside in London, with which
iad some acquaintance; there he lived in Cornhill,
Kitte and his daughter Calote, for many long years.
oegan to expand his poem into the B-text, wherein
the last days of Edward III. in the words—'ʒif I
iile' (4. 177), and also explicitly to the dearth in the
f April, 1370, when Chichester was mayor; a dearth
xcessive rains in the autumn of 1369. Chichester
1369 (probably in October) and was still mayor in
iey's Memorials of London, p. 344, he is mentioned

year 1362, which was formerly called 1361, when the year
t to begin till March. See, for these a lusions, **3**. 186, 188
4.

When these various assertions come to be tested, it is easily
found that, as Professor Pearson says, 'the only known family of
Langlands has a very distinct history in connection with Somersetshire, Devonshire, and Dorsetshire, but never comes to view
in the Midland Counties.' I remember finding the name over
and over again in MS. Wood 1, in the Bodleian Library, but
always in connexion with the neighbourhood of East Brent in
Somersetshire. See also MS. Addit. 5937, fol. 54 b, in the British
Museum. But any trace of a Langland family in the Midland
Counties is so entirely absent that the name ought perhaps to be
given up; at least such is the conclusion to which we seem to
be led, though I cannot bring myself to disregard the old MS.
notes. On the other hand, there are two places called Langley,
from either of which the poet may have been named. One
is the hamlet of Langley in the very parish of Shipton-under-
Wychwood just mentioned; and there was a family of Langleys
of which Professor Pearson says—' The Langleys of Oxfordshire
have not yet, we believe, found place in any county history. But
their pedigree is abundantly proveable. They emerge into history
with Thomas de Langley, who gives King John a hundred marks
and a palfrey in 1213 to replace Thomas Fitzhugh in the guardian-
ship of Wychwood Forest (*Rot. de Fin.* 485). From that time the
Langleys, William, Thomas, John, John, and Thomas successively,
were wardens of Wychwood, and owned land in Shipton-under-
Wychwood as early as 1278, and as late as 1362 (*Rot. Hundred.*
ii. 739; *Inquis. post Mortem*, ii. 252). But the last Thomas died
beforé the thirty-sixth year of Edward III., and was succeeded by
his cousin and heir, Simon Verney (*Inquis. post Mortem*, ii. 252,
290).' This is quite sufficient to connect the name of Langléy
with Shipton, but does not quite solve the difficulty, as the poet
probably did not belong to so good a family. The other hamlet
is Langley near Acton Burnel, in Shropshire; adjoining which is
the hamlet of Ruckley or Rokele, which may be identified with
Rokayle. 'We find in Shropshire,' says Professor Pearson, ' that
younger members of the Burnel family were occasionally known
as Burnels de Langley (*Inquis. post Mortem*, i. 12, 253); that there
were other Langleys on the estate or in the employ of the Burne]

family; and that even the name of Rokeyle may be traced in one instance with high probability to the Welsh border (*Yearbook of* 32 Edw. I. 298). . . . . . A William de Langley was a tenant of William Burnel in 1228 (*Testa de Nevill*, 57). A Robert de Langley receives fifty marks due to Robert Burnel, afterwards Chancellor, in 1272 (*Exchequer Issues*, 87). A Robert de Langley was instituted clerk of *Rokesley* chapel some time between 1311 and 1349 (Eyton's *Shropshire*, vi. 147). Again, Henry de Rokesley and Richard de Waleys, whose name indicates a Welshman, both claimed to descend from Robert Paytevin; and one of the few Paytevins who can be traced was a follower of Roger de Mortimer, the lord of Cleobury Mortimer (*Parliamentary Writs*, iv. 1269). Seemingly therefore there were two families, one of Langley and one of Rokesle, who lived in adjoining hamlets, attached to the same manor, and of whom one was connected with the service of the Burnels, the other more remotely with the Mortimers, as being related to one of their dependants. Here then we perhaps get a clue to the poet's birth at Cleobury Mortimer, which was a possession of the Mortimers (*Inquis. post Mortem*, i. 190, ii. 224). It remains to explain the connection with Shipton-under-Wychwood. Edward Burnel (born 1287, d. 1315) married Alicia, daughter of Hugh de Despenser, of whom we only know that she survived him (Eyton's *Shropshire*, vi. 135). And a Hugh de Despenser died in 1349, seized of the manor of Shipton-under-Wychwood (*Inquis. post Mortem*, ii. 160; Kennett's *Parochial Antiquities*, ii. 102). Now, whether the poet's ancestor was a Langley or a Rokesle, it seems easy from what has gone before to understand why he first held a farm under the Mortimers and afterwards under the Despensers. In fact, there was a group of great families connected by birth or position in Shropshire and Oxfordshire, and a group of small families who were naturally linked with their fortunes.'—North British Review, April 1870, p. 244. From all this it seems tolerably clear that, of the hamlets named Langley, either the Shropshire one or the Oxfordshire one may be considered as giving the poet his name, since the family seems to have removed from one to the other. There is yet one more consideration that establishes, perhaps, a slight con-

nection between Wychwood and Mal
poet talks of his having been ' put to
ceived a clerical education, we may f
his early days in one of the priories at
priory at Great Malvern, or at the
which was considered as 'in one
the church at Worcester' (Abinge
Cathedral, p. 225). Now the H
tioned as dying in 1349, when La
years old, was son of the too fa
younger' (put to death Nov. 29,
sister and co-heir of Gilbert de
that marriage had obtained t
the manors of Malvern and Wy
same lord (see Sir H. Nicolas's
these traces are, they agree so
probable that we are upon the
more point that may be obse
visit to London. This is, tha
not appear in London, we do
1386, Adam Langele was a b
' in Macellas (*sic*), infra w
A.D. 1395, we find another
butcher, namely, ' Robertus
capellanus, London', [who
shope in Les Flesshambles i
mentum in parochia Sancti
de 6s. exeunt' de quodam
Beatæ Marie' (*Inquis. pos*
theorise yet further, and
or William made pers plc
had a brother named Ro
have assisted him. But
perhaps to stop here. I
is not wholly free from

k The Church of St. Nic
gate Street.

For
the poe
the info
his life
I shall
the resu
At the
years of
at Cleob
school (p
or schola
at the ag
out any t
to Edwar
of Edwar
treaty of
also most
place on
the poem
whilst wan
part rightl
troduction
dering abou
with whom
not long aft
he already
with his wife
In 1377, he
he alludes to
regne any w
dry month o
due to the
was elected i
1370. In Ri

1 That is, th
was supposed n
4. 45; and 5. I

as being mayor in that very month of April in that very year in the words—'Afterwards, on the 25th day of April in the year above-mentioned, it was agreed by John de Chichestre, Mayor,' &c. It is important to insist upon this, because the MS. followed by Mr. Wright, in company with many inferior ones, has a corrupt reading which turns the words—'A þousande and thre hondreth· tweis *thretty* and ten' into 'twice *twenty* and ten,' occasioning a great difficulty, and misleading many modern writers and readers, since the same mistake occurs in Crowley's edition. Fortunately, the Laud MS. 581 and MS. Rawl. Poet. 38 set us right here, and all difficulty now vanishes; for it is easily ascertained that Chichester was mayor in 1369-70, and at no other time, having never been re-elected. Stowe and other old writers have the right date. In the C-text, written at some time after 1390, the poet represents himself (apparently) as having left London, and in the commencement of Passus VI. gives us several particulars concerning himself, wherein he alludes to his own tallness, saying that he is too 'long' to stoop low, and has also some remarks concerning the sons of freemen which imply that he was himself the son of a franklin or freeman, and born in lawful wedlock. He wore the clerical tonsure, probably as having taken minor orders, and earned a precarious living by singing the *placebo, dirige*, and 'seven psalms' for the good of men's souls; for, ever since his friends died who had first put him to school, he had found no kind of life that pleased him except to be in 'these long clothes,' and by help of such (clerical) labour as he had been bred up to he had contrived not only to live '*in* London, but *upon* London' also. The supposition that he was married (as he says he was) may perhaps explain why he never rose in the church. He has many allusions to his extreme poverty. Lastly, in the poem of 'Richard the Redeles,' he describes himself as being in Bristol in the year 1399, when he wrote his last poem. This poem is but short, and in the only MS. wherein it exists, terminates abruptly in the middle of a page, and it is quite possible that it was never finished. This is the last trace of him, and he was then probably about sixty-seven years of age, so that he may not have long survived the accession of Henry IV. In personal appearance, he was so tall that he obtained the nickname of 'Longe Wille,' as he tells us in the line—

'I have lyued in londe,' quod I ᐧ 'my name is Longe wille ᵐ.'

This nickname may be paralleled from Mr. Riley's Memorials of London, p. 457, where we read of John Edward, 'otherwise called Longe Jacke,' under the date 1382; and it is to the purpose to observe further, that the poet Gascoigne was commonly called 'Long George,' from his tallness. In Passus 15 (B-text) Will says that he was loath to reverence lords or ladies, or persons dressed in fur, or wearing silver ornaments; he never would say 'God save you' to serjeants whom he met, for all of which proud behaviour, then very uncommon, people looked upon him as a fool. It requires no great stretch of imagination to picture to ourselves the tall gaunt figure of Long Will in his long robes and with his shaven head, striding along Cornhill, saluting no man by the way, minutely observant of the gay dresses to which he paid no outward reverence. It ought also to be observed how very frequent are his allusions to lawyers, to the law-courts at Westminster, and to legal processes. He has a mock-charter, beginning with the ordinary formula *Sciant præsentes et futuri* (see p. 18), a form of making a will (see p. 70), and in one passage (B-text, Pass. XI) he speaks with such scorn of a man who draws up a charter badly, who interlines it or leaves out sentences, or puts false Latin in it, that I think we may fairly suppose him to have been conversant with the writing out of legal documents, and to have eked out his subsistence by the small sums received for doing so. The various texts of the poem are so consistent, and the different MSS. agree so well together, that I fully believe he was his own scribe in the first instance, though we cannot now point to any MS. as an autograph. Nevertheless, the very neatly written MS. Laud 581 is so extremely correct as regards the *sense*, and is marked for correction on account of such very minute errors, that we may be sure he must himself have perused it ⁿ.

Respecting the poem itself there are some excellent remarks

ᵐ See Wright's edition, p. 304, where 'quod *I*' is printed 'quod *he*'; an error which a collation of many MSS. has removed.

ⁿ After carefully considering the question from every point, I think it quite possible that it is indeed an autograph.

in the works of Mr. Marsh and Dean Milman, which I cannot do better than transcribe here, in part. But the reader should consult the books themselves.

In Mr. Marsh's lectures on the Origin and History of the English Language, 8vo, 1862, p. 296, we read as follows:—

'Every great popular writer is, in a certain sense, a product of his country and his age, a reflection of the intellect, the moral sentiment, and the prevailing social opinions of his time. The author of Piers Ploughman, no doubt, embodied in a poetic dress just what millions felt, and perhaps hundreds had uttered in one fragmentary form or another. His poem as truly expressed the popular sentiment, on the subjects it discussed, as did the American Declaration of Independence the national thought and feeling on the relations between the Colonies and Great Britain. That remarkable document disclosed no previously unknown facts, advanced no new political opinions, proclaimed no sentiment not warranted by previous manifestations of popular doctrine and the popular will, employed perhaps even no new combination of words, in incorporating into one proclamation the general results to which the American head and heart had arrived. Nevertheless, Jefferson, who drafted it, is as much entitled to the credit of originality, as he who has best expressed the passions and emotions of men in the shifting scenes of the drama or of song.

'The Vision° of Piers Ploughman thus derives its interest, not from the absolute novelty of its revelations, but partly from its literary form, partly from the moral and social bearings of its subject—the corruptions of the nobility and of the several departments of the government, the vices of the clergy and the abuses of the church—in short, from its connection with the actual life and opinion of its time, into which it gives us a clearer insight than many a laboured history. Its dialect, its tone, and its poetic dress alike conspired to secure to the Vision a wide circulation among the commonalty of the realm, and by formulating—to use a favourite word of the day—sentiments almost universally felt, though but dimly apprehended, it brought them

He means the *Liber*, the whole poem

into distinct consciousness, and thus prepared the English people for the reception of the seed, which the labours of Wycliffe and his associates were already sowing among them[p] . . . .

'The Vision of the Ploughman furnishes abundant evidence of the familiarity of its author with the Latin Scriptures, the writings of the fathers, and the commentaries of Romish expositors, but exhibits very few traces of a knowledge of Romance literature. Still the proportion of Norman-French words, or at least of words which, though of Latin origin, are French in form, is quite as great as in the works of Chaucer[q]. The familiar use of this mixed vocabulary, in a poem evidently intended for the popular ear, and composed by a writer who gives no other evidence of an acquaintance with the literature of France[r], would, were other proof wanting, tend strongly to confirm the opinion I have before advanced, that a large infusion of French words had been, not merely introduced into the literature, but incorporated into the common language of England; and that only a very small proportion of those employed by the poets were first introduced by them.

'The poem, if not altogether original in conception, is abundantly so in treatment. The spirit it breathes, its imagery, the turn of thought, the style of illustration and argument it employs, are as remote as possible from the tone of Anglo-Saxon poetry, but exhibit the characteristic moral and mental traits of the Englishman, as clearly and unequivocally as the most national portions of the works of Chaucer or of any other native writer.

'The Vision has little unity of plan, and indeed—considered as a satire against many individual and not obviously connected abuses in church and state—it needed none. But its aim and

[p] In other words, Long Will was certainly a *prophet*, a speaker-out.

[q] The Prologue to Piers the Plowman and the first 420 lines of Chaucer's Prologue alike contain 88 per cent. of Anglo-Saxon words. See Marsh, Lectures on English, 1st Series, p. 124. The number of French words in our author is considerable. It is common to meet with the remark that Piers the Plowman is singularly free from any admixture of French; but the remark is false, as the reader may see for himself.

[r] He knew something of French, and quotes a couple of French proverbs. More than this, he appears to have read Le Chastel d'Amour and the poems of Rutebuef (see note to 5. 594), and a poem on Antichrist by Huon de Meri (R. 20. 52).

purpose are one. It was not an expostulation with temporal and spiritual rulers, not an attempt to awaken their consciences or excite their sympathies, and thus induce them to repent of the sins and repair the wrongs they had committed; nor was it an attack upon the theology of the Church of Rome, or a revolutionary appeal to the passions of the multitude. It was a calm, allegorical exposition of the corruptions of the state, of the church, and of social life, designed, not to rouse the people to violent resistance or bloody vengeance, but to reveal to them the true causes of the evils under which they were suffering, and to secure the reformation of those grievous abuses, by a united exertion of the moral influence which generally accompanies the possession of superior physical strength.'

In Dean Milman's History of Latin Christianity, vol. vi. p. 536 (ed. 1855), occurs the following excellent passage.

' Before Chaucer, even before Wycliffe, appeared with his rude satire, his uncouth alliterative verse, his homely sense, and independence of thought, the author of Piers Ploughman's Vision *. This extraordinary manifestation of the religion, of the language, of the social and political notions, of the English character, of the condition, of the passions and feelings of rural and provincial England †, commences, and with Chaucer and Wycliffe completes the revelation of this transition period, the reign of Edward III. Throughout its institutions, language, religious sentiment, Teutonism is now holding its first initiatory struggle with Latin Christianity. In Chaucer is heard a voice from the court, from the castle, from the city, from universal England. All orders of society live in his verse, with the truth and originality of individual being, yet each a type of every rank, class, every religious and social condition and pursuit. And there can be no doubt that his is a voice of freedom, of more or less covert hostility to the hierarchial system, though more playful and with a poet's genial appreciation of all which was true, healthful, and beautiful in the old faith. In Wycliffe is heard a voice from the Uni-

---

* This title is wrong, as has been shewn; he means ' The Book concerning Piers the Plowman.'
† We may certainly say also—of the lower classes in the city of London.

versity, from the seat of theology and scholastic philosophy, from the centre and stronghold of the hierarchy; a voice of revolt and defiance, taken up and echoed in the pulpit throughout the land against the sacerdotal domination. In the Vision of Piers Ploughman is heard a voice from the wild Malvern Hills, the voice, it should seem, of an humble parson, or secular priest. He has passed some years in London, but his home, his heart is among the poor rural population of central Mercian England. . . . . Whoever he was, he wrote in his provincial idiom, in a rhythm perhaps from the Anglo-Saxon times familiar to the popular ear; if it strengthened and deepened that feeling, no doubt the poem was the expression of a strong and wide-spread feeling. It is popular in a broader and lower sense than the mass of vernacular poetry in Germany and England. . . .

'The Visionary is no disciple, no precursor of Wycliffe in his broader religious views: the Loller of [the author of] Piers Ploughman is no Lollard; he applies the name as a term of reproach for a lazy indolent vagrant. The poet is no dreamy speculative theologian; he acquiesces seemingly with unquestioning faith in the Creed and in the usages of the Church. He is not profane but reverent as to the Virgin and the Saints. Pilgrimages, penances, oblations on the altar, absolution, he does not reject, though they are all nought in comparison with holiness and charity; on Transubstantiation and the Real Presence and the Sacraments, he is almost silent, but his silence is that of submission, not of doubt. It is in his intense absorbing moral feeling that he is beyond his age: with him outward observances are but hollow shows, mockeries, hypocrisies without the inward power of religion. It is not so much in his keen cutting satire on all matters of the Church as his solemn installation of Reason and Conscience as the guides of the self-directed soul, that he is breaking the yoke of sacerdotal domination; in his constant appeal to the plainest, simplest Scriptural truths, as in themselves the whole of religion, he is a stern reformer. The sad serious Satirist, in his contemplation of the world around him, the wealth of the world and the woe, sees no hope, but in a new order of things, in which if the hierarchy shall subsist, it shall subsist in a form, with powers, in a spirit totally opposite to that which now rules mankind. The mysterious Piers the Plough-man seems to designate from what quarter that Reformer is to arise [u]. . . . .

'With Wycliffe, with the spiritual Franciscans, Langland ascribes all the evils, social and religious, of the dreary world to the wealth of the Clergy, of the Monks, and the still more incongruous wealth of the Mendicants. With them, he asserts the right, the duty, the obligation of the temporal Sovereign to despoil the hierarchy of their corrupting and fatal riches . . . With the Fraticelli, to him the fatal gift of Constantine was the doom of true religion; with them he almost adores poverty, but it is industrious down-trodden rustic poverty; not that of the impostor beggar, common in his days, and denounced as sternly as by the political economy of our own, still less of the religious mendicant. Both these are fiercely excluded from his all-embracing charity.

'Langland is Antipapal, yet he can admire an ideal Pope, a general pacificator, reconciling the Sovereigns of the world to universal amity. It is the actual Pope, the Pope of Avignon or of Rome, levying the wealth of the world to slay mankind, who is the subject of his bitter invective. The Cardinals he denounces with the same indignant scorn; but chiefly the Cardinal Legate, whom he has seen in England riding in his pride and pomp, with lewdness, rapacity, merciless extortion, insolence in his train. Above all, his hatred (it might seem that on this all honest English indignation was agreed) is against the Mendicant orders. Of the older monks there is almost total silence. For St. Benedict, for St. Dominic, for St. Francis he has the profoundest reverence. But it is against their degenerate sons that he arrays his allegorical Host; the Friars furnish every impersonated vice, are foes to every virtue: his bitterest satire, his

---

[u] A sentence here follows, which is based on a misconception. The phrase 'Piers pardon the Ploughman' involves a very curious grammatical construction (not uncommon in Early English), and signifies 'the pardon of (or given by) Piers the Ploughman.' But Dean Milman treats it as a *proper name*, 'Piers-Pardon-Ploughman,' which it cannot possibly be. Elsewhere we have ' Piers berne the Plowman,' meaning *Piers the Ploughman's barn.*

keenest irony (and these weapons he wields with wonderful poetic force) are against their dissoluteness, their idleness, their pride, their rapacity, their arts, their lies, their hypocrisy, their delicate attire, their dainty feasts, their magnificent buildings, even their proud learning; above all their hardness, their pitiless-ness to the poor, their utter want of charity, which with Lang-land is the virtue of virtues.

'Against the clergy he is hardly less severe; he sternly con-demns their dastardly desertion of their flocks, when during the great plague they crowded to London to live an idle life; that idle life he describes with singular spirit and zest. Yet he seems to recognise the Priesthood as of Divine institution. Against the whole host of officials, pardoners, summoners, archdeacons, and their functionaries; against lawyers, civil as well as ecclesiastical, he is everywhere fiercely and contemptuously criminatory.

'His political views are remarkable. He has a notion of a king ruling in the affections of the people, with Reason for his chancellor, Conscience for his justiciary. On such a king the commonalty would cheerfully and amply bestow sufficient revenue for all the dignity of his office, and the exigencies of the state, even for his conquests. No doubt that commonalty would first have absorbed the wealth of the hierarchy. He is not absolutely superior to that hatred of the French, nor even to the ambition for the conquest of France engendered by Edward's wars and his victories. And yet his shrewd common sense cannot but see the injustice and cruelty of those aggressive and sanguinary wars.'

After some remarks upon the language and the allegory of the poem, (some of which require to be slightly modified to make them absolutely accurate,) and a slight sketch of the general plan of the poem considered as a whole, Dean Milman sums up the whole matter in the following just words :—

'The poet who could address such opinions, though wrapt up in prudent allegory, to the popular ear, to the ear of the peasantry of England; the people who could listen with delight to such strains, were far advanced towards a revolt from Latin Christianity. Truth, true religion, was not to be found with, it was not known by, Pope, Cardinals, Bishops, Clergy, Monks, Friars. It was to be sought by man himself, by the individual man, by the poorest man, under the sole guidance of Reason, Conscience, and of the Grace of God, vouchsafed directly, not through any intermediate human being, or even Sacrament, to the self-directing soul. If it yet respected all existing doctrines, it respected them not as resting on traditional or sacerdotal authority. There is a manifest appeal throughout, an unconscious installation of Scripture alone, as the ultimate judge; the test of everything is a moral and purely religious one, its agreement with holiness and charity.'

It should be remembered that several of the above remarks apply in particular to the C-text, which Dr. Milman seems to have examined the most attentively, doubtless because it is the longest and fullest. There are several points about the poem which render caution on the reader's part very necessary, if he would avoid being misled. One is, that the effect of its double revision has been to introduce occasional anachronisms. Thus, when the poet speaks of Reason as being set on the bench between the king and his son, he referred originally to Edward III. and the Black Prince, as the remark was made in 1362; but when the line was allowed to stand without change in the later versions, as occurring in a part of the poem which was not very much altered, the allusion was lost, and it must be taken merely as a general expression signifying that Reason was placed in a seat of dignity. Again, the allusion to the king's fear of death in the words '3if I regne any while' is of less force when retained in the C-text than when first composed and inserted in the B-text. The usual date assigned to the poem, 1362, is very misleading; for all depends upon which form of the poem is in question. It was in hand and subject to variation during twenty or thirty years, the date 1362 expressing merely the time of its commencement. Hence William was, in fact, absolutely contemporaneous with Chaucer, and cannot fairly be said to have preceded him. A comparison between these two great writers is very instructive; it is soon perceived that each is, in a great measure, the supplement of the other, notwithstanding the sentiments which they have in common. Chaucer describes the rich more fully than the poor, and shows us the holiday-making, cheerful, genial phase of English life; but William pictures the homely poor in their ill-fed, hard-working condition, battling against hunger, famine, injustice, oppression, and all the stern realities and hardships that tried them as gold is tried in the fire. Chaucer's satire often raises a good-humoured laugh; but William's is that of a man who is constrained to speak out all the bitter truth, and it is as earnest as is the cry of an injured man who appeals to Heaven for vengeance. Each, in his own way, is equally admirable, and worthy to be honoured by all who prize highly the English character and our own land. The extreme earnestness of our author and the obvious truthfulness and blunt honesty of his character are in themselves attractive, and lend a value to all he utters, even when he is evolving a theory or wanders away into abstract questions of theological speculation. It is in such a poem as his that we get a real insight into the inner every-day life of the people, their dress, their diet, their wages, their strikes, and all the minor details which picture to us what manner of men they were [x].

One very curious variation occurs in the character of Piers the Plowman himself. In the A-text, he is merely the highest type of the honest small farmer, whose practical justice and Christianity are so approved of by truth (who is the same with God the Father), that he is entrusted with a bull of pardon of more value than even the Pope's. But towards the conclusion of the B-text, the poet strikes a higher note, and makes him the type of the human nature in its highest form of excellence, the human flesh within whom dwelt the divine soul of Christ our Saviour. By a sort of parody upon the text in 1 Cor. x. 4, he asserts that *Petrus est Christus*, that Piers is Christ, and he likens the Saviour to a champion who fights in Piers' armour, that is to say, in human flesh—*humana natura*. When the fact is once fully perceived that, in a part of the poem, Piers is actually identified with our Lord and Saviour, the notion of imagining

[x] Some of these remarks are repeated from my introduction to the Early English Text Society's edition, vol. i. p. iv.

him to have been *an old English author* stands revealed in all its complete and irreverent absurdity.

The reader should beware also of being much influenced by the mention of the Malvern Hills. The name of William of Malvern has been proposed for the poet, in order to meet the objection that his surname is not certainly known. In my opinion, such a name is hardly a fit one, as likely to add to the numerous misconceptions already current concerning him. One great merit of the poem is, that it chiefly exhibits London life and London opinions, which are surely of more interest to us than those of Worcestershire. He does but mention Malvern three times, and those three passages may be found within the compass of the first eight Passus of Text A. But how numerous are his allusions to London! He not only speaks of it several times, but he frequently mentions the law courts of Westminster; he was familiar with Cornhill, East Cheap, Cock Lane in Smithfield, Shoreditch, Garlickhithe, Stratford, Tyburn, and Southwark, all of which he mentions in an off-hand manner. He mentions no river but the Thames, which is with him simply synonymous with river; for in one passage he speaks of two men thrown into the Thames, and in another he says that rich men are wont to give presents to the rich, which is as superfluous as if one should fill a tun with water from a fresh river, and then pour it into the Thames to render it fuller ⁷. To remember the London origin of a large portion of the poem is the true key to the right understanding of it.

It is impossible to give here an adequate sketch of that portion of English history which the poem illustrates, but it is very important that its close connection with history should be ever borne in mind. I will merely adduce one instance of this, one to which Mr. Wright has well drawn attention, and upon which I would lay even more stress than he has done. I allude to the

---

⁷ The words 'to woke with Temese' (see Wright's edition, p. 315), seem to mean 'to wet the Thames with.' *Woke*, left insufficiently explained by Mr. Wright, seems to mean to wet, to moisten, such appearing to be the sense required in another passage, in C. xv. 25. See my Notes to Piers Plowman (E. E. T. S.), p. 287. However, this is still uncertain, and further evidence is required.

rebellion under Wat Tyler. It is most evident that Langland himself was intensely loyal; if he would not reverence men whom he saw going about in rich clothing, he had a most profound reverence and even affection for the king. In the Prologue to his poem upon Richard II., whom he rates soundly and spares not, he commences with words of most tender and even touching remonstrance; it evidently goes to his heart that he should be compelled by a sense of duty to administer a severe reproof to 'his sovereign, whose subject he ought to be.' He nowhere recommends or encourages revolutionary ideas, but the contrary, and he never could have intended his words to have roused the flame of rebellion. But the outspoken manner of them was just that which delighted the populace; his exaltation of the ploughman was gladly seized upon, and his bold words perverted into watchwords of insurgency. He had but lately elaborated his second text of the poem, when John Balle, 'the crazy priest of Kent,' wrote the following remarkable letter to the commons of Essex.—' John Schep, som tyme Seynt Marie prest of ȝorke, and nowe of Colchestre, greteth welle Johan Nameles, and Johan the Mullere, and Johan Cartere, and biddeth hem that thei ware of gyle of borugh, and stondeth togiddir in Goddis name, and biddeth *Peres Plouȝman* go to his werke, and chastise well Hobbe the robber, and taketh with ȝou Johan Trewman, and all his felaws, and no mo, and loke schappe ȝou to on heued, and no mo.

> Johan the Muller heth ygrownde smal, smal, smal;
> The Kyngis sone of hevene shalle paye for alle.
> Be ware or ye be wo,
> Knoweth ȝour frende from ȝoure foo,
> Haveth ynowe, and seythe 'Hoo';
> And *do welle* and *bettre*, and fleth synne,
> And seketh pees, and holde therynne;

And so biddeth Johan Trewman and alle his felawes.' For writing which, John Balle was drawn, hung, and quartered, July 15, 1381, just one month after Wat Tyler had been cut down by Sir William Walworth. See Thomæ Walsingham Historia Anglicana, ed. Riley, vol. ii. p. 33. The reader will remark the mention, not only of *Peres Plowman*, but of *do-welle* and *bettre*; besides which, the name of *Schep* (or shepherd) was probably adopted from the second line of the prologue, and the name of *Trewman* was possibly suggested by William's **Tomme** *Trew-tonge* (4. 17).

It will probably assist the reader to have before him a general sketch of one of the forms of the Poem. Taking the B-text of it, it may be divided, as before explained, into two parts, viz. Piers the Plowman, properly so called, the whole of which is here printed, and the Vision of Do-wel, Do-bet, and Do-best. The former consists of an Introductory Prologue and Seven Passus, and can be subdivided into two distinct portions, which may be called: (1) The Vision of the Field Full of Folk, of Holy Church, and of Lady Meed, occupying the Prologue and Passus I–IV; and (2) the Vision of the Seven Deadly Sins and of Piers the Plowman[z], occupying Passus V–VII.

I. *Vision of the Field Full of Folk, of Holy Church, and of Lady Meed.*

In the *Prologue*, the author describes how, weary of wandering, he sits down to rest upon Malvern Hills, and there falls asleep and dreams. In his vision, the world and its people are represented to him by a field full of folk, busily engaged in their avocations. The field was situate between the tower of Truth, who is God the Father, and the dungeon which is the abode of evil spirits. In it there were ploughmen and spendthrifts, anchorites, merchants, jesters, beggars, pilgrims, hermits, friars, a pardoner with his bulls, and priests who deserted their cures. There was also a king, to whom an angel speaks words of advice. Then was seen suddenly a rout of rats and mice, conspiring to bell the cat, from doing which they were dissuaded by a wise mouse. There were also lawsergeants, burgesses, tradesmen, labourers, and taverners touting for custom.

Passus I. Presently, he sees a lovely lady, of whom he asks the meaning of the tower. She tells him it is the abode of the Creator, who provides men with the necessaries of life. The dungeon is the castle of Care, where lives the Father of Falseness.

---

[z] Piers is *never once mentioned* till we come to Pass. V. 544.

He prays the lady to disclose her name, and she tells him she is Holy Church, and instructs him how great a treasure Truth is, how Lucifer fell through pride, that faith without works is dead, and that the way to heaven lies through Love.

Passus II. He asks how he may know Falsehood. She bids him turn, and see both Falsehood and Flattery (Favel). Looking aside, he sees, not them alone, but a woman in glorious apparel. He is told that she is the Lady Meed (i.e. Reward or Bribery), who is to be married to Falsehood on the morrow. Holy Church then leaves him. The wedding is arranged, and Simony and Civil read a deed respecting the property with which False-hood and Meed are to be endowed. Theology objects to the marriage, and disputes its legality; whereupon it is agreed that all must go to Westminster to have the question decided. All the parties ride off to London, Meed being mounted upon a sheriff, and Falsehood upon a 'sisour.' Guile leads the way, and they soon reach the king's court, who vows that he will punish Falsehood if he can catch him. Whereupon all run away, except Meed alone, who is taken prisoner.

Passus III. Lady Meed is now brought before the king. The justices assure her that all will go well. To seem righteous, she confesses to a friar and is shriven, offering to glaze a church-window by way of amendment, immediately after which she advises mayors and judges to take bribes. The king proposes that she shall marry Conscience; but Conscience refuses, and exposes her faults. She attempts to retaliate and to justify herself; but Conscience refutes her arguments, quotes the example of Saul to show the evil of covetousness, and declares that Reason shall one day reign upon earth and punish all wrong-doers. To this is appended a description of the year of jubilee, and a caution about reading texts in connection with the context, neither of which things appears in the A-text.

Passus IV. Hereupon the king orders Reason to be sent for; who comes, accompanied by Wit and Wisdom. At this moment Peace enters with a complaint against Wrong. Wrong, knowing the complaint to be true, wins over Wit and Wisdom to his side, by Meed's help, and offers to buy Peace off with a present.

Reason, however, is firm and will shew no pity, but advises the king to act with strict justice. The king is convinced, and prays Reason to remain with him for ever afterwards.

II. *The Vision of the Seven Deadly Sins, and of Piers the Plowman.*

Passus V. Here the dreamer awakes, but not for long; he soon falls asleep over his prayers, and has a second dream, wherein he again sees the field full of folk, and Reason[a] preaching to the assembled people, reminding them that the late tempest and pestilences were judgments of God. Many are affected by the sermon, and begin to repent and confess their sins. Of these, the first is Pride, who makes a vow of humility. The second is Luxury or Lechery, who vows henceforth only to drink water. The third is Envy, who confesses his evil thoughts and his attempts to harm his neighbours. The fourth is Wrath, a friar, whose aunt was a nun, and who was both cook and gardener to a convent, and incited many to quarrel. The fifth, Avarice, who confesses how he lied, cheated, and lent money upon usury, and who, not understanding the French word *restitution*, thought that it was another term for stealing. The sixth, Gluttony, who (on his way to church) is tempted into a London ale-house, of the interior of which the author gives a most life-like picture, as distinct as a drawing by Hogarth. Glutton also repents and vows amendment, but not till after he has first become completely drunk and afterwards felt ashamed of himself. The seventh is Sloth, a priest who knows rimes about Robin Hood better than his prayers, and can find a hare in a field more readily than he can read the lives of the saints. Robert the robber too repents, and prays for forgiveness, and Repentance makes supplication for all the penitents[b]. Then all set out to seek after Truth, but no one knows the way. Soon they meet with a palmer, who had sought the shrines of many saints, but never that of one named *Truth*. At this juncture Piers the Plowman for the first time appears, declaring that he knows

---

[a] In the A-text, it is *Conscience* who preaches.
[b] In the A-text, Passus VI begins here, at l. 520 of our text.

Truth well, and will tell them the way, which he then describes.

Passus VI. The pilgrims still ask for a guide, and Piers says he will shew them, when he has ploughed his half-acre. Meanwhile, he gives good advice to ladies and to a knight. Before starting, he makes his will, and then sets all who come to him to hard work. Many shirk their work, but are reduced to subordination by the sharp treatment of Hunger. Next follow some most curious and valuable passages concerning the diet of the poor, strikes for higher wages, and the discontents engendered by a brief prosperity.

Passus VII. At this time Truth (i.e. God the Father) sends Piers a bull of pardon, especially intended for kings, knights, bishops, and the labouring poor, and even for some lawyers and merchants, in a less degree. A priest disputes the validity of Piers' pardon, and wants to see it. The dispute between him and Piers is so violent that the dreamer awakes, and the poem of Piers the Plowman (properly so called) ends with a fine peroration on the small value of the pope's pardons, and the superiority of a righteous life over mere trust in indulgences, at the Last Great Day.

The poem of *Do-well* is much more discursive, and is far too full of matter to admit of a brief summary of it; it contains many passages of great interest and importance. In one of these occurs the curious prophecy, that a king would one day come and beat the religious orders for breaking their rules, and then should the abbot of Abingdon receive a knock from the king, and incurable should be the wound; a passage which excited great interest in the days of Henry VIII. In another passage is the reference to the mayoralty of John Chichester. The poem of *Do-bet* has a long and most singular prologue, containing, among other things, a reference to the Mahometan religion and the duty of Christians to convert the Saracens to the true faith. The poem itself is on a uniform and settled plan, designed to point out that Jesus is the only Saviour of men. It seems to me most admirable, both in conception and execution. We are introduced to Faith, personated by Abraham, and to Hope, both of whom

pass by the wounded man who has been stripped by thieves.
But Love, who is the Good Samaritan, and none other than
Jesus in the dress of Piers the Ploughman, alone has compassion
on him and saves his life. With growing power and vividness,
the poem describes the death of Christ, the struggle between
Life and Death and between Light and Darkness, the meeting
together of Truth and Mercy, Righteousness and Peace, whilst
the Saviour rests in the grave; a triumphant description of the
descent of Christ into hell, and His victory over Satan and Lucifer,
till the poet wakes in ecstacy, with the joyous peal of the bells
ringing in his ears on the morning of Easter day. And I cannot
refrain from adding here my conviction, that there are not many
passages in English poetry which are so sublime in their conception as this 18th Passus. Some of the lines are rudely and quaintly
expressed, but there are also many of great beauty and power,
and which buoyantly express the glorious triumph of Christ.
But alas! the poem of *Do-best* reveals how far off the end yet is.
The Saviour leaves earth, and Antichrist descends upon it. The
Church is assailed by many foes, and can scarcely hold her own;
diseases assail all mankind; death 'pashes' to the dust kings and
knights, emperors and popes, and many a lovely lady; old age
can scarce bear up against despair; Envy hates Conscience, and
hires flattering friars to salve Conscience with soothing but deadly
remedies, till Conscience, hard beset by Pride and Sloth, cries
out to Contrition to help him; but Contrition still slumbers,
benumbed by the deadly potions he has drunk. With a last
effort Conscience arouses himself, and seizes his pilgrim's staff,
determined to wander wide over the world till he shall find Piers
the Plowman. And the dreamer awakes in tears.

Dr. Whitaker once suggested that the poem is not perfect,
that it must have been designed to have a more satisfactory
ending, and not one so suggestive of disappointment and gloom.
I am convinced that this opinion is most erroneous; not so much
because all the MSS. have here the word *Explicit*, as from the
very nature of the case. What other ending can there be? or
rather, the end is not yet. We may be defeated, yet not cast
down; we may be dying, and yet live. We are all still pilgrims

upon earth. *That* is the truth which the author's mighty genius would impress upon us in his parting words. Just as the poet awakes in ecstacy at the end of the poem of Do-bet, where he dreams of that which has been already accomplished, so here he wakes in tears, at the thought of how much remains to be done. So far from ending carelessly, he seems to me to have ceased speaking at the right moment, and to have managed a very difficult matter with consummate skill.

METRE OF THE POEM.

The last consideration that requires attention is the form of the poem, as regards its metre and language.

The metre is that known as *alliterative*, the only metre which in the earliest times was employed in Anglo-Saxon poetry. It also resembles the older kind of alliterative poetry in being entirely without rime. Poems thus composed may be printed either in short lines or long ones, as is most convenient. I have adopted the system of long lines, as Early English poems in this metre and of this period are invariably written in long lines in the MSS., except when written continuously, as we write prose. Every long line is divided into two short lines or half-lines by a pause, the position of which is marked in the MSS. by a point (sometimes coloured red), or by a mark resembling a paragraph mark (¶) or inverted D (ᗞ), coloured red and blue alternately. In some MSS., but these are generally inferior ones, the mark is entirely omitted. It is also not infrequently misplaced. In the present volume the position of the pause is denoted by a raised full-stop, and the reader will find that it almost invariably points out the right place for a slight rest in reading, and in very many places is equivalent to a comma in punctuation. If we employ the term *loud* syllables to denote those syllables which are more strongly accented and are of greater weight and importance, and *soft* syllables to denote those having a slighter stress or none at all, we may briefly state the chief rules of alliterative verse, as employed by our author and other writers of his time, in the following manner.

1. Each half-line contains two or more loud syllables, two being the usual number. More than two are frequently found in the first half-line, but rarely in the second.

2. The initial-letters which are common to two or more of these loud syllables being called the *rime-letters*, each line should have two *rime-letters* in the first, and one in the second half. The two former are called *sub-letters*, the latter the *chief-letter*.

3. The chief-letter should begin the *former* of the two loud syllables in the second half-line. If the line contain only two rime-letters, it is because one of the sub-letters is dispensed with.

4. If the chief-letter be a consonant, the sub-letters should be the same consonant, or a consonant expressing the same sound. If a vowel, it is sufficient that the sub-letters be also vowels; they need not be the same, and in practice are generally different. If the chief-letter be a combination of consonants, such as *sp, ch, str,* and the like, the sub-letters frequently present the same combination, although the recurrence of the first letter only would be sufficient.

These rules are easily exemplified by the opening lines of the prologue. (The secondary, or slighter accents, are not marked)

> 'In a sómer séson · whan sóft was the sónnë,
> I shópe me in shróudës · as I a shépe wérë,
> In hábite as an héremite · vnhóly of wórkës,
> Went wýde in þis wórld · wóndres to hére.
> Ac on a Máy mórnynge · on Máluerne húllë,
> Me byfél a férly · of fáiry, me thóu3të;
> I was wéry forwándred · and wént me to réstë
> Vnder a bróde bánkë · bi a bórnës sídë,
> And ás I láy and léned · and lóked in þe wáteres,
> I slómbred in a slépyng · it swéyued so mérye.'

Line 1 has *s* for its rime-letter; the sub-letters begin *somer* and *seson*; the chief-letter begins *soft*. The *s* beginning *sonne* may be regarded as superfluous and accidental.

Line 2 shews *sh* used as a rime-letter. The syllables marked with a diæresis are to be fully sounded, and counted as distinct syllables. The *e* at the end of *shope* merely shows that the preceding *o* is long, and is not syllabic.

Line 3 is very regular; it reminds us that the *vn-* in *vnholy* is a mere prefix, and that the true base of the word is *holy*, beginning with *h*.

In line 4, the initial *W* in *Went* is superfluous.

In line 5, two loud syllables, viz. *May* and the first of *mornynge*, come together. This is rare, and not pleasing.

In line 6, *by-* in *byfel* is a mere prefix; and so is *for-* in *forwandred* in line 7.

In line 8, the *b* in *bi* is unnecessary to the alliteration.

In line 9, if a stress be laid upon *as*, there will be three loud syllables in the first half-line.

In line 10, the chief-letter is *s*, but the sub-letters exhibit the combination *sl*.

The less forcible or secondary accents, not here accounted for, cause considerable difficulty. A few variations may be noticed.

(*a*) The chief-letter may begin the *second* loud syllable of the second half-line; as,—

'Vnkýnde to her kýn · and to állë crístene;' I. 190.

(*b*) Sometimes there are two rime-letters in the second half-line, and one in the first. Such lines are rare; I give an example from the A-text of the poem, Pass. ii. l. 112:—

'Týle he had sýluer · for his sáwes and his sélynge.'

(*c*) The chief-letter is sometimes omitted; but this is a great blemish. Thus, in l. 34 of the Prologue, nearly all the MSS. have *synneles*, instead of *giltles*, which is the reading of MS. R. 3. 14 in Trinity College, Cambridge.

(*d*) By a bold license, the rime-letter is sometimes found at the beginning of *soft* or subordinate syllables, as in the words *for*, *whil*, in the lines:—

'Þanne I fráinëd hir fáirë · for hým þat hir mádë;' I. 58.
'And with hím to wónye with wó · whil gód is in héuene;' 2. 106.

(*e*) It may be noted that *k* seems to have been sounded before *n*; hence *kn* is alliterated with *k*, as in Pass. 5. l. 1. Also, *w* seems to have been sounded before *r*, so that *wr* is alliterated with *w*; see 3. 182. Both these peculiarities are found in other alliterative poems. But there is a third peculiarity which is very scarce else-where, except in Richard the Redeles, viz. the alliteration of *f* with *v*, as in Prol. 194, 2. 60, 5. 443. This in itself furnishes an argument for the common authorship of Richard and Piers the Plowman.

Some of the above examples certainly tend to shew that William was not very particular about his metre. He frequently neglects to observe the strict rules, and evidently considered metre of less importance than the sense. This remark will suffice to dismiss the subject, since, for more perfect specimens of the metre, the poems of the Anglo-Saxon period should be studied. Of the poems in unrimed alliterative metre which are most nearly contemporaneous with Piers the Plowman, some of the principal are William of Palerne, and a fragment of a poem on Alexander (both edited by myself for the Early English Text Society in the same volume), Pierce the Ploughman's Crede, 'Richard the Redeles,' Two poems (one upon Cleanness, and another upon Patience), edited by Mr. Morris for the Early English Text Society in 1864, The Destruction of Jerusalem, &c. For further information, see my essay on Alliterative Poetry in vol. iii. of the Percy Folio MS., edited by Hales and Furnivall.

LANGUAGE OF THE POEM.

As regards the language of the poem, the first point is the dialect. This is certainly of a mixed character, as it exhibits the plural forms in *-en* in the indicative mood (which are a mark of Midland dialect), and also plural forms in *-eth* (which mark the Southern). This peculiarity is by no means confined to the particular MS. here printed, but is the case with most other MSS. which I have examined. Thus, in Pass. iii. ll. 80, 81, we find—

'For þise aren men on þis molde · þat moste harme worch*eth*
To þe pore peple · þat parcel-mele bugg*en* [buy].'

This mixture of the *-eth* ending in *worcheth*, and the *-en* ending in *buggen*, occurs in at least six other MSS., and a careful ex-amination of many MSS. has convinced me that such an admixture of dialect is an essential mark of the poem, and of the dialect spoken by its composer. There are many traces of West of England speech also, and even some of Northern, but the latter may possibly be rightly considered as common to both North and West. The reader will therefore do well to remember that he has here to deal with a dialect of a peculiarly uncertain character, and that he cannot therefore always draw certain conclusions. At the same time, the dialect is far from being such as to cause much difficulty by the introduction of uncommon words. The language is fairly intelligible after a slight amount of patience has been bestowed upon the first few hundred lines, and the occasional occurrence of hard words is chiefly due to the extraordinary extent of the author's vocabulary.

Dr. Morris well observes, in his Introduction to 'Chaucer's Prologue,' &c., in the Clarendon Press Series—that the number of Norman-French words in Chaucer is so great that 'he has been accused of corrupting the language by a large and unnecessary admixture of Norman-French terms. But Chaucer, with few exceptions, employed only such terms as were in use in the *spoken* language, and stamped them with the impress of his genius, so that they became current coin of the literary realm.' That this remark is true is shewn by the fact that William does the very same thing, employing Norman-French words freely whenever he wishes to do so.

As regards the **orthography**, it may be remarked that the scribe of the Laud MS. seems to have added many final *e*'s where the rules would not lead us to expect them, and has omitted many where they seem necessary. This is due, either to carelessness on his part, or to a peculiar orthographical system, or to the fact that the dialect is of a mixed character and more uncertain. The first supposition alone hardly suffices, as most MSS. of the B-text exhibit like irregularities. The chief points of the grammar are so well explained in the Introduction to Mr. Morris's Chaucer (Clarendon Press Series), pp. xxxi–xlii, that a very brief summary of some of them may be sufficient here.

The scribe uses þ to represent *th*. In a great many cases he distinguishes between the sound of *th* in *thin*, and the sound of *th* in *thine.* He denotes the former by *th* written at length, as in *precheth, thinketh,* and the like, and the latter by þ, as in þe, þat, þanne, and the like. This is his usual custom; but there are several instances of the contrary. He also uses ʒ, as usual, with the sound of *y* at the beginning of a word, as in ʒe, ʒoure, and with the guttural sound of *gh* in the middle of a word, as in thouʒte, nauʒt. He employs very few contractions, all of which are here denoted by italics. Most of these involve the letter *r;* thus a curl above the line, which is really a corruption of the old form of *e,* stands for *er* or *re;* as in bet*ter,* prech*ed*[c]. An *i* above the line means *ri,* as in c*ri*st. A roughly written *a* means *ra,* as in g*ra*ce. A roughly written *v* means *vr* or *ur,* as in hono*ur.* A *p* with a straight stroke through the tail means *per* or *par,* as in *per*soun, *par*fyt. A *p* with a curling stroke below means *pro,* as in *pro*fyt. A straight stroke above a letter means *n* or *m,* as in mo*m*me, ma*n*, where the stroke is over *o* and *a* respectively. A few words are written shortly, as lr̄e for le*tt*re, cō̄e for co*mun*e, qd for qu*o*d. When these contractions and a few others of rare occurrence are mastered, the difficulty of reading MSS. is not great. To read them correctly *in all cases* comes by practice only.

NOUNS[d].

Number. The nominative plural ends commonly in *-es,* as in *shroudes, workes;* sometimes in *s,* as in *bidders,* or in *z,* as in *diamantz.* This *z* is written exactly like ʒ, the symbol for *y* or *gh.* For *-es, -is* is sometimes found, as in *wittis;* and very rarely, *-us,* as in *folus.* Some few plurals are in *-en,* as *sustren, chylderen.* A few nouns, such as *folk,* which were originally neuter, have no termination in the plural. *Gees, men,* are examples of plurals formed by vowel-change; *fete* and *feet* are various spellings of the plural of *foot.*

Case. The genitive singular ends in *-es,* sometimes corrupted

---

[c] It is only when it occurs after *p,* that it means *re.* This is because 'per' can be denoted otherwise, viz. by drawing a stroke across the tail of the *p.*

[d] These remarks are chiefly copied and adapted from Mr. Morris's Chaucer.

into *-is*, as in *cattes, cattis*; other endings are very rare. The genitive plural sometimes ends in *-en* or *-ene*, as in *clerken, kyngene. Childryn* is also a genitive plural. The instances of these more unusual forms are readily found by help of the references in the Glossarial Index. *Mannus* (for *men's*) occurs once only. The dative case singular commonly ends in *-e*, as in *to beddë.*

ADJECTIVES.

The distinction between definite and indefinite adjectives is difficult to follow, owing to the irregularity of the alliterative rhythm; and the scribe, not having much to guide him, may have been at fault sometimes, and has certainly added many final *-e*'s after a long vowel, which he never intended to be pronounced as a separate syllable. He even writes *fete* for *feet*, *shope* for *shoop*, where there is no doubt about the final *e* being silent, and intended to be non-syllabic. Plural adjectives should end in *-e*, and commonly do so, as *alle*. The reduplication of a consonant when a syllable is added is worth notice; thus *alle* is the plural of *al*, just as *shullen* is the plural of the auxiliary verb *shal*. Very rarely, plural adjectives of French origin end in *-es*; I believe that *cardinales vertues* is the sole instance; cf. the phrase *maistres freres*[*]. The comparative of *heigh* (high) is *herre*, the superlative *hexte*. Adjectives and adverbs ending in *-ly* sometimes form their comparatives and superlatives in *-loker*, *-lokest*, as *lightloker*, *lightlokest.*

PRONOUNS.

The pronouns are the same as in Chaucer; but, besides *sche*, the older form *heo* is *also* used[†]; and, besides *þei*, the older form *hij* (*by*). These are instances of a confusion or admixture of dialect. *Their* is denoted by *here, her,* or *hir*; *them* by *hem*. The dative case is used with impersonal verbs, as *me byfel, him likede.* The pronoun *thou* is often written *tow*, and at the same time

---

[*] *Maistris liers* occurs in Pecock's Repressor, ed. Babington, p. 478.
[†] The form in Chaucer is *sche*, and never *heo.*

joined to its verb, as *seestow*, seest thou, *repentedestow*, repentedst thou. The genitive of *who* is written *whas*, 2. 18. *Vch a*
or *eche a* is used for each; *which a* for what sort of a; pl. *whiche*,
what sort of.

VERBS.

It is chiefly here that the Laud MS. (in all other respects
superior to the rest) exhibits irregularities; several of which,
however, are found also in other good MSS. of the B-class. The
indicative plural ends both in *-en* and *-eth*, as *geten*, *conneth*;
a variety which has been already noted. The past tense of weak
verbs, which should end in *-ede*, commonly ends in *-ed* only, and
this not only in the singular, but in the plural, as *pleyed*; yet
sometimes even the full plural form *-eden* occurs, as in *lyueden*.
The student will learn much by contrasting the various endings
in William's popular poem (which probably in all its forms exhibited the language rather of the educated poorer classes than
that of the more wealthy), with the more regular endings found
in good MSS. of Chaucer [g]. I can only point out a few of the
most striking peculiarities, and refer to Dr. Morris's Introduction
to Chaucer, and to his Grammatical Introduction to 'Specimens
of Early English' for further information, and to his Historical
Outlines of English Accidence for full tables of verbal forms.

The abbreviated forms *sit* (for *sitteth*), *rit* (for *rideth*), *halt* (for
holdeth), and the like, occur here as in Chaucer. So also *bit* for
biddeth, *rest* for *resteth*, *fet* for *fedeth*.

In weak verbs, which should form their past tenses in *-de* or
-te, the final *-e* is often dropped. Thus *went* is used for *wente*.

In strong verbs, which should terminate (in the first and third
persons singular of the past tense) in a consonant, we often find
an *-e* added to lengthen the vowel, as already explained (p. xlii).
Thus *I shope* is written for *I shop* or *I shoop*. The plural commonly has the correct termination *-en*, as in *wonnen*, *chosen*.

---

[g] The Vernon MS., containing many other poems besides Piers the
Plowman, is, upon the whole, tolerably regular in its forms; but this is the
only MS. that is so, and the uniformity is due to the fact that the scribe of it
has turned everything (wherever he could) into the *Southern* dialect.

In the infinitive mood, some verbs are found with the ending -*ie* or -*ye*, as *shonye, stekye, louye*; and the final -*e* is sometimes dropped, as in *eracchy*. This ending, which the West Midland and Southern dialects had in common, seldom occurs in Chaucer, except in a few words like *herie*, to praise, *tilye*, to till.

The present participles end in -*yng*, as *lybbyng, worchyng, wandryng*; but the ending -*inde* occurs occasionally in the MSS. The prefix *y-* is frequently found before past participles, and sometimes even before past tenses; see **Y-** in the Glossary.

The anomalous verbs and negative verbs (such as *nam* for *am not, nelle* for *will not*), adverbs, &c., are much the same as in Chaucer.

There is one error in syntax which, in more passages than one, is so well supported by MS. authority, that we can hardly suppose it not to have been due to the author himself. It is, that he uses a singular verb with a plural noun, especially the verb *is* or *was*. A clear example is in Pass. v. 99.

Few things are more important than to pay great attention to the true force of adverbs, prepositions, and conjunctions; till these are mastered, the construction of sentences is left quite uncertain; and when a sentence appears difficult, it is often because such small words have not been understood. Thus *there* frequently means *where*; *then* = than; *thanne* = then. *Bi* often = with reference to, and *of* often = by. *Vp* = upon, *vntil* = unto. *Or* or *ar* = ere, before; *als* = as; *but* = except; *ac* = but; *ʒif* = if; *sithen* = since. It is a common error to assign to words, especially words of this class, the meanings which they have *now*. For instance, *als* is seen to be another form of *also*, and it is therefore supposed to mean *also*; but it more commonly has the *old* meaning of *al so*, i. e. just as. The preposition *with* often has a very odd position in the sentence; see note to Pass. ii. 31. *An* is written for *and*; and, conversely, *and* for *an*, if.

GENERAL HINTS.

Several mistakes are frequently made by those who are beginning to study Middle English, which are worth mention, in order to put the student on his guard.

1. It is common to disregard the spelling, and look upon it as lawless. It is true that it was not uniform, but the scribes had a law nevertheless, for their general object was to represent sounds, and the spelling is phonetic, not conventional. The variations in spelling arose from the variety of ways in which sounds can be represented. Thus *i* and *y* were considered as interchangeable, and it is a mere chance which is used.

2. The difficulty of Middle English has been much exaggerated. Though it may take years to become a sound scholar, a very fair knowledge of it may be picked up in a few weeks, and is of great utility; for more grammar can thus be learnt in a short time than by reading any amount of grammatical treatises that ignore the older forms of the language.

3. Many words are regarded as entirely obsolete which are nevertheless still preserved in provincial dialects.

4. Old words are often wrongly taken in their modern sense. Thus, to *allow* does not mean to *permit*, but to *approve of*, the root being the Latin *laudare*. Again, *to take* is supposed always to mean *to receive*; whereas it commonly means *to give*.

5. Some forget to apply and make the most of such knowledge as they really possess. Thus, in the phrase 'the *quick* and the dead,' every one knows that *quick* means *living*. Such knowledge should be put to good use; let it be remembered that *quick* is almost sure to mean *living* in Early English, and then it will not wrongly be supposed to mean *quick*.

SELECT BIBLIOGRAPHY

BIBLIOGRAPHICAL.

Wells, J. E., *A Manual of the Writings in Middle English,* 1050–1400, New Haven, &c., 1916; Supplement, 1919.

EDITIONS.

Langland, *The Vision of William concerning Piers Plowman,* &c., ed. W. W. Skeat, 4 vols. Early English Text Society, 1867–85.

Langland, *The Vision of William concerning Piers Plowman,* &c., ed. W. W. Skeat, 2 vols., Oxford, 1886.

SPECIAL STUDIES.

Early English Text Society, original Series, Nos. 135[b] and 139[b, c, d, e]. Articles on the authorship of *Piers Plowman,* by J. M. Manly, J. J. Jusserand, R. W. Chambers, H. Bradley, London, 1908 and 1910. [Discussions on the question whether the various forms of *Piers Plowman* represent the work of one or of several writers. The question is still open.]

Bradley H., *Who was John But?* Mod. Lang. Review. viii (1913) 88.

Chambers, R. W., *The Original Form of the A-Text of 'Piers Plowman'.* Mod. Lang. Rev. vi. (1911) 302.

Jusserand, J. J., *Les Anglais au Moyen Âge: L'Épopée mystique de Will. Langland.* Paris, 1893. English transl. (revised) London, 1894.

Knott, T. H., *An Essay toward the Critical Text of the A-Version of 'Piers Plowman'.* Mod. Phil. XII. 389 ff.

DICTIONARIES.

A New English Dictionary on Historical Principles, ed. Sir J. A. H. Murray, H. Bradley, W. A. Craigie, C. T. Onions, Oxford, 1888.

Stratmann, F. A., *A Middle English Dictionary,* new edn. by H. Bradley, Oxford, 1891.

Skeat, W. W., *Etymological Dictionary of the English Language,* revised edn. 1910.

Skeat, W. W., *A Concise Etymological Dictionary of the English Language,* Oxford, 1911.

CONTEMPORARY AUTHORS.

Chaucer, Geoffrey, *Complete Works*, ed. Skeat, 1895 [Oxford Poets].

Chaucer, Geoffrey, *Complete Works*, ed. Pollard, A. W., (and others) [Globe edition] London, 1903.

Gower, John, *Complete Works*, ed. G. C. Macaulay, 4 vols. Oxford 1899–1902.

Wyclif, John, *Select English Works*, ed. T. Arnold, 3 vols; Oxford, 1869–71.

Wyclif, John, *The English Works hitherto unprinted*, ed. F. D. Mathew, E.E.T.S. 1880.

Political Songs of England (John to Edward II), ed. T. Wright. Camden Society, 1839.

Political Songs of England (Edward III to Richard III), ed. T. Wright, Rolls Series, 2 vols., 1859–61.

STUDIES OF THE PERIOD.

Capes, W. W., *The English Church in the Fourteenth and Fifteenth Centuries*, London, 1909.

Chadwick, D., *Social Life in the Days of Piers Plowman*, Cambridge, 1922.

Coulton, G. G., *Chaucer and his England*, London, 1908.

Cutts, E. L., *Scenes and Characters of the Middle Ages*, London, 1872; 3rd. edn. 1911.

Jusserand, J. J., *English Wayfaring Life in the Middle Ages* (transl. L. Toulmin Smith), London, 1889; revised edn. 1921.

Ker, W. P., *English Literature, Medieval*, London, 1912.

Lingard, John, *A History of England (to 1688)*, 8 vols., 1819–30.

Mediaeval England: being a new and enlarged edition of F. P. Barnard's *Companion to English History (Middle Ages)*. Oxford, 1923.

Oman, Sir Charles Wm. C., *The Great Revolt of 1381*, Oxford, 1906.

Riley, H. T., *Memorials of London and London Life (1270–1419)*, London, 1868.

Sisam, K. and Tolkien, J. R. R., *Fourteenth Century Verse and Prose*, Oxford, 1921.

Traill, H. D. and Mann, J. S., *Social England*, esp. vol. ii (1274–1509). London, 1902.

Trevelyan, G. M., *England in the Age of Wycliffe*, London, 1899, new edn. 1909.

CHRONOLOGICAL TABLE.

Edward II deposed (3. 126*)	Jan. 20, 1327.
Edward III begins to reign	Jan. 25, 1327.
Edward II murdered (3. 126)	Sept. 21, 1327.
Langland born	about 1332.
Chaucer born	1340.
Coinage of nobles (3. 45)	1343 or 1344.
Battle of Creçy (12. 107)	Aug. 26, 1346.
First great pestilence	May 31, 1348 to Sept. 29, 1349.
Treaty of Brétigny (3. 188)	May 8, 1360.
Second great pestilence	Aug. 15, 1361 to May 3, 1362.
Great storm of wind (5. 14)	Saturday, Jan. 15, 1362.
A-text of *Piers the Plowman* written	1362.
Third great pestilence	July 2 to Sept. 29, 1369.
John Chichester mayor of London (13. 271)	Oct. 1369 to Oct. 1370.
A fourth pestilence (13. 248)	1375 and 1376.
Death of the Black Prince	June 8, 1376.
Jubilee of Edward's accession (3. 297)	Feb. 1377.
Death of Edward III	June 21, 1377.
Speech of the Duke of Lancaster, in his own vindication	Oct. 13, 1377.
B-text of *Piers the Plowman* written	1377.
Schism of the Popes	Sept. 21, 1378.
Wycliffe's translation of the Bible (8. 90)	about 1380.
Wat Tyler's rebellion	June 1381.
Chaucer writes his Canterbury Tales	about 1387.
C-text of *Piers the Plowman* written	probably about 1393.
Gower's *Confessio Amantis*	about 1390.
Richard II taken prisoner	Aug. 18, 1399.
Poem of '*Richard the Redeles*'	Sept. 1399.
Richard II formally deposed	Sept. 30, 1399.
Death of Chaucer	1400.
Probable date of death of **Langland**	about 1400.

* These numbers denote the lines of the poem in which the events mentioned are referred to.

THE VISION OF WILLIAM

'PIERS THE PLOWMAN.'

INCIPIT LIBER DE PETRO PLOWMAN.

Prologus.

IN a somer seson · whan soft was the sonne,
  I shope me in shroudes · as I a shepe were,
In habite as an heremite · vnholy of workes,
Went wyde in þis world · wondres to here.
Ac on a May mornynge · on Maluerne hulles,   5
Me byfel a ferly · of fairy, me thouȝte ;
I was wery forwandred · and went me to reste
Vnder a brode banke · bi a bornes side,
And as I lay and lened · and loked in þe wateres,
I slombred in a slepyng · it sweyued so merye.   10
    Thanne gan I to meten · a merueilouse sweuene,
That I was in a wildernesse · wist I neuer where;
As I bihelde in-to þe est · an hiegh to þe sonne,
I seigh a toure on a toft · trielich ymaked;
A depe dale binethe · a dongeon þere-Inne,   15
With depe dyches & derke · and dredful of sight.
A faire felde ful of folke · fonde I there bytwene,
Of alle maner of men · þe mene and þe riche,
Worchyng and wandryng · as þe worlde asketh

Some putten hem to þe plow · pleyed ful selde,   20
In settyng and in sowyng · swonken ful harde,
And wonnen that wastours · with glotonye destruyeth.
    And some putten hem to pruyde · apparailed hem þere-
        after,
In contenaunce of clothyng · comen disgised.
    In prayers and in penance · putten hem manye,   25
Al for loue of owre lorde · lyueden ful streyte,
In hope forto haue · heueneriche blisse ;
As ancres and heremites · that holden hem in here selles,
And coueiten nought in contre · to kairen aboute,
For no likerous liflode · her lykam to plese.   30
    And somme chosen chaffare · they cheuen the bettere,
As it semeth to owre syȝt · that suche men thryueth ;
And somme murthes to make · as mynstralles conneth,
And geten gold with here glee · giltles, I leue.
Ac iapers & iangelers · Iudas chylderen,   35
Feynen hem fantasies · and foles hem maketh,
And han here witte at wille · to worche, ȝif þei sholde ;
That Poule precheth of hem · I nel nought preue it here ;
Qui turpiloquium loquitur · is luciferes hyne.
    Bidders and beggeres · fast aboute ȝede,   40
With her belies and her bagges · of bred ful ycrammed;
Fayteden for here fode · fouȝten atte ale ;
In glotonye, god it wote · gon hij to bedde,
And risen with ribaudye · tho roberdes knaues ;
Slepe and sori sleuthe · seweth hem eure.   45
    Pilgrymes and palmers · pliȝted hem togidere
To seke seynt Iames · and seyntes in rome.
Thei went forth in here wey · with many wise tales,
And hadden leue to lye · al here lyf after.
I seigh somme that seiden · þei had ysouȝt seyntes :   50
To eche a tale þat þei tolde · here tonge was tempred to lye,

More þan to sey soth · it semed bi here speche.

Heremites on an heep · With hoked staues,
Wenten to Walsyngham · and here wenches after ;
Grete lobyes and longe · that loth were to swynke,　　　55
Clotheden hem in copis · to ben knowen fram othere ;
And shopen hem heremites · here ese to haue.

I fonde þere Freris · alle þe foure ordres,
Preched þe peple · for profit of hem-seluen,
Glosed þe gospel · as hem good lyked,　　　60
For coueitise of copis · construed it as þei wolde.
Many of þis maistres Freris · mowe clothen hem at lykyng,
For here money and marchandise · marchen togideres.
For siþ charite haþ be chapman · and chief to shryue lordes
Many ferlis han fallen · in a fewe ȝeris.　　　65
But holychirche and hij · holde better togideres,
The most myschief on molde · is mountyng wel faste.

Þere preched a Pardonere · as he a prest were,
Brouȝte forth a bulle · with bishopes seles,
And seide þat hym-self myȝte · assoilen hem alle　　　70
Of falshed of fastyng · of vowes ybroken.

Lewed men leued hym wel · and lyked his wordes,
Comen vp knelyng · to kissen his bulles ;
He bonched hem with his breuet · & blered here eyes,
And rauȝte with his ragman · rynges and broches ;　　　75
Thus þey geuen here golde · glotones to kepe.

.　　　.　　　.　　　.　　　.　　　.

Were þe bischop yblissed · and worth bothe his eres,
His seel shulde nouȝt be sent · to deceyue þe peple.
Ac it is nauȝt by þe bischop · þat þe boy precheth,　　　80
For the parisch prest and þe pardonere · parten þe siluer,
That þe poraille of þe parisch · sholde haue, ȝif þei nere.

Persones and parisch prestes · pleyned hem to þe bischop,
Þat here parisshes were pore · siþ þe pestilence tyme,

To haue a lycence and a leue · at London to dwelle,   85
And syngen þere for symonye · for siluer is swete.

Bischopes and bachelers · bothe maistres and doctours,
Þat han cure vnder criste · and crounyng in tokne
And signe þat þei sholden · shryuen here paroschienes,
Prechen and prey for hem · and þe pore fede,   90
Liggen in London · in lenten, an elles.
Somme seruen þe kyng · and his siluer tellen,
In cheker and in chancerye . chalengen his dettes
Of wardes and wardmotes · weyues and streyues.

And some seruen as seruantz · lordes and ladyes,   95
And in stede of stuwardes · sytten and demen.
Here messe and here matynes · and many of here oures
Arn don vndeuoutlych; · drede is at þe laste
Lest crist in consistorie · acorse ful manye.
I parceyued of þe power · þat Peter had to kepe,   100
To bynde and to vnbynde · as þe boke telleth,
How he it left wiþ loue · as owre lorde hight,
Amonges foure vertues · þe best of all vertues,
Þat cardinales ben called · & closyng ȝatis,
Þere crist is in kyngdome · to close and to shutte,   105
And to opne it to hem · and heuene blisse shewe.
Ac of þe cardinales atte Courte · þat cauȝt of þat name,
And powei presumed in hem · a Pope to make,
To han þat power þat peter hadde · inpugnen I nelle;
For in loue and letterure · þe eleccioun bilongeth,   110
For-þi I can and can nauȝte · of courte speke more.

Þanne come þere a kyng · knyȝthod hym ladde,
Miȝt of þe comunes · made hym to regne,
And þanne cam kynde wytte · and clerkes he made,
For to conseille þe kyng · and þe comune saue.   115
The kyng and knyȝthode · and clergye bothe
Casten þat þe comune · shulde hem-self fynde.

Þe comune contreued · of kynde witte craftes,
And for profit of alle þe poeple · plowmen ordeygned,
To tilie and trauaile · as trewe lyf askeþ.   120
Þe kynge and þe comune · and kynde witte þe thridde
Shope lawe & lewte · eche man to knowe his owne.

Þanne loked vp a lunatik · a lene þing with-alle,
And knelyng to þe kyng · clergealy he seyde ;
' Crist kepe þe, sire kyng · and þi kyngriche,   125
And leue þe lede þi londe · so leute þe louye,
And for þi riȝtful rewlyng · be rewarded in heuene !'

And sithen in þe eyre an hiegh · An angel of heuene
Lowed to speke in latyn— · for lewed men ne coude
Iangle ne iugge · þat iustifie hem shulde,   130
But suffren & seruen— · for-thi seyde þe angel,
' *Sum Rex, sum Princeps* · *neutrum fortasse deinceps ;—*
O qui iura regis · *Christi specialia regis,*
Hoc quod agas melius · *iustus es, esto pius !*
Nudum ius a te · *vestiri vult pietate ;*   135
Qualia vis metere · *talia grana sere.*
Si ius nudatur · *nudo de iure metatur ;*
Si seritur pietas · *de pietate metas !*'

Thanne greued hym a Goliardeys · a glotoun of wordes,
And to þe angel an heiȝ · answered after,   140
' *Dum rex a regere* · *dicatur nomen habere,*
Nomen habet sine re · *nisi studet iura tenere.*'

And þanne gan alle þe comune · crye in vers of latin,
To þe kynges conseille · construe ho-so wolde—
' *Precepta Regis* · *sunt nobis vincula legis.*'   145

Wiþ þat ran þere a route · of ratones at ones,
And smale mys myd hem · mo þen a þousande,
And comen to a conseille · for here comune profit;
For a cat of a courte · cam whan hym lyked,
And ouerlepe hem lyȝtlich · and lauȝte hem at his wille, 150

And pleyde wiþ hem perilouslych · and possed hem aboute.
' For doute of dyuerse dredes · we dar nouȝte wel loke ;
And ȝif we grucche of his gamen · he wil greue vs alle,
Cracche vs, or clowe vs · and in his cloches holde,
That vs lotheth þe lyf · or he lete vs passe.   155
Myȝte we wiþ any witte · his wille withstonde,
We myȝte be lordes aloft · and lyuen at owre ese.'

    A raton of renon · most renable of tonge,
Seide for a souereygne · help to hym-selue ;—
' I haue ysein segges,' quod he · ' in þe cite of london   160
Beren biȝes ful briȝte · abouten here nekkes,
And some colers of crafty werk ; · vncoupled þei wenden
Boþe in wareine & in waste · where hem leue lyketh ;
And otherwhile þei aren elles-where · as I here telle.
Were þere a belle on here beiȝ · bi Iesu, as me thynketh, 165
Men myȝte wite where þei went · and awei renne !
And riȝt so,' quod þat ratoun · ' reson me sheweth,
To bugge a belle of brasse · or of briȝte syluer,
And knitten on a colere · for owre comune profit,
And hangen it vp-on þe cattes hals · þanne here we mowen
Where he ritt or rest · or renneth to playe.   171
And ȝif him list for to laike · þenne loke we mowen,
And peren in his presence · þer-while hym plaie liketh,
And ȝif him wrattheth, be ywar · and his weye shonye.'

    Alle þis route of ratones · to þis reson þei assented.   175
Ac þo þe belle was ybouȝt · and on þe beiȝe hanged,
Þere ne was ratoun in alle þe route · for alle þe rewme of
        Fraunce,
Þat dorst haue ybounden þe belle · aboute þe cattis nekke,
Ne hangen it aboute þe cattes hals · al Engelonde to wynne ;
And helden hem vnhardy · and here conseille feble,   180
And leten here laboure lost · & alle here longe studye.

    A mous þat moche good · couthe, as me thouȝte,

Stroke forth sternly · and stode biforn hem alle,
And to þe route of ratones · reherced þese wordes ;
' Thou3 we culled þe catte · 3ut sholde þer come another, 185
To cracchy vs and al owre kynde · þou3 we crope vnder
　　benches.
For-þi I conseille alle þe comune · to lat þe catte worthe,
And be we neuer so bolde · þe belle hym to shewe ;
For I herde my sire seyn · is seuene 3ere ypassed,
Þere þe catte is a kitoun · þe courte is ful elyng ;　　　　190
Þat witnisseth holiwrite · who-so wil it rede,
　　　　Ve terre vbi puer rex est, &c.
For may no renke þere rest haue · for ratones bi ny3te ;
Þe while he caccheþ conynges · he coueiteth nou3t owre
　　caroyne,
But fet hym al with venesoun · defame we hym neuere.
For better is a litel losse · þan a longe sorwe,　　　　195
Þe mase amonge vs alle · þou3 we mysse a schrewe.
For many mannus malt · we mys wolde destruye,
And also 3e route of ratones · rende mennes clothes,
Nere þat cat of þat courte · þat can 3ow ouerlepe ;
For had 3e rattes 3owre wille · 3e couthe nou3t reule 3owre-
　　selue.　　　　　　　　　　　　　　　　　　　　　　　200
I sey for me,' quod þe mous · ' I se so mykel after,
Shal neuer þe cat ne þe kitoun · bi my conseille be greued,
Ne carpyng of þis coler · þat costed me neure.
And þou3 it had coste me catel · biknowen it I nolde,
But suffre as hym-self wolde · to do as hym liketh,　　　205
Coupled & vncoupled · to cacche what thei mowe.
For-þi vche a wise wi3te I warne · wite wel his owne.'—
　　What þis meteles bemeneth · 3e men þat be merye,
Deuine 3e, for I ne dar · bi dere god in heuene !
　　3it houed þere an hondreth · in houues of selke,　　210
Seriauntz it semed · þat serueden atte barre,

Pldeden for penyes · and poundes þe lawe,
And nouȝt for loue of owre lorde · vnlese here lippes onis.
Þow myȝtest better mete þe myste · on maluerne hulles,
Þan gete a momme of here mouthe · but money were
   shewed.   215

 Barones an burgeis · and bonde-men als
I seiȝ in þis assemble · as ȝe shul here after.
Baxsteres & brewesteres · and bocheres manye,
Wollewebsteres · and weueres of lynnen,
Taillours and tynkeres · & tolleres in marketes,   220
Masons and mynours · and many other craftes.
Of alkin libbyng laboreres · lopen forth somme,
As dykers & delueres · þat doth here dedes ille,
And dryuen forth þe longe day · with ' *Dieu vous saue, Dame
   Emme !* '

Cokes and here knaues · crieden, ' hote pies, hote !   225
Gode gris and gees · gowe dyne, gowe ! '

 Tauerners vn-til hem · tolde þe same,
' White wyn of Oseye · and red wyn of Gascoigne,
Of þe Ryne and of þe Rochel · þe roste to defye.'—
Al þis seiȝ I slepyng · and seuene sythes more.   230

PASSUS I.

Passus Primus de visione.

WHAT this montaigne bymeneth · and þe merke dale,
 And þe felde ful of folke · I shal ȝow faire schewe.
A loueli ladi of lere · in lynnen yclothed,
Come down fram a castel · and called me faire,
And seide, 'Sone, slepestow · sestow þis poeple,   5
How bisi þei ben · abouten þe mase?
Þe moste partie of þis poeple · þat passeth on þis erthe,
Haue þei worschip in þis worlde · þei wilne no better;
Of other heuene þan here · holde þei no tale.'

 I was aferd of her face · þeiȝ she faire were,   10
And seide, 'mercy, Madame · what is þis to mene?'
'Þe toure vp þe toft,' quod she · 'treuthe is þere-Inne,
And wolde þat ȝe wrouȝte · as his worde techeth;
For he is fader of feith · fourmed ȝow alle,
Bothe with fel and with face · and ȝaf ȝow fyue wittis   15
Forto worschip hym þer-with · þe while þat ȝe ben here.
And þerfore he hyȝte þe erthe · to help ȝow vchone
Of wollen, of lynnen · of lyflode at nede,
In mesurable manere · to make ȝow at ese;

 And comaunded of his curteisye · in comune þree þinges;
Arne none nedful but þo · and nempne hem I thinke,   21
And rekne hem bi resoun · reherce þow hem after.
That one is vesture · from chele þe to saue,
And mete atte mele · for myseise of þi-selue.

And drynke whan þow dryest · ac do nouȝt out of resoun, 25
That þow worth þe werse · whan þow worche shuldest.

    ·   ·   ·

For-þi drede delitable drynke · and þow shalt do þe bettere;
Mesure is medcyne · þouȝ þow moche ȝerne. 35
It is nauȝt al gode to þe goste · þat þe gutte axeþ,
Ne liflode to þi likam · þat leef is to þi soule.
Leue not þi likam · for a lyer him techeth,
That is þe wrecched worlde · wolde þe bitraye.
For þe fende and þi flesch · folweth þe to-gidere, 40
This and þat sueth þi soule · and seith it in þin herte;
And for þow sholdest ben ywar · I wisse þe þe beste.'
    'Madame, mercy,' quod I · 'me liketh wel ȝowre wordes,
Ac þe moneye of þis molde · þat men so faste holdeth,
Telle me to whom, Madame · þat tresore appendeth?' 45
    'Go to þe gospel,' quod she · 'þat god seide hym-seluen,
Tho þe poeple hym apposed · wiþ a peny in þe temple,
Whether þei shulde þer-with · worschip þe kyng Sesar.
And god axed of hem · of whome spake þe lettre,
And þe ymage ilyke · þat þere-inne stondeth? 50
" *Cesaris,*" þei seide · " we sen hym wel vchone."
" *Reddite cesari,*" quod god · " þat *cesari* bifalleth.
Et que sunt dei, deo · or elles ȝe done ille."
For riȝtful reson · shulde rewle ȝow alle,
And kynde witte be wardeyne · ȝowre welthe to kepe, 55
And tutour of ȝoure tresore · and take it ȝow at nede;
For housbonderye & hij · holden togideres.'
Þanne I frained hir faire · for hym þat hir made,
'That dongeoun in þe dale · þat dredful is of siȝte,
What may it be to mene · ma-dame, I ȝow biseche?' 60
    'Þat is þe castel of care · who so cometh þerinne
May banne þat he borne was · to body or to soule.
Þerinne wonieth a wiȝte · þat wronge is yhote,

Fader of falshed · and founded it hym-selue.
Adam and Eue · he egged to ille,   65
Conseilled caym · to kullen his brother ;
Iudas he iaped · with iuwen siluer,
And sithen on an eller · honged hym after.
He is letter of loue · and lyeth hem alle ;
That trusten on his tresor · bitrayeth he sonnest.'   70

   Thanne had I wonder in my witt · what womman it were
þat such wise wordes · of holy writ shewed ;
And asked hir on þe hieȝe name · ar heo þennes ȝeode,
What she were witterli · þat wissed me so faire ?

   'Holicherche I am,' quod she · 'þow ouȝtest me to knowe,
I vnderfonge þe firste · and þe feyth tauȝte,   76
And brouȝtest me borwes · my biddyng to fulfille,
And to loue me lelly · þe while þi lyf dureth.'

   Thanne I courbed on my knees · and cryed hir of grace,
And preyed hir pitousely · prey for my synnes,   80
And also kenne me kyndeli · on criste to bileue,
That I miȝte worchen his wille · þat wrouȝte me to man ;
'Teche me to no tresore · but telle me þis ilke,
How I may saue my soule · þat seynt art yholden ?'

   'Whan alle tresores aren tried,' quod she · 'trewthe is
     þe best ;   85
I do it on *deus caritas* · to deme þe soþe ;
It is as derworth a drewery · as dere god hym-seluen.

   Who-so is trewe of his tonge · & telleth none other,
And doth þe werkis þer-with · and wilneth no man ille,
He is a god bi þe gospel · agrounde and aloft,   90
And ylike to owre lorde · bi seynte lukes wordes.
þe clerkes þat knoweþ þis · shulde kenne it aboute.
For cristene and vncristne · clameþ it vchone.

   Kynges & kniȝtes · shulde kepe it bi resoun,
Riden and rappe down · in reumes aboute,   95

And taken *trangressores* · and tyen hem faste,
Til treuthe had ytermyned · her trespas to þe ende.
And þat is þe *professioun* appertly · þat appendeth for knyȝtes,
And nouȝt to fasten a fryday · in fyue score wynter ;
But holden wiþ him & with hir · þat wolden al treuthe,   100
And neuer leue hem for loue · ne for lacchyng of syluer.

　　For Dauid in his dayes · dubbed kniȝtes,
And did hem swere on here swerde · to serue trewthe eu*er*e,
And who-so passed þat poynte · was *apostata* in þe ordre.

　　But criste kingene kynge · kniȝted ten,   105
Cherubyn and seraphin · suche seuene and an othre,
And ȝaf hem myȝte in his maieste · þe muryer hem þouȝte ;
And ouer his mene meyne · made hem archangeles,
Tauȝte hem bi þe Trinitee · treuthe to knowe,
To be buxome at his biddyng · he bad hem nouȝte elles. 110

　　Lucifer wiþ legiounes · lerned it in heuene,
But for he brake buxumnesse · his blisse gan he tyne,
And fel fro þat felawship · in a fendes liknes,
In-to a depe derke helle · to dwelle þere for eure ;
And mo þowsandes wiþ him · þan man couthe noumbre 115
Lopen out wiþ Lucifer · in lothelich forme,
For þei leueden vpon hym · þat lyed in þis manere :

　　　　Ponam pedem in aquilone, et similis ero altissimo.

　　And alle þat hoped it miȝte be so · none heuene miȝte hem
　　　　holde,
But fellen out in fendes liknesse · nyne dayes togideres,
Til god of his goodnesse · gan stable and stynte,   120
And garte þe heuene to stekye · and stonden in quiete.

　　Whan thise wikked went out · wonderwise þei fellen,
So*m*me in eyre, so*m*me in erthe · & so*m*me in helle depe ;
Ac lucifer lowest · lith of hem alle ;
For pryde þat he pult out · his peyne hath none ende ; 125
And alle þat worche with wronge · wenden hij shulle

After her deth day · and dwelle wiþ þat shrewe.
Ac þo þat worche wel · as holiwritt telleth,
And enden, as I ere seide · in treuthe, þat is þe best,
Mowe be siker þat her soule · shal wende to heuene,   130
Þer treuthe is in Trinitee · and troneth hem alle.
For-þi I sey, as I seide ere · bi siȝte of þise textis,
Whan alle tresores arne ytried · treuthe is þe beste.
Lereth it þis lewde men · for lettred men it knowen,
Þat treuthe is tresore · þe triest on erþe.'   135
  ' Ȝet haue I no kynde knowing,' quod I · ' Ȝet mote ȝe kenne
      me better,
By what craft in my corps · it comseth, and where.'
  ' Þow doted daffe,' quod she · ' dulle arne þi wittes ;
To litel latyn þow lernedest · lede, in þi ȝouthe ;
      Heu michi, quod sterilem duxi vitam iuuenilem !
  It is a kynde knowyng,' quod she · ' þat kenneth in þine
      herte   140
For to louye þi lorde · leuer þan þi-selue ;
No dedly synne to do · dey þouȝ þow sholdest :
This I trowe be treuthe · who can teche þe better,
Loke þow suffre hym to sey · and sithen lere it after.
  For thus witnesseth his worde · worche þow þereafter ; 145
For trewthe telleþ þat loue · is triacle of heuene ;
May no synne be on him sene · þat vseth þat spise,
And alle his werkes he wrouȝte · with loue as him liste ;
And lered it Moises for þe leuest þing · and moste like to
      heuene,
And also þe plante of pees · moste precious of vertues.   150
  For heuene myȝte nouȝte holden it · it was so heuy of
      hym-self,
Tyl it hadde of þe erthe · yeten his fylle.
  And whan it haued of þis folde · flesshe & blode taken,
Was neuere leef vpon lynde · liȝter þer-after,

And portatyf and persant · as þe poynt of a nedle,   155
That myȝte non armure it lette · ne none heiȝ walles.

For-þi is loue leder · of þe lordes folke of heuene,
And a mene, as þe Maire is · bitwene þe kyng and þe
    comune ;
Riȝt so is loue a ledere · and þe lawe shapeth,
Vpon man for his mysdedes · þe merciment he taxeth.   160
And for to knowe it kyndely · it comseth bi myght,
And in þe herte þere is þe heuede · and þe heiȝ welle ;

For in kynde knowynge in herte · þere a myȝte bigynneth.
And þat falleth to þe fader · þat formed vs alle,
Loked on vs with loue · and lete his sone deye   165
Mekely for owre mysdedes · to amende vs alle ;
And ȝet wolde he hem no woo · þat wrouȝte hym þat peyne,
But mekelich with mouthe · mercy he bisouȝte
To haue pite of þat poeple · þat peyned hym to deth.

Here myȝtow see ensamples · in hym-selue one,   170
That he was miȝtful & meke · and mercy gan graunte
To hem þat hongen him an heiȝ · and his herte þirled.

For-thi I rede ȝow riche · haueth reuthe of þe pouere ;
Thouȝ ȝe be myȝtful to mote · beth meke in ȝowre werkes.

For þe same mesures þat ȝe mete · amys other elles,   175
ȝe shullen ben weyen þer-wyth · whan ȝe wende hennes ;
        Eadem mensura qua mensi fueritis, remecietur vobis.

For þouȝ ȝe be trewe of ȝowre tonge · and trewliche wynne,
And as chaste as a childe · þat in cherche wepeth,
But if ȝe louen lelliche · and lene þe poure,
Such goed as god ȝow sent · godelich parteth,   180
ȝe ne haue na more meryte · in masse ne in houres,
Þan Malkyn of hire maydenhode · þat no man desireth.

For Iames þe gentil · iugged in his bokes,
That faith with-oute þe faite · is riȝte no þinge worthi,
And as ded as a dore-tree · but ȝif þe dedes folwe ;   185

Fides sine operibus mortua est, &c.

For-thi chastite with-oute charite · worth cheyned in helle;
It is as lewed as a laumpe · þat no liȝte is Inne.

Many chapeleynes arne chaste · ac charite is awey;
Aren no men auarouser*e* þan hij · whan þei ben auaunced;   190
Vnkynde to her kyn · and to alle cristene,
Chewen here charite · and chiden after more.
Such chastite wiþ-outen charite · worth cheyned in helle!

Many curatoures kepen hem · clene of here bodies,
Thei ben acombred wiþ coueitise · þei konne nouȝt don it
   fram hem,
So harde hath auarice · yhasped hem togideres.   195
And þat is no treuthe of þe trinite · but treccherye of helle,
And lernyng to lewde men · þe latter for to dele.

For-þi þis wordes · ben wryten in þe gospel,
Date & dabitur vobis · for I dele ȝow alle.
And þat is þe lokke of loue · and lateth oute my grace,   200
To conforte þe careful · acombred wiþ synne.

Loue is leche of lyf · and nexte owre lorde selue,
And also þe graith gate · þat goth in-to heuene;
For-þi I sey, as I seide · ere by þe textis,
Whan alle tresores ben ytryed · treuthe is þe beste.   205
Now haue I tolde þe what treuthe is · þat no tresore is
   bettere,
I may no lenger lenge þe with now loke þe owre lorde!'   207

PASSUS II.

YET I courbed on my knees · and cryed hir of grace,
And seide, 'mercy, Madame · for Marie loue of heuene,
That bar þat blisful barne · þat bouȝte vs on þe Rode,
Kenne me bi somme crafte · to knowe þe fals.'

   'Loke vppon þi left half · and lo where he standeth,   5
Bothe fals and fauel · and here feres manye!'

   I loked on my left half · as þe lady me taughte,
And was war of a womman · wortheli yclothed,
Purfiled with pelure · þe finest vpon erthe,
Y-crounede with a corone · þe kyng hath non better.   10
Fetislich hir fyngres · were fretted with golde wyre,
And þere-on red rubyes · as red as any glede,
And diamantz of derrest pris · and double manere safferes,
Orientales and ewages · enuenymes to destroye.

   Hire robe was ful riche · of red scarlet engreyned,   15
With ribanes of red golde · and of riche stones ;
Hire arraye me rauysshed · suche ricchesse saw I neuere ;
I had wondre what she was · and whas wyf she were.

   'What is þis womman,' quod I · 'so worthily atired ?'
'That is Mede þe Mayde, quod she · 'hath noyed me ful
   oft,   20
And ylakked my lemman · þat lewte is hoten,
And bilowen hire to lordes · þat lawes han to kepe.
In þe popis paleys · she is pryue as my-self,

But sothenesse wolde nouȝt so · for she is a bastarde.

For fals was hire fader · þat hath a fykel tonge, 25
And neuere sothe seide · sithen he come to erthe.

And Mede is manered after hym · riȝte as kynde axeth;

> *Qualis pater, talis filius; bona arbor bonum fructum facit.*

I auȝte ben herre þan she · I cam of a better.

Mi fader þe grete god is · and grounde of alle graces,
O god with-oute gynnynge · & I his gode douȝter, 30
And hath ȝoue me mercy · to marye with my-self;
And what man be merciful · and lelly me loue,
Schal be my lorde and I his leef · in þe heiȝe heuene.

And what man taketh Mede · myne hed dar I legge,
That he shal lese for hir loue · a lappe of *caritatis.* 35
How construeth dauid þe kynge · of men þat taketh Mede,
And men of þis molde · þat meynteneth treuthe,
And how ȝe shal saue ȝow-self · þe Sauter bereth witnesse,

> *Domine, quis habitabit in tabernaculo tuo, &c.*

And now worth þis Mede ymaried · al to a mansed schrewe,

To one fals fikel-tonge · a fendes biȝete; 40
Fauel þorw his faire speche · hath þis folke enchaunted,
And al is lyeres ledyng · þat she is þus ywedded.

To-morwe worth ymade · þe maydenes bruydale,
And þere miȝte þow wite, if þow wolt · which þei ben alle
That longeth to þat lordeship · þe lasse and þe more. 45
Knowe hem þere if þow canst · and kepe þi tonge,
And lakke hem nouȝt, but lat hem worth · til lewte be iustice,
And haue powere to punyschen hem; · þanne put forth þi resoun.

Now I bikenne þe criste,' quod she · 'and his clene moder,
And lat no conscience acombre þe · for coueitise of Mede.' 50

Thus left me þat lady · liggyng aslepe,

And how Mede was ymaried · in meteles me þouȝte,
Þat alle þe riche retenauns · þat regneth with þe false
Were boden to þe bridale · on bothe two sydes,
Of alle maner of men · þe mene and þe riche.   55
To marie þis maydene · was many man assembled,
As of kniȝtes and of clerkis · and other comune poeple,
As sysours and sompnours · Shireues and here clerkes,
Bedelles and Bailliues · and brokoures of chaffare,
Forgoeres and vitaillers · and vokates of þe arches ;   60
I can nouȝt rekene þe route · þat ran aboute mede.

 Ac Symonye and cyuile · and sisoures of courtes
Were moste pryue with Mede · of any men, me þouȝte.
Ac fauel was þe first · þat fette hire out of boure,
And as a brokour brouȝte hir · to be with fals enioigned.   65
Whan Symonye and cyuile · seiȝ here beire wille,
Thei assented for siluer · to sei as bothe wolde.
Thanne lepe lyer forth, and seide · ' lo here ! a chartre,
That gyle with his gret othes · gaf hem togidere,'
And preide cyuile to se · and symonye to rede it.   70
Thanne Symonye and cyuile · stonden forth bothe,
And vnfoldeth þe feffement · þat fals hath ymaked,
And þus bigynneth þes gomes · to greden ful heiȝ :—
         ' *Sciant presentes & futuri, &c.*

 Witeth and witnesseth · þat wonieth vpon þis erthe,
Þat Mede is y-maried · more for here goodis,   75
Þan for ani vertue or fairenesse · or any free kynde.
Falsenesse is faine of hire · for he wote hire riche ;
And fauel with his fikel speche · feffeth bi þis chartre
To be prynces in pryde · and pouerte to dispise,
To bakbite, and to bosten · and bere fals witnesse,   80
To scorne and to scolde · and sclaundere to make,
Vnboxome and bolde · to breke þe ten hestes ;—
     And þe Erldome of enuye · and Wratthe togideres,

With þe chastelet of chest · and chateryng-oute-of-resou*n*,
Þe counte of coueitise · and alle þe costes aboute,   85
That is, vsure and auarice · alle I hem graunte,
In bargaines and in brokages · with al þe borghe of theft.'

   .   .   .   .   .   .

  ' Glotonye he gaf hem eke · and grete othes togydere,
And alday to drynke · at dyuerse tauernes,
And there to iangle and to iape · and iugge here euene-
    cristene,
And in fastyng-dayes to frete · ar ful tyme were.   95
And þanne to sitten and soupen · til slepe hem assaille ;

   .   .   .   .   .   .

Tyl sleuth and slepe · slyken his sides ;
And þanne wanhope to awake hym so · with no wille to
    amende,
For he leueth be lost · þis is here last ende.   100
  And þei to haue and to holde · and here eyres after,
A dwellyng with þe deuel · and dampned be for eure,
Wiþ al þe purtenaunces of purgatorie · in-to þe pyne of helle.
Ʒeldyng for þis þinge · at one ʒeres ende,
Here soules to Sathan · to suffre with hym peynes,   105
And with him to wonye with wo · whil god is in heuene.'
  In witnesse of which þing · wronge was þe first,
And Pieres þe pardonere · of paulynes doctrine,
Bette þe bedel · of Bokyngham-shire,
Rainalde þe Reue · of Rotland sokene,   110
Munde þe Mellere · and many moo other.
' In þe date of þe deuil · þis dede I assele,
Bi siʒte of Sire Simonye · and cyuyles leue.'
  Þenne tened hym theologye · whan he þis tale herde,
And seide to cyuile · ' now sorwe mot þow haue,   115
Such weddynges to worche · to wratthe with treuthe ;
And ar þis weddyng be wrouʒte · wo þe bityde !

For Mede is moylere · of amendes engendred,
And god graunteth to gyf · Mede to treuthe,
And þow hast gyuen hire to a gyloure · now god gyf þe
　　sorwe !   120
Thi tixt telleth þe nouȝt so · treuthe wote þe sothe,
For *dignus est operarius* · his hyre to haue,
And þow hast fest hire to fals · fy on þi lawe !
For al by lesynges þow lyuest · and lecherouse werkes,
Symonye and þi-self · schenden holicherche,   125
Þe notaries and ȝee · noyeth þe peple,
Ȝe shul abiggen it bothe · bi god þat me made !
Wel ȝe witen, wernardes · but if ȝowre witte faille,
That fals is faithlees · and fikel in his werkes,
And was a bastarde y-bore · of belsabubbes kynne.   130
And Mede is moylere · a mayden of gode,
And myȝte kisse þe kynge · for cosyn, an she wolde.

　　For-þi worcheth bi wisdome · and bi witt also,
And ledeth hire to londoun · þere lawe is yshewed,
If any lawe wil loke · þei ligge togederes.   135
And þouȝ Iustices iugge hir · to be ioigned with fals,
Ȝet beth war of weddyng · for witty is truthe,
And conscience is of his conseille · and knoweth ȝow vchone ;
And if he fynde ȝow in defaute · and with þe fals holde,
It shal bisitte ȝowre soules · ful soure atte laste !'   140
　　Here-to assenteth cyuile · ac symonye ne wolde,
Tyl he had siluer for his seruise · and also þe notaries.
　　Thanne fette fauel forth · floreynes ynowe,
And bad gyle to gyue · golde al aboute,
And namelich to þe notaries · þat hem none ne faille,   145
And feffe false-witnes · with floreines ynowe ;
' For he may mede amaistrye · and maken at my wille.'
　　Tho þis golde was gyue · grete was þe þonkynge
To fals and to fauel · for her faire ȝiftes,

And comen to conforte · fram care þe fals,　　　　150
And seiden, ' certis, sire · cesse shal we neuere
Til Mede be þi wedded wyf · þorw wittis of vs alle.
For we haue Mede amaistried · with owre mery speche,
That she graunteth to gon · with a gode wille,
To Londoun to loke · ȝif þat þe lawe wolde　　　155
Iugge ȝow ioyntly · in ioye for euere.'

　　Thanne was falsenesse fayne · and fauel as blithe,
And leten sompne alle segges · in schires aboute,
And bad hem alle be bown · beggeres and othere,
To wenden wyth hem to Westmynstre · to witnesse þis
　　dede.　　　　　　　　　　　　　　　　160
　　Ac þanne cared þei for caplus · to kairen hem þider,
And fauel fette forth þanne · folus ynowe ;
And sette Mede vpon a Schyreue · shodde al newe,
And fals sat on a sisoure · þat softlich trotted,
And fauel on a flaterere · fetislich atired.　　165
　　Tho haued notaries none · annoyed þei were,
For Symonye and cyuile · shulde on hire fete gange.
　　Ac þanne swore Symonye · and cyuile bothe,
That sompnoures shulde be sadled · and serue hem vchone,
And lat apparaille þis prouisoures · in palfreis wyse ;—　170
' Sire Symonye hym-seluen · shal sitte vpon here bakkes.
　　Denes and suddenes · drawe ȝow togideres,
Erchdekenes and officiales · and alle ȝowre Regystreres,
Lat sadel hem with siluer · owre synne to suffre,
As auoutrie and deuorses · and derne vsurye,　　175
To bere bischopes aboute · abrode in visytynge.
　　Paulynes pryues · for pleyntes in þe consistorie,
Shul serue my-self · þat cyuile is nempned ;
And cartesadel þe comissarie · owre carte shal he lede.
　　·　　　·　　　·　　　·　　　·　　　·　　　180
　　And maketh of lyer a longe carte · to lede alle þese othere,

As Freres and faitours · þat on here fete rennen.'
And thus fals and fauel · fareth forth togideres,
And Mede in þe myddes · and alle þise men after.

I haue no tome to telle · þe taille þat hem folweth,   185
Of many maner man · þat on þis molde libbeth;
Ac gyle was forgoer · and gyed hem alle.

Sothenesse seiȝ hym wel · and seide but a litel,
And priked his palfrey · and passed hem alle,
And come to þe kynges courte · and conscience it tolde,   190
And conscience to þe kynge · carped it after.

'Now by cryst,' quod þe kynge · · 'and I cacche myȝte
Fals or fauel · or any of his feres,
I wolde be wroke of þo wrecches · þat worcheth so ille,
And don hem hange by þe hals · and alle þat hem meynteneth!
Shal neure man of molde · meynprise þe leste,   196
But riȝte as þe lawe wil loke · late falle on hem alle.'

And comanded a constable · þat come atte furst,
To 'attache þo tyrauntz · for eny thynge, I hote,
And fettereth fast falsenesse · for enykynnes ȝiftes,   200
And gurdeth of gyles hed · and lat hym go no furthere.
And ȝif ȝe lacche lyer · late hym nouȝt ascapen
Er he be put on þe pilorye · for eny preyere, I hote;
And bryngeth Mede to me · maugre hem alle.'

Drede atte dore stode · and þe dome herde,   205
And how þe kynge comaunded · constables and seriantz,
Falsenesse and his felawschip · to fettren an to bynden.
Þanne drede went wiȝtliche · and warned þe fals,
And bad hym flee for fere · and his felawes alle.

Falsenesse for fere þanne · fleiȝ to þe freres,   210
And gyle doþ hym to go · agast for to dye.
Ac marchantz mette with hym · and made hym abide,
And bishetten hym in here shope · to shewen here ware,
And apparailled hym as a prentice · þe poeple to serue.

Liȝtliche lyer · lepe awey þanne,   215
Lorkynge thorw lanes · to-lugged of manye.
He was nawhere welcome · for his manye tales,
Ouer al yhowted · and yhote trusse;
Tyl pardoneres haued pite · and pulled hym in-to house.
They wesshen hym and wyped hym · and wonden hym in
    cloutes,   220
And sente hym with seles · on sondayes to cherches,
And gaf pardoun for pens · poundmel aboute.

   .   .   .   .

Spiceres spoke with hym · to spien here ware,   225
For he couth of here craft · and knewe many gommes.
  Ac mynstralles and messageres · mette with hym ones,
And helden hym an half-ȝere · and elleuene dayes.
  Freres with faire speche · fetten hym þennes,
And for knowyng of comeres · coped hym as a frere.   230
Ac he hath leue to lepe out · as oft as hym liketh,
And is welcome whan he wil · and woneth wyth hem oft.
  Alle fledden for fere · and flowen in-to hernes,
Saue Mede þe Mayde · na mo durst abide.
Ac trewli to telle · she trembled for drede,
And ek wept and wronge · whan she was attached.   236

PASSUS III

Passus tertius.

NOW is Mede þe Mayde · and namo of hem alle
 With bedellus & wiþ bayllyues · brouȝt bifor þe kyng.
The kyng called a clerke · can I nouȝt his name,
To take Mede þe mayde · and make hire at ese.
'I shal assaye hir my-self · and sothelich appose   5
What man of þis molde · þat hire were leueste.
And if she worche bi my witte · and my wille folwe,
I wil forgyue hir þis gilte · so me god help !'

  Curteysliche þe clerke þanne · as þe Kyng hight,
Toke Mede bi þe Middel · and brouȝte hir in-to chaumbre, 10
And þere was myrthe and mynstralcye · Mede to plese.

  They þat wonyeth in Westmynstre · worschiped hir alle ;
Gentelliche wiþ ioye · þe Iustices somme
Busked hem to þe boure · þere þe birde dwelled,
To conforte hire kyndely · by clergise leue,   15
And seiden, 'mourne nought, Mede · ne make þow no sorwe,
For we wil wisse þe kynge · and þi wey shape,
To be wedded at þi wille · and where þe leue liketh,
For al conscience caste · or craft, as I trowe !'

  Mildeliche Mede þanne · mercyed hem alle   20
Of þeire gret goodnesse · and gaf hem vchone
Coupes of clene golde · and coppis of siluer,
Rynges with rubies · and ricchesses manye,
The leste man of here meyne · a motoun of golde.

Thanne lauȝte þei leue · þis lordes, at Mede.   25
  With that comen clerkis · to conforte hir þe same.
And beden hire be blithe · 'for we beth þine owne,
For to worche þi wille · þe while þow myȝte laste.'
Hendeliche heo þanne · bihight hem þe same,
To 'loue ȝow lelli · and lordes to make,   30
And in þe consistorie atte courte · do calle ȝowre names ;
Shal no lewdnesse lette · þe leode þat I louye,
That he ne worth first auanced · for I am biknowen
Þere konnyng clerkes · shul clokke bihynde.'

  Þanne come þere a confessoure · coped as a Frere,   35
To Mede þe mayde · he mellud þis wordes,
And seide ful softly · in shrifte as it were,

   ·   ·   ·   ·   ·   ·   ·

' Theiȝ falsenesse haued yfolwed þe · al þis fyfty wyntre,
I shal assoille þe my-selue · for a seme of whete,   40
And also be þi bedeman · and bere wel þi message,
Amonges kniȝtes and clerkis · conscience to torne.'

  Thanne Mede for here mysdedes · to þat man kneled,
And shroue hire of hire shrewednesse · shamelees, I trowe,
Tolde hym a tale · and toke hym a noble,   45
Forto ben hire bedeman · and hire brokour als.

  Thanne he assoilled hir sone · and sithen he seyde,
' We han a wyndowe a wirchyng · wil sitten vs ful heigh ;
Woldestow glase þat gable · and graue þere-inne þi name,
Siker sholde þi soule be · heuene to haue.'   50
' Wist I that,' quod þat womman · ' I wolde nouȝt spare
For to be ȝowre frende, frere · and faille ȝow neure ;

  ·   ·

And I shal keure ȝowre kirke · ȝowre cloystre do maken,   60
Wowes do whiten · and wyndowes glasen,
Do peynten and purtraye · and paye for þe makynge,
That eury segge shal seyn · I am sustre of ȝowre hous.'

Ac god to alle good folke · suche *grauynge* defendeth,
To writen in wyndowes · of here wel dedes,   65
On auenture pruyde be peynted þere · and pompe of þe
    worlde ;
For crist knoweþ þi conscience · and þi kynde wille,
And þi coste and þi coueitise · and who þe catel ouȝte.
    For-þi I lere ȝow, lordes · leueþ suche werkes,
To writen in wyndowes · of ȝowre wel dedes,   70
Or to greden after goddis men · whan ȝe delen doles ;
An auenture ȝe han ȝowre hire here · and ȝoure heuene als ;
    Nesciat sinistra quid faciat dextra.
Lat nouȝte þi left half · late ne rathe,
Wyte what þow worchest · with þi riȝt syde ;
For þus bit þe gospel · gode men do here almesse.   75
    Meires and maceres · that menes ben bitwene
Þe kynge and þe *comune* · to kepe þe lawes,
To punyschen on pillories · and pynynge-stoles
Brewesteres and bakesteres · bocheres and cokes ;
For þise aren men on þis molde · þat moste harme worcheth
To þe pore peple · þat parcel-mele buggen.   81
    For they poysou*n* þe peple · priueliche and oft,
Thei rychen þorw regraterye · and rentes hem buggen
With þat þe pore people · shulde put in here wombe ;
For toke þei on trewly · þei tymbred nouȝt so heiȝe,   85
Ne bouȝte non burgages · be ȝe ful certeyne.
    Ac Mede þe Mayde · þe Maire hath bisouȝte,
Of alle suche sellers · syluer to take,
Or presentz with-oute pens · as peces of siluer,
Ringes or other ricchesse · þe regrateres to maynetene.   90
    'For my loue,' quod that lady · 'loue hem vchone,
And soffre hem to selle · somdele aȝeins resoun.'
    Salamon þe sage · a sarmou*n* he made,
For to amende Maires · and men þat kepen lawes,

And tolde hem þis teme · þat I telle thynke ;   95
  Ignis deuorabit tabernacula eorum qui libenter accipiunt
   munera, &c.
Amonge þis lettered ledes · þis latyn is to mene,
That fyre shal falle, and brenne · al to blo askes
The houses and þe homes · of hem þat desireth
ȝiftes or ȝeresȝyues · bi-cause of here offices.

 The kynge fro conseille cam · and called after Mede,   100
And ofsent hir alswythe · with seriauntes manye,
That brouȝten hir to bowre · with blisse and with ioye.

 Curteisliche þe kynge þanne · comsed to telle,
To Mede þe mayde · melleth þise wordes :
' Vnwittily, womman ! · wrouȝte hastow oft,   105
Ac worse wrouȝtestow neure · þan þo þow fals toke.
But I forgyue þe þat gilte · and graunte þe my grace ;
Hennes to þi deth day · do so namore !

 I haue a knyȝte, conscience · cam late fro biȝunde ;
ȝif he wilneth þe to wyf · wyltow hym haue ?'   110
' ȝe, lorde,' quod þat lady · ' lorde forbede elles !
But I be holely at ȝowre heste · lat hange me sone !'

 And þanne was conscience calde · to come and appiere
Bifor þe Kynge and his conseille · as clerkes and othere.
Knelynge, conscience · to þe kynge louted,   115
To wite what his wille were · and what he do shulde.

 ' Woltow wedde þis womman,' quod þe kynge · ' ȝif I wil
  assente,
For she is fayne of þi felawship · for to be þi make ?'

 Quod conscience to þe kynge · ' cryst it me forbede !
Ar I wedde suche a wyf · wo me bityde !   120
For she is frele of hir feith · fykel of here speche,
And maketh men mysdo · many score tymes ;
Truste of hire tresore · treieth ful manye.
Wyues and widewes · wantounes she techeth,

And lereth hem leccherye · that loueth hire ȝiftes.   125
Ȝowre fadre she felled · þorw fals biheste,
And hath apoysounde popis · and peired holicherche.

        ·   ·   ·   ·   ·   ·   ·

Sisoures and sompnoures · suche men hir preiseth ;
Shireues of shires · were shent ȝif she nere ;
For she doþ men lese here londe · and here lyf bothe.   135
She leteth passe prisoneres · and payeth for hem ofte,
And gyueth þe gailers golde · and grotes togideres,
To vnfettre þe fals · fle where hym lyketh ;
And takeþ þe trewe bi þe toppe · and tieth hym faste,
And hangeth hym for hatred · þat harme dede neure.   140
    To be cursed in consistorie · she counteth nouȝte a russhe ;
For she copeth þe comissarie · and coteth his clerkis ;
She is assoilled as sone · as hir-self liketh,
And may neiȝe as moche do · in a moneth one,
As ȝowre secret seel · in syx score dayes.   145
For she is priue with þe pope · prouisoures it knoweth,
For sire symonye and hir-selue · seleth hire bulles.
    She blesseth þise bisshopes · þeiȝe þey be lewed,
Prouendreth persones · and prestes meynteneth,
To haue lemmannes and lotebies · alle here lif-dayes,   150
And bringen forth barnes · aȝein forbode lawes.
There she is wel with þe kynge · wo is þe rewme,
For she is fauorable to the fals · and fouleth trewthe ofte.
    Bi ihesus, with here ieweles · ȝowre iustices she shendeth,
And lith aȝein þe lawe · and letteth hym þe gate,   155
That feith may nouȝte haue his forth · here floreines go so
        þikke.
She ledeth þe lawe as hire list · and louedayes maketh,
And doth men lese þorw hire loue · þat lawe myȝte wynne,
Þe mase for a mene man · þouȝ he mote hir eure.
Lawe is so lordeliche · and loth to make ende,   160

With-oute presentz or pens · she pleseth wel fewe.

　Barounes and burgeys · she bryngeth in sorwe,
And alle þe comune in kare · þat coueyten lyue in trewthe ;
For clergye and coueitise · she coupleth togideres.
Þis is þe lyf of that lady · now lorde ȝif hir sorwe !　　165
And alle that meynteneth here men · meschaunce hem bityde !
For pore men mowe haue no powere · to pleyne hem þouȝ
　　þei smerte ;
Suche a maistre is Mede · amonge men of gode.'

　Thanne morned Mede · and mened hire to the kynge,
To haue space to speke · spede if she myȝte.　　170

　The kynge graunted hir grace · with a gode wille ;
' Excuse þe, ȝif þow canst · I can namore seggen,
For conscience acuseth þe · to congey þe for euere.'

　' Nay, lorde,' quod þat lady · ' leueth hym þe worse,
Whan ȝe wyten witterly · where þe wronge liggeth ;　　175
There þat myschief is grete · Mede may helpe.
And þow knowest, conscience · I cam nouȝt to chide,
Ne depraue þi persone · with a proude herte.
Wel þow wost, wernard · but ȝif þow wolt gabbe,
Þow hast hanged on myne half · elleuene tymes,　　180
And also griped my golde · gyue it where þe liked ;
And whi þow wratthest þe now · wonder me thynketh.
Ȝit I may, as I myȝte · menske þe with ȝiftes,
And mayntene þi manhode · more þan þow knoweste.

　Ac þow hast famed me foule · bifor þe Kynge here.　　185
For kulled I neuere no kynge · ne conseilled þer-after,
Ne dede as þow demest · I do it on þe kynge !

　In normandye was he nouȝte · noyed for my sake ;
Ac þow þi-self sothely · shamedest hym ofte,
Crope in-to a kaban · for colde of þi nailles,　　190
Wendest þat wyntre · wolde haue lasted euere,
And draddest to be ded · for a dym cloude,

And hiedest homeward · for hunger of þi wombe.

Witþ-out pite, piloure · pore men þow robbedest,
And bere here bras at þi bakke · to caleys to selle.   195
There I lafte with my lorde · his lyf for to saue,
I made his men meri · and mornyng lette.
I batered hem on þe bakke · and bolded here hertis,
And dede hem hoppe, for hope · to haue me at wille.
Had I ben Marschal of his men · bi Marie of heuene!   200
I durst haue leyde my lyf · and no lasse wedde,
He shulde haue be lorde of þat londe · a lengthe and a brede,
And also Kyng of þat kitthe · his kynne for to helpe,
Þe leste brolle of his blode · a barounes pere!

Cowardliche þow, conscience · conseiledst hym þennes,   205
To leuen his lordeship · for a litel siluer,
That is þe richest rewme · þat reyne ouer houeth!

It bicometh to a kynge · þat kepeth a rewme,
To ȝiue Mede to men · þat mekelich hym serueth,
To alienes and to alle men · to honoure hem with ȝiftes;   210
Mede maketh hym biloued · and for a man holden.
Emperoures and Erlis · and al manere lordes,
For ȝiftes, han ȝonge men · to renne and to ride.
The pope and alle prelatis · presentz vnderfongen,
And medeth men hem-seluen · to meyntene here lawes.   215
Seruauntz for her seruise · we seth wel þe sothe,
Taken Mede of here maistre · as þei mowe acorde.
Beggeres for here biddynge · bidden men Mede;
Mynstralles for here murthe · mede þei aske.
Þe kynge hath mede of his men · to make pees in londe;
Men þat teche chyldren · craue of hem mede.   221
Prestis þat precheth þe poeple · to gode, asken mede,
And masse-pans and here mete · at þe mele tymes.
Alkynnes crafty men · crauen Mede for here prentis;
Marchauntz and Mede · mote nede go togideres;   225

No wiȝte, as I wene · with-oute Mede may libbe.'

Quod þe kynge to conscience · 'bi criste! as me thynketh,
Mede is wel worthi · þe maistrye to haue!'

'Nay,' quod conscience to þe Kynge · and kneled to þe
erthe,

'There aren two manere of Medes · my lorde, with ȝowre
leue.   230

Þat one, god of his grace · graunteth, in his blisse,
To þo þat wel worchen · whil þei ben here.

The prophete precheth þer-of · and put it in þe sautere,

Domine, quis habitabit in tabernaculo tuo ?

"Lorde, who shal wonye in þi wones · and with þine holi
seyntes,

Or resten on þi holy hilles?" · þis asketh dauid ;   235

And dauyd assoileth it hym-self · as þe sauter telleth,

Qui ingreditur sine macula, & operatur iusticiam,

"Tho þat entren of o colour · and of on wille,
And han wrouȝte werkis · with riȝte and with reson ;
And he þat ne vseth nauȝte · þe lyf of vsurye,
And enfourmeth pore men · and pursueth treuthe ;   240

*Qui pecuniam suam non dedit ad vsuram, & munera
super innocentem, &c. ;*

And alle þat helpeth þe innocent · and halt with þe riȝtful,
With-oute mede doth hem gode · and þe trewthe helpeth"—
Suche manere men, my lorde · shal haue þis furst Mede
Of god, at a grete nede · whan þei gone hennes.

There is an-other Mede mesurelees · þat maistres desireth;
To meyntene mysdoers · Mede þei take ;   246

And þere-of seith þe sauter · in a salmes ende,

*In quorum manibus iniquitates sunt, dextera eorum
repleta est muneribus ;*

And he þat gripeth her golde · so me god helpe!
Shal abie it bittere · or þe boke lyeth!

Prestes and *per*sones · þat plesynge desireth,   250
That taketh Mede and moneie · for messes þat þei syngeth,
Taketh here mede here · as Mathew vs techeth;

    Amen, amen, receperunt mercedem suam.

That laboreres and lowe folke · taketh of her maistres,
It is no manere Mede · but a mesurable hire.
In marchandise is no mede · I may it wel a-vowe;   255
It is a *per*mutaciou*n* apertly · a penyworth for an othre.

Ac reddestow neuere *Regum* · þow recrayed Mede,
Whi þe veniaunce fel · on Saul and on his children?
God sent to Saul · bi Samuel þe p*r*ophete,
Þat agag*e* of amalek*e* · and al his peple aftre   260
Shulde deye for a dede · þat done had here eldres.

  " For-þi," seid Samuel to Saul · " god hym-self hoteth
The be boxome at his biddynge · his wille to fulfille :
Wende to amalec with þyn oste · and what þow fyndest þere,
    slee it;
Biernes and bestes · brenne hem to ded;   265
Wydwes and wyues · wo*m*men and children,
Moebles and vnmoebles · and al þat þow my3te fynde,
Brenne it, bere it nou3te awey · be it neuere so riche
For mede ne for moneie; · loke þow destruye it,
Spille it and spare it nou3te · þow shalt spede þe bettere." 270

  And for he coueyted her catel · and þe kynge spared,
Forbare hym and his bestes bothe · as þe bible witnesseth,
Otherwyse þan he was · warned of þe p*r*ophete,
God seide to Samuel · þat Saul shulde deye,
And al his sede for þat synne · shenfullich ende.   275
Such a myschief Mede · made Saul þe kynge to haue,
That god hated hym for euere · and alle his eyres after.
The color*um* of þis cas · kepe I nou3te to shewe;
An auenture it noyed men · none ende wil I make.
For so is þis worlde went · wiþ hem þat han power*e*,   280

That who-so seyth hem sothes · is sonnest yblamed.

I, conscience, knowe þis · for kynde witt me it tauȝte,
Þat resoun shal regne · and rewmes gouerne;
And riȝte as agag hadde · happe shul somme.
Samuel shal sleen hym · and Saul shal be blamed,   285
And dauid shal be diademed · and daunten hem alle,
And one cristene kynge · kepen hem alle.

   Shal na more Mede · be maistre, as she is nouthe,
Ac loue and lowenesse · and lewte togederes,
Þise shul be maistres on molde · treuthe to saue.   290

   And who-so trespasseth ayein treuthe · or taketh aȝein his
      wille,
Leute shal don hym lawe · and no lyf elles.
Shal no seriaunt for here seruyse · were a silke howue,
Ne no pelure in his cloke · for pledyng atte barre.
Mede of mys-doeres · maketh many lordes,   295
And ouer lordes lawes · reuleth þe rewmes.

   Ac kynde loue shal come ȝit · and conscience togideres,
And make of lawe a laborere · suche loue shal arise,
And such a pees amonge þe peple · and a perfit trewthe,
Þat iewes shal wene in here witte · and waxen wonder glade,
Þat Moises or Messie · be come in-to þis erthe,   301
And haue wonder in here hertis · þat men beth so trewe.

   Alle þat bereth baslarde · brode swerde or launce,
Axe other hachet · or eny wepne ellis,
Shal be demed to þe deth · but if he do it smythye   305
In-to sikul or to sithe · to schare or to kulter;
      Conflabunt gladios suos in vomeres, &c.;
Eche man to pleye with a plow · pykoys or spade,
Spynne, or sprede donge · or spille hym-self with sleuthe.

   Prestes and persones · with *placebo* to hunte,
And dyngen vpon dauid · eche a day til eue.   310
Huntynge or haukynge · if any of hem vse,

His boste of his benefys · worth bynome hym after.
Shal neither kynge ne knyȝte · constable ne Meire
Ouer-lede þe comune · ne to þe courte sompne,
Ne put hem in panel · to don hem pliȝte here treuthe,   315
But after þe dede þat is don · one dome shal rewarde,
Mercy or no mercy · as treuthe wil acorde.

    Kynges courte and comune courte · consistorie and
       chapitele,
Al shal be but one courte · and one baroun be iustice;
Thanne worth trewe-tonge, a tidy man · þat tened me
       neuere.   320
Batailles shal non be · ne no man bere wepne,
And what smyth þat ony smytheth · be smyte þer-with to dethe;
     Non leuabit gens contra gentem gladium, &c.

    And er þis fortune falle · fynde men shal þe worste,
By syx sonnes and a schippe · and half a shef of arwes;
And þe myddel of a mone · shal make þe iewes to torne,   325
And saracenes for þat siȝte · shulle synge *gloria in ex-
    celsis, &c.*,
For Makomet & Mede · myshappe shal þat tyme;
     For, *melius est bonum nomen quam diuicie multe.*'

    Also wroth as þe wynde · wex Mede in a while,
'I can no latyn,' quod she · 'clerkis wote þe sothe.
Se what Salamon seith · in Sapience bokes,   330
That hij þat ȝiueth ȝiftes · þe victorie wynneth,
& moche worschip had þer-with · as holiwryt telleth,
     Honorem adquiret qui dat munera, &c.'

    'I leue wel, lady,' quod conscience · 'þat þi latyne be
       trewe;
Ac þow art like a lady · þat redde a lessoun ones,
Was, *omnia probate* · and þat plesed here herte,   335
For þat lyne was no lenger · atte leues ende.
Had she loked þat other half · and þe lef torned,

She shulde haue founden fele wordis · folwyng þer-after,
Quod bonum est tenete; · treuthe þat texte made!
  And so ferde ȝe, madame! · ȝe couthe namore fynde, 340
Tho ȝe loked on sapience · sittynge in ȝoure studie.
Þis tixte þat ȝe han tolde · were gode for lordes,
Ac ȝow failled a cunnyng clerke · þat couthe þe lef haue
    torned!
And if ȝe seche sapience eft · fynde shal ȝe þat folweth,
A ful teneful tixte · to hem þat taketh Mede, 345
And þat is, *animam autem aufert* · *accipientium, &c.*:
And þat is þe taille of þe tixte · of þat þat ȝe schewed,
Þat, þeiȝe we wynne worschip · and wiþ mede haue victorie,
Þe soule þat þe sonde taketh · bi so moche is bounde.' 349

PASSUS IV.

Passus quartus de visione, vt supra.

'CESSETH,' seith þe kynge · 'I suffre ȝow no lengere.
    Ȝe shal sauȝtne for sothe · and serue me bothe.
Kisse hir,' quod þe kynge · 'conscience, I hote.'
  'Nay, bi criste,' quod conscience · 'congeye me for euere !
But resoun rede me þer-to · rather wil I deye !'   5
  'And I comaunde þe,' quod þe Kynge · to conscience þanne,
'Rape þe to ride · and resoun þow fecche ;
Comaunde hym þat he come · my conseille to here.
For he shal reule my rewme · and rede me þe beste,
And acounte with þe, conscience · so me cryst helpe,   10
How þow lernest þe peple · þe lered and þe lewede.'
  'I am fayne of þat forwarde ' · seyde þe freke þanne,
And ritt riȝte to resoun · and rowneth in his ere,
And seide as þe kynge badde · and sithen toke his leue.
  'I shal arraye me to ride,' quod resoun · 'reste þe a
    while '—   15
And called catoun his knaue · curteise of speche,
And also tomme trewe-tonge- · tell-me-no-tales-
Ne-lesyng-to-lawȝe-of- · for-I-loued-hem-neuere—
'And sette my sadel vppon suffre- · til-I-se-my-tyme,
And lete warrok it wel · with witty-wordes gerthes,   20
And hange on hym þe heuy brydel · to holde his hed lowe,
For he wil make wehe · tweye er he be there.'
  Thanne conscience vppon his caple · kaireth forth faste,

And resou*n* with hym rit · rownynge togideres,
Whiche maistries Mede · maketh on þis erthe.   25
 One waryn wisdom · And witty his fere
Folwed hem faste · for þei haued to done
In þe cheker and at þe chauncerie · to be discharged of
    þinges ;
And riden fast, for resou*n* · shulde rede hem þe beste,
For to saue hem, for siluer · fro shame and fram harmes.   30
 And conscience knewe hem wel · þei loued coueitise,
And bad resou*n* ride faste · and recche of her noither,
' Þere aren wiles in here wordes · and with Mede þei dwelleth ;
There as wratthe and wranglyng is · þere wynne þei siluer ;
 Ac þere is loue and lewte · þei wil nou3te come þere ;   35
    Contricio & infelicitas in vijs eorum, &c.
Þei ne gyueth nou3te of god · one gose wynge,
    Non est timor dei ante oculos eorum.
For, wot god, þei wolde do more · for a dozeine chickenes,
Or as many capones · or for a seem of otes,
Þan for loue of owre lorde · or alle hise leue seyntes.
For-þi, resou*n*, lete hem ride · þo riche, bi hem-seluen,   40
For conscience knoweth hem nou3te · ne cryst, as I trowe.'
And þanne resou*n* rode faste · þe ri3te hei3e gate,
As conscience hym kenned · til þei come to þe kynge.
 Curteisliche þe kynge þanne · come a3ein resou*n*,
And bitwene hym-self and his sone · sette hym on benche, 45
And wordeden wel wyseli · a gret while togideres.
 And þanne come pees in-to p*ar*lement · and put forth a
    bille,
How wronge a3eines his wille · had his wyf taken.
      ·   ·   ·   ·   ·   ·
' Bothe my gees & my grys · his gadelynges feccheth ;   51
I dar nou3te for fere of hym · fy3te ne chyde.
He borwed of me bayard · he brou3te hym home neure,

Ne no ferthynge þer-fore · for nauȝte I couthe plede.

He meyneteneth his men · to morther myne hewen,　　　55

Forstalleth my feyres · and fiȝteth in my chepynge,

And breketh vp my bernes dore · and bereth aweye my
　　　whete,

And taketh me but a taile · for ten quarteres of otes ;

And ȝet he bet me þer-to · and lyth bi my Mayde,

I nam nouȝte hardy for hym · vneth to loke.'　　　60

　　The kynge knewe he seide sothe · for conscience hym
　　　tolde,

Þat wronge was a wikked luft · and wrouȝte moche sorwe.

　　Wronge was afered þanne · and wisdome he souȝte

To make pees with his pens · and profered hym manye,

And seide, ' had I loue of my lorde þe kynge · litel wolde I
　　　recche,　　　65

Theiȝe pees and his powere · pleyned hym eure !'

　　Þo wan wisdome · and sire waryn þe witty,

For þat wronge had ywrouȝte · so wikked a dede,

And warned wronge þo · with such a wyse tale ;

' Who-so worcheth bi wille · wratthe maketh ofte ;　　　70

I seye it bi þi-self · þow shalt it wel fynde.

But if Mede it make · þi myschief is vppe,

For bothe þi lyf and þi londe · lyth in his *grace*.'

　　Thanne wowed wronge · wisdome ful ȝerne,

To make his pees w*it*h his pens · handi-dandi payed.　　　75

Wisdome and witte þanne · wenten togideres,

And toke Mede myd hem · mercy to winne.

　　Pees put forþ his hed · and his panne blody ;

' Wyth-outen gilte, god it wote · gat I þis skaþe,

Conscience and þe comune · knowen þe sothe.'　　　80

　　Ac wisdom and witt · were about faste

To ouercome þe kyng · with catel, ȝif þei myȝte.

　　Þe kynge swore, bi crist · and bi his crowne bothe,

Þat wronge for his werkis · sholde wo þolye,
And comaunded a constable · to casten hym in yrens,   85
' And late hym nouȝte þis seuene ȝere · seen his feet ones.'

' God wot,' quod wysdom · ' þat were nauȝte þe beste ;
And he amendes mowe make · late meynprise hym haue ;
And be borwgh for his bale · and biggen hym bote,
And so amende þat is mysdo · and euermore þe bettere.'   90

Witt acorded þer-with · and seide þe same :
' Bettere is þat bote · bale adoun brynge,
Þan bale be ybette · & bote neuere þe bettere.'

And þanne gan Mede to mengen here · and mercy she
     bisought,
And profred pees a present · al of pure golde :   95
' Haue þis, man, of me,' quod she · ' to amende þi skaþe,
For I wil wage for wronge · he wil do so namore.'

Pitously pees þanne · prayed to þe kynge
To haue mercy on þat man · þat mys-did hym so ofte :
' For he hath waged me wel · as wysdome hym tauȝte,   100
And I forgyue hym þat gilte · with a goode wille,
So þat þe kynge assent ; · I can seye no bettere ;
For Mede hath made me amendes · I may namore axe.'

' Nay,' quod þe Kynge þo · ' so me cryst helpe !
Wronge wendeth nouȝte so awaye · arst wil I wite more ;   105
For loupe he so liȝtly · laughen he wolde,
And efte þe balder be · to bete myne hewen ;
But resoun haue reuthe on hym · he shal rest in my stokkes,
And þat as longe as he lyueth · but lowenesse hym borwe.'

Somme men redde Resoun þo · to haue reuthe on þat
     schrewe,   110
And for to conseille þe kynge · and conscience after,
That Mede moste be meynpernour · resoun þei bisouȝte.

' Rede me nouȝte,' quod resoun · ' no reuthe to haue,
Til lordes and ladies · louien alle treuthe,

And haten **al** harlotrye · to heren it, or to mouthen **it**; 115
Tyl pernelles p*u*rfil · be put in here hucche ;
And childryn cherissyng · be chastyng with ȝerdes ;
And harlotes holynesse · be holden for an hyne ;
Til clerken coueitise be · to clothe þe pore and to fede,
And religious romares · *recordare* in here cloistres, 120
As seynt Benet he*m* bad · Bernarde and Frau*n*ceys ;
And til prechoures p*r*echyng · be pr*e*ued on hem-seluen ;
Tyl þe kynges conseille · be þe co*mune* profyte ;
Tyl bisschopes baiardes · ben beggeres chambres,
Here haukes and her houndes · helpe to pore Religious ; 125

And til seynt Iames be souȝte · þere I shal assigne,
That no man go to Galis · but if he go for euere ;
And alle Rome-renneres · for robberes of byȝonde
Bere no siluer ouer see · þat signe of kynge sheweþ,
Noyther graue ne vngraue · golde noither siluer, 130
Vppon forfeture of þat fee · who-so fynt hym at Douere,
But if it be marchau*n*t or his man · or messagere with l*ett*eres,
Prouysou*r*e or prest · or penaunt for his synnes.

And ȝet,' q*u*od resou*n*, ' bi þe Rode · I shal no reuthe haue,
While Mede hath þe maistrye · in þis moot-halle. 135
Ac I may shewe ensaumples · as I se other-while ;
I sey it by my-self,' q*u*od he · ' and it so were
That I were kynge with crowne · to kepen a Rewme,
Shulde neuere wronge in þis worlde · þat I wite myȝte,
Ben vnpunisshed in my power*e* · for peril of my soule ! 140
Ne gete my grace for giftes · so me god saue !
Ne for no Mede haue mercy · but mekenesse it make.

For *nullum malum* þe man · mette with *inpunitum*,
And badde *nullum bonum* · be *irremuneratum*.

Late ȝowre confessoure, sire Kynge · construe þis vnglosed ; 145
And ȝif ȝe worken it in werke · I wedde myne eres,

That lawe shal ben a laborere · and lede a-felde donge,
And loue shal lede þi londe · as þe lief lyketh!'

Clerkes þat were confessoures · coupled hem togideres,
Alle to construe þis clause · and for þe kynges profit,   150
Ac nouȝte for conforte of þe comune · ne for þe kynges soule.

For I seiȝe mede in the moot-halle · on men of lawe wynke,
And þei lawghyng lope to hire · and lafte resoun manye.

Waryn wisdome · wynked vppon Mede,
And seide, 'Madame, I am ȝowre man · what so my mouth
     iangleth;   155
I falle in floreines,' quod þat freke · 'an faile speche ofte.'

Alle riȝtful recorded · þat resoun treuthe tolde,
And witt acorded þer-with · and comended his wordes,
And þe moste peple in þe halle · and manye of þe grete,
And leten mekenesse a maistre · and Mede a mansed
     schrewe.   160

Loue lete of hir liȝte · and lewte ȝit lasse,
And seide it so heiȝe · þat al þe halle it herde,
'Who-so wilneth hir to wyf · for welth of her godis,
But he be knowe for a koke-wolde · kut of my nose!'

Mede mourned þo · and made heuy chere.   165

   ·   ·   ·   ·   ·   ·   ·

Ac a sysoure and a sompnoure · sued hir faste,
And a schireues clerke · byschrewed al þe route,
'For ofte haue I,' quod he · 'holpe ȝow atte barre,
And ȝit ȝeue ȝe me neuere · þe worthe of a russhe.'   170

The kynge called conscience · and afterwardes resoun,
And recorded þat resoun · had riȝtfullich schewed,
And modilich vppon Mede · with myȝte þe Kynge loked,
And gan wax wrothe with lawe · for Mede almoste had shent
     it,
And seide, 'þorw ȝowre lawe, as I leue · I lese many chetes;
Mede ouer-maistrieth lawe · and moche treuthe letteth.   176

Ac resoun shal rekene with ȝow · ȝif I regne any while,
And deme ȝow, bi þis day · as ȝe han deserued.
Mede shal nouȝte meynprise ȝow · bi þe Marie of heuene !
I wil haue leute in lawe · and lete be al ȝowre ianglyng,   180
And as moste folke witnesseth wel · wronge shal be demed.'

   Quod conscience to þe kynge · 'but the comune wil assent,
It is ful hard, by myn hed · here-to to brynge it,
Alle ȝowre lige leodes · to lede þus euene.'

   'By hym þat rauȝte on þe rode' · quod resoun to þe kynge,
'But if I reule þus ȝowre rewme · rende out my ribbes !   186
ȝif ȝe bidden buxomnes · be of myne assente.'

   'And I assent,' seith þe kynge · 'by seynte Marie my lady,
Be my conseille comen · of clerkis and of erlis.
Ac redili, resoun · þow shalt nouȝte ride fro me,   190
For as longe as I lyue · lete þe I nelle.'

   'I am aredy,' quod resoun · 'to reste with ȝow euere,
So conscience be of owre conseille · I kepe no bettere.'
'And I graunt,' quod the kynge · 'goddes forbode it faile !
Als longe as owre lyf lasteth · lyue we togideres.'   195

PASSUS V.

Passus quintus de Visione.

THE kyng and his knightes · to the kirke wente
    To here matynes of þe day · and þe masse after.
Þanne waked I of my wynkynge · and wo was with-alle,
Þat I ne hadde sleped sadder · and yseiȝen more.
Ac er I hadde faren a fourlonge · feyntise me hente,   5
That I ne myȝte ferther a-foot · for defaute of slepynge ;
And sat softly adown · and seide my bileue,
And so I babeled on my bedes · þei brouȝte me a-slepe.

    And þanne saw I moche more · þan I bifore tolde,
For I say þe felde ful of folke · þat I bifore of seyde,   10
And how resoun gan arrayen hym · alle þe reume to preche,
And with a crosse afor þe kynge · comsed þus to techen.

    He preued þat þise pestilences · were for pure synne,
And þe southwest wynde · on saterday at euene
Was pertliche for pure pryde · and for no poynt elles.   15
Piries and plomtrees · were puffed to þe erthe,
In ensample, ȝe segges · ȝe shulden do þe bettere.
Beches and brode okes · were blowen to þe grounde,
Torned vpward her tailles · in tokenynge of drede,
Þat dedly synne at domesday · shal fordon hem alle.   20

    Of þis matere I myȝte · mamely ful longe,
Ac I shal seye as I saw · so me god helpe !
How pertly afor þe poeple · resoun gan to preche.

    He bad wastoure go worche · what he best couthe,

And wynnen his wastyng · with somme manere crafte.   25
   And preyed peronelle · her purfyle to lete,
And kepe it in hir cofre · for catel at hire nede.
   Thomme stowue he tauȝte · to take two staues,
And fecche felice home · fro þe wyuen pyne.
   He warned watt · his wyf was to blame,   30
Þat hire hed was worth halue a marke · his hode nouȝte worth
    a grote.
And bad bette kut · a bow other tweyne,
And bete betoun þer-with · but if she wolde worche.
   And þanne he charged chapmen · to chasten her childeren ;
' Late no wynnynge hem forweny · whil þei be ȝonge,   35
Ne for no pouste of pestilence · plese hem nouȝte out of
    resoun.
   My syre seyde so to me · and so did my dame,
Þat þe leuere childe · þe more lore bihoueth,
And Salamon seide þe same · þat Sapience made,
    Qui parcit virge, odit filium.
Þe Englich of þis latyn is · who-so wil it knowe,   40
Who-so spareth þe sprynge · spilleth his children.'
   And sithen he preyed prelatz · and prestes to-gideres,
' Þat ȝe prechen to þe peple · preue it on ȝowre-seluen,
And doth it in dede · it shal drawe ȝow to good ;
If ȝe lyuen as ȝe leren vs · we shal leue ȝow þe bettere.'   45
   And sithen he radde Religioun · here reule to holde—
' Leste þe kynge and his conseille · ȝowre comunes appayre,
And ben stuwardes of ȝowre stedes · til ȝe be ruled bettre.'
   And sithen he conseilled þe kynge · þe comune to louye,
' It is þi tresore, if tresoun ne were · and triacle at þi nede.'
And sithen he prayed þe pope · haue pite on holicherche,   51
And er he gyue any grace · gouerne firste hym-selue.
   ' And ȝe that han lawes to kepe · late treuthe be ȝowre
    coueytise,

More þan golde or other gyftes · if ȝe wil god plese ;
For who-so contrarieth treuthe · he telleth in þe gospel, 55
That god knoweth hym nouȝte · ne no seynte of heuene ;
    Amen dico vobis, nescio vos.

And ȝe þat seke seynte Iames · and seintes of Rome,
Seketh seynt treuthe · for he may saue ȝow alle ;
Qui cum patre & filio · þat feire hem bifalle
Þat suweth my sermon ;' · and þus seyde resoun. 60
Thanne ran repentance · and reherced his teme,
And gert wille to wepe · water with his eyen.

SUPERBIA.

Peronelle proude-herte · platte hir to þe erthe,
And lay longe ar she loked · and 'lorde, mercy !' cryed,
And byhiȝte to hym · þat vs alle made, 65
She shulde vnsowen hir serke · and sette þere an heyre
To affaiten hire flesshe · þat fierce was to synne :
' Shal neuere heiȝe herte me hente · but holde me lowe,
And suffre to be myssayde— · and so did I neuere.
But now wil I meke me · and mercy biseche, 70
For al þis I haue · hated in myne herte.'

LUXURIA.

Þanne lecchoure seyde 'allas !' · and on owre lady he
  cryed,
To make mercy for his mis-dedes · bitwene god and his
  soule,
With þat he shulde þe saterday · seuene ȝere þere-after,
Drynke but myd þe doke · and dyne but ones. 75

INUIDIA.

Enuye with heuy herte · asked after schrifte,
And carefullich *mea culpa* · he comsed to shewe.

He was as pale as a pelet · in þe palsye he semeð,
And clothed in a caurimaury · I couthe it nouȝte discreue ;
In kirtel and kourteby · and a knyf bi his syde;   80
Of a freres frokke · were þe forsleues.
And as a leke hadde yleye · longe in þe sonne,
So loked he with lene chekes · lourynge foule.

    His body was to-bolle for wratthe · þat he bote his lippes,
And wryngynge he ȝede with þe fiste · to wreke hym-self he
            þouȝte   85
With werkes or with wordes · whan he seighe his tyme.
Eche a worde þat he warpe · was of an Addres tonge,
Of chydynge and of chalangynge · was his chief lyflode,
With bakbitynge and bismer · and beryng of fals witnesse ;
Þis was al his curteisye · where þat euere he shewed hym.   90
    'I wolde ben yshryue,' quod þis schrewe · 'and I for shame
            durst ;
I wolde be gladder, bi god · þat gybbe had meschaunce,
Than þouȝe I had þis woke ywonne · a weye of essex chese.

    I haue a neighbore neyȝe me · I haue ennuyed hym ofte,
And lowen on hym to lordes · to don hym lese his siluer,   95
And made his frendes ben his foon · thorw my false tonge ;
His grace and his good happes · greueth me ful sore.
Bitwene many and many · I make debate ofte,
Þat bothe lyf and lyme · is lost þorw my speche.
And whan I mete him in market · þat I moste hate,   100
I hailse hym hendeliche · as I his frende were ;
For he is douȝtier þan I · I dar do non other.
Ac hadde I maystrye and myȝte · god wote my wille !
    And whan I come to þe kirke · and sholde knele to þe
            Rode,
And preye for þe poeple · as þe prest techeth,   105
For pilgrimes and for palmers · for alle þe poeple after,
Þanne I crye on my knees · þat cryste ȝif hem sorwe

Þat baren awey my bolle · and my broke schete.

  Awey fro þe auter þanne · turne I myn eyghen,
And biholde how Eleyne · hath a newe cote;　　　　110
I wisshe þanne it were myne · and al þe webbe after.

  And of mennes lesynge I laughe · þat liketh myn herte;
And for her wynnynge I wepe · and waille þe tyme,
And deme þat hij don ille · þere I do wel worse;
Who-so vndernymeth me here-of · I hate hym dedly after.
I wolde þat vche a wyght · were my knaue,　　　　116
For who-so hath more þan I · þat angreth me sore.
And þus I lyue louelees · lyke a luther dogge,
That al my body bolneth · for bitter of my galle.

  I my3te nou3te eet many 3eres · as a man ou3te,　　120
For enuye and yuel wille · is yuel to defye.
May no sugre ne swete þinge · asswage my swellynge,
Ne no *diapenidion* · dryue it fro myne herte,
Ne noyther schrifte ne shame · but ho-so schrape my mawe?'
    '3us, redili,' q*u*od repentaunce · and radde hym to þe
        beste,　　　　125
'Sorwe of synnes · is sauacioun of soules.'

  'I am sori,' q*u*od þat segge · 'I am but selde other,
And þat maketh me þus megre · for I ne may me venge.
Amonges Burgeyses haue I be · dwellynge At Londou*n*,
And gert bakbitinge be a brocoure · to blame mennes ware.
Whan he solde and I nou3te · þanne was I redy　　131
To lye and to loure on my neighbore · and to lakke his
        chaffare.
I wil amende þis, 3if I may · þorw my3te of god almy3ty.'

IRA.

  Now awaketh wratthe · with two whyte eyen,
And nyuelynge with þe nose · and his nekke hangynge.　135
    'I am wrath,' q*u*od he · 'I was sum-tyme a frere,

And þe couentes Gardyner · for to graffe ympes;
On limitoures and listres · lesynges I ymped,
Tyl þei bere leues of low speche · lordes to plese,
And sithen þei blosmed obrode · in boure to here shriftes.
And now is fallen þer-of a frute · þat folke han wel leuere 141
Schewen her schriftes to hem · þan shryue hem to her
    *per*sones.
    And now persones han parceyued · þat Freres parte with
    hem,
Þise possessioneres preche · and depraue freres, 144
And freres fyndeth hem in defaute · as folke bereth witnes,
That whan þei preche þe poeple · in many place aboute,
I, wrath, walke with hem · and wisse hem of my bokes.
Þus þei speken of sp*iri*tualte · þat eyther despiseth other,
Til þei be bothe beggers · and by my sp*iri*tualte libben,
Or elles alle riche · and riden aboute. 150
I, wrath, rest neuere · þat I ne moste folwe
This wykked folke · for suche is my grace.
    I haue an aunte to nonne · and an abbesse bothe,
Hir were leuere swowe or swelte · þan suffre any peyne.
I haue be cook in hir kichyne · and þe couent serued 155
Many monthes with hem · and with monkes bothe.
I was þe priouresses potagere · and other poure ladyes,
And made hem ioutes of iangelynge · þat dame Iohanne was
    a bastard,
And dame Clarice a kniʒtes douʒter · ac a kokewolde was
    hire syre,
And dame Peronelle a prestes file · Priouresse worth she
    neuere. 160

   ·   ·   ·   ·   ·   ·   ·

    Of wykked wordes I, wrath · here wortes I-made,
Til "þow lixte" and "þow lixte" · lopen oute at ones,
And eyther hitte other · vnder þe cheke; 164

Hadde þei had knyues, bi cryst · her eyther had killed other.

Seynt Gregorie was a gode pope · and had a gode forwit,
Þat no priouresse were prest · for þat he ordeigned.
Þei had þanne ben *infamis* þe firste day · þei can so yuel hele
    conseille.

Amonge monkes I miȝte be · ac many tyme I shonye;
For þere ben many felle frekis · my feres to aspye,   170
Bothe Prioure an supp*riour*e · and owre *pater abbas;*
And if I telle any tales · þei taken hem togyderes,
And do me faste frydayes · to bred and to water,
And am chalanged in þe chapitelhous · as I a childe were,

For-þi haue I no lykyng · with þo leodes to wonye.   176
I ete there vnthende fisshe · and fieble ale drynke;
Ac other while, whan wyn cometh · whan I drynke wyn
    at eue,
I haue a fluxe of a foule mouthe · wel fyue dayes after.
Al þe wikkednesse þat I wote · bi any of owre bretheren,   180
I couth it in owre cloistre · þat al owre couent wote it.'

'Now repent þe,' quod Repentau*n*ce · 'and reherce þow
    neure
Conseille þat þow cnowest · bi contenau*n*ce ne bi riȝte;
And drynke nouȝte ouer delicatly · ne to depe noyther,
Þat þi wille bi cause þer-of · to wrath myȝte torne.   185
Esto sobrius,' he seyde · and assoilled me after,
And bad me wilne to wepe · my wikkednesse to amende.

AUARICIA.

And þanne cam coueytise · can I hym nouȝte descryue,
So hungriliche and holwe · sire Heruy hym loked.
He was bitelbrowed · and baberlipped also,   190
With two blered eyghen · as a blynde hagge;
And as a letheren purs · lolled his chekes,

Wel sydder þan his chyn · þei chiueled for elde ;
And as a bondman of his bacou*n* · his berde was bidraueled.
With an hode on his hed · a lousi hatte aboue,　　　195
And in a tauny tabarde · of twelue wynter age,
Al totorne and baudy · and ful of ly*s* crepynge ;
But if þat a lous couthe · haue lopen þe bettre,
She sholde nou3te haue walked on þat welche · so was it
　　　thredebare.
　　'I haue ben coueytouse,' q*uo*d þis caityue · 'I biknowe it
　　　here ;　　　　　　　　　　　　　　　　　　　　200
For some tyme I serued · Symme atte Stile,
And was his prentis ypli3te · his profit to wayte.
First I lerned to lye · a leef other tweyne,
Wikkedlich to weye · was my furst lessou*n*.
To Wy and to Wynchestre · I went to þe faire,　　　205
With many maner*e* marchandise · as my Maistre me hi3te ;
Ne had þe g*ra*ce of gyle · ygo amonge my ware,
It had be vnsolde þis seuene 3ere · so me god helpe !
　　Thanne drowe I me amonges draperes · my donet to lerne,
To drawe þe lyser alonge · þe lenger it semed ;　　　210
Amonge þe riche rayes · I rendred a lessou*n*,
To broche hem with a paknedle · and plaited hem togyderes,
And put hem in a presse · and pynned hem þerinne,
Tyl ten 3erdes or twelue · hadde tolled out threttene.
　　My wyf was a webbe · and wollen cloth made ;　　　215
She spak to spynnesteres · to spynnen it oute.
Ac þe pounde þat she payed by · poised a q*uarter*ou*n* more,
Than myne owne auncer*e* · who-so wey3ed treuthe.
　　I bou3te hir barly malte · she brewe it to selle,
Peny-ale and podyng-ale · she poured togideres　　　220
For laboreres and for low folke ; · þat lay by hym-selue.
　　The best ale lay in my boure · or in my bedchambre,
And who-so bu*m*med þer-of · bou3te it þer-after,

A galoun for a grote · god wote, no lesse;
And ȝit it cam in cupmel · þis crafte my wyf vsed.   225
Rose þe regratere · was hir riȝte name;
She hath holden hokkerye · al hire lyf-tyme.

Ac I swere now, so the ik · þat synne wil I lete,
And neuere wikkedliche weye · ne wikke chaffare vse,
But wenden to Walsyngham · and my wyf als,   230
And bidde þe Rode of bromeholme · brynge me oute of dette.'

'Repentedestow þe euere,' quod repentance · 'ne restitucioun madest?'

'Ȝus, ones I was herberwed,' quod he · 'with an hep of
chapmen,

I roos whan þei were arest · and yrifled here males.'

'That was no restitucioun,' quod repentance · 'but a
robberes thefte,   235

Þow haddest be better worthy · be hanged þerfore
Þan for al þat · þat þow hast here shewed.'

'I wende ryflynge were restitucioun,' quod he · 'for I
lerned neuere rede on boke,

And I can no frenche in feith · but of þe ferthest ende of
norfolke.'

'Vsedestow euere vsurie,' quod repentaunce · 'in alle þi
lyf-tyme?'   240

'Nay, sothly,' he seyde · 'saue in my ȝouthe.

I lerned amonge lumbardes · and iewes a lessoun,
To wey pens with a peys · and pare þe heuyest,
And lene it for loue of þe crosse · to legge a wedde and lese
it;

Suche dedes I did wryte · ȝif he his day breke.   245

I haue mo maneres þorw rerages · þan þorw *miseretur &
comodat.*

I haue lent lordes · and ladyes my chaffare,
And ben her brocour after · and bouȝte it my-self.

Eschaunges and cheuesances · with suche chaffare I dele,

And lene folke þat lese wol · a lyppe at eu*er*y noble.   250

And with lumbardes *lett*res · I ladde golde to Rome,

And toke it by taille here · and tolde hem þere lasse.'

'Lentestow euere lordes · for loue of her mayntenaunce ?'

'ȝe, I haue lent lordes · loued me neuere after,

And haue ymade many a knyȝte · bothe mercere &
    draper*e*,   255

þat payed neuere for his prentishode · nouȝte a peire gloues.'

'Hastow pite on pore men · þat mote nedes borwe ?'

'I haue as moche pite of pore men · as pedler*e* hath of
    cattes,

þat wolde kille hem, yf he cacche hem myȝte · for coueitise
    of her*e* skynnes.'

'Artow manlyche amonge þi neiȝbores · of þi mete and
    drynke ?'   260

'I am holden,' quod he 'as hende · as hounde is in
    kychyne,

Amonges my neighbores, namelich · such a name ich haue.'

'Now god lene neure,' quod repentance · 'but þow repent
    þe rather,

Þe grace on þis grounde · þi good wel to bisette,

Ne þine ysue after þe · haue ioye of þat þow wynnest,   265

Ne þi excecutours wel bisett · þe siluer þat þow hem leuest ;

And þat was wonne with wronge · with wikked men be
    despended.

For were I frere of þat hous · þere gode faith and charite is,

I nolde cope vs with þi catel · ne owre kyrke amende,

Ne haue a peny to my pitaunce · of þyne, bi my soule
    hele,   270

For þe best boke in owre hous · þeiȝe brent golde were þe
    leues,

And I wyst wytterly · þow were suche as þow tellest,

Or elles þat I kouþe knowe it · by any kynnes wise.

Seruus es alterius · cum fercula pinguia queris,

Pane tuo pocius · vescere, liber eris.   275

    Thow art an vnkynde creature · I can þe nouȝte as-
        soille ;

Til þow make restitucioun · and rekne with hem alle,

And sithen þat resoun rolle it · in þe regystre of heuene,

That þow hast made vche man good · I may þe nouȝte
        assoille ;

        Non dimittitur peccatum, donec restituatur ablatum, &c.

For alle þat haue of þi good · haue god my trouthe !   280

Ben holden at þe heighe dome · to helpe þe to restitue.

And who so leueth nouȝte þis be soth · loke in þe sauter
    glose,

In *miserere mei deus* · where I mene treuthe ;

        Ecce enim veritatem dilexisti, &c.

    Shal neuere werkman in þis worlde · þryue wyth þat þow
        wynnest ;

Cum sancto sanctus eris · construe me þat on englische.'   285

    Thanne wex þat shrewe in wanhope · and walde haue
        hanged him-self,

Ne hadde repentaunce þe rather · reconforted hym in þis
    manere,

' Haue mercye in þi mynde · and with þi mouth biseche it,

For goddes mercye is more · þan alle hise other werkes ;

        Misericordia eius super omnia opera eius, &c.

    And al þe wikkednesse in þis worlde · þat man myȝte
        worche or thynke,   290

Ne is no more to þe mercye of god · þan in þe see a glede ;

        Omnis iniquitas quantum ad misericordiam dei, est quasi
        sintilla in medio maris.

    For-þi haue mercy in þi mynde · and marchandise, leue it

For þow hast no good grounde · to gete þe with a wastel,

But if it were with thi tonge · or ellis with þi two hondes.
For þe good þat þow hast geten · bigan al with falsehede, 295
And as longe as þow lyuest þer-with · þow 3eldest nou3te, but
    borwest.
   And if þow wite neuere to whiche · ne whom to restitue,
Bere it to þe bisschop · and bidde hym of his *grace*,
Bisette it hym-selue · as best is for þi soule.
For he shal answere for þe · at þe heygh dome, 300
For þe and for many mo · þat man shal 3if a rekenynge,
What he lerned 3ow in lente · leue þow none other,
And what he lent 3ow of owre lordes good · to lette 3ow fro
    synne.'

GULA.

  Now bigynneth glotoun · for to go to schrifte,
And kaires hym to-kirke-ward · his coupe to schewe. 305
   Ac Beton þe brewestere · bad hym good morwe,
And axed of hym with þat · whiderward he wolde.
  'To holi cherche,' quod he · 'forto here masse,
And sithen I wil be shryuen · and synne namore.'
   'I haue gode ale, gossib,' quod she · 'glotown, wiltow
    assaye?' 310
'Hastow au3te in þi purs · any hote spices?'
   'I haue peper and piones,' quod she · 'and a pounde of
    garlike,
A ferthyngworth of fenel-seed · for fastyngdayes.'
   Þanne goth glotoun in · and grete othes after;
Cesse þe souteresse · sat on þe benche, 315
Watte þe warner · and hys wyf bothe,
Tymme þe tynkere · and tweyne of his prentis,
Hikke þe hakeneyman · and hughe þe nedeler,
Clarice of cokkeslane · and þe clerke of þe cherche,
Dawe þe dykere · and a dozeine other; 320

Sire Piers of Pridie · and Peronelle of Flaundres,
A ribibour, a ratonere · a rakyer of chepe,
A ropere, a redyngkyng · and Rose þe dissheres,
Godfrey of garlekehithe · and gryfin þe walshe,
And vpholderes an hepe · erly bi þe morwe 325
Geuen glotoun with glad chere · good ale to hansel.

   Clement þe cobelere · cast of his cloke,
And atte new faire · he nempned it to selle;
Hikke þe hakeneyman · hitte his hood after,
And badde bette þe bochere · ben on his side. 330
Þere were chapmen y-chose · þis chaffare to preise;
Who-so haueth þe hood · shuld haue amendes of þe cloke.

   Two risen vp in rape · and rouned togideres,
And preised þese penyworthes · apart bi hem-selue;
Þei couth nouȝte bi her conscience · acorden in treuthe, 335
Tyl Robyn þe ropere · arose bi þe southe,
And nempned hym for a noumpere · þat no debate nere,
For to trye þis chaffare · bitwixen hem þre.

   Hikke þe hostellere · hadde þe cloke,
In couenaunte þat Clement · shulde þe cuppe fille, 340
And haue Hikkes hode hostellere · and holde hym yserued;
And who-so repented rathest · shulde arise after,
And grete sire glotoun · with a galoun ale.

   Þere was laughyng and louryng · and 'let go þe cuppe,'
And seten so til euensonge · and songen vmwhile, 345
Tyl glotoun had y-globbed · a galoun an a Iille.

·   ·   ·   ·   ·   ·   ·

He myȝte neither steppe ne stonde · er he his staffe hadde;
And þanne gan he go · liche a glewmannes bicche,
Somme tyme aside · and somme tyme arrere,
As who-so leyth lynes · forto lacche foules. 355
   And whan he drowgh to þe dore · þanne dymmed his
     eighen,

He stumbled on þe thresshewolde · an threwe to þe erthe.
Clement þe cobelere · cauȝte hym bi þe myddel,
For to lifte hym alofte · and leyde him on his knowes ;   359

    .   .   .   .   .

    With al þe wo of þis worlde · his wyf and his wenche
Baren hym home to his bedde · and brouȝte hym þerinne.
And after al þis excesse · he had an accidie,   366
Þat he slepe saterday and sonday · til sonne ȝede to reste.
Þanne waked he of his wynkyng · and wiped his eyghen ;
Þe fyrste worde þat he warpe · was, 'where is þe bolle ?'
His wif gan edwite hym þo · how wikkedlich he lyued,   370
And repentance riȝte so · rebuked hym þat tyme :

    'As þow with wordes and werkes · hast wrouȝte yuel in þi
        lyue,
Shryue þe and be shamed þer-of · and shewe it with þi mouth.'

    'I, glotoun,' quod þe gome · 'gylti me ȝelde,
Þat I haue trespassed with my tonge · I can nouȝte telle how
        ofte,   375
Sworen 'goddes soule' · and 'so god me help and halidom,'
Þere no nede ne was · nyne hundreth tymes ;

    And ouer-seye me at my sopere · and some tyme at nones,
Þat I glotoun girt it vp · er I hadde gone a myle,
And y-spilte þat myȝte be spared · and spended on somme
        hungrie ;   380
Ouerdelicatly on fastyng-dayes · drunken and eten bothe,
And sat some tyme so longe þere · þat I slepe and ete at
        ones.
For loue of tales, in tauernes · to drynke þe more, I dyned,
And hyed to þe mete er none · whan fastyng-dayes were.'

    'This shewyng shrifte,' quod repentance · 'shal be meryte
        to þe.'   385
    And þanne gan glotoun grete · and gret doel to make
For his lither lyf · þat he lyued hadde,

And avowed to fast— · 'for hunger or for thurst
Shal neuere fisshe on þe fryday · defien in my wombe,
Tyl abstinence myn aunte · haue ʒiue me leue ;   390
And ʒit haue I hated hir · al my lyf-tyme.'

ACCIDIA.

Þanne come sleuthe al bislabered · *with* two slymy eiʒen,
'I most sitte,' seyde þe segge · 'or elles shulde I nappe ;
I may nouʒte stonde ne stoupe · ne with-oute a stole knele.'

  ·   ·   ·   ·   ·   ·   ·

'What I awake, renke I' quod repentance · 'and rape þe to
    shrifte.'
  'If I shulde deye bi þis day · me liste nouʒte to loke ;   400
I can' nouʒte p*er*fitly my pat*er-nost*er · as þe prest it syngeth,
But I can rymes of Robyn hood · and Randolf erle of
    Chestre,
Ac neither of owre lorde ne of owre lady · þe leste þat euere
    was made.
  I haue made vowes fourty · and for-ʒete hem on þe morne ;
I parfourned neure penaunce · as þe prest me hiʒte,   405
Ne ryʒte sori for my synnes · ʒet was I neuere.
And ʒif I bidde any bedes · but if it be in wrath,
Þat I telle with my tonge · is two myle fro myne herte.
I am occupied eche day · haliday and other,
With ydel tales atte ale · and otherwhile in cherches ;   410
Goddes peyne and his passiou*n* · ful selde þynke I þer*e*-on.
  I visited neuere fieble men · ne fettered folke in puttes,
I haue leuere here an harlotrie · or a somer-game of souteres,
Or lesynges to laughe at · and belye my neighbore,
Þan al þat euere Marke made · Mathew, John, & lucas. 415
And vigilies and fastyng-dayes · alle þise late I passe,

  ·   ·   ·   ·   ·   ·   ·

Tyl matynes and masse be do · and þanne go to þe freres ;

Come I to *ite, missa est* · I holde me yserued.

I nam nouȝte shryuen some tyme · but if sekenesse it
    make,   420

Nouȝt tweies in two ȝere · and þanne vp gesse I schryue me.

    I haue be prest and persoun · passynge thretti wynter,

ȝete can I neither solfe ne synge · ne seyntes lyues rede ;

But I can fynde in a felde · or in a fourlonge an hare,

Better þan in *beatus vir* · or in *beati omnes*   425

Construe oon clause wel · and kenne it to my parochienes.

I can holde louedayes · and here a Reues rekenynge,

Ac in canoun ne in þe decretales · I can nouȝte rede a lyne.

    ȝif I bigge and borwe it · but ȝif it be ytailled,

I forȝete it as ȝerne · and ȝif men me it axe   430

Sixe sithes or seuene · I forsake it with othes,

And þus tene I trewe men · ten hundreth tymes.

    And my seruauntz some tyme · her salarye is bihynde,

Reuthe is to here þe rekenynge whan we shal rede acomptes ;

So with wikked wille and wraththe · my werkmen I paye. 435

    ȝif any man doth me a benfait · or helpeth me at nede,

I am vnkynde aȝein his curteisye · and can nouȝte vnder-
    stonde it ;

For I haue and haue hadde · some dele haukes maneres,

I nam nouȝte lured with loue · but þere ligge auȝte vnder þe
    thombe.

    The kyndenesse þat myne euene-cristene · kidde me
    fernyere,   440

Sixty sythes I, sleuthe · haue forȝete it sith,

In speche and in sparynge of speche · yspilte many a tyme

Bothe flesche & fissche · and many other vitailles ;

Bothe bred and ale · butter, melke, and chese

Forsleuthed in my seruyse · til it myȝte serue noman.   445

    I ran aboute in ȝouthe · and ȝaf me nouȝte to lerne,

And euere sith haue be beggere · for my foule sleuthe ;

Heu michi, quod sterilem · vitam duxi Iuuenilem !'

　‘ Repentestow þe nauȝte ?’ quod repentance · and riȝte with
　　þat he swowned,
Til *vigilate* þe veille · fette water at his eyȝen,　　　　　450
And flatte it on his face · and faste on hym criede,
And seide, ‘ware þe fram wanhope · wolde þe bitraye.
“I am sori for my synnes” · sey so to þi-selue,
And bete þi-selue on þe breste · and bidde hym of grace ;
For is no gult here so grete · þat his goodnesse nys more.’

　　Þanne sat sleuthe vp · and seyned hym swithe,　　　456
And made avowe to-fore god · for his foule sleuthe,
‘ Shal no sondaye be þis seuene ȝere · but sykenesse it lette,
Þat I ne shal do me er day · to þe dere cherche,
And heren matines and masse · as I a monke were.　　460
Shal none ale after mete · holde me þennes,
Tyl I haue euensonge herde · I behote to þe Rode.
And ȝete wil I ȝelde aȝein · if I so moche haue,
Al þat I wikkedly wan · sithen I wytte hadde.

　　And þough my liflode lakke · leten I nelle,　　　465
Þat eche man ne shal haue his · ar I hennes wende :
And with þe residue and þe remenaunt · bi þe Rode of
　　chestre !
I shal seke treuthe arst · ar I se Rome !’
　　Robert þe robbere · on *reddite* lokede,
And for þer was nouȝte wher-of · he wepe swithe sore.　470
Ac ȝet þe synful shrewe · seyde to hym-selue,
‘ Cryst, þat on caluarye · vppon þe crosse deydest,
Tho dismas my brother · bisouȝte ȝow of grace,
And haddest mercy on þat man · for *memento* sake,
So rewe on þis robbere · þat *reddere* ne haue,　　　475
Ne neuere wene to wynne · with crafte, þat I owe.
But for þi mykel mercy · mitigacioun I biseche ;
Ne dampne me nouȝte at domesday · for þat I did so ille.’

What bifel of þis feloun · I can nouȝte faire schewe,
Wel I wote he wepte faste · water with boþe his eyen,   480
And knowleched his gult · to cryst ȝete eftsones,
Þat *penitencia* his pyke · he shulde polsche newe,
And lepe with hym ouer londe · al his lyf-tyme.

.   .   .   .   .   .

And þanne had repentaunce reuthe · and redde hem alle
     to knele,   485
'For I shal biseche for al synful · owre saueoure of *grace*,
To amende vs of owre mysdedes · and do mercy to vs alle.
     Now god,' quod he, 'þat of þi goodnesse · gonne þe
     worlde make,
And of nouȝte madest auȝte · and man moste liche to þi-
     selue,
And sithen suffredest for to synne · a sikenesse to vs alle,   490
And al for þe best, as I bileue · what euere þe boke telleth,
     O felix culpa ! o necessarium peccatum ade ! &c.
For þourgh þat synne þi sone · sent was to þis erthe,
And bicam man of a mayde · mankynde to saue,
And madest þi-self with þi sone · and vs synful yliche,
     Faciamus hominem ad ymaginem et similitudinem
     nostram ;
     Et alibi : qui manet in caritate, in deo manet, & deus
     in eo ;
And sith with þi-self sone · in owre sute deydest   495
On godefryday for mannes sake · at ful tyme of þe daye,
Þere þi-self ne þi sone · no sorwe in deth feledest ;
But in owre secte was þe sorwe · and þi sone it ladde,
     Captiuam duxit captiuitatem.
Þe sonne for sorwe þer-of · les syȝte for a tyme
Aboute myddday, whan most liȝte is · and mele-tyme of
     seintes ;   500
Feddest with þi fresche blode · owre forfadres in derknesse,

Populus qui ambulabat in tenebris, vidit lucem magnam ;
And thorw þe liȝte þat lepe oute of þe · lucifer was blent,
And blewe alle þi blissed · in-to þe blisse of paradise.

Þe thrydde daye after · þow ȝedest in owre sute,
A synful Marie þe seighe · ar seynte Marie þi dame,   505
And al to solace synful · þow suffredest it so were :
   Non veni vocare iustos, set peccatores ad penitenciam.
And al þat Marke hath ymade · mathew, Iohan, and lucas,
Of þyne douȝtiest dedes · were don in owre armes ;
   Verbum caro factum est, et habitauit in nobis.
And bi so moche, me semeth · þe sikerere we mowe
Bydde and biseche · if it be þi wille,   510
Þat art owre fader and owre brother · be merciable to vs,
And haue reuthe on þise Ribaudes · þat repente hem here
   sore,
Þat euere þei wratthed þe in þis worlde · in worde, þouȝte, or
   dedes.'

Þanne hent hope an horne · of *deus, tu conuersus viuificabis*
   nos,
And blew it with *Beati quorum* · *remisse sunt iniquitates,*   515
Þat alle seyntes in heuene · songen at ones,
   Homines & iumenta saluabis, quemadmodum multiplicasti
     misericordiam tuam, deus, &c.

A thousand of men þo · thrungen togyderes ;
Criede vpward to cryst · and to his clene moder,
To haue grace to go with hem · treuthe to seke.

Ac þere was wyȝte non so wys · þe wey þider couthe,   520
But blustreden forth as bestes · ouer bankes and hilles,
Til late was and longe · þat þei a lede mette,
Apparailled as a paynym · in pylgrymes wyse.
He bare a burdoun ybounde · with a brode liste,
In a withewyndes wise · ywounden aboute.   525
A bolle and a bagge · he bare by his syde ;

An hundreþ of ampulles · on his hatt seten,
Signes of synay · and shelles of galice ;
And many a cruche on his cloke · and keyes of Rome,
And þe vernicle bifore · for men shulde knowe,   530
And se bi his signes · whom he souȝte hadde.

Þis folke frayned hym firste · fro whennes he come ?

'Fram synay,' he seyde · 'and fram owre lordes sepulcre ;
In bethleem and in babiloyne · I haue ben in bothe,
In ermonye, in Alisaundre · in many other places.   535
Ȝe may se bi my signes · þat sitten on myn hatte,
Þat I haue walked ful wyde · in wete and in drye,
And souȝte gode seyntes · for my soules helth.'

'Knowestow ouȝte a corseint · þat men calle treuthe ?
Coudestow auȝte wissen vs þe weye · where þat wy
    dwelleth ?'   540

'Nay, so me god helpe !' · seide þe gome þanne,
'I seygh neuere palmere · with pike ne with scrippe
Axen after hym er · til now in þis place.'

'Peter !' quod a plowman · and put forth his hed,
'I knowe hym as kyndely · as clerke doþ his bokes ;   545
Conscience and kynde witte · kenned me to his place,
And deden me suren hym sikerly · to serue hym for euere,
Bothe to sowe and to sette · þe while I swynke myghte.
I haue ben his folwar · al þis fifty wyntre ;
Bothe ysowen his sede · and sued his bestes,   550
With-Inne and with-outen · wayted his profyt.
I dyke and I delue · I do þat treuthe hoteth ;
Some tyme I sowe · and some tyme I thresche,
In tailoures crafte and tynkares crafte · what treuthe can
    deuyse,
I weue an I wynde · and do what treuthe hoteth.   555

For þouȝe I seye it my-self · I serue hym to paye ;
Ich haue myn huire of hym wel · and otherwhiles more ;

He is þe prestest payer · þat pore men knoweth ;
He ne with-halt non hewe his hyre · þat he ne hath it at
    euen.
He is as low as a lombe · and loueliche of speche,   560
And ȝif ȝe wilneth to wite · where þat he dwelleth,
I shal wisse ȝow witterly · þe weye to his place.'
    ' ȝe, leue Pieres,' quod þis pilgrymes · and profered hym
    huire
For to wende with hem · to treuthes dwellyng place.
    ' Nay, bi my soules helth,' quod pieres · and gan forto
    swere,   565
'I nolde fange a ferthynge · for seynt Thomas shryne !
Treuthe wolde loue me þe lasse · a longe tyme þere-after !
Ac if ȝe wilneth to wende wel · þis is þe weye thider,
Þat I shal say to ȝow · and sette yow in þe soþe.
    ȝe mote go þourgh mekenesse · bothe men and wyues, 570
Tyl ȝe come in-to conscience · þat cryst wite þe sothe,
Þat ȝe louen owre lorde god · leuest of alle þinges,
And þanne ȝowre neighbores nexte · in non wise apeyre
Otherwyse þan þow woldest · he wrouȝte to þi-selue.
    And so boweth forth bi a broke · beth-buxum-of-
    speche,   575
Tyl ȝe fynden a forth · ȝowre-fadres-honoureth,
    Honora patrem & matrem, &c. :
Wadeþ in þat water · and wascheth ȝow wel þere,
And ȝe shul lepe þe liȝtloker · al ȝowre lyf-tyme.
And so shaltow se swere-nouȝte- · but-if-it-be-for-nede-
And-namelich-an-ydel- · þe-name-of-god-almyȝti.   580
    Þanne shaltow come by a crofte · but come þow nouȝte
    þere-Inne ;
That crofte hat coueyte-nouȝte- · mennes-catel-ne-her-wyues·
Ne-none-of-her-seruauntes- · þat-noyen-hem-myȝte.
Loke ȝe breke no bowes þere · but if it be ȝowre owne.

Two stokkes þere stondeth · ac stynte ȝe nouȝte þere,   585
They hatte stele-nouȝte, ne-slee-nouȝte · stryke forth by
    bothe ;
And leue hem on þi left halfe · and loke nouȝte þere-after ;
And holde wel þyne haliday · heighe til euen.
Thanne shaltow blenche at a berghe · bere-no-false-witnesse,
He is frithed in with floreines · and other fees many ;   590
Loke þow plukke no plante þere · for peril of þi soule.

   Þanne shal ȝe se sey-soth- · so-it-be-to-done-
In-no-manere-ellis-nauȝte- · for-no-mannes-biddynge.

   Þanne shaltow come to a courte · as clere as þe sonne,
Þe mote is of mercy · þe manere aboute,   595
And alle þe wallis ben of witte · to holden wille oute ;
And kerneled with crystendome · man-kynde to saue,
Boterased with bileue-so- · or-þow-beest-nouȝte-ysaued.

   And alle þe houses ben hiled · halles and chambres,
With no lede, but with loue · and lowe-speche-as-bre-
    theren.   600
Þe brugge is of bidde-wel- · þe-bette-may-þow-spede ;
Eche piler is of penaunce · of preyeres to seyntes,
Of almes-dedes ar þe hokes · þat þe gates hangen on.

   Grace hatte þe gateward · a gode man for sothe,
Hys man hatte amende-ȝow · for many man him knoweth ; 605
Telleth hym þis tokene · þat treuthe wite þe sothe ;
'I parfourned þe penaunce · þe preest me enioyned,
And am ful sori for my synnes · and so I shal euere,
Whan I þinke þere-on · þeighe I were a pope.'

   Biddeth amende-ȝow meke him · til his maistre ones,   610
To wayue vp þe wiket · þat þe womman shette,
Tho Adam and Eue · eten apples vnrosted;

      Per euam cunctis clausa est, & per mariam virginem
      iterum patefacta est ;
For he hath þe keye and þe cliket · þouȝ þe kynge slepe.

And if grace graunte þe · to go in in þis wise,
Þow shalt see in þi-selue · treuthe sitte in þine herte,   615
In a cheyne of charyte · as þow a childe were,
To suffre hym and segge nouȝte · aȝein þi sires wille.

   Ac bewar þanne of wrath-þe · þat is a wikked shrewe,
He hath enuye to hym · þat in þine herte sitteth ;
And pukketh forþ pruyde · to prayse þi-seluen.   620
Þe boldnesse of þi bienfetes · maketh þe blynde þanne,
And þanne worstow dryuen oute as dew · and þe dore closed,
Kayed and cliketed · to kepe þe with-outen ;
Happily an hundreth wyntre · ar þow eft entre.
Þus myght þow lesen his loue · to late wel by þi-selue,   625
And neuere happiliche efte entre · but grace þow haue.

   Ac þere aren seuene sustren · þat seruen treuthe euere,
And aren porteres of þe posternes · that to þe place longeth.
Þat one hat abstenence · and humilite an other,
Charite and chastite · ben his chief maydenes,   630
Pacience and pees · moche poeple þei helpeth,
Largenesse þe lady · heo let in ful manye ;
Heo hath hulpe a þousande oute · of þe deueles ponfolde.

   And who is sibbe to þis seuene · so me god helpe !
He is wonderliche welcome · and faire vnderfongen.   635
And but if ȝe be syb · to summe of þise seuene,
It is ful harde bi myne heued,' quod Peres · ' for any of ȝow
        alle
To geten ingonge at any gate þere · but grace be þe more.'

   ' Now, bi cryst,' quod a cutpurs · ' I haue no kynne þere !'
' Ne I,' quod an apewarde · ' bi auȝte þat I knowe !'   640
   ' Wite god,' quod a wafrestre · ' wist I þis for sothe,
Shulde I neuere ferthere a fote · for no freres prechynge.'

   ' Ȝus,' quod Pieres þe plowman · and pukked hem alle to
        gode,
' Mercy is a maydene þere · hath myȝte ouer hem alle ;

H

And she is syb to alle synful · and her sone also; 645
And þoruȝe þe helpe of hem two · (hope þow none other),
Þow myȝte gete grace þere · bi so þow go bityme.'
 'By seynt Poule,' quod a pardonere · 'perauenture I be
  nouȝte knowe þere,
I wil go fecche my box with my breuettes · and a bulle with
  bisshopes lettres !'
'By cryst,' quod a comune womman · 'þi companye wil I
  folwe,
Þow shalt sey I am þi sustre · I ne wot where þei bicome.' 651

PASSUS VI.

Passus Sextus.

'THIS were a wikked way · but who-so hadde a gyde
   That wolde folwen vs eche a fote;' · þus þis folke hem
   mened.
Quatʒ Perkyn þe plouman · 'bi seynt Peter of Rome,
I haue an half acre to erye · bi þe heighe way;
Hadde I eried þis half acre · and sowen it after,   5
I wolde wende with ʒow · and þe way teche.'
   'Þis were a longe lettynge' · quod a lady in a sklayre,
'What sholde we wommen · worche þere-whiles?'
   'Somme shal sowe þe sakke,' quod Piers · 'for shedyng of
   þe whete;
And ʒe, louely ladyes · with ʒoure longe fyngres,   10
Þat ʒe han silke and sendal · to sowe, whan tyme is,
Chesibles for chapelleynes · cherches to honoure.
   Wyues and wydwes · wolle & flex spynneth,
Maketh cloth, I conseille ʒow · and kenneth so ʒowre
   douʒtres;
Þe nedy and þe naked · nymmeth hede how hij liggeth, 15
And casteth hem clothes · for so comaundeth treuthe.
For I shal lene hem lyflode · but ʒif þe londe faille,
Flesshe and bred bothe · to riche and to pore,
As longe as I lyue · for þe lordes loue of heuene.
   And alle manere of men · þat þorw mete and drynke
   lybbeth,   20

Helpith hym to worche wiȝtliche · þat wynneth ȝowre fode.'

'Bi crist,' quod a knyȝte þo · 'he kenneth vs þe best ;
Ac on þe teme trewly · tauȝte was I neuere.
Ac kenne me,' quod þe knyȝte · 'and, bi cryst, I wil assaye !'

'Bi seynt Poule,' quod Perkyn · 'ȝe profre ȝow so faire,   25
Þat I shal swynke and swete · and sowe for vs bothe,
And oþer laboures do for þi loue · al my lyf-tyme,
In couenaunt þat þow kepe · holikirke and my-selue
Fro wastoures and fro wykked men · þat þis worlde struyeth.

    And go hunte hardiliche · to hares and to foxes,   30
To bores and to brockes · þat breketh adown myne hegges,
And go affaite þe faucones · wilde foules to kille ;
For suche cometh to my croft · and croppeth my whete.'

    Curteislich þe knyȝte þanne · comsed þise wordes,
'By my power, Pieres,' quod he · 'I pliȝte þe my treuthe   35
To fulfille þis forward · þowȝ I fiȝte sholde ;
Als longe as I lyue · I shal þe mayntene.'

    'Ȝe, and ȝit a poynt,' quod Pieres · 'I preye ȝow of more ;
Loke ȝe tene no tenaunt · but treuthe wil assent.
And þowgh ȝe mowe amercy hem · late mercy be taxoure,   40
And mekenesse þi mayster · maugre medes chekes ;
And þowgh pore men profre ȝow · presentis and ȝiftis,
Nym it nauȝte, an auenture · ȝe mowe it nauȝte deserue ;
For þow shalt ȝelde it aȝein · at one ȝeres ende,
In a ful perillous place · purgatorie it hatte.   45

    And mysbede nouȝte þi bonde-men · þe better may þow
        spede ;
Þowgh he be þyn vnderlynge here · wel may happe in heuene,
Þat he worth worthier sette · and with more blisse,
Þan þow, bot þou do bette · And lyue as þow shulde ;
        Amice, ascende superius.

For in charnel atte chirche · cherles ben yuel to knowe,   50
Or a kniȝte fram a knaue þere · knowe þis in þin herte.

And þat þow be trewe of þi tonge · and tales þat þow hatie,
But-if þei ben of wisdome or of witte · þi werkmen to chaste.
Holde with none harlotes · ne here nouȝte her tales,
And nameliche atte mete · suche men eschue ;   55
For it ben þe deueles disoures · I do þe to vnderstande.'
  'I assente, bi seynt Iame' · seyde þe kniȝte þanne,
'Forto worche bi þi wordes · þe while my lyf dureth.'
    'And I shal apparaille me,' quod Perkyn · 'in pilgrimes
        wise,
And wende with ȝow I wil · til we fynde treuthe;   6c
    And cast on me my clothes · yclouted and hole,
My cokeres and my coffes · for colde of my nailles,
And hange myn hoper at myn hals · in stede of a scrippe;
A busshel of bredcorne · brynge me þer-inne ;
For I wil sowe it my-self · and sitthenes wil I wende   65
To pylgrymage as palmers don · pardoun forto haue.
    Ac who so helpeth me to erie · or sowen here ar I wende,
Shal haue leue, bi owre lorde · to lese here in heruest,
And make hem mery þere-mydde · maugre who-so bigrucch-
        eth it.
    And alkyn crafty men · þat konne lyuen in treuthe,   70
I shal fynden hem fode · þat feithfulliche libbeth.
    Saue Iakke þe iogeloure · and Ionet of þe stues,
And danyel þe dys-playere · and denote þe baude,
And frere þe faytoure · and folke of his ordre,
And Robyn þe Rybaudoure · for his rusty wordes.   75
Treuthe tolde me ones · and bad me tellen it after,
Deleantur de libro viuentium · I shulde nouȝte dele with hem ;
For holicherche is hote of hem · no tythe to take,
    Quia cum iustis non scribantur ;
They ben ascaped good auenture · now god hem amende !'
    Dame worche-whan-tyme-is · Pieres wyf hiȝte,   8c
His douȝter hiȝte do-riȝte-so- · or-þi-dame-shal-þe-bete,

His sone hiȝte suffre-þi-souereynes- · to-hauen-her-wille-
Deme-hem-nouȝte-for-if-þow-doste-'þow-shalt-it-dere-abugge.
' Late god yworth with al · for so his worde techeth ;

For now I am olde and hore · and haue of myn owen,   85
To penaunce and to pilgrimage · I wil passe with þise other.
For-þi I wil, or I wende · do wryte my biqueste.
In dei nomine, amen · I make it my-seluen.
He shal haue my soule · þat best hath yserued it,
And fro þe fende it defende · for so I bileue,   90
Til I come to his acountes · as my *credo* me telleth,
To haue a relees and a remissioun · on þat rental, I leue.

Þe kirke shal haue my caroigne · and kepe my bones ;
For of my corne and catel · he craued þe tythe.
I payed it hym prestly · for peril of my soule,   95
For-thy is he holden, I hope · to haue me in his masse,
And mengen in his memorye · amonge alle crystene.

My wyf shal haue of þat I wan · with treuthe and nomore,
And dele amonge my douȝtres · and my dere children.
For þowghe I deye to-daye · my dettes ar quitte,   100
I bare home þat I borwed · ar I to bedde ȝede.

And with þe residue and þe remenaunte · bi þe Rode of
      Lukes !
I wil worschip þer-with · treuthe by my lyue,
And ben his pilgryme atte plow · for pore mennes sake.
My plow-fote shal be my pyk-staf · and picche atwo þe
      rotes,   105
And helpe my culter to kerue · and clense þe forwes.'

Now is perkyn and his pilgrymes · to þe plowe faren ;
To erie þis halue acre · holpyn hym manye.
Dikeres & delueres · digged vp þe balkes ;
Þere-with was perkyn apayed · and preysed hem faste.   110
Other werkemen þere were · þat wrouȝten ful ȝerne,
Eche man in his manere · made hym-self to done.

And some to plese perkyn · piked vp þe wedes.

At heighe pryme peres · lete þe plowe stonde,

To ouersen hem hym-self; · and who-so best wrouȝte,   115

He shulde be huyred þer-after · whan heruest-tyme come.

And þanne seten somme · and songen atte nale,

And hulpen erie his half acre · with 'howl trolli-lolli!'

'Now, bi þe peril of my soule!' quod Pieres · al in pure
tene,

'But ȝe arise þe rather · and rape ȝow to worche,   120

Shal no greyne þat groweth · glade ȝow at nede;

And þough ȝe deye for dole · þe deuel haue þat reccheth!'

Tho were faitoures aferde · and feyned hem blynde,

Somme leyde here legges aliri · as suche loseles conneth,

And made her mone to pieres · and preyde hym of *grace*:   125

'For we haue no lymes to laboure with · lorde, y-graced be
ȝe!

Ac we preye for ȝow pieres · and for ȝowre plow bothe,

Þat god of his grace · ȝowre grayne multiplye,

And ȝelde ȝow of ȝowre almesse · þat ȝe ȝiue vs here;

For we may nouȝte swynke ne swete · suche sikenesse vs
eyleth.'   130

'If it be soth,' quod pieres, 'þat ȝe seyne · I shal it sone
asspye!

Ȝe ben wastoures, I wote wel · and treuthe wote þe sothe!

And I am his olde hyne · and hiȝte hym to warne

Which þei were in þis worlde · his werkemen appeyred.

Ȝe wasten þat men wynnen · with *tra*uaille and with
tene,   135

Ac treuthe shal teche ȝow · his teme to dryue,

Or ȝe shal ete barly bred · and of þe broke drynke.

But if he be blynde or broke-legged · or bolted with yrnes,

He shal ete whete bred · and drynke with my-selue,

Tyl god of his goodnesse · amendement hym sende.   140

Ac ȝe myȝte trauaille as treuthe wolde · and take mete &
　　huyre
To kepe kyne in þe felde · þe corne fro þe bestes,
Diken or deluen · or dyngen vppon sheues,
Or helpe make morter · or bere mukke a-felde.

　　In lecherye and in losengerye · ȝe lyuen, and in sleuthe, 145
And al is þorw suffrance · þat veniaunce ȝow ne taketh.

　　Ac ancres and heremytes · þat eten noȝt but at nones,
And namore er morwe · myne almesse shul þei haue,
And of my catel to cope hem with · þat han cloistres and
　　cherches.
Ac robert renne-aboute · shal nowȝte haue of myne,　　150
Ne posteles, but þey preche conne · and haue powere of þe
　　bisschop;
They shal haue payne and potage · and make hem-self at
　　ese,
For it is an vnresonable Religioun · þat hath riȝte nouȝte of
　　certeyne.'

　　And þanne gan a wastoure to wrath hym · and wolde haue
　　yfouȝte,
And to Pieres þe plowman · he profered his gloue;　　155
A Brytonere, a braggere · a-bosted pieres als—

　　·　　　·　　　·　　　·　　　·　　　·　　　·

'Wiltow or neltow · we wil haue owre wille,
Of þi flowre and of þi flessche · fecche whan vs liketh,
And make vs myrie þer-myde · maugre þi chekes!'　　160
　　Thanne Pieres þe plowman · pleyned hym to þe knyȝte,
To kepe hym, as couenaunte was · fram cursed shrewes,
And fro þis wastoures wolueskynnes · þat maketh þe worlde
　　dere:
'For þo waste and wynnen nouȝte · and þat ilke while
Worth neuere plente amonge þe poeple · þer-while my plow
　　liggeth.'　　　　　　　　　　　　　　　　165

Curteisly þe knyȝte þanne · as his kynde wolde,
Warned wastoure · and wissed hym bettere,
'Or þow shalt abugge by þe lawe · by þe ordre þat I bere!'
  'I was nouȝt wont to worche,' quod wastour · 'and now wil
    I nouȝt bigynne!'—
And lete liȝte of þe lawe · and lasse of þe knyȝte,   170
And sette Pieres at a pees · and his plow bothe,
And manaced pieres and his men · ȝif þei mette eft sone.
  'Now, by þe peril of my soule!' quod pieres · 'I shal
    apeyre ȝow alle!'
And houped after hunger · þat herd hym atte firste:
A-wreke me of þise wastoures,' quod he · 'þat þis worlde
    schendeth!'   175
  Hunger in haste þo · hent wastour bi þe mawe,
And wronge hym so bi þe wombe · þat bothe his eyen
    wattered;
He buffeted þe Britoner · aboute þe chekes,
Þat he loked like a lanterne · al his lyf after.
He bette hem so bothe · he barste nere here [ribbes;] 180
Ne hadde Pieres with a pese-lof · preyed hunger to cesse,
They hadde ben doluen bothe · ne deme þow non other.
'Suffre hem lyue,' he seyde · 'and lete hem ete with hogges,
Or elles benes and bren · ybaken togideres,
Or elles melke and mene ale' · þus preyed pieres for hem. 185
  Faitoures for fere her-of · flowen in-to bernes,
And flapten on with flayles · fram morwe til euen,
That hunger was nouȝt so hardy · on hem for to loke,
For a potful of peses · þat peres hadde ymaked.
An heep of heremites · henten hem spades,   190
And ketten here copes · and courtpies hem made,
And wenten as werkemen · with spades and with schoueles,
And doluen and dykeden · to dryue aweye hunger.
  Blynde and bedreden · were botened a þousande,

Þat seten to begge syluer · sone were þei heled. 195
For þat was bake for bayarde · was bote for many hungry,
And many a beggere for benes · buxome was to swynke,
And eche a pore man wel apayed · to haue pesen for his
  huyre,
And what pieres preyed hem to do · as prest as a sperhauke.
And þere-of was peres proude · and put hem to werke, 200
And ȝaf hem mete as he myȝte aforth · and mesurable huyre.
  Þanne hadde peres pite · and preyed hunger to wende
Home in-to his owne erde · and holden hym þere.
'For I am wel awroke now · of wastoures, þorw þi myȝte.
Ac I preye þe, ar þow passe' · quod Pieres to hunger, 205
'Of beggeres and of bidderes · what best be to done?
For I wote wel, be þow went · þei wil worche ful ille;
For myschief it maketh · þei beth so meke nouthe,
And for defaute of her fode · þis folke is at my wille.
Þey are my blody brethren,' quod pieres · 'for god bouȝte
  vs alle ; 210
Treuthe tauȝte me ones · to louye hem vchone,
And to helpen hem of alle þinge · ay as hem nedeth.
And now wolde I witen of þe · what were þe best,
And how I myȝte amaistrien hem · and make hem to
  worche.' 214
  'Here now,' quod hunger · 'and holde it for a wisdome:
Bolde beggeres and bigge · þat mowe her bred biswynke,
With houndes bred and hors bred · holde vp her hertis,
Abate hem with benes · for bollyng of her wombe ;
And ȝif þe gomes grucche · bidde hem go swynke,
And he shal soupe swettere · whan he it hath deseruid. 220
  And if þow fynde any freke · þat fortune hath appeyred,
Or any maner fals men · fonde þow suche to cnowe ;
Conforte hem with þi catel · for crystes loue of heuene,
Loue hem and lene hem · so lawe of god techeth:—

Alter alterius onera portate.

And alle maner of men · þat þow myȝte asspye,   225
That nedy ben, and nauȝty · helpe hem with þi godis,
Loue hem and lakke hem nouȝte · late god take þe
    veniaunce;
Theigh þei done yuel · late þow god y-worþe:—
    Michi vindicta, & ego retribuam.
And if þow wilt be gracious to god · do as þe gospel techeth,
And biloue þe amonges low men · so shaltow lacche grace,
    Facite vobis amicos de mamona iniquitatis.'
  'I wolde nouȝt greue god,' quod piers · 'for al þe good on
    grounde;   231
Miȝte I synnelees do as þow seist?' · seyde pieres þanne.
  'Ȝe, I bihote þe,' quod hunger · 'or ellis þe bible lieth;
Go to Genesis þe gyaunt · þe engendroure of vs alle;
"*In sudore* and swynke · þow shalt þi mete tilye,   235
And laboure for þi lyflode" · and so owre lorde hyȝte.
And sapience seyth þe same · I seigh it in þe bible;
"*Piger pro frigore* · no felde nolde tilye,
And þerfore he shal begge and bidde · and no man bete his
    hunger."
  Mathew with mannes face · mouthed þise wordes,   240
Þat *seruus nequam* had a nam · and for he wolde nouȝte chaf-
    fare,
He had maugre of his maistre · for euermore after;
And binam hym his Mnam · for he ne wolde worche,
And ȝaf þat Mnam to hym · þat ten Mnames hadde,
And with þat he seyde · þat holicherche it herde,   245
"He þat hath shal haue · and helpe þere it nedeth,
And he þat nouȝt hath, shal nouȝt haue · and no man hym
    helpe;
And þat he weneth wel to haue · I wil it hym bireue."
  Kynde witt wolde · þat eche a wyght wrouȝte

Or in dykynge or in deluynge · or trauaillynge in preyeres,   250
Contemplatyf lyf or actyf lyf · cryst wolde men wrouȝte.
Þe sauter seyth in þe psalme · of *beati omnes*,
Þe freke þat fedeth hym-self · with his feythful laboure,
He is blessed by þe boke · in body and in soule:

> *Labores manuum tuarum, &c.'*

'Ȝet I prey ȝow,' quod pieres · '*par charite*, and ȝe kunne
Eny leef of lechecraft · lere it me, my dere.   256
For somme of my seruauntz · and my-self bothe
Of al a wyke worche nouȝt · so owre wombe aketh.'

   'I wote wel,' quod hunger · ' what sykenesse ȝow eyleth,
Ȝe han maunged ouer-moche · and þat maketh ȝow grone. 260
Ac I hote þe,' quod hunger · 'as þow þyne hele wilnest,
Þat þow drynke no day · ar þow dyne somwhat.
Ete nouȝte, I hote þe · ar hunger þe take,
And sende þe of his sauce · to sauoure with þi lippes;
And kepe some tyl soper-tyme · and sitte nouȝt to longe, 265
Arise vp ar appetit · haue eten his fulle.
Lat nouȝt sire surfait · sitten at þi borde;
Leue him nouȝt, for he is lecherous · and likerous of tonge,
And after many manere metes · his maw is afyngred.

   And ȝif þow diete þe þus · I dar legge myne eres,   270
Þat phisik shal his furred hodes · for his fode selle,
And his cloke of calabre · with alle þe knappes of golde,
And be fayne, bi my feith · his phisik to lete,
And lerne to laboure with londe · for lyflode is swete;
For morthereres aren mony leches · lorde hem amende! 275
Þei do men deye þorw here drynkes · ar destine it wolde.'

   'By seynt Poule,' quod pieres · 'þise aren profitable
        wordis!
Wende now, hunger, whan þow wolt · þat wel be þow euere!
For þis is a louely lessoun · lorde it þe for-ȝelde!'

   'By-hote god,' quod hunger · 'hennes ne wil I wende,   280

Til I haue dyned bi þis day · and ydronke bothe.'
  ' I haue no peny,' q*u*od peres · ' poletes forto bigge,
Ne neyther gees ne grys · but two grene cheses,
A fewe cruddes and creem · and an hauer cake,
And two loues of benes and bran · y-bake for my fauntis.
And ʒet I sey, by my soule · I haue no salt bacou*n*,   286
Ne no kokeney, bi cryst · coloppes forto maken.
Ac I haue p*er*cil and porettes · and many kole-plantes,
And eke a cow and a kalf · and a cart-mare
To drawe a-felde my donge · þe while þe drought lasteth. 290
And bi þis lyflode we mot lyue · til lammasse tyme;
And bi þat, I hope to haue · heruest in my croft;
And þanne may I diʒte þi dyner · as me dere liketh.'
Alle þe pore peple þo · pesecoddes fetten,
Benes and baken apples · þei brouʒte in her lappes, 295
Chibolles and cheruelles · and ripe chiries manye,
And p*ro*fred peres þis p*re*sent · to plese with hunger.
  Al hunger eet in hast · and axed after more.
Þanne pore folke for fere · fedde hunger ʒerne   299
With grene poret and pesen · to poysou*n* hunger þei þouʒte.
By þat it neighed nere heruest · newe corne cam to chepynge;
Þanne was folke fayne · and fedde hunger with þe best,
With good ale, as glotou*n* tauʒte · and gerte hunger go slepe.
  And þo wolde wastour nouʒt werche · but wandren aboute,
Ne no begger ete bred · þat benes Inne were,   305
But of coket or clerematyn · or elles of clene whete;
Ne none halpeny ale · in none wise drynke,
But of þe best and of þe brounest · þat in borgh*e* is to selle.
  Laboreres þat haue no lande · to lyue on but her handes,
Deyned nouʒt to dyne a-day · nyʒt-olde wortes.   310
May no peny-ale hem paye · ne no pece of bakou*n*,
But if it be fresch flesch other fische · fryed other bake,
And þat *chaude* or *plus chaud* · for chillyng of here mawe.

And but if he be heighlich huyred · ellis wil he chyde,
And þat he was werkman wrouȝt · waille þe tyme,   315
Aȝeines catones conseille · comseth he to iangle :—
    Paupertalis onus pacienter ferre memento.

He greueth hym aȝeines god · and gruccheth aȝeines
    resoun,
And þanne curseth he þe kynge · and al his conseille after,
Suche lawes to loke · laboreres to greue.
Ac whiles hunger was her maister · þere wolde none of hem
    chyde,   320
Ne stryue aȝeines his statut · so sterneliche he loked.
  Ac I warne ȝow, werkemen · wynneth while ȝe mowe,
For hunger hiderward · hasteth hym faste,
He shal awake with water · wastoures to chaste.
Ar fyue ȝere be fulfilled · suche famyn shal aryse,   325
Thorwgh flodes and þourgh foule wederes · frutes shul faille,
And so sayde saturne · and sent ȝow to warne :
Whan ȝe se þe sonne amys · and two monkes hedes,
And a Mayde haue þe maistrie · and multiplie bi eight,
Þanne shal deth withdrawe · and derthe be iustice,   330
And dawe þe dyker · deye for hunger,
But if god of his goodnesse · graunt vs a trewe.   332

PASSUS VII.

TREUTHE herde telle her-of · and to peres he sent,
  To taken his teme · and tulyen þe erthe,
And purchaced hym a pardoun · *a pena & a culpa,*
For hym, and for his heires · for euermore after.
And bad hym holde hym at home · and eryen his leyes,   5
And alle þat halpe hym to erie · to sette or to sowe,
Or any other myster · þat myʒte pieres auaille,
Pardoun with pieres plowman · treuthe hath ygraunted.

  Kynges and knyʒtes · þat kepen holycherche,
And ryʒtfullych in reumes · reulen þe peple,   10
Han pardoun thourgh purgatorie · to passe ful lyʒtly,
With patriarkes and prophetes · in paradise to be felawes.

  Bisshopes yblessed · ʒif þei ben as þei shulden,
Legistres of bothe þe lawes · þe lewed þere-with to preche,
And in as moche as þei mowe · amende alle synful,   15
Aren peres with þe apostles · (þis pardoun Piers sheweth),
And at þe day of dome · atte heigh deyse to sytte.

  Marchauntz in þe margyne · hadden many ʒeres,
Ac none *a pena & a culpa* · þe Pope nolde hem graunte,
For þei holde nouʒt her halidayes · as holicherche techeth, 20
And for þei swere by her soule · and 'so god moste hem
    helpe,'
Aʒein clene conscience · her catel to selle.

  Ac vnder his secret seel · treuthe sent hem a lettre,

That þey shulde bugge boldely · þat hem best liked,

And sithenes selle it aӡein · and saue þe wynnynge,   25

And amende *mesondieux* þere-myde · and myseyse folke helpe,

And wikked wayes · wiӡtlich hem amende;

And do bote to brugges · þat to-broke were,

Marien maydenes · or maken hem nonnes;

Pore peple and prisounes · fynden hem here fode,   30

And sette scoleres to scole · or to somme other craftes;

Releue Religioun · and renten hem bettere;—

'And I shal sende ӡow my-selue · seynt Michel myn archangel,

Þat no deuel shal ӡow dere · ne fere ӡow in ӡowre deyinge,

And witen ӡow fro wanhope · if ӡe wil þus worche,   35

And send ӡowre sowles in safte · to my seyntes in ioye.'

Þanne were Marchauntz mery · many wepten for ioye,

And preyseden pieres þe plowman · þat purchaced þis bulle.

Men of lawe lest pardoun hadde · þat pleteden for Mede,

For þe sauter saueth hem nouӡte · such as taketh ӡiftes,   40

And namelich of innocentz · þat none yuel ne kunneth;

    Super innocentem munera non accipies.

Pledoures shulde peynen hem · to plede for such, an helpe,

Prynces and prelates · shulde paye for her trauaille;

    A regibus & pryncipibus erit merces eorum.

Ac many a iustice an iuroure · wolde for Iohan do more,

Þan *pro dei pietate* · leue þow none other!   45

Ac he þat spendeth his speche · and spekeþ for þe pore

Þat is Innocent and nedy · and no man appeireth,

Conforteth hym in þat cas · with-oute coueytise of ӡiftes,

And scheweth lawe for owre lordes loue · as he it hath lerned,

Shal no deuel at his ded-day · deren hym a myӡte,   50

Þat he ne worth sauf and his sowle · þe sauter bereth witnesse;

Domine, quis habitabit in tabernaculo tuo, &c.

Ac to bugge water, ne wynde · ne witte, ne fyre þe fierthe,
Þise foure þe fader of heuene · made to þis folde in comune;
Þise ben treuthes tresores · trewe folke to helpe,
Þat neuere shal wax ne wanye · with-oute god hymselue.   55

Whan þei drawen on to deye · and Indulgences wolde haue,
Her pardoun is ful petit · at her partyng hennes,
Þat any Mede of mene men · for her motyng taketh.
Ȝe legistres and lawyeres · holdeth þis for treuthe,
Þat, ȝif þat I lye · Mathew is to blame,   60
For he bad me make ȝow þis · and þis prouerbe me tolde,
       Quodcumque vultis vt faciant vobis homines, facite eis.

Alle lybbyng laboreres · þat lyuen with her hondes,
Þat trewlich taken · and trewlich wynnen,
And lyuen in loue and in lawe · for her lowe hertis,
Haueth þe same absolucioun · þat sent was to peres.   65

Beggeres ne bidderes · ne beth nouȝte in þe bulle,
But if þe suggestioun be soth · þat shapeth hem to begge.
For he þat beggeth or bit · but if he haue nede,
He is fals with þe fende · and defraudeth the nedy,
And also he bigileth þe gyuere · ageines his wil.   70
For if he wist he were nouȝte nedy · he wolde ȝiue þat an
       other,
Þat were more nedy þan he · so þe nediest shuld be hulpe.
Catoun kenneth men þus · and þe clerke of þe stories,
Cui des, videto · is catounes techynge,
And in the stories he techeth · to bistowe þyn almes;   75
       Sit elemosina tua in manu tua, donec studes cui des.

Ac Gregori was a gode man · and bad vs gyuen alle
Þat asketh, for his loue · þat vs alle leneth :—
       Non eligas cui miserearis, ne forte pretereas illum qui
              meretur accipere. Quia incertum est pro quo Deo
              magis placeas.

I

For wite ȝe neuere who is worthi · ac god wote who hath
  nede,
In hym þat taketh is þe treccherye · if any tresoun wawe;
For he þat ȝiueth, ȝeldeth · and ȝarketh hym to reste,   80
And he þat biddeth, borweth · and bryngeth hym-self in dette.
For beggeres borwen euermo · and her borghe is god almyȝti,
To ȝelden hem þat ȝiueth hem · and ȝet vsure more:

> *Quare non dedisti peccuniam meam ad mensam, vt ego*
> *veniens cum vsuris exegissem illam?*

For-þi biddeth nouȝt, ȝe beggeres · but if ȝe haue gret nede;
For who-so hath to buggen hym bred · þe boke bereth
  witnesse,   85
He hath ynough þat hath bred ynough · þough he haue nouȝt
  elles:

> *Satis diues est, qui non indiget pane.*

Late vsage be ȝowre solace · of seyntes lyues redynge,
Þe boke banneth beggarie · and blameth hem in þis manere:

> *Iunior fui, etenim senui; et non vidi iustum derelictum,*
> *nec semen eius querens panem.*

For ȝe lyue in no loue · ne no lawe holde;   89
Many of ȝow ne wedde nouȝt . þe wommen þat ȝe with delen,

  .   .   .   .

And bryngeth forth barnes · þat bastardes men calleth.   92
Or þe bakke or some bone · he breketh in his ȝouthe,
And sitthe gon faiten with ȝoure fauntes · for euermore after.
Þere is moo mysshape peple · amonge þise beggeres,   95
Þan of alle maner men · þat on þis molde walketh;
And þei þat lyue þus here lyf · mowe lothe þe tyme,
Þat euere he was man wrouȝt · whan he shal hennes fare.

Ac olde men & hore · þat helplees ben of strengthe,
And women with childe · þat worche ne mowe,   100
Blynde and bedered · and broken here membres,
Þat taketh þis myschief mekelych · as meseles and othere,

Han as pleyne pardoun · as þe plowman hym-self;
For loue of her lowe hertis · owre lorde hath hem graunted
Here penaunce and her purgatorie · here on þis erthe.   105
   'Pieres,' quod a prest þo · 'þi pardoun most I rede,
For I wil construe eche clause · and kenne it þe on engliche.'
   And pieres at his preyere · þe pardoun vnfoldeth,
And I bihynde hem bothe · bihelde al þe bulle.
Al in two lynes it lay · and nouȝt a leef more,   110
And was writen riȝt þus · in witnesse of treuthe:

> *Et qui bona egerunt, ibunt in vitam eternam;*
> *Qui vero mala, in ignem eternum.*

   'Peter!' quod þe prest þo · 'I can no pardoun fynde,
But "dowel, and haue wel · and god shal haue þi sowle,
And do yuel, and haue yuel · hope þow non other
But after þi ded-day · þe deuel shal haue þi sowle!"'   115
   And pieres for pure tene · pulled it atweyne,

> And seyde, '*si ambulauero, in medio vmbre mostis, non*
> *timebo mala; quoniam tu mecum es.*

I shal cessen of my sowyng,' quod pieres · 'and swynk
   nouȝt so harde,
Ne about my bely-ioye · so bisi be namore!
Of preyers and of penaunce · my plow shal ben her-after,
And wepen whan I shulde slepe · þough whete-bred me
   faille.   120
Þe prophete his payn ete · in penaunce and in sorwe,
By þat þe sauter seith · so dede other manye;
Þat loueth god lelly · his lyflode is ful esy:

> *Fuerunt michi lacrime mee panes die ac nocte.*

   And, but if Luke lye · he lereth vs bi foules,
We shulde nouȝt be to bisy · aboute þe worldes blisse;   125
Ne solliciti sitis · he seyth in þe gospel,
And sheweth vs bi ensamples · vs selue to wisse.
Þe foules on þe felde · who fynt hem mete at wynter?

Haue þei no gernere to go to · but god fynt hem alle.'

'What I' quod þe prest to perkyn · 'peter I as me þinketh,
Þow art lettred a litel · who lerned þe on boke ?'   131

   'Abstinence þe abbesse,' quod pieres · 'myne a. b. c. me
     tauȝte,

And conscience come afterward · and kenned me moche
     more.'

   'Were þow a prest, pieres,' quod he · 'þow miȝte preche
     where þow sholdest,

As deuynour in deuynyte · with *dixit insipiens* to þi teme.' 135

   'Lewed lorel I' quod Pieres · 'litel lokestow on þe bible,

On salomones sawes · selden þow biholdest,

     Eice derisores et iurgia cum eis, ne crescant, &c.'

Þe prest and perkyn · apposeden eyther other,

And I þorw here wordes a-woke · and waited aboute,

And seighe þe sonne in þe south · sitte þat tyme,   14○

Metelees and monelees · on Maluerne hulles,

Musyng on þis meteles ; · and my waye ich ȝede.

   Many tyme þis meteles · hath maked me to studye

Of þat I seigh slepyng · if it so be myȝte,

And also for peres þe plowman · ful pensyf in herte,   145

And which a pardoun peres hadde · alle þe peple to conforte,

And how þe prest impugned it · with two propre wordes.

Ac I haue no sauoure in songewarie · for I se it ofte faille ;

Catoun and canonistres · conseilleth vs to leue

To sette sadnesse in songewarie · for, *sompnia ne cures.* 150

   Ac for þe boke bible · bereth witnesse,

How danyel deuyned · þe dremes of a kynge,

Þat was nabugodonosor · nempned of clerkis.

Daniel seyde, 'sire Kynge · þi dremeles bitokneth,

Þat vnkouth knyȝtes shul come · þi kyngdom to cleue; 155

Amonges lowere lordes · þi londe shal be departed.'

And as danyel deuyned · in dede it felle after,

Þe kynge lese his lordship · and lower men it hadde.

  And ioseph mette merueillously · how þe mone and þe
    sonne,

And þe elleuene sterres · hailsed hym alle.   160

Þanne Iacob iugged · iosephes sweuene :

' *Beau filtz,*' quod his fader · ' for defaute we shullen,

I my-self and my sones · seche þe for nede.'

  It bifel as his fader seyde · in pharaoes tyme,

Þat ioseph was iustice · egipte to loken,   165

It bifel as his fader tolde · his frendes þere hym souȝte.

And al þis maketh me · on þis meteles to þynke ;

  And how þe prest preued · no pardoun to dowel,

And demed þat dowel · indulgences passed,

Biénnales and triennales · and bisschopes *let*tres,   170

And how dowel at þe day of dome · is dignelich vnderfongen,

And passeth al þe pardoun · of seynt petres cherche.

  Now hath þe pope powere · pardoun to graunte þe peple

With-outen eny penaunce · to passen in-to heuene;

Þis is owre bileue · as lettered men vs techeth,   175

      Quodcumque ligaueris super terram, erit ligatum et in
        celis, &c.

And so I leue lelly · (lordes forbode ellis !)

Þat pardoun and penaunce · and preyeres don saue

Soules þat haue synned · seuene sithes dedly.

Ac to trust to þise triennales · trewly me þinketh,

Is nouȝt so syker for þe soule · certis, as is dowel.   180

  For-þi I rede ȝow, renkes · þat riche ben on þis erthe,

Vppon trust of ȝowre tresoure · triennales to haue,

Be ȝe neuere þe balder · to breke þe ten hestes;

And namelich, ȝe maistres · mayres and iugges,

Þat han þe welthe of þis worlde · and for wyse men ben
    holden,   185

To purchace ȝow pardoun · and þe popis bulles.

At þe dredeful dome · whan dede shullen rise,
And comen alle bifor cryst · acountis to ȝelde,
How þow laddest þi lyf here . and his lawes keptest,
And how þow dedest day bi day · þe dome wil reherce ;   190
A poke ful of pardoun þere   ne prouinciales le*tt*res,
Theigh ȝe be founde in þe fraternete · of alle þe foure ordres,
And haue indulgences double-folde · but if dowel ȝow help,
I sette ȝowre patentes and ȝowre pardounȝ · at one pies hele !

  For-þi I conseille alle cristene · to crye god mercy,   195
And Marie his moder · be owre mene bitwene,
Þat god gyue vs grace here · ar we gone hennes,
Suche werkes to werche · while we ben here,
Þat after owre deth-day · dowel reherce,
At þe day of dome · we dede as he hiȝte.   200

Explicit visio willelmi de petro plowman.

CRITICAL NOTES.

The text is printed exactly as it stands in MS. Laud 581, excepting in the following instances, where improvements have been suggested by a collation of the text with several other MSS. See note to prol. 39 just below.

Prologue, l. 20. Here we must read *putten*, as in l. 23; but the Laud MS. has *put* in this line.

34. *giltles* is taken from the text printed by Crowley. The MSS. have *synneles.*

39. The words *is luciferes hyne* are omitted in MS. Laud, but are found in the MS. in Trinity College, Cambridge, and in many others. I shall in future denote the Laud MS. by the letter L; the Trinity College MS. by T; MS. Rawlinson Poet. 38, by R; the Oriel MS. by O; and the Cambridge folio MS. (Dd. I. 17) by C.

41. *belies;* so in T; but most MSS., including LCO, read *bely.* *bagges;* L has *bagge,* but TCO have the plural form.

67. *myschief;* misspelt *mychief* in L.

99. *consistorie;* so in TCO; spelt *constorie* in L.

140. *answered;* so in CTO; but LR have the present tense, *answeres.* I may here note that when two or three MSS., as CTO, are mentioned together, I give the *spelling* of the one which stands *first.*

147. The form *myd* (found in MS. T) suits the alliteration; but L and others read *with.*

151. MSS. LT omit the second *hem;* but it occurs in RCO, and should be retained.

179. L omits *it,* which is retained in all the other MSS.

186. L has *croupe* instead of *crope,* which is the reading in R; C has *crepe;* T. has *cropen.*

197. The curious (West-Midland) spelling *mannus* is found both in L and R; other MSS. read *mannes.*

215. *money* is misspelt *monoy* in L in this place, but is rightly spelt elsewhere in our MS.

224. *longe;* so in TCO; but L has *dere.* MSS. of the A-class read *longe.*

226. *and* is miswritten *a* in L; MS. C has *an,* which is very commonly used instead of *and*, and shews that the final *d* was frequently not sounded.

Passus I, l. 37. The words *þat leef is to þi soule Leue not þi likam* are wrongly omitted in LTC; but they are found in RO, and in MSS. of the A-class. The omission was clearly due to the repetition of the word *likam*.

41. *sueth*; so in R. The other readings hardly make sense; they are—*seest*, L ; *seeþ*, TO ; *seiþ* in MS. L. 4. 14 in the Cambridge University Library. Many MSS. of the A-class read *schendeth*, which means *harm*. *Sueth* means *pursue*.

81. *kenne*; so in TCRO; L corruptly has *kende*.

107. *muryer*; so in CT. In L it is curiously spelt *murger*, and in R *murgur*.

139. The Latin quotation is evidently a hexameter, and hence *quod* is the right reading; but nearly all the MSS. (including L) have *quia*. The reading *quod* is adopted from a MS. in the Cambridge University Library, of which the class-mark is Ff. 5. 35.

145. For *worche* (which occurs in C and O) MS. L reads *worcheth*, which produces a false concord ; *worcheth* is plural, but *þow* is singular.

150. *plante*. MSS. of the A-class shew this to be the right reading. MS. L and most others of the B-class have *plente*.

Passus II, l. 27. In the Latin quotation, LTO have *bonus* instead of *bona*. The latter occurs in C.

59. Our MS. has *chaffre* here; but see Prol. l. 31.

87. For *borghe*, the reading in C and R, L has the false spelling *borgthe*. Two MSS., T and O, have *burghe*. *Borghe, burghe* are various spellings of the word now spelt *borough* or *burgh*.

116. *weddynges*; so in TRO; L has *wendynges*.

118. *engendred*; so in TO; LCR read *engendreth*.

165. *flaterere*; so in TCRO; but L has *flatere*.

175. *deuorses*. In both LR we find *deuoses*, by a curious omission of the *r*. C has *deuorses*, T *diuorces*, and O *deuorces*.

227. *mynstralles*. This is of course right, but MS. L has *mynstalles* (omitting *r*) both here and in a later passage.

Passus III, l. 17. L omits *wil*, retained in RT.

48. Instead of *ful*, as in other MSS., L has *wel*.

61. *whiten*; so in C; spelt *whitten* in L.

73. *ne* ; so in TCR; L has *no*.

95. *thynke*; miswritten *thynko* in L.

97. *brenne*; so in TCO; preferable to *berne* in L.

98. L omits *þat*, retained in other MSS.

107. L. omits *þe*, found in RTO, in the last two of which it is spelt *þes*.

127. L omits the second *and*, found in TRO.

187. L omits *it*, found in TRO.

227. *Quod*; so in TCRO; L has *Quaþ*.

251, 269. *moneie ;* so in C ; L has *mone.*

252. *receperunt ;* so in O ; most MSS. (L included) have *recipiebant.*

304. *other,* R ; corruptly spelt *orther* in L.

322. *smytheth,* TO ; *smyteth* in L ; *smithie,* R.

337, 338. *she ;* so in TC ; L corruptly has *ʒe.*

Passus IV. After l. 9 the MSS. of the B-class have lost a line, retained in the MSS. of the A-class, and in Crowley's printed text. It is—

        Of Mede and of other mo · and what man shal her wed.

24. *rit* O ; *ryt* T ; *rydes* C ; badly spelt *ritte* in L.

27. *for þei ;* retained in TO ; L omits.

128. *byʒonde ;* spelt *byʒende* in L.

186. *ribbes ;* so in the Vernon MS. (A-text) ; *guttes,* L and MSS. of B-class.

Passus V, l. 13. *were ;* so in T ; but most MSS. have *was.*

29. *felice ;* so in TRCO ; spelt *filice* in L.

76. *schrifte ;* L has *scrifte* ; but see l. 124.

105. *poeple ;* L has *pople* here, but *poeple* in the next line.

108. *baren ;* so in O ; T has *beren* ; L has *bar.*

143. *han ;* so in T ; L omits *han,* and some MSS. insert it *before* the word *persones,* to the detriment of the sense.

154. *suffre ;* so in most MSS., but spelt *soeffre* in L.

189. *Heruy ;* so in most MSS., but LCR have *Henri* or *henry.*

212. *paknedle ;* so in most MSS., but L has *batnedle.*

213. *pynned.* Badly spelt *pyned* in L.

214. *hadde ;* omitted in LR, but supplied in other MSS.

224. *no ;* so in other MSS., L has *na.*

232. *Repentedestow ;* so in T ; L has *Repentestow.*

236. The first *be* is omitted in L, by mistake.

253. L has *Lenestow,* but T has *Lentestow.*

272. L has *telleth,* by mistake ; *tellest* is in TCR.

273. This line is from the Cambridge MS. ; L omits it.

280, 281. For the first *haue* LR have *hath,* and for *Ben* they have *Is.* I follow CTO.

291. L omits *quasi,* but it is in TCOR.

312. For *she,* L has *he,* by a slip. Cf. l. 310.

338. From the Oriel MS. and C ; LTR omit this line.

357. *stumbled ;* so in TCO ; *trembled,* L ; *tremled,* R.

370. *wif ;* so in TO ; *witte,* L ; *wit,* C.

388. L omits *to,* which occurs in TCO.

434. L omits *þe,* which occurs in TCO.

440. *fernyere ;* so in TC ; L has *farnere.*

441. *forʒete ;* miswritten *foʒete* in L.

447. *haue* is supplied from C ; in TO we find *haue I* ; L omits it.

448. *quod ;* so in R ; miswritten *quia* in L, which spoils the scansion.

514. *nos ;* not in L ; supplied from R.

549. *fifty;* so in TCO; *fourty* in LR. Cf. Pass. vi. 85.

557. *of hym;* supplied from R; LTCO omit.

569. Supplied from C and O; omitted by LTR.

586. *hatte;* so in CR; *hiȝte,* W. L has *hat,* which is the sing. form.

590. *fees;* so in TCR; *foes,* L; *foos,* O.

600. *With;* so in TRO; L. has *Wit.*

611. *wayue.* The word may also be read *wayne* in the MSS.

612. *cunctis,* C; *cuntis,* L; only R retains *iterum.*

613. *cliket;* so in TC; LR have *clikat.*

623. *cliketed;* so in C; spelt *clikated* in L.

627. *aren;* so in R; L has *ar.*

Passus VI, l. 6. *wolde;* so in TO; LR have *wil.*

9. L omits *þe* before *sakke;* the other MSS. retain it.

49. This line is from C; LTRO omit it.

138. *or,* TCRO; *and,* L; in the first instance.

147. *noȝt,* TCO; LR omit it.

180. *ribbes;* so in the Vernon MS.; others have *guttes.*

206. L omits *to,* which other MSS. retain.

223. *hem;* so in RO; LT have *hym.*

228. *y-worthe;* so in T; LR have the inferior spelling *aworthe;* CO have *worthe.* For *vindicta,* all the MSS. have *vindictam.*

229. *wilt;* so in TCO; L has *wil.*

230. *biloue;* so in TCO; *bilow* in L; *bylowe* in R.

243. L omits *hym* by mistake.

323. L omits the *r* in *hiderward,* by mistake.

325. *ȝere;* so in E; *ȝeer* in O; LTC omit it.

Passus VII, l. 16. *þis;* so in TCO; LR have *þus.*

25. *wynnynge;* miswritten *wynnyge* in L.

75. LR omit the first *tua,* which TCO retain.

77. In the Latin quotation, for *Deo* (as in T), LCRO have *Deum.*

83. In the quotation, *exegissem* is from CR; L has *exigerem;* TO have *exigere.* The last word, *illam,* is not in the MSS. I have supplied it from the Vulgate.

88. LTR omit *querens panem;* OC retain it.

94. *And;* miswritten *A* in L.

115. *But;* so in TCO; L and R have *þat.*

137. In the quotation, *Eice* (the old spelling of *Ejice*) is from O; LTRC wrongly have *Ecce.*

183. *ten;* so in CRO; LT have *x.*

187. *dede;* so in TCR; L has *ded.*

NOTES.

[The text generally follows MS. Laud Misc. 581, as explained in the Critical Notes.]

Title. The English title is a translation of the title found in numerous MSS., viz. 'Visio Willelmi de Petro Plowman.' The first division of the poem, or *Prologue*, is marked by the Latin word *Prologus* in *one* MS. only; in most others, it has no heading. In our Laud MS., however, we find here 'Incipit liber de petro plowman,' nearly obliterated.

1. *soft*, mild, warm.

2. *I shope me*, &c.; I put myself into clothes, as if I were a shepherd, i. e. I put on (rough) clothes, so that I looked like a shepherd. *Shope*, lit. shaped; the phrase *I shope me* generally means *I got myself ready*, as in *he shope hym for to walken*, he got ready to set off walking; Pass. xi. l. 404. We know that *shepe* here means shepherd, because *shepherd* is the reading of many MSS. It more often means *sheep*, but a few instances of the signification *shepherd* occur. Thus, in an old and very rude hexameter which gives the names of the leaders in Wat Tyler's rebellion, we have

'Jak *Chep*, Tronche, Jon Wrau, Thom Myllere, Tyler, Jak Strawe;'

where another reading for *Chep* is *Schep*. See Political Poems, ed. Wright, vol. i. p. 230. This statement has been questioned, but Dr. Morris assures me he has seen *schepe* used for *shepherd* more than once, and so have I; but we have both lost the references. Still there need be no doubt about it: compare the Chaucerian word *hunte* in the sense of *hunter*. So too we find *prisune* used to mean, not a gaol, but a *prisoner;* Genesis and Exodus, ed. Morris, l. 2044. In the same poem *prisuner* also occurs, but it means the gaoler; l. 2042. So again *message* means *messenger*, in the MSS. of Chaucer's Man of Lawes Tale, l. 333. And again, in the Ancren Riwle, p. 212, last line, occurs the remarkable form *slep*, meaning 'a sleeper.' But the most sure confirmation of the above interpretation is in the fact that, *since the first edition of this work was published*, the word has been discovered still existing in Lincolnshire. *Shep* for ' shepherd' is given in Mr. Peacock's Glossary of Words used in Manley and Corringham. More than this, I have recovered one of my lost references. The expression 'A *chepys* croke,' i. e. a shepherd's crook, occurs in Lydgate's 'Chorl and Bird,' as printed in Ashmole's Theatrum Chemicum, p. 223.

It will be observed, that I have, in relation to the word *shope*, quoted from

Passus *eleven.* **Properly** speaking, the poem has but *seven* Passus ; but in all MSS. of the B-class, it is followed by another poem, entitled *Vita De Dowel, Do-bet, et Do-best,* and the two are taken together so as to form one long poem, comprising a Prologue and twenty Passus. The name of the whole work, both parts together, is *Liber de petro plowman,* as distinct from the *Visio,* yet inclusive of it. For the meaning of A-class, B-class, C-class, see the Preface.

3. *In habite as an heremite.* The simple shepherd's dress resembled that of a hermit. *Vnholy of workes.* This Dr. Whitaker paraphrases by—'not like an anchorite who keeps his cell, but like one of those unholy hermits who wander about the world to hear and see wonders.' Or it may simply be supposed to be inserted parenthetically, and to express the author's opinion of hermits in general; an opinion which he elsewhere repeats more than once. Cf. l. 28, and note to l. 53.

5. *May mornynge;* readers of Chaucer will remember how fond he is (like other Early English poets) of the month of May. *On a May morning* is nearly equivalent to *once upon a time.* *Malverne hulles;* the poet mentions Malvern hills three times, here, at the end of this Prologue, and in Pass. vii. It may be that the first sketch of the poem was composed in that locality; but, at the time when it was re-cast into the shape here printed, he may have been living in London. At any rate, it is certain that he was at that time very familiar with London, and we may consider London as being the *real scene* of the greater part of the poem. The importance of this remark will be seen as we advance.

6. *A ferly,* a wonder. Cf. 'And I will show you *ferlies* three ;' Sir W. Scott : Ballad of Thomas the Rhymer. *Of fairy,* due to fairy contrivance. See Tyrwhitt's note to l. 6441 of the Cant. Tales. *Me thoughte,* it seemed to me. There is a difference in form between A.S. *hit þincð,* it seems (G. *es dünkt*) and A.S. *þencan,* to think (G. *denken*). Several other verbs bear a similar construction ; thus, another reading for *þow dryest* (Pass. i. 25) is *þe drieth,* i. e. it drieth thee, thou art dry.

7. *Forwandred,* tired out by wandering. See Glossary. *Went me,* turned me, went ; to *wend* originally meant to *turn.* Mr. Hales suggests that *me* is here an ethic dative, as it so commonly is in our old dramatists. I do not think that it is so in this particular passage, but remain of the opinion that *went me* is for *turned myself.* So in Cædmon, ed Thorpe, p. 56, l. 28 ; Ancren Riwle, p. 52 ; and the phrase *wend thee* in a quotation in Halliwell's Dict. s. v. *Disposed.* And again, *himzelue wende* in Spec. of Eng. ed. Morris and Skeat, Pt. II. p. 105, l. 226. But the clearest example is in the Ayenbite of Inwyt, ed. Morris, p. 180—'ase þe wedercoc þet is ope [*upon*] þe steple, þet *him went* mid eche winde.' Cf. *shope me* in l. 2 ; and see l. 57.

10. *Sweyued so merye,* sounded so pleasantly.

11. *Meten,* to dream ; *sweuene,* a dream. Another word for a dream is *metels,* or *meteles.* See the Glossary.

13. *Bihelde into the est*, looked towards the east, on high, towards the sun.

14. *Seigh*, saw. The tower on the toft is explained (Pass. i. 12) as being the abode of Truth, i. e. of God the Father; and it may remind us of Bunyan's Celestial City. Truth's abode is afterwards minutely described (Pass. v. 594).

15. The dungeon in the deep dale is explained (Pass. i. 61) as being the castle of Care, or the abode of Falsehood or Lucifer. In the Chester Plays, ed. Wright, p. 10, the Creator is made to say—

> 'The worlde, that is bouth voyde and vayne
>   I forme in the formacion,
>   With a *dongion of darckenes*,
>   Which never shall have endinge.'

17. *A faire felde.* The fair field is the world (Matt. xiii. 38). The poet's vision surveys heaven, hell, and the world. *Fonde*, found.

19. *As the worlde asketh*, as the way of the world requires. In many other places, *aske* answers to our modern *require*.

20. *Pleyed.* It should rather be *pleyeden*, or at least *pleyede*, but I have observed that *-ed* is constantly used as a *plural* ending, not only in the Laud MS., but in many others. In the Oriel MS., the ending *-eden* is found almost invariably. Cf. *lyueden* in l. 26.

21. *Settyng*, planting. *Swonken*, laboured. *Ful*, very; used like the German *viel*, though etymologically related to *voll*.

22. *That*, that which; and won that which wasteful men expend in gluttony.

24. *Contenaunce*, outward appearance. *Disgised*, decked out in strange guise. See a curious passage in Chaucer's Persone's Tale (*de superbia*) about the 'strangeness and *disgisines*' of precious clothing.

25. A few MSS. have *To* instead of *In*; the sense is the same.

26. *Ful streyte*, very strictly. Observe that *-e* is a common adverbial ending.

27. *Heueneriche*, of the kingdom of heaven. This is an instance of a neuter noun forming the genitive case in *-e*. This genitive in *-e* is not common, except in the case of *feminine* nouns.

28. *Ancres*, anchorites. The *Ancren Riwle*, i. e. the Rule of Anchoresses, is the name of a prose work written in the early part of the thirteenth century. The word *ancre* is both masculine and feminine.

29. *Kairen*, wander, go up and down. Frequently confused with *carien* in the MSS., both here and in other passages.

30. *For no*, &c., for (the sake of) any luxurious living, to please their body. Double negatives, like the *no* here following *nought*, are very common.

31. *Cheuen*, succeed.

34. *Giltles.* Most MSS. read *synneles*; but this is not so suitable for the alliteration. Langland here speaks of the guiltless or honest minstrels, who

played instruments merely to gain a livelihood; but this class of men had a bad name, and he proceeds to satirize the unscrupulous jesters and slanderers. The subject of *minstrels* is very fully treated of in Ritson's Ancient Romances, vol. i, in Warton's History of English Poetry, Percy's Reliques, &c. See also Chambers' Book of Days, i. 430. Ritson tells us that the instruments they used were the harp, fiddle, bagpipe, pipe, tabour, cittern, hurdygurdy, bladder (or canister) and string, and, possibly, the Jew's-harp. The minstrels of King Edward III.'s household played the trumpet, cytole, pipe, tabret, clarion, and fiddle. When men or women were conveyed to the pillory, it was common to hire minstrels to accompany them, no doubt to call people's attention to them, and to heighten their disgrace. Much is to be learnt about them from Langland's poem, as he mentions them frequently, and in Pass. xiii. there is a long description of a minstrel who also gained a livelihood by selling cakes. Another name for them is *gleemen*. *Jangelers* (chatterers), *Jesters* (tale-tellers), *Japers* (jesters), *Disours* (story-tellers), *Jougleors* or *Jugglers* (*joculatores*), all belong to the same fraternity. Cf. Pass. ii. 93, 94. See also Tyrwhitt's note on Chaucer, Cant. Tales, 11453.

36. Feign fancies for themselves, and make fools of themselves, and (yet) have their wit at their will, (able) to work if they were obliged. The sentence is elliptical, and incomplete: we must mentally connect with the next line by saying—'*as for such fellows*, that which Paul preaches about them, I will not prove it (or adduce it) here; (else might I be blameworthy myself, since) he who speaks slander is Lucifer's servant.' The text of S. Paul which Langland does *not* quote is *Qui non laborat, non manducet* (2 Thess. iii. 10), which is written in the margin of the Oriel MS. The quotation *Qui, &c.,* is *not* from S. Paul, nor does Langland say that it is; yet it has some resemblance to Eph. v. 4, Col. iii. 8.

40. *Yede*, went. In a long note in Warton's Hist. Eng. Poetry, vol. ii. p. 73 (ed. 1840), it is argued that *yede* corresponds to the A.S. *éode*, went, and not to *ge-éode*, which is *said* to be transitive only. That is, the *y* does not *here* answer to the A.S. prefix *ge-*, but is the effect of a phonetic spelling, in the same way as we so often find *yale, yerthe*, for *ale, earth*. On the other hand, *ge-éode* is often intransitive, and explains the *y* in *y-ede* much more simply.

41. *Her*, their. The bag or wallet was the beggar's inseparable companion, and was used for receiving the broken pieces of meat and bread bestowed upon him as alms. They also always carried a *bourdon*, or *staff*.

'That maketh beggares go with *bordon* and *bagges*.'

Song of the Husbandman; see Polit. Songs (Camd. Soc. 1839), p. 150. *Ycrammed*, crammed, the *y-* being the A.S. prefix *ge-*.

42. *Atte*, at the. It is also written *at the, at then*, or *atten*; and very frequently *atten ale* is written *atte nale*. So also *at the nende* for *at then ende*. *Then* or *ten* is the dative of the article; hence this corruption is generally found after a preposition. Another similar corruption is *the tone, the tother*,

from *that one, that other* ; where the *t* is the sign of the neuter gender, as in *tha-t, i-t* ; compare the Latin *d* in *i-d, quo-d, illu-d*. *Ale* here means an *ale-house*, and such is the best interpretation of it in Launce's speech in Two Gent. of Verona, ii. 5.—' Thou hast not so much charity in thee as to go *to the ale* with a Christian ;' for only just above Launce says again—' If thou wilt, go with me *to the ale-house*.' See Staunton's Shakesp. vol. i. p. 43.

43. *Hij,* they. Written for *hy,* a variation of *hi,* just as *ij* is written for *ii* or *y* in Dutch.

44. Compare

> ' And ryght as *Robertes men* · raᴋen [*wander*] aboute,
> At feires & at ful ales · & fyllen the cuppe.'
>
> Pierce the Plowmans Crede, l. 72.

' Robartes men, or Robertsmen, were a set of lawless vagabonds, notorious for their outrages when Piers Plowman was written. The statute of Edw. III. (an. reg. 5, c. xiv.) specifies " divers manslaughters, felonies, and robberies, done by people that be called *Roberdesmen, Wastours,* and *drawlacches.*" And the statute of Richard II. (an. reg. 7, c. v.) ordains, that the statute of King Edward concerning *Roberdesmen* and *drawlacches* should be rigorously observed. Sir Edward Coke (Instit. iii. 197) supposes them to have been originally the followers of *Robin Hood* in the reign of Richard I. See Blackstone's Comm. bk. iv. ch. 17.'—Warton's Hist. Eng. Poetry, vol. ii. p. 95, ed. 1840. William of Nassyngton says that they tried the latches of people's doors, contrived to get into houses, and then extorted money either by telling some lying tale or playing the bully. See Pass. v. 402, and the confession of *Robert the robber* in the same Passus. See also Pass. vi. 154.

45. *Eure=evre,* ever. In early MSS., *u* is frequently written to denote the *v*-sound, and conversely words *commencing* with *u* are frequently written with *v,* as *vp, vnto.* These slight difficulties are easily mastered, and there is no reason for suppressing them, as is commonly done by editors.

46. *Palmers.* See note to Pass. v. l. 523.

47. *Seynt James,* or Santiago. His shrine at Compostella, in Galicia, was a famous place of pilgrimage; see Southey's poem of The Pilgrim to Compostella. Cf. Pass. iv. 126; and Chaucer's Prologue, ed. Morris, l. 466. See a good popular account of him in Chambers' Book of Days, ii. 120 (July 25). A book called The Stacyons of Rome and The Pilgrim's Sea-voyage (ed. Furnivall, 1867, for the Early English Text Society), well illustrates this passage. Rome abounded with shrines at which several thousands of years of remission from purgatory could be obtained. The Sea-voyage is a satire upon the inconveniences of the pilgrimage to Compostella. One of the questions put to Lord Cobham at his trial was this—' Holy chirche hath determyned that it is needeful to a crystyn man to go a pylgrimage to holy placeys, and there specyally to worschype holy relyques of seyntes, apostlys, martires, confessourys, and alle seyntes approved be the chirche of Rome. How fele ȝe thys artycle ?'—Fasciculus Zizaniorum, p. 442.

53. See the chapter on Hermits in Cutts, Scenes and Characters of the Middle Ages, pp. 93–151. Cf. Pass. vi. 147, 190.

54. Our Lady of Walsingham's shrine was much resorted to; its celebrity almost surpassed that of St. Thomas's shrine at Canterbury. In Blomefield's Norfolk (v. 839) we read that King Henry VIII. walked barefoot from Barsham to this shrine [no very great distance] and presented Our Lady with a necklace of great value. He also tells us that the common people had an idea that the Milky Way pointed towards Walsingham, and they called it *Walsingham-way* accordingly. It is remarkable that the Milky Way is, in Spain, called *the road to Santiago*; see Quart. Rev. Oct. 1873; p. 464. The obvious reason for the name is that the road was as crowded with pilgrims as the Milky Way with stars. The Wycliffites opposed such pilgrimages, and especially that to Walsingham. Ruins of the convent, with two wells called the 'wishing-wells,' are still to be seen at Old Walsingham, Norfolk. The monastery was founded for Augustinian or Black Canons. See Chambers' Book of Days, i. 795, ii. 8, 174.

55. *Lobyes*, lubbers. *Longe*, tall. 'Ther goeth a comen prouerbe: That he which hath ones ben in an abbey, wyll euer more after be slouthefull; for the whiche cause they ben called of many men *Abbey loutes* or *lubbers*;' A Supplicacyon for the Beggars, by Simon Fish, ed. Furnivall (E. E. T. S.), p. 15.

56. In Chaucer's Monkes Prologue, the *cope* is the mark of a *monk*; in Pierce the Ploughman's Crede, it is that of a *mendicant friar*. In Chaucer's Prologue, the Frere has a semi-cope. See also l. 61.

57. *And shopen hem*, and arrayed themselves as; see l. 2.

58. The four Orders of mendicant friars are severely satirized in The Ploughman's Crede; see notes in my edition on ll. 29, 486. They were the Carmelites (white friars), Augustines (Austin friars), Jacobins or Dominicans (black friars), and Minorites (gray friars). They are easily remembered by Wycliffe's jest upon them. He takes the initial letters C, A, I, M, to form the word *Caim*, which was the usual spelling of *Cain* at that date, and declares them to be *of Cain's kin*. To be *of Cain's kin* or *of Judas' kin* (see l. 35 above), was a proverbial expression equivalent to being *children of Satan*.

60. To *glose* is to comment upon. The commentaries often strayed from and superseded the text. See Chaucer, Sompnoures Tale, l. 80. *As hem good lyked*, as it pleased them well. *Lyked* is very frequently thus employed as an impersonal verb. *Hem* is the dative case. *Good* is properly an adjective, but is used here with an adverbial force.

62. *maistres Freres*, master-friars. The two nominatives plural are in apposition. *At lykyng*, at their liking, as they like.

64. 'Since Love has turned pedlar.' This alludes to the money received by friars for hearing confessions. Besides this, the friars literally resembled pedlars when they carried about with them knives and pins to give away to women. See the description of the *Frere* in Chaucer's Prologue.

66. 'Except Holy Church and they [the friars] hold better together, the

greatest mischief on earth will be increasing very fast.' The regular friars and secular clergy were so far from 'holding together,' that they quarrelled fiercely as to the right of hearing confessions. See Pass. v. 143.

68. See Chaucer's description of a *Pardonere*, in his Prologue; the conclusion of the Pardoner's Tale; and Massingberd's English Reformation, p. 127.

70. *Assoilen*, absolve.

71. *Of falshed of fastyng*, of breaking their vows of fasting. The first *of* belongs to *assoilen*.

72. *Lewed*, unlearned; it exactly answers, in sense, perhaps in etymology, to the modern adj. *lay*. *Leued hym wel*, believed him entirely.

74. *He bonched*, &c.; lit. he banged them with his brevet, and bleared their eyes. We should now say, he thrust his brevet in their faces. The word is *bouched* in Mr. Wright's edition, but my collation of MSS. shews this to be an error; and, indeed, no such word as *bouch* exists. To *blear one's eye* is a common phrase for to blind, delude, cajole.

> 'For al thy waityng, *blered is thyn ye*.'
>
> Chaucer's Manc. Tale, l. 148.

> 'Wyth fantasme, and fayrye,
> Thus sche *blerede hys yye*.'
>
> Ly Beaus Disconus, l. 1432; Ritson's Met. Rom. vol. ii.

75. *Ragman*; properly a catalogue or roll of names; here applied to the charter or bull with numerous bishops' seals. But for the explanation of many of the harder words, the reader must be referred to the Glossary.

78. 'Were the bishop a truly holy man, and worth (i.e. fit to have) both his ears, his seal would not be sent (to the pardoner, for him) to deceive the people with.' The expression *yblissed*, blessed, is used for truly righteous, as appears more clearly from Pass. vii. l. 13, which see. The phrase 'worth both his ears' is a satirical expression, signifying that the person so spoken of is one of some worth, and not like one whose ears and eyes are of no particular use to him.

80. 'Yet it is not against the bishop that the young fellow preaches; for (often) the parish-priest and he (agree to) divide the silver, which the poor people would else get.' Sometimes, instead of quarrelling, the priest and pardoner compounded matters. Chaucer, however, in his Prologue, l. 704, makes the pardoner more than a match for the parson, and represents him as cheating both the parish-priest and his flock too. *Not by the bischop* might also mean not by the bishop's leave, but the two lines above shew that the pardoner really obtained such leave. Hence we must consider it as slightly humorous, meaning—'But you may be sure that it is never against the bishop (or with reference to the bishop) that he preaches.' For examples of *by* in this sense, see 1 Cor. iv. 4, and Mr. Wright's Bible Wordbook. Or else *by* means 'by leave of.'

82. *3if þei nere*, if they were not; i. e. if there were no such people; if it were not for them.

83. *Pleyned hem*, made their complaints; lit. complained themselves, *hem* being here used reflexively. For other examples of *pleyne* followed by *hem*, see the Glossarial Index.

84. *Pestilence tyme*, time of pestilence; cf. note to iii. 19. There were three great pestilences which were long remembered; we may even count a fourth. For the dates of the two first, see note to Pass. v. l. 13 ; the third lasted from July 2 to Sept. 29, 1369. The first was also called the *great* pestilence, and is probably here meant. In Pass. v. 13, William speaks of *these pestilences*, obviously with reference to the *first and second* ones.—Cf. Chaucer, Prol. 442.

85. *To have*, i. e. and petitioned the bishop that they might have. Cf. Chaucer, Prologue, where he says of the good parish priest,

> ' He sette not his benefice to huyre . . . .
> And ran to *Londone*, unto seynte Poules,
> *To seeken him a chaunterie for soules.*'

87. The whole of the passage in ll. 87–209 is peculiar to the B-text of the poem, and is not found in the A-text, or earliest draught. It is of much interest and importance, and refers entirely to *London* ; it was probably inserted here because London has just been mentioned.

88. *Crounyng*, tonsure. See Mrs. Jameson, Legends of Monastic Orders, p. xxxii ; Wyclif's Works, ed. Arnold, iii. 447.

91. ' Lie (i. e. lodge, dwell) in London during Lent, and at other times.'

92. *Tellen*, count. Formerly, the three principal courts of law, the King's Bench, the Common Pleas, and the Exchequer, had a separate jurisdiction. The Exchequer decided only such cases as related to the collection of the revenue, and hence the ecclesiastics who held office in it are said here to *challenge*, i. e. to *claim* the King's debts from the various *wards* or divisions of the city. The *wardmote* is the court, or *meeting*, held in each ward. They also claimed for the King all *waifs* and *strays*, i. e. property without an owner and strayed cattle. But see *streyues* in the Glossary.

> ' Summe beth in ofice wid the king, and gaderen tresor to hepe,
> And the fraunchise of holi cherche hii laten ligge slepe.'

> Political Songs (Camd. Soc. 1839), p. 325.

We read also in the Complaint of the Ploughman (Polit. Poems, i. 325), the following account of the ' canons seculer : '—

> ' They have great prebendes and dere,
> Some two or three, and some mo ;
> A personage to ben a playing fere,
> And yet they *serve the King also*,
> And let to ferme all that fare
> To whom that woll most give therefore ; ' &c.

95. Wycliffe complains in the same strain—' But our Priests ben so busie about wordlie [*worldly*] occupation, that they seemen better Baylifs or Reues, than ghostlie Priests of Jesu Christ. For what man is so busie about

marchandise, and other wordly doings, as bene Preists that showld bee light of heauenlie life to al men about them.'—Two Treatises against Friars ed. James, p. 16. And see Wyclif's Works, ed. Arnold, iii. 215, 277, 335. In Pecock's Repressor, ii. 324, 366, is an answer to the charge brought by the Wycliffites that some bishops and abbots held courts and decided causes.

97. *Messe*, mass; *oures*, hours, or prayers repeated at stated times of the day. Cf. Pass. i. 181.

98. *Drede is*, there is a fear, it is to be feared.

99. *Consistorie*, also frequently spelt *constorie*, a church council or assembly of prelates. It is here used of the Last Great Assembly held by Christ at the day of Judgment.

102. I. e. Peter deputed the power of the Keys to the four cardinal virtues, viz. to Prudence, Temperance, Fortitude, and Justice. The old English names are Sleight, Temperance, Strength, and Doom; see Ayenbite of Inwyt p. 124, where we read further that—'Thise uour uirtues byeth y-cleped cardinals, uor thet hi byeth he*gh*est amang the uirtues, huer-of the yealde [*old*] filosofes speke. Vor be thise uour uirtues the man gouerneth himzelue ine thise wordle, as the apostles gouerneth holy cherche be his cardinals.' In Pass. xix. Conscience reproves evildoers by telling them that without the cardinal virtues they will be lost; whereupon a shameless vicar replies that if so, many a man will be lost, and that he never knew a 'cardinal' but such as came from the pope. The same play upon the word occurs here. So in Shakesp. Hen. VIII, iii. 1. 103—

'Upon my soul, two reverend *cardinal virtues!*
But *cardinal sins* and hollow hearts I fear ye.'

104. *Closyng ȝatis*, closing gates. This is a sort of translation of the Latin *cardinalis*, which is derived from *cardo*, a hinge. The power of the keys is, as it were, made for the moment into a power of the hinges.

105. *There, &c.*, where Christ reigns. This sense of *there* should be carefully observed. Cf. l. 190.

107. *Atte Courte*, at the court, sc. of Rome. *Cauȝt of*, received.

111. I *can* speak more, for I have much I could say about them; yet I *cannot* speak more, out of reverence, for the power of electing a pope is a high and holy thing. Such seems to be William's meaning.

112. Tyrwhitt supposed that this part of the poem was written after the death of the Black Prince, when his son Richard was heir-apparent. In fact, the date of composition of this portion of the poem seems to be the earlier part of the year 1377. Line 113 is very significant. In many MSS., ll. 113 and 195 are underscored as worthy of attention.

114. *Kynde wytte* (a common phrase in our author) is what we now call *common sense*, i.e. natural intelligence.

117. *Hem-self fynde*, provide for themselves. *Hem-self* is ambiguous. It

may mean that the king and his knights decided that the commons ought to support *them*, or that they ought to support *themselves*. The latter is more immediately meant; cf. Chaucer, Nonne Prestes Tale, l. 9.

118. *Of kynde witte craftes*, handicrafts that could be pursued by help of common intelligence. Besides the king, knights, clergy, and commons there was a fifth class, of ploughmen, &c., mere tillers of the soil, who were looked upon as inferior to the rest. Yet the importance of agriculture among the crafts was well recognised.

123. I have no doubt that the *lunatic* is *William himself*. He is here expressing his favourite loyal hope that the king may so govern as to be beloved by all loyal subjects. For the use of *lunatic* there are three reasons : (1) it conveys a touch of satire, as though it were a mad thing to hope for ; (2) a *lunatic* is privileged to say strange things ; and (3) he expressly declares, at the beginning of Pass. xv, that people considered him a *fool*, and that he *raved*. This opinion he bitterly adopts. He makes the lunatic, however, speak *clergealy*, i. e. like a scholar. The word *thing* does not necessarily imply contempt ; it merely signifies a creature, a person. Cf. ' For he was a ful dughti *thing* ;' Cursor Mundi, C-text, l. 8182 ; ed. Morris.

126. *Leue*, grant. No two words have been more hopelessly confused than *leue* and *lene*. See *Leue* in the Glossary. The line means—' And grant thee to govern thy land, so that loyalty (i. e. thy lieges) may love thee.'

128. The angel descends and begins to speak, but only in Latin, since common people ought not to be told how to justify themselves ; all who could not understand Latin or French had best suffer and serve. The angel's reproof to the king is in Leonine or riming verses, of which the first is a hexameter, and the first four words of it are quoted as from the mouth of the king himself. The remaining six are alternate hexameters and pentameters, and contain the angel's charge to the king. The verses may have been composed by William himself, and may be thus translated.

(You say) ' I am a king, I am a prince,' (but you will be) neither perhaps hereafter.

O thou who dost administer the special laws of Christ the King,
That thou mayst do this the better, as you are just, be merciful !
Naked justice requires to be clothed by thee with mercy,
Whatever crops thou wouldst reap, such be sure to sow.
If justice is stripped bare, let it be meted to thee of naked justice ;
If mercy is sown, mayest thou reap of mercy !

It may be added, that long pieces of advice to kings are common at this period of English. Thus, in Gower's Confessio Amantis, lib. vii, is a long disquisition on politics. Again, there is Occleve's poem, entitled De Regimine Principum. Both these, and many like them, are founded on a spurious treatise ascribed to Aristotle, and entitled Secretum Secretorum.

Gower, like William, addresses his advice to Richard II, and with much freedom. So also Chaucer, in his Balade on Lack of Steadfastness. See Warton; Hist. E. P. ii. 230; ed. 1840.

139. *Goliardeys.* 'Un goliardois, Fr.; *Goliardus*, or *Goliardensis*, Lat. This jovial sect seems to have been so called from Golias, the real or assumed name of a man of wit, towards the end of the thirteenth century, who wrote the Apocalypsis Goliæ, and other pieces in burlesque Latin rimes, some of which have been falsely attributed to Walter Map . . . In several authors of the thirteenth century, quoted by Du Cange, the *Goliardi* are classed with the *joculatores et buffones.*'—Tyrwhitt; note on l. 562 of Chaucer's Cant. Tales. But it would appear that *Golias* is the sole invention of Walter Map, and that the original 'Golias' poems are really his. He named his imaginary Bishop Golias after the Philistine slain by David; not without some reference, perhaps, to the O. Fr. *goule*, Lat. *gula*, gluttony. Soon after, *Goliardus* meant a clerical buffoon; later still, it meant any *jougleur*, or any teller of ribald stories; in which sense it is used by Chaucer. See Morley's English Writers, vol. i. p. 586. William's *Goliardeys* is a glutton of words, one full of long pieces which he could recite; cf. the Latin phrase *helluo librorum.* He is here made to quote, in an altered form, two lines which are also found as under:—

> 'O rex, si rex es, rege te, vel eris sine re, rex;
> Nomen habes sine re, nisi te recteque regas, rex.'
>
> Political Poems, ed. Wright, i. 278.

Compare also—

> 'Legem quoque dicimus regis dignitatem
> Regere; nam credimus esse legem lucem,
> Sine qua concludimus deviare ducem.'
>
> Political Songs (Camd. Soc.), p. 115.

Also—

> 'Non a regnando rex est, sed iure regendo.'
>
> Political Poems, i. 57.

143. The commons are not supposed to have understood the angel's advice given in Latin, but they just knew as much as was good for them to know; they could say—

> 'Precepta regis sunt nobis vincula legis.'

146. This well-known fable, of the rats and mice trying to hang a bell round the cat's neck, is nowhere so well told as here. Mr. Wright says— 'The fable is found in the old collection, in French verse of the fourteenth century, entitled Ysopet; and M. Robert has also printed a Latin metrical version of the story from a MS. of the same century. La Fontaine has given it among his fables.' It is a well-known story in Scottish history, that this fable was narrated by Lord Gray to the conspirators against the favourites of King James III, when Archibald, Earl of Angus, exclaimed, 'I am he who will bell the cat;' from which circumstance he obtained the name of

Archibald Bell-the-Cat; see Marmion, note 2 Y. In the present instance, the rats are the burgesses and more influential men among the commons; the mice, those of less importance. The cat can be no other than the old King Edward III, whilst the kitten is Richard, his grandson, afterwards Richard II. On the death of the Black Prince, which took place on June 8, 1376, his son Richard became heir-apparent. The date of this part of the present version of the poem seems to be the early part of 1377, shortly before the death of Edward on June 21 of that year. Compare the note to Pass. iii. 298, where there is evidently a reference to the proclamation of Edward's jubilee in February of the same year. Hence the date is limited to the months of March, April, and May, 1377; which gives us a very close approximation. I am indebted to some excellent remarks on this subject by M. J. J. Jusserand, who published some 'Observations sur la Vision de Piers Plowman' at Paris, in 1879.

152. *Doute* in Old English almost always means *fear*, as here. *Loke*, look about us; cf. l. 172.

153. 'And if we grumble about his play,' &c.

155. *Vs lotheth*, it loathes us, i. e. we loathe; cf. l. 174. *Or*, ere.

157. *Aloft*, on high, above his reach.

158. *Renable*, contracted from *resonable*. Thus, in Myrc's Duties of a Parish Priest (ed. Peacock, 1868), the Cotton MS. has 'renabulle tonge' where the Douce MS. has 'resonable.' But it was often regarded as if formed from the verb *renne*, to run; hence it is still used in Norfolk in the form *runnable*; i. e. glib, loquacious. In the following it has, apparently, the older meaning:

> 'Hir maners might no man amend;
> *Of tong* she was *trew and renable*,
> And of hir semblant soft and stabile.'

Ywaine and Gawaine, l. 208; in Ritson's Met. Rom. vol. i. p. 10. So also *renably* for *reasonably* in Chaucer, C. T. 7091. The C-text has *resonable*.

159. 'For a sovereign remedy for himself;' i. e. as far as he was himself concerned. Cf. *for me*, l. 201.

161. *Bighes*, necklaces. *Colers of crafty werk*, collars of skilful workmanship; alluding to the gold or metal chains, such as are still worn by sheriffs, &c.

164. And at other times they are elsewhere, viz. away from London, living in retirement.

180. 'And thought themselves not daring enough,' &c.

181. *Leten*, considered, esteemed; cf. Pass. iv. l. 160.

185. *Sholde*, would; as in l. 79 above.

185. *To lat the catte worthe*, to let the cat be, to let it alone. *Worthe* is the A. S. *weorðan*, to be. When Alexander tamed Bucephalus, we read that

'Soone hee leapes on-loft ' and *lete hym worthe*
To fare as hym lyst faine ' in feelde or in towne.'
William of Palerne, &c. ; ed. Skeat, 1867; p. 216.

189. *Is seuene ȝere ypassed*, i. e. seven years have past, seven years ago.

190. The expressive word *elyng, elenge*, or *ellinge*, still common in Kent, includes the meanings *sad* and *solitary*. Henry VIII, in a letter to Anne Bullen, speaks of ' his *ellengness* since her departure;' Hearne's edition of Avesbury, p. 360. The word is used both by Chaucer and Occleve.

191. '*Væ tibi, terra, cujus rex puer est, et cujus principes mane come-dunt;*' Ecclesiastes x. 16. In MS. Digby 53 is a note to this effect—

Þar þe child is kinge and þe cuerl [*churl*] is alderman, and þe wale [*stranger*] biscop, wa þene lede [*wo to the people*] ; unde versus,

'Ve populo cujus puer est rex, censor agrestis,
Exterus antistes ; hii mala multa movent.'

A similar saying is attributed to Beda; O. Eng. Miscellany, ed. Morris, p. 184. When Robert Crowley reprinted *Piers Plowman*, in the time of *Edward VI*, he added, for obvious reasons, this sidenote : 'Omnium doc-tissimorum suffragio, dicuntur hec de lassiuis, fatuis, aut ineptis principibus, non de etate tenellis. Quasi dicat, ubi rex puerilis est.' In this and other quotations, I follow the peculiar spellings of the originals. The use of *e* for *æ* in Latin words is very common.

192. The wise mouse here suggests that the rats want keeping in order themselves, and that it is a pity that the true cat (i. e. the king, in this instance) is only a kitten. Also the cat may sometimes be expected to go out catching rabbits, and meanwhile he will let the rats and mice alone. ' Better a little loss than a long sorrow; (for there would, if the king died, be) confusion amongst us all, though we be rid of a tyrant.' William uses *the mase* to mean *confusion, bewilderment* ; l. 196 is explanatory of the ' long sorrow ' mentioned above. *Mysse*=lose, be without.

197. ' We mice, the lower order of commons, would eat up many men's malt, and ye rats, the burgesses, would tear men's clothes, &c.' These lines are almost prophetical. The rising of the peasantry under Wat Tyler took place but a short time afterwards, in June, 1381.

199. ' Were it not for that cat belonging to that court.'

201. *For me*, for myself; cf. note to l. 159. *After*, afterwards.

202. Observe how *the cat* (Edward III) is here distinguished from *the kitten* (Richard, heir apparent).

203. *Ne carpyng of*, nor shall there be any more talking about. Supply *shal be* from the line above. *Costed me neure*, would never have cost me anything ; for I would not have subscribed to it.

204. And, even if I *had* subscribed, I would not own it, but would submit to let him do as he likes ; both he and the kitten may catch what they can.

209. *Deuine ȝe*, guess ye the meaning ; I dare not.

210. The rest of the Prologue is found in Text A, as well as in the later

ones. The law-sergeants are here spoken of. 'Lawyers were originally priests and of course wore the tonsure; but when the clergy were forbidden to intermeddle with secular affairs, the lay lawyers continued the practice of shaving the head, and wore the coif for distinction's sake. It was at first made of linen, and afterwards of *white silk*;' British Costume, p. 126. It was a sort of skullcap; Strutt, Manners and Customs, iii. 76. The white silk hoods are again alluded to in Pass. iii. l. 293.

212. *Pleteden,* pleaded. This verb is derived from the O. Fr. *plet,* a plea, which is corrupted from the Lat. *placitum,* an opinion. Hence *plead* and *please* are from the same root. By the statute of 36 Edw. III, c. 15 (A.D. 1362), it was enacted that pleadings should henceforward be conducted in English, but recorded in Latin. They were not *recorded* in English till the fourth year of George II. The *penny* was an important coin in the time of Edward III; but it should be observed that *any* coin, such as a florin, could be sometimes called a penny, in which case a *half-penny* would mean the half-florin, and a *farthing* (*fourth-ing*) the fourth part of the florin. See note to Pass. ii. 143. There is a satirical poem in praise of 'Sir Peny,' who was much sought after by all men, including lawyers.

> 'Sir Peny mai ful mekil availe
>   To tham that has nede of cownsail,
>   Als sene is in assise.'
>   Hazlitt : Early Popular Poetry, i. 165.

213. *Vnlese,* unloose, unclose.

214. 'Thou mightest better measure the mist on Malvern hills than get a *mum* out of their mouth, unless money should be exhibited.' A *mum* is anything approaching to a word, a *mumble.* The whole of this passage is imitated by Lydgate;

> 'Unto the common place [*pleas*] I yode thoo,
>   Where sat one with a *sylken hoode*;
>   I dyd hym reverence, for I ought to do so,
>   And told my case as well as I coode,
>   How my goods were defrauded me by falshood.
>   *I gat not a mum of his mouth* for my meed,
>   And for *lack of mony,* I myght not spede.'

Lydgate's London Lyckpeny; Specimens of English, 1394–1597, ed. Skeat, p. 24.

216. *An,* and. Both spellings are common.

218. *Brewesteres,* female brewers. 'The trade of brewing was confined almost wholly to females, and was reckoned among the callings of low repute.'—Note to Liber Albus, ed. H. T. Riley; p. 307. At p. 312 of the same we read, 'If any *brewer* or *brewster,*' &c. Cf. Pass. v. 306.

219. *Wollewebsteres,* female weavers of linen. But the distinction between *webbe,* a male weaver, and *webstere,* a female weaver, is not always made. Thus, in Pass. v. 215 we find—

> 'My wyf was a *webbe* ' and wollen cloth made.'

222. 'Of labourers of every kind there leapt forth some.' For *alkin* we sometimes find *alle kyn, alle kynne, alles kinnes,* and even the odd-looking form *alle skinnes.* The full form is *alles kynnes,* of every kind. It is in the genitive case. The word *labourers* in the Statutes of Edward III is comprehensive, including masons, bricklayers, tilers, carpenters, ditchers, diggers, &c.; Liber Albus, pp. 288, 635.

224. *Dieu vous saue, dame Emme!* God save you, dame Emma! Evidently the refrain of some low popular song. In another place (B. xiii. 340) William speaks of 'dame Emme of Shoreditch,' which was a low locality.

226. 'Good pigs and geese! let's go and dine!' It was the practice thus to tout for custom, standing outside the shop-door. In the same way the taverners kept crying out, 'White wine! Red wine!' &c. Here again Lydgate copies from William :—

> 'Cokes, to me they toke good entent,
> *Called me nere, for to dyne;*
> And profered me good brede, ale, and wyne . . .
> Then I hied me into Est Chepe;
> One cries *ribes of befe, and many a pie;*
> Pewtar potts they clatteryd on a heape;
> Ther was harpe, pipe, and sawtry,' &c.

London Lyckpeny; MS. Harl. 542.

The above text differs somewhat from the other copy in MS. Harl. 367, printed in Specimens of English, 1394–1579, ed. Skeat, pp. 25, 26.

228. White and red wines, chiefly imported from France, were common ; see Chaucer's Pardoner's Tale. Though *Osey* is said to come from Portugal in the first volume of Hackluyt's Voyages, p. 188, yet the name is certainly a corruption of *Alsace.* Thus *Ausoy* is written for Alsace frequently in the Romance of Partenay, and Roquefort explains the O. Fr. *Aussay* to mean *Alsatia.* It seems to have been a sweet, straw-coloured wine. The wines of Gascony, of the Rhine, and of Rochelle, need no explanation. *The roste to defye,* to digest the roast meat. This is well illustrated by the following oft-quoted passage :—

> 'Ye shall have rumney and malmesyne,
> Both ypocrasse, and vernage wyne,
> Mount rose and wyne of Greke,
> Both algrade, and respice eke,
> Antioche, and bastarde,
> Pyment also, and garnarde,
> Wyne of Greke, and muscadell,
> Both clarè, pyment, and *Rochell;*
> The reed your stomach to *defye,*
> And pottes of *Osey* set you by.'

Squyr of lowe degre; Ritson's Met. Rom. iii. **176.**

NOTES TO PASSUS I.

Passus, a portion or ' fytte ' of a poem. In an entertainment given to Queen Elizabeth at Kenilworth, a minstrel was to have sung a song, &c. After singing a portion, he was to have made ' a pauz and a curtezy, for *primus passus*,' i. e. to signify that the first part was over. See Ritson's Met. Rom. vol. i. p. ccxxii. Compare—

> ' Thus passed is the *first pas* · of this pris tale.'
>
> William of Palerne, l. 161.

1. *Bymeneth*, signifies.

3. *A loueli ladi of lere*, i. e. *A ladi, loueli of lere*, A lady, lovely of countenance.

5. *Sone;* some copies read *Wille*, the poet's name. *Slepestow*, sleepest thou ; *sestow*, seest thou. The suffix -*tu* for þu, thou, is found in A.S. after the letter *t*, as in *scealtu* = *scealt* þu, shalt thou. So here, *slepestow* = *slepest-tow* = *slepest thou.*

6. *Mase*, confused medley of people. Cf. note to iii. 159.

8. *Haue thei worschip*, if they have honour. *Wilne*, desire ; different both from *wille*, intend, and *wyssche*, wish.

9. *Holde thei no tale*, they keep no account, they regard not.

11. *What is this to mene*, what is the meaning of this ; or, how is this to be explained? *To mene* takes the place of A.S. *gerund*, where *to* is a preposition governing the dative case, and *mene* is for *mǽnanne*, a dative formed from the infinitive *mǽnan*, to mean. Thus *to mǽnanne* is, literally, *for a meaning*.

12. *Vp*, upon. The tower is that mentioned in the Prologue, l. 14. *Truth* is here synonymous with the *Father of Faith*, i. e. God the Father and Creator.

15. *Fyue wittis*, five senses, viz. of hearing, sight, *speech*, smelling, feeling, according to the enumeration in Grosteste's Castle of Love. But for *speech* we commonly have *tasting*. In Pass. xiv. 53, is the passage—

> ' Bi so that thow be sobre · of syȝte and of tonge,
>
> In etynge and in handlynge · and in alle thi *fyue wittis*.'

Compare Tennyson's Song of the Owl :—

> ' Alone and warming his *five wits*,
>
> The white owl in the belfry sits.'

17. *Hyghte*, commanded. *To help yow of*, to provide you with.

20. *In comune three thinges*, three things in common ; these are clothing, meat, and drink. ' The chief thing for life is water, and bread, and clothing, and an house to cover shame.' Ecclus. xxix. 21 ; cf. xxxix. 26. Hence, in Spenser, F. Q. i. x. 37–39, the first three of the seven beadmen supply lodging, meat, drink, and clothing.

23. *From chele*, &c., to keep thee from a chill.

24. *For myseise*, as a remedy against disease or discomfort. This curious use of *for* is worth notice. It is sufficiently common; cf. vi. 62.

26. *That thow worth*, so that thou become the worse for it.

35. 'Moderation is a remedy, though thou yearn for much.' The same line reappears in Richard the Redeles, ii. 139, a poem which I attribute to the author of Piers Plowman :—

'But mesure is a meri mene, þou3 men moche yerne.'

Cf. Deposition of Rich. II. (Camd. Soc.), p. 12. 'Mesure is a mery mene' is quoted as a proverb by Skelton and Heywood. Another form of it is *Measure is treasure;* Dyce's Skelton, ii. 238, 241.

36, 37. This means—Not all which the body desires is good for the soul, nor is all that is dear to the soul a source of life to the body.

38. 'Believe not thy body, for a liar—this wretched world—teaches it, and would betray thee.'

41. 'Both this (the fiend) and that (thy flesh) pursue thy soul, and sug-gest things to thy heart.'

42. *Ywar*, wary. This is an instance of the prefix *y-*, the A.S. *ge-*, being prefixed to an adjective. It is the A.S. *gewær*, wary, cautious, from which our *aware* seems to have been corrupted, though its form would correspond better to the A.S. *on ware*, in caution, on guard. *I wisse*, I teach, is to be distinguished from the adverb *I-wis*, certainly, with which it is only too often confounded; and both again are different from *I wot*, I know, and *I wiste*, I knew, which are from the verb *to wit*.

46. 'Go to the gospel, (and see there) that which God said himself.'

49. 'And God (i. e. Jesus) enquired of them—of whom spake the superscription.'

50. *Ilyke*, like; see note to l. 42. The word *was* is understood before *Ilyke*, but is not in the MSS. of the B-text. But it is found in those of the A-text.

52. 'Et ait illis Jesus: Cujus est imago hæc, et superscriptio? Dicunt ei, Cæsaris. Tunc ait illis: Reddite ergo quæ sunt Cæsaris, Cæsari; et quæ sunt Dei, Deo.' Matt. xxii. 20, 21 (Vulgate).

55. *Kynde witte*, common sense; cf. Prol. 114.

56. ' And Common Sense should be preserver of your treasure, and should bestow it on you in your need.'

57. *Housbonderye*, economy; as in Shakespeare, Macbeth, ii. 1. 5, 'There's husbandry in heaven,' because no stars were out. The line signifies that 'economy and they (viz. reason and wit) hold well together.' *Hij*, put for *hy*, they. *Holden togideres;* see note to Prol., l. 66.

58. *For hym*, for the sake of Him who made her.

59. The dungeon is that spoken of in Prol., l. 15.

62. *To body*, so as to possess a body. Cf. l. 82, where *wroughte me to man* means *wrought me so that I became a man.*

64. *And founded it*, and *he* founded it. Here *it* refers to *falsehood*, not to the *castle of care;* for, with our author, to *found* is to *originate*.

66. *Caym*, Cain. See note to Prol., l. 58.

67. *Iuwen*, of Jews. The gen. pl. ending is *-en* or *-ene;* see l. 105.

68. The idea that Judas hanged himself upon an *elder* occurs in Shakespeare, Love's Labour's Lost, v. 2 ; and in Ben Jonson—'He shall be your *Judas*, and you shall be his *elder-tree* to hang on;' Every Man out of Hum. iv. 4. See Nares. On the other hand, we read that 'the *Arbor Judæ* is thought to be that whereon Judas hanged himself, and not upon the *elder-tree*, as it is vulgarly said;' Gerrard's Herbal, ed. Johnson, p. 1428; quoted by Brand, Pop. Ant. iii. 283. Mr. Wright points out a passage in Sir John Maundeville, who says that the very elder-tree was still in existence when he visited Jerusalem; see p. 93 of Halliwell's edition.

69. *Letter*, stopper, hinderer, destroyer. *Lyeth hem*, lieth to them.

70. *That*, Those who.

73. *Yeode*, or *yede*, went. See note to Prol., l. 40.

74. *Wissed*, taught. See note to l. 42.

76. *I vnderfonge þe*, I received thee, viz. at baptism.

77. *Borwes*, sureties, viz. the sponsors in baptism.

82. *Wroughte me to man*, shaped me so that I became a man. There are other instances of this phrase. Cf. l. 62.

83. *Teche me to*, direct me to. *Teach* is here used in its original sense, to indicate, point out by a *token* or sign. *This ilke*, this same, this very thing. The word *tresore* alludes to l. 45; the dreamer now alters his question.

84. 'Tell me, thou who art considered holy, how may I save my soul?'

86. *I do it on deus caritas*, I appeal to the text *God is love* (1 John iv. 8) as my authority. Cf. Pass. iii. 187.

88. *None other*, nothing else but the truth. The Vernon MS. has *not elles*.

90. *Bi the gospel*, by what the gospel says, according to the gospel. In the next line we are referred to St. Luke, that is, to the parable of the unjust steward, where those to whom are to be committed the 'true riches' are taught to be faithful in that which is least; Luke xvi. 10–13. See also Luke viii. 21.

93. Christians and heathens alike claim to learn the truth.

96. *Transgressores* is marked in the MSS. as a Latin word. Latin words are strongly underlined, frequently with a *red* stroke.

98. *Appendeth for*, pertains to. Another reading is *apendeth to*.

99. *A Fryday*, one single Friday. *A Friday* generally means *on Friday*, but not here. Another reading is *o*, i. e. one. Cf. 'all of *a* size.'

100. *Him and hir*, i. e. every man and woman; as in Ch. Man of Lawes Tale, 460 (Cant. Tales, 4880).

102. *David*, &c. This may refer to 1 Sam. xxii. 2, to 1 Chron. xi. 1–3, or, still more probably, to 1 Chron. xii. 17, 18. When King Horn was dubbed a knight, as told in the romance of that name, he was girt with a sword, his spurs were fastened on him, and he was set upon a white steed. A few lines lower, at l. 105, we find Christ described as knighting the angels.

104. An *apostata* was one who quitted his order *after* he had completed the year of his noviciate. This is very clearly shewn by the following statement of a novice,—

> 'Out of the ordre thof I be gone,
> *Apostata* ne am I none,
> Of *twelve* monethes me wanted *one*,
> *And odde days nyen or ten.*'

Monumenta Franciscana, p. 606.

The writer of this was one who had been a novice in the order of St. Francis, but left it to become a Wycliffite. See my preface to Pierce the Ploughman's Crede, p. xiii.

105. *Kyngene kynge*, king of kings. The genitive plural in *-ene* is from the A. S. ending *-ena*, as in *Witena gemót*, meeting of wits (wise men). Wycliffe says, in speaking of true religion, that—' Jesu Christ and his Apostles bene chiefe *knights* thereof, and after them Holy Martirs and Confessours'; Two Treatises against Friers, ed. James, p. 19. So too Chaucer, C. T., Group G, 383 (Second Nonnes Tale).

Ten; so in all the MSS., otherwise we should have expected *nine;* for the angels were generally distributed into three hierarchies of three orders each: first, seraphim, cherubim, and thrones; second, dominions, virtues, and powers; third, principalities, archangels, and angels. William here enumerates the seraphim and cherubim, *seven such orders more*, and *one other*. But the *one other* is the order over which Lucifer presided, as implied by l. 111. This makes up the *ten* orders, as having been the *original* number. And that this is the true explanation is rendered certain by a passage in Early English Homilies, ed. Morris, 1868, p. 219, where the preacher enumerates the nine orders, and adds that the *tenth* order revolted and became evil; that the elder of the tenth order was called ' *leoht berinde*,' i. e. lightbearing or Lucifer, who was beautifully formed, but who grew moody and said that he would sit in the *north part* of heaven, and be equal to the Almighty. For this sin he was driven out of heaven with his host. It must be added, that this *tenth* order was *above*, not *below*, the other nine; for the Franciscan Friars used to call themselves the Seraphic Order, having installed their founder, St. Francis, ' *above* the Seraphim, *upon the throne from which Lucifer fell.*' See Southey's Book of the Church, ed. 1848, p. 182. Speaking of the Chester Mystery of the Fall of Lucifer, Dean Milman says,—' This drama, performed by the guilds in a provincial city in England, solves the insoluble problem of the origin of evil through the intense pride of

Lucifer. God himself is present on the scene; *the nine Orders* remonstrate against the overweening haughtiness of Lucifer, who, with the devils, is cast down into the dark dungeon prepared for them.' Hist. of Lat. Christ. vi. 409. See also the Ormulum, i. 34; Chambers's Book of Days, i. 635; Mr. Kitchin's note on Spenser's Faerie Queene, i. 12. 39; Warton's Hist. Eng. Poetry, ed. Hazlitt, iii. 233, note 4, &c. Allusions to this fall of Lucifer are very common; see the beginning of Chaucer's Monkes Tale; Wycliffe's Two Treatises, p. 35; Ayenbite of Inwyt, ed. Morris, 1868, p. 182; Genesis and Exodus, ed. Morris, 1865, p. 3; Cædmon, ed. Thorpe, p. 18, &c. See a long note by myself in Notes and Queries, 3rd S. xii. 110; and cf. note to l. 118.

107. *The muryer*, the more pleasant it seemed to them.

118. *Ponam pedem*, &c. An inexact quotation from Isaiah xiv. 13, 14: ' In cœlum conscendam, super astra Dei exaltabo solium meum, sedebo in monte testamenti, in lateribus aquilonis. Ascendam super altitudinem nubium; similis ero Altissimo.' It is curious that wherever the fall of Lucifer is mentioned, as in most of the places cited in the note above, there is mention also of Lucifer's sitting in the *north*. We find it even in Milton, P. L. v. 755-760:

> ' At length into the limits of the *north*
> They came; and Satan to his royal *seat*,
>
> .   .   .   .   .   .
>
> The palace of great *Lucifer*,' &c.

So in Skelton's Colin Clout:

> 'Some say ye sit in trones [thrones]
> Like princes *aquilonis*.'

So in the Anglo-Saxon Version of the Hexameron of St. Basil, ed. Norman, 1849, p. 16, which agrees closely with Isaiah. In Chaucer's Freres Tale, 115, the fiend lives 'in the north contre.' In Text C of Piers Plowman, William inquires *why* Lucifer chose the *north* side, but fears he shall offend *Northern men* if he says much about it. Yet he hints that the north is the place for cold and discomfort, and suitable enough for the fallen angel. In the Icelandic Gylfaginning we find—' niðr ok norðr liggr Helvegr,' i.e. ' downwards and *northwards* lieth the way to Hell.'

119. *Nyne dayes*. So Milton—'Nine days they fell'; P. L. vi. 871.

123. Mr. Wright says—' In the Master of Oxford's Catechism, written early in the fifteenth century, and printed in Reliquiæ Antiquæ, vol. i. p. 231, we have the following question and answer — C. Where be the anjelles that God put out of heven, and bycam devilles? M. Som into hell, and som reyned in the skye, and som in the erth, and som in waters and in wodys.' This was an easy way of accounting for all classes of fairies, some of whom were supposed to be not malignant; for the fallen spirits were supposed to be not all equally wicked. The Rosicrucians, in like manner, placed the

sylphs in the air, the gnomes in the earth, the salamanders in the fire, the nymphs in the water; and as Pope says, in his Introduction to the Rape of the Lock—'The gnomes, or demons of earth, delight in mischief; but the sylphs, whose habitation is the air, are the best-conditioned creatures imaginable.'

125. *Pult out*, put out, put forth, exhibited.

132. The texts are, *Reddite Cæsari*, l. 52, and *Deus caritas*, l. 86. This line is repeated at l. 204. *Bi siȝte*, according to the evidence.

134. *Lereth it this lewde men*, Teach it to these unlearned men. To *lere* is to teach, *lerne* to learn. *Lerne* sometimes also means *to teach*, as in prov. English, but *lere* is never (I think) to *learn* in our author, as it is in Chaucer. *This* and *thise* are both used as plurals of *this*.

136. *Kynde knowing*, natural understanding.

137. *Craft*, power, potentiality. *Comseth*, commenceth, originates.

139. I have not yet traced the original of this Latin rimed (or Leonine) hexameter; it recurs at v. 448.

140. Here the '*kynde knowyng*' is identified with conscience. *Kenneth*, makes known, makes manifest.

146. *Triacle*. 'Theriaca, from which *treacle* is a corruption, is the name of a nostrum, invented by Andromachus, who was physician to Nero'; Bacon's Advancement of Learning, ed. Wright; note at p. 296. A full account of the word is given by Professor Morley, in his Library of Eng. Literature, part i. p. 21.

147. *That spice*, that species, that kind of remedy for sin. It refers to *love*, which is the theme of the succeeding context.

149. *Lered it Moises*, taught it Moses; viz. in Deut. vi. 5, x. 12, &c.

150. *Plante*, plant. MSS. of the A-type have *plaunte, plante, plonte*, &c., which can only mean *plant*. *Plente* (which is another reading) would mean plenty, fulness. See the Critical Note.

151. *It*, sc. love; here used of the love of Christ, which heaven could not contain, till it had 'eaten its fill of the earth,' i. e. participated in the human nature by Incarnation. When it had taken flesh and blood, it became light as a linden-leaf, and piercing as a needle.

154. 'As light as leaf on linden' was an old proverb. It occurs in Chaucer's Clerkes Tale, Group E, 1211. The leaves of the tree are easily stirred by the wind.

160. *He*, i. e. love. *The merciment taxeth*, assesses (or imposes) the fine. Cf. vi. 40, where *amercy*=fine, and *taxoure*=assessor. *Fines* were of fixed amount; but *amerciaments* were arbitrarily imposed.

161. *To knowe it kyndely*, to understand it by natural reason; cf. ll. 136, 140. In Pass. ix, near the beginning, there is a description of the castle of *Caro* (man's body), which is guarded by the constable *Inwit* (conscience); and it is said of Inwit and the five senses that—

'In the herte is hir home · and hir moste reste;' l. 55.

164. *That falleth*, &c. That belongs to the Father, i. e. it is God the Father who implanted Conscience in man's heart.

167. *He*, sc. God the Son.

170. *One*, alone; dat. case of *on*, one, A. S. *án.*

173. Compare—

'Cogitate, diuites, qui uel quales estis,
    Quod in hoc iudicio facere potestis,' &c.

              Poems of Walter Map, ed. Wright, p. 53.

176. *Eadem.* &c. Matthew vii. 2; Luke vi. 38. *Remecietur* is no mis-print. Some Latin words are not always spelt alike in old MSS. Thus *scintilla* is frequently spelt *sintilla*, as in Pass. v. 291, and *commodat* is spelt *comodat*, as in Pass. v. 246.

177. *A childe*, &c. This probably means a babe who is being baptized, baptism being sometimes accompanied by tears on the part of the infant.

179. *Lene the poure*, lend to the poor. *Poure* is for *povre*, more frequently spelt *pouere*, i.e. *povere.*

182. *Malkyn* was a proverbial name for an unchaste slattern. It occurs in Chaucer's Man of Lawes Prologue, l. 30.

185. For *dore-tre* some MSS. have *dore-nayl*. Note that *tre* is expressly used here, as elsewhere in Old English, in the sense of wood that is cut down and dead. So too in the modern *axle-tree*; so that *dore-tre* means a door-post. *As dead as a door-nail* is still a common proverb, but it is older even than William's poem, as it occurs twice in the alliterative romance of William of Palerne, written about A.D. 1350. The Vulgate edition of the Bible has—'Sicut enim corpus sine spiritu mortuum est, ita et fides sine operibus mortua est.' S. Jacob. ii. 26.

186. *Worth*, shall be. The present is often used for the future in Middle English, as in Anglo-Saxon. We even find in our Bibles, ' we also go with thee,' John xxi. 3. This line is repeated below, l. 192.

187. Dan Michel, in his Ayenbite of Inwyt (ed. Morris, p. 233), says that virginity without love is as a lamp without oil, and refers to the parable of the foolish virgins. No doubt William also was thinking of that parable.

191. *Chewen here charite*, &c. They chew up their charity; i. e. they eat up what they should give away, and then cry out for more. This striking expression, *chewen charite*, was copied from William by his imitator, the author of the Ploughman's Crede; see the *Crede*, ed. Skeat, l. 663.

194. *Thei ben*, i. e. and yet they are.

197. *And lernyng*, &c.; and an instruction to unlearned men, to distribute (alms) all the later, i. e. to put off giving away. For the sense of *dele*, see l. 199.

199. *Date et dabitur vobis* (S. Luke vi. 38) is the commencement of the verse already partially quoted above; see l. 176.

203. *Graith gate* direct way. The expression occurs in the History of Wallace, v. 135,

For thair sloith-hund the *graith gate* till him yeid;'
i.e. their sleuth-hound went straight towards him. Cf. Pass. iv. 42.

204. Repeated from above; see ll. 132, 133.

207. *Lenge the with,* linger with thee. *Loke the,* guard thee; i.e. may our Lord guard thee!

PASSUS II.

5, 6. 'See where he [Falsehood] stands; and not he only, but Favel [Flattery] also, and their many companions.' Occleve, in his De Regimine Principum, ed. Wright, pp. 106, 111, describes *favelle* or flattery, and says —'In wrong preisyng is all his craft and arte.' Cf. Wiat's 2nd Satire, l. 67, in Specimens of English, ed. Skeat.

8. *A womman.* Here William carefully describes the Lady Meed, who represents both Reward in general, and Bribery in particular; the various senses of *Meed* are explained in iii. 230-256. Female dress at this date was very extravagant, and we may compare with the text the following remarks in Lingard's History. ' Her head was encircled with a turban or covered with a species of mitre of enormous height, from the summit of which ribbons floated in the air like the streamers from the head of a mast. Her tunic was half of one colour, and half of another: a zone deeply embroidered, and richly ornamented with gold, confined her waist, and from it were suspended in front two daggers in their respective pouches;' vol. iv. p. 91. This part of Piers Plowman appears in the early text of 1362, otherwise William's description of Meed would have served admirably for Alice Perrers, who obtained a grant of Queen Philippa's jewels, and ' employed her influence to impede the due administration of justice in favour of those who had purchased her protection;' and against whom the following ordinance was made in 1376: ' Whereas complaint has been brought before the king, that some women have pursued causes and actions in the king's courts by way of maintenance, and for *hire and reward*, which thing displeases the king, the king forbids that any woman do it hereafter; and in particular Alice Perrers,' &c. See Lingard, iv. 142. Indeed it is very likely that William perceived this likeness in revising his poem, for the description of Meed's clothing is amplified in the B-text, and he *adds* the *very* significant line,

'I had wondre *what she was* · and *whas wyf she were.*'
How Alice treated King Edward in his last illness is well known. Whitaker suggests that the Lady Meed is the original of Spenser's *Lady Munera;* see Spenser, F. Q. bk. v. c. ii. st. 9.

9. *Pelure,* fur. The laws about the kinds of furs to be worn by different ranks were very minute. Furred hoods, in particular, were much in fashion.

14. *Enuenymes to destroye.* It was a common belief that precious stones could cure diseases, and that they were as antidotes against poisons. Thus ' Richard Preston, citizen and grocer, gave to the shrine of St. Erkenwald

his *best sapphire stone,* for *curing of infirmities of the eyes,*' &c.; note in
Milman's Lat. Christ. vi. 375; where Milman quotes from Dugdale, p. 21.
So also, in the Ancren Riwle, pp. 134-136, ed. Morton, Christ is likened to
the *agate* which the poison of sin cannot approach.

15. *Engreyned,* i.e. dyed of a fast colour. See the note in Smith's Student's
Manual of English Literature, by P. Marsh, p. 55. Add to the illustrations
there given the following :—" In crammasyn cled and *granyt violat;*' Gawin
Douglas, in Specimens of English, ed. Skeat, p. 127.

19. *What,* who. But it implies something more, viz. what sort of a
person. So in Layamon, l. 13844, 'Ich the wullen cuðen *what* cnihtes we
beoð,' i.e. 'I will inform thee what knights (what sort of knights) we
are.' This is spoken by Hengist, who then proceeds to describe himself
and his companions fully.

20. *Mede,* i.e. Meed, or Reward; but here used in a bad sense, as the personification of Bribery. In the twelfth year of Henry III a common seal was
granted to the city of London, and it was ordered that any one who shewed
reasonable cause should be permitted to use it, 'and that no *mede* schulde be
take no [*nor*] payed of eny man in no manner wyse for the said seall;' Chron.
of London, p. 13. It is just in this sense that William uses it.

21. *Lewte,* Loyalty. William arrays Love, Loyalty, Soothness, Reason,
Conscience, Wisdom, and Wit on the one side, and Meed (daughter of False),
Wrong, Favel or Flattery, Simony, Civil, Liar, and Guile upon the other.
Wisdom and Wit waver in their allegiance, but are won back again. Lines
27-38 are not in the A-text.

27. *As kynde axeth,* as nature requires or provides. For *bona* some MSS.
have *bonus,* for the sake of euphony, much as in French we have *mon* for
ma before nouns beginning with a vowel.

30. *O god,* one God. Wright's text has *So,* but it is a misprint for *Oo.*

31. *To marye with myself;* we should now arrange the words *to marry my-
self with.* *With* in Middle English is always near its verb, a puzzling arrangement to a learner. So in the *Crede,* 'to coueren with our bones,' l. 116.
So, in l. 116 below, *to wratthe with treuthe* means 'to anger Truth with.'
Mercy is here the dowry which Holy Church brings to the man who
espouses her.

38. See Ps. xv. 1 (called xiv. in the Vulgate).

39. *Mansed,* cursed. The word *maused* in Mr. Wright's text is a mis-
print, as he explains in a note on p. 537, and in his Glossary.

43. *Bruydale,* bride-ale or bridal. An *ale* means a feast merely. There
were leet-ales, scot-ales, church-ales, clerk-ales, bid-ales, and bride-ales. The
bride-ales were so called because the bride brewed some ale for her wedding-
day, which her friends purchased at a high price, by way of assisting her and
amusing themselves at the same time. This led to abuses, and we find in
the court-roll of Hales Owen, in the 15th year of Elizabeth, an order ' that
persons brewing wedding-ale to sell, should not brew above 12 strike of malt
at most.' See Brand's Popular Antiquities, ed. Ellis, ii. 144.

47. *Lat hem worth,* &c. ; let them be, till Loyalty be a justice. Cf. note to Prologue, l. 187.

49. *I bikenne the criste,* I commend thee to Christ ; *criste* is the dative case of *crist.*

50. *For,* on account of; ' on account of greediness of reward.'

59. *Brokoures.* In the reign of Edward I. a law was passed that 'no one shall be *broker,* but those who are admitted and sworn before the Mayor.' Liber Albus, ed. Riley, p. 505.

62. In Passus xx. the church is described as assailed by numerous enemies. One is *Simony,* who causes good faith to flee away, and falseness to abide, and who boldly vanquishes much of the wit and wisdom of Westminster Hall by the use of many a bright noble. He is also there described as contriving divorces. By *Cyuile* is meant one skilled in the civil law.

A *sisour* was (1) a person deputed to hold assizes; and (2) a juror, though not quite in the modern sense. See Polit. Songs, ed. Wright, p. 344; Tale of Gamelyn, l. 871.

65. *Brokour* is here used in the general sense of a contriver of bargains, a match-maker. *Brokage* (l. 87) is a treaty made by an agent.

66. *Here beire wille,* the will of them both. See *Beire* in the Glossary.

73. *Hei₃,* loudly ; ' to cry out very loudly,' ' to proclaim aloud.'

74. The form of this mock charter may be compared with that of the charter whereby the Black Prince was invested, in 1362 (the very year in which William wrote the first version of his poem) with the principality of Acquitaine. It is given at length in Barnes's Life of Edward III.

76. *Free kynde,* liberal nature, liberality of nature, generosity. Cf. *fredom* = liberality, in Chaucer, Prol. 46. Or it may mean ' gentle blood.'

78. *Feffeth,* grants to them ; lit. *enfeoffs,* i. e. invests them with a fief or fee.

80. *To bakbite,* to defame. See note to v. 89.

85. ' The County of Covetousness, and all the coasts around it ; ' where *coasts* = borders, neighbouring country. See Matt. viii. 34.

95. *Frete,* to eat, viz. before the proper time for eating arrived.

98. Here is a sudden change from the plural to the singular; *his* seems to refer to Falsehood. In l. 100 there is a sudden change to the plural again, since *here* means *their.* But other passages show that *his* and *hym* may be used indefinitely, as we now use *one's* and *one.*

102. *A dwellyng,* a habitation ; the acc. after *holde.*

103. *In-to* (*invariably* in Lowland Scotch, and *occasionally* in old English) has the force of *in* merely.

104. *3eldyng,* giving up in return. Cf. the phrase ' to yield a crop;' Cymb. iv. 2. 180. See Pass. v. 296.

108. *Of Paulynes doctrine,* of the doctrine (or order) of the Paulines. In the same yere [1310] began the order of *Paulyns,* that is to say, Crowched Freres.'—A Chronicle of London (edited in 1827, and published by Longmans), p. 43. But Matthew Paris says that the order of Crutched Friars came into England A.D. 1244. In a poem called the Image of Ypo-

crisie, written about A.D. 1533, a list is given of orders of *monks*, which includes the *Paulines*, the Antonines, Bernardines, Celestines, &c. The C-text
has, *Of Paulynes queste*, i. e. of the Paulines' inquest or jury; observe also
that the word *Paulynes* occurs again below, l. 177, in connection with
ecclesiastical law-courts.

109. *Bedel.* ' The duties of the beadle, in ancient times, lay more on the
farm than in the law-court. . . . In many places, the bedelry and the hay-
wardship were held together by one person,' &c. See Nooks and Corners of
English Life, by Timbs; p. 233. The oath of the Bedels is given at p. 272
of the Liber Albus. They were to suffer no persons of ill repute to dwell in
the ward of which they were bedels, to return good men upon inquests, not
to be regrators themselves, nor to suffer things to be sold secretly. And at
p. 289 of the same we find—' Item, that the *bedel* have a good horn, and
loudly sounding.' It is remarkable that in Text C, William changed
Bokyngham-shire (which may merely have been chosen for the alliteration)
into ' *Banbury soken*.' This may have been an intentional fling at the beadle
of Banbury, with whom he may have quarrelled. For it is to be noted that
Banbury is at no great distance from Shipton-under-Wychwood, where
William's father is said to have farmed land.

122. *Dignus est enim operarius mercede sua* ; Luke x. 7.

128. *But if* might very well have been printed *but-if*, with a hyphen, as
it is here practically *one* word, with the meaning *except*.

129. *Fikel*, treacherous, *not* changeable ; so also in iii. 121. Cf. Havelok,
ed. Skeat, l. 1210.

132. *For cosyn*, as if she were his cousin. *An she wolde*, if she wished.

137. *Witty is truthe*, wise is Truth. It must be remembered that Truth
means God the Father, as in Pass. i. 12.

140. *Bisitte*, sit close to, oppress. *Soure*, bitterly, lit. sourly ; *not* sorely ;
cf. note to Selections from Chaucer, ed. Skeat, Group. B, l. 2012.

143. *Floreines*, florins ; the name of which is derived from the city of
Florence. We read in Fabyan (ed. Ellis, p. 455) under the year 1343—' In
this yere also, kynge Edward made a coyne of fine gold, and named it the
floryne, that is to say, the peny of the value of vis. viii*d.*, the halfe peny of
the value of iiis. iiii*d.*, and the farthinge of the value of xx*d.*, which coyne
was ordeyned for his warris in Fraunce; for the golde thereof was not so fine
as was the noble, which he before in his xiiii. yere of his reygne had causyd
to be coyned.' So in Thomas Walsingham, vol. i. p. 262, ed. Riley. The
value of a *noble* was also 6*s.* 8*d.* See note to Pass. iii. 45. Both *florin*
and *noble* are mentioned by Chaucer.

160. *Westmynstre.* William seems to have been very familiar with the
courts of law at Westminster, as appears from the present and two following
Passus. In Pass. xx, we again find him speaking of the 'false folk' who
repair ' to Westmynstre.' The number of statutes enacted there in the reign
of Edward III is considerable. See Liber Albus, p. 470.

162. Those who had horses could anticipate others at the court, by performing the journey more quickly, and they could thus obtain a first audience and administer a bribe. In a poem on The Evil Times of Edward II we have—

> 'Coveytise *upon his hors* he wole *be sone there*,
> And bringe the bishop silver, and rounen in his *ere*.'
>
> Polit. Songs (Camd. Soc.), p. 326.

William, however, supposes sheriffs and sisours to serve for horses, puts saddles on the sompnours, and turns provisors into palfreys.

173–175. 'As for archdeacons, &c., cause men to saddle them with silver, in order that they may permit our sin, whether it be adultery or divorces, or secret usury.'

177. *Paulines pryues.* It may be that *pryues* is here the plural adjective, agreeing with *Paulines*, as French adjectives not unfrequently take *s* in the plural. If so, the phrase means 'the confidential Paulines.' Otherwise, it must mean 'the confidential men of the Paulines' fraternity'; which comes to much the same thing. The MSS. of the A-class read *Paulines peple*, i.e. the people of the Paulines. Cf. note to l. 108.

185. *Tome,* leisure. The adjective *toom* means empty. *Toom tabard* (empty tabard) was a nickname given to the king of Scotland, John Baliol, on account of his little wit. It occurs in Burns' Halloween: 'Because he gat the *toom* dish thrice,' &c. In William of Palerne, l. 3778, the bodies of the slain in battle are collected and borne

> 'til the tentis, til thei might haue · *tom* hem to berie.'

And again, in the Destruction of Troy (E. E. T. S.), l. 43, the author says—

> 'Of his trifuls to telle I haue no *tome* nowe.'

192. *And,* if. *And* is often written for *an,* if; and conversely, *an* is often written for the copulative conjunction *and,* as in l. 207. The fact is, that *an* and *and* are two forms of the same word. The use of *and* in the sense of *if* is found in Icelandic, in which the word is spelt *enda.*

196. *Meynprise,* furnish bail, be security for. A person arrested for debt or any other personal action might find *mainprise* or bail, before the sheriffs or their clerks thereunto deputed. The person finding bail was called a *mainpernour,* lit. a taker by the hand, by metathesis from *mainpreneur.* See Liber Albus, p. 177; and cf. Pass. iv. ll. 88 and 112.

200. *Enykynnes yiftis,* gifts of any kind. *Enykynnes* is the genitive singular, and is also spelt *enys kynnys,* or even assumes the odd form *eny skynnys.* Cf. note to Prol. 222.

203. *For eny preyere,* in spite of any prayer. Cf. l. 230.

205. *Dome,* sentence decision. Cf. Chaucer, Prol. 323.

211. *Doth hym to go,* prepares himself to depart. The compassion shewn to Guile by merchants, and to Liar by pardoners, grocers, and friars, is a brilliant touch of satire.

213. *Shope.* For pictures of London *shops*, see Chambers' Book of Days, i. 350.

218. 'Everywhere hooted at, and bidden to pack off.' *Ouer al* is here just like the German *überall*.

230. *For knowyng of comeres*, to prevent recognition by strangers.

236. *Wronge*, wrung her hands. *Attached*, arrested; but the person arrested might find sureties for his appearance. Liber Albus, pp. 73, 77.

PASSUS III.

13. *Somme* must here be considered as partitive, and equivalent to *some of them.* I have reason to know that the explanation of *somme* as 'together,' given in former editions of this book, is wrong.

19. *Conscience caste or craft*, Conscience's contrivance or art. 'In O. E. of the fifteenth century, if the noun ended in a sibilant or was followed by a word beginning with a sibilant, the possessive sign was dropt; as, a *goose* egg, the *river* side;' Morris, Hist. Outlines of Eng. Accidence, p. 102. Cf. Prol. l. 84.

22. *Coupes, coppis.* The MSS. carefully distinguish between the spellings of these words, and for the latter some read *peces*. They must not then be confused if we can help it. The M. E. *coupe* is borrowed from the O. F. *coupe*, which is the Lat. *cupa*, a tub, cask. Cotgrave explains the F. *coupe* as meaning 'a cup, goblet, or mazer,' where a *mazer* is a kind of bowl. The M. E. *coppe*, from A. S. *coppa*, is from Low Lat. *cuppa*, a secondary form from *cupa*, and means a cup. Hence, probably, the sense is 'large bowls of pure gold and cups of silver.' I think it must be admitted that the poet seems to have been driven by alliteration into making a distinction without much apparent difference, unless custom had established some distinction between the French *coupe* and the A. S. *cuppa*. The phrase '*coupes* of golde' occurs in the Ayenbite of Inwyt, ed. Morris, p. 35, and Dr. Morris explains it by *cups*, though there is nothing in the context to render this explanation absolutely certain. About the word *coppis* there is no difficulty. It is equivalent to *peces* (see l. 89), and therefore means simply *cups*. Way, in the Promptorium Parvulorum, quotes the following—'A *pece* of siluer or of metalle, *crater, cratera*.—'*Crater, vas vinarium*, a pyece or wyne cuppe.'—'*Pece*, to drinke in, *tasse*. Pece, a cuppe, *tasse, hanap*.' It was called *pece* to distinguish it from the *pot* or large flagon.

> 'A capone rosted broght she sone.
> A clene klath, and brede tharone,
> And a *pot* with riche wine,
> And a *pece* to fill it yne.'
>
> Ywaine and Gawin, l. 757 (Ritson's Met. Rom. i. 33)

24. *Motoun.* ‘ Ye shall vnderstande that a *moton* is a coyne vsed in Fraunce and Brytaygne, and is of value, after the rate of sterlynge money, upon v s., or thereabout.’—Fabyan’s Chronicles, ed. Ellis, p. 468. It was so called from its bearing an impression of a *lamb;* on the other side was a figure of St. John the Baptist.—Memorials of London, ed. Riley, p. 297.

25. *Laughte thei leue at,* they took leave of. *To lacche leue,* to take leave, is a common phrase. The taking of bribes seems to have been a common failing with justices at this time. Compare—

> ‘ Hoc facit pecunia Quam omnis fere curia jam duxit in uxorem ;
> Sunt justiciarii Quos favor et denarii alliciunt a jure.’

Polit. Songs (Camd. Soc.), p. 225.

In particular, ladies seem to have had great influence :

> ‘ Sed si quædam nobilis Pulcra, vel amabilis,
>   cum capite cornuto, auro circumvoluto,
> Accedat ad judicium, Hæc expedit negotium, ore suo muto.’

Ibid. p. 226.

See also note above, Pass. ii. 8.

31. *Do calle,* (I will) cause your names to be called over. So also *do peynten,* (I will) cause to be painted, in l. 62 below.

32. *Shal no lewdnesse lette,* no ignorance shall hinder.

34. ‘ Where really skilful clerks will limp along behind in the rear.’ See *Clokke* in Glossary.

35. *Frere.* The knowing ones went to confession to a *friar* rather than to a parish priest. Wycliffe complains of this, saying—‘ For commonlie if there be anie cursed Jurour [swearer], extortioner, or avoutrer [adulterer], he will not be shriuen at his owne Curate, but go to a flattering Friar, that will assoile him falsly, for a little mony by yeare, though he be not in wil to make restitution, and leaue his cursed sinne.’ Two treatises against Friars, ed. James, 1608 ; p. 53.

45. *Toke hym a noble.* Tyrwhitt remarks (note to Cant. Tales, 13852), that—‘ *to take,* in our old language, is also used for *to take to, to give* as in l. 13334,

> He *toke* me certain gold, I wote it well.’

Whether the *noble* or *florin* was first coined, and what was the exact value of them, seem somewhat doubtful, unless we can depend upon the statement of Fabyan quoted above, Pass. ii. 143, and upon the following statement of the same, under the year 1339,—‘ In this yere also the kynge chaungyd his coyne, and made the noble & the halfe noble of the value of vi s. viii d., which at this day is worthe viii s. ix d. or x d., & the halfe noble after the rate, if they kepe the trewe weyght,’ &c. There is a similar statement in A Chronicle of London, p. 57, under the fourteenth year of Edward III, which seems, as in Fabyan, to signify 1339 rather than 1340 :—‘ also the kyng made the coyne of goold : that is for to seyne, the *noble,* the halfe noble, and the ferthyng.’ Walsingham gives the date 1343 for the coinage of *florins;* but some consider the true date to be 1344. In the English Cyclopædia, under the heading *Coin,* we are told that—' it is from Edward III that the series of English gold coins really commences, for no more occurs till 1344, when that prince struck florins. The half and quarter-florin were struck at the same time. The florin was then to go for *six shillings,* though now it would be intrinsically worth nineteen. This coin being inconvenient, as forming no aliquot part of larger ideal denominations, seems to have been withdrawn. None have yet been found, but a few quarter-florins are preserved in cabinets, and one half-florin is known. In consequence, in the same year, the noble was published, of *6 s. 8 d.* value, forming half a mark, then the most general ideal form of money. The obverse represents the king standing on a vessel, asserting the dominion of the sea. The noble was also·attended by its half and quarter. This coin, sometimes called the *rose noble,* together with its divisions, continued the only gold coin, till the angels of Edward IV, 1465, and the angelets or half-angels, were substituted in their place. Henry V. is said to have diminished the noble, still making it go for its former value. Henry VI restored it to its size, and caused it to pass for 10 s., under the new name of ryal,' &c. William clearly intimates that *florins* were by no means scarce, and this seems at first sight to contradict that which is said above. But the fact is simply, that most of the florins were coined abroad, chiefly at Florence; and it was ordered that florins de Escu, and florins of Florence, should be current along with the sterlings, according to their value. See Ruding's Annals of the Coinage.

48. *A wyndowe.* A list of people who glazed windows for a new church of the Friars Minors is given in Monumenta Franciscana, p. 515. One of the names of subscribers to the expense is that of Isabella, mother of Edward III. The practice of glazing windows is satirized also by William's imitator in the *Crede,* ll. 123–128. It was usual to introduce portraits of the benefactors in stained glass. *Wil sitten vs,* will ' sit ' us very highly; we should now say—will *stand* us in a very high amount, i. e. will cost us a great deal.

67. *Thi kynde wille, and thi coste;* thy natural disposition, and thy expenses.

71. *Or to greden after goddis men,* or to cry out for God's men, i. e. to send for the friars. *Nesciat sinistra,* &c.; Matt. vi. 3.

75. *Bit,* biddeth; so *ritt,* contracted form of *rideth,* Pass. iv. 13, where most MSS. have *ryt* or *rit,* and one has *ridith;* and again *halt,* for *holdeth,* in l. 241 below. Mr. Wright's edition has *by,* a misprint for *byt.*

78. *Pillories.* Under the xvth year of Edward IV, Fabyan tells us that —'this yere this mayer [Robert Basset, salter] dyd sharp correccion vpon bakers for makynge of lyght brede, in so moche that he sette dyuerse vpon the pyllory, ... and a woman named Agnes Deyntie was also there punysshed for sellyng of false myngyd [mixed] butter.' Lydgate has a ballad about Fraudulent Millers and Bakers, whose true heritage is the pillory (MS. Harl. 2255). *Pynynge-stoles,* stools of punishment, also called *cucking-*

stools. The *cucking-stool* was a seat of ignominy; see Chambers' Book of Days, i. 211. 'In Scotland, an ale-wife who exhibited bad drink to the public was put upon the *Cock stule,* and the ale, like such relics of John Girder's feast as were totally uneatable (see Bride of Lammermoor), was given to the poor folk.' It was different from the *ducking-stool,* which was a punishment for scolds. See Brand; Popular Antiquities, iii. 102 (note), and 103. Brand seems to confound the two. See also a long note in Hudibras, ed. Bell, vol. i. p. 231. Cf. note to Pass. iv. 126.

81. *Parcel-mele,* by small parcels, i. e. retail.

83. *Regraterye,* selling by retail. The wholesale dealer was called an *Engrosser* (whence our *grocer*), because he sold in the *gross* or *great* piece. The retail dealer was called a *Regrater* or *Regrateress;* cf. Pass. v. 226. The frauds and adulterations of the *regraters* were a constant source of annoyance, and were continually being complained of. Compare—

> 'Si status conspicimus, nullus excusatur :
> Quod in shopis venditur, male mensuratur ;
> Quilibet perjurio vel fraude lucratur,' &c.

> Monumenta Franciscana, ed. Brewer, p. 593.

Engrossers and *Regraters* are not to cause dearness of victuals; Riley's Liber Albus, p. 547. Cotgrave explains O. F. *regrateur* by ' an huckster; mender, dresser, scowrer, trimmer up of old things for sale.'

85. *Tymbred nought,* would not have built.

89. *Presentz.* Presents made, not in money, but in silver cups, &c.

95. The quotation is not from Solomon, but from Job. xv. 34:—' fire shall consume the tabernacles of bribery.'

99. ʒeresʒyues, lit. yeargifts. ' *Jeresgive* [read *Yeresgive*] is a toll or fine taken by the king's officers on a person's entering an office ; or rather, a sum of money or *bribe, given to them to connive at extortion or other offence in him that gives it.* (See Chart. Hen. II. ; fourth Chart. Hen. III. ; and ninth Chart. Hen. III.) ;' Privilegia Londini, by W. Bohun, of the Middle Temple, 1723; qu. in N. and Q. 4 S. iv. 560. This definition perfectly suits the present passage, but we may fairly assume, from the form of the word, that it once meant an *annual* donation, like the modern Christmas-box. It came to be so troublesome that we find special exemptions from it, as in the following : ' Also, that the city of London shall be quit of *Brudtol,* and *Childewite,* and *Yeresgive,* and *Scotale* ;' Liber Albus, ed. Riley, pp. 117, 138.

100. *The kynge.* This passage is retained even in the latest version, which is later than 1380. But the description was originally intended for Edward III, for whom it is much more suitable. See notes to ll. 126 and 186.

126. Alluding to the deposition and death of Edward II.

137. *Grotes,* lit. great coins, perhaps because, until they were coined, there was no silver coin larger than the penny ; but the name arose in Bremen. ' In this yere [1349] the kynge caused to be coyned grotes and half grotes, the

whiche lacked of the weyghte of his former coyne, ii. *s.* vi *d.* in a *li.* [*libra*, pound] Troy.'—Fabyan, p. 461. The *groat* should have been equal to four silver pennies, but was only equal to about three and a half. A drawing of one may be seen in Knight's Pictorial Hist. England, i. 837.

146. *Provisors.* A writ summoning one to appear for contempt of the sovereign was called *præmunire*, from its first word. 'Numerous statutes have defined what shall be such a contempt as amounts to a præmunire. Most of the earlier are directed against *provisors*, as they were called, or persons who purchased from Rome provisions for holding abbeys or priories, &c., before those benefices were vacant (25 Edw. III, Stat. 5, c. 22. Stat. 6), or for exemption from obedience to their proper ordinary (2 Hen. IV, c. 3) or bulls for exemptions from tithes,' &c.—English Cyclopædia, *s. v.* Præmunire. William seems to allude to the purchase of sees in particular, as he speaks of 'these bishops,' l. 148.

155. 'And lieth against the law, and hindereth it (in its) way.' *Gate* = way, as in i. 203. *Forth* in l. 156 signifies passage, means of egress.

157. *Louedayes.* Days on which extra services were rendered to the lord in seed-time or harvest were sometimes called boon-days or love-days ; 'but it more commonly meant a law-day, a day set apart for a leet or manorial court, a day of final *concord* and *reconciliation:*' as we read in the Coventry Mysteries :—

> 'Now is the *love-day* mad of us foure fynially,
>   Now may we leve in pes as we were wonte.'

'Hock-day was usually set apart for a *love-day*, law-day, or court-leet.'— Timbs' Nooks and Corners of English Life, pp. 224, 228. [Hock-day was the second Tuesday after Easter.] William uses the term again, Pass. v. l. 427, and it occurs in Chaucer, Prol., l. 258. It was so called because the object was the amicable settlement of differences.

159. *The mase,* &c. 'It is bewilderment for a poor man, though he plead here ever.' Some MSS. have *plede* instead of *mote;* several omit *hir,* which is also spelt *hire, here, heer.* The verb *to hear* is also sometimes spelt *hire.* Cf. l. 167.

164. *Clergye* most frequently means *learning*, as opposed to *lewdness*, ignorance. It probably means so here, as bribery makes clever men covetous.

174. It is a mark of respect for Meed to address the king in the plural number, and a mark of familiarity or contempt to address Conscience in the singular. This distinction is very carefully observed by Chaucer, William, and the author of William of Palerne.

180. *Hanged on myne half*, hung upon my side, clung to my party. The word is *never* here written *hals* [neck] in MSS. of the 'B-class, although, curiously enough, the Vernon MS. has *nekke*, probably by mistake.

183. *Yit I may,* &c. 'Yet I may perhaps, as far as I might have the power, honour thee with gifts.'

186. Cf. l. 126. Meed here repudiates the charge, and appeals to the king himself (Edward III).

188. This alludes to Edward's wars in Normandy, and, in particular, to the treaty sealed at Bretigny, near Chartres, on the 8th of May, 1360. Edward renounced his claim to the crown of France, and his claim to Normandy, Anjou, Touraine, and Maine, and restored all his conquests except Calais and Guisnes; but reserved Poitou, Guienne, and the county of Ponthieu. The dauphin agreed to pay, for the ransom of his father King John, the sum of 3,000,000 scutes (*escus*) or crowns of gold. See Lingard, iv. 118; Thomas Walsingham, i. 290; Fabyan, p. 471. The sufferings of the English in their previous retreat from Paris to Bretagne were very great, and they encountered a most dreadful tempest near Chartres, with violent wind and heavy hail. Hence the allusions in the text to the cold, to the lengthening out of winter till May, to the dim cloud, and to the famine from which the army suffered. 'It is to be noted,' says Stow, 'that the 14 day of April, and the morrow after Easter Day (1360), King Edward with his host lay before the city of Paris; which day was full dark of mist and hail, and so bitter cold, that many men died on their horsebacks with the cold; wherefore unto this day it hath been called the *Black Monday*.' Meed suggests that instead of exacting money, Edward should have foregone it, or even have paid some, to secure to himself the kingdom of France. The articles agreed to at Bretigny were never fulfilled.

190. *For colde*, i.e. to keep off the cold. See note to vi. 62.

200. *Marschal.* 'When the king summoned his military tenants, the earl constable and earl mareschal held the principal command under the sovereign; but in armies raised by contract, he appointed two or more mareschals, whose duty it was to array the forces and to direct their movements.'—Lingard, iv. 190.

220. *The kynge hath mede*, &c. The context shews that *mede* is here to be taken in a good sense. It must therefore refer to the king's lawful tribute, and not to the fact that even the king sometimes accepted a bribe to make peace between neighbours.

224. *Alkynnes crafty men*, skilled men (craftsmen) of every kind.

230. Here Conscience distinguishes between the two meanings of Meed, viz. (1) divine reward, shewn by God to well-doers, and (2) corruption or bribery.

233. This and the two next quotations are from Psalm xv, called Ps. xiv in the Vulgate.

236. *Assoileth it*, solves the question.

237. *Of o colour*, of one colour, pure, spotless.

240. The quotation ends—*innocentem non accepit.*

241. *Halt*, holdeth; cf. *bit*, biddeth, &c.

247. Ps. xxvi. 10 (xxv. 10 in the Vulgate).

252. Matt. vi. 5. Most MSS. read *recipiebant.*

257. *Regum,* the book *of Kings;* i.e. the first book, generally called the first book of Samuel. See 1 Sam. xv.

258. There is no apparent alliteration, but William considers *v* and *f* to answer to one another, as in Pass. ii. 60, so that *veniaunce* rimes to *fei*; in the second half of the verse the alliteration fails.

261. See Exod. xvii. 8 for the sin of Amalek.

262, 263. *Hoteth the be boxome,* bids thee to be obedient.

267. Cf. 'Movable good, as cuppe, or chalice, mytir, bacul, or *unmovable good,* as hous, feeld, wode'; Pecock's Repressor, ii. 386.

279. 'In case it should annoy men, I will make *no* ending,' i.e. draw no conclusion.

284. *Somme,* to some; dat. plural.

291. *His wille,* the will of Truth, i.e. of God.

292. *Leute,* &c. 'Loyalty and no one else, shall execute the law upon him.' See *Lyf* in the Glossary.

293. *Silke howue,* (white) silk hood. Cf. note to Prol. 210.

295. *Of mysdoeres,* out of misdoers, from amongst misdoers.

296. *Ouer lordes lawes,* superseding lords' laws.

298. With this line Pass iii., in the A-text, abruptly terminates. The admirable addition here made was suggested, I feel confident, by the recent proclamation of a *jubilee,* in the last year of Edward III (Feb. 1377), proclaimed because the king had attained the *fiftieth* year of his reign. Taking his cue from this, the poet hopes that the new reign of Richard II, soon to begin, may usher in a new era of perfect peace; but, in l. 323, he suddenly prophesies that certain rather unlikely events will first happen, thus revealing his fear that no such good time was really at hand. I find this suggestion confirmed by a similar passage in John of Bridlington's pretended prophecies, bk. iii. c. viii.; cf. note to l. 323.

303. *Baslarde.* 'Temp. Rich. II, civilians wore swords called *baselards* or *badelaires.* Example; monument of a civilian, King's Sombourne Church, Hants, 1380.'—Godwin's Handbook of English Archæology, p. 261. 'The *baselard* was of two kinds, straight and curved ... By Statute 12 Rich. II, c. vi, it was provided that—"null servant de husbandrie ou laborer ne servant de artificer ne de vitailler porte desore enavant *baslard,* dagger, nespee [*nor sword*] sur forfaiture dicelle." Priests were strictly inhibited from wearing this instrument of war, but the rule was constantly broken.'—Note by Peacock to Myrc's Instructions for Parish Priests (Early English Text Society). The frequent enactments against the wearing of weapons by civilians, &c., in the reigns of Edward III and Richard II, show how often this law was disregarded. See Liber Albus, pp. 335, 554, 555. See also note to l. 309, below.

306. See Isaiah ii. 4, quoted in note to l. 322.

307. *Pykoys,* a mattock; now cleverly corrupted to 'pick-axe.'

309. To hunt (not with hounds, but) with *placebo* means to be diligent

in singing *placebo*, i. e. in studying the breviary.   In Pass. **xv.** we find the
author speaking of ploughing with *placebo* :—

> 'Sire Johan and sire Geffrey · hath a girdel of silver,
>
> A *baselard* or a ballok-knyf · with botons over-gilte,
>
> Ac a porthors, that sholde be his plow · *placebo* to sigge,
>
> Hadde he nevere service to save silver therto · seith it with ydel
> wille.'   Piers Pl. ed. Wright, p. 302; or ed. Skeat, B. **xv.** 120.

A later spelling of *porthors* is *portous;* it means a breviary.   The *placebo*
was the Office for the Dead at Vespers, which began—' *Placebo* domino in
regione viventium' (Ps. cxvi. 9, or cxv. 9 in the Vulgate).   To 'sing *placebo*'
came to be used in a humorous sense, to signify complaisance.   Hence the
name *Placebo* for a flattering character in Chaucer's Marchauntes Tale.

316. *After the dede,* according to the deed; cf. 'neither reward us *after*
our iniquities' in the Litany.

322. Isaiah ii. 4: 'Et judicabit gentes, et arguet populos multos: et con-
flabunt gladios suos in vomeres, et lanceas suas in falces: non levabit gens
contra gentem gladium, nec exercebuntur ultra ad prælium.'   Cf. Wyclif's
Works, ed. Arnold, i. 321, 322.

323. Fanciful prophecies were then in vogue; see those of John of Bridlington, in Political Poems, ed. Wright, vol. i.   William has another similar
one at the end of Pass. **vi.**   This present one merely vaguely hints at a final
time when Jews and Mahometans shall be converted.   Line 325 is easily
explained.   The *middle of a moon* is the *full moon*, and *to turn* in M. E.
means to be converted.   It means—thoughts upon the Paschal full moon
will convert the Jews.   As to the *six suns,* compare ' three suns' in 3 Hen. VI.,
ii. 1. 25.

327. Prov. xxii. 1.

330. The question is not from the book of Wisdom, but from Prov. xxii.
9.   Meed quotes only *half* of it, for which Conscience reproves her, and
quotes the rest, l. 345.   The full verse is—' Victoriam et honorem acquiret
qui dat munera ; animam autem aufert accipientium.'

333. *I leue wel,* I well believe, I fully grant.

334. The lady read but *half* the text.   It is—' Omnia autem probate,
quod bonum est tenete.'   1 Thess. **v.** 21.

342. *Were gode,* would be good.

344. *Seche sapience eft,* refer to the book of Wisdom [Proverbs] again.

349. *Sonde,* gift.   Conscience here adds the rest of the quotation, which
Meed, less accurate, had omitted.

PASSUS IV.

5. *But resoun rede me,* unless Reason advise me.

17. *Tomme trewe-tonge ;* mentioned before, Pass. iii. 320.

18. *Lesyng,* leasing, lying, an idle tale to laugh at.

'Trofels sal i yow nane tell,
    Ne *lesinges* forto ger [make] yow lagh.'
                    Ywaine and Gawin (Ritson's Met. Rom.), l. 150.

19. Reason tells his servant Cato (so named, probably, from Dionysius Cato, whom our author often quotes) to put a saddle upon Patience, and to restrain Patience further by means of girths and a heavy bridle, as he will be sure to shew signs of impatience before long. To *make wehe* is to make a neighing sound, to neigh, *wehe* being an imitation of that sound, as in the Welsh *wihi*. In the Ayenbite of Inwyt (ed. Morris, 1868, p. 204) is a similar passage. 'Thanne the bodiliche wyttes byeth ase thet hors thet yernth wyth-oute bridle zuo thet hit deth falle his lhord. Ac the herte chaste ham ofhalt mid the bridle of skele;' i. e. then the bodily wits are as the horse that runneth without bridle, so that it causes its lord to fall. But the chaste heart restrains them with the bridle of discernment.

25. *Whiche*, what sort of, what kind of; a common meaning of *whiche*.

31–41. These lines are not in the earliest version (A-text).

34. *There as*, there where. *Contricio*, &c. This quotation and the next are from Ps. xiv. 7 (xiii. 3, Vulgate):—'Contritio et infelicitas in viis eorum, et viam pacis non cognoverunt: non est timor Dei ante oculos eorum.'

45. *His sone*, Edward the Black Prince, a great favourite with the people. He did not leave England to take possession of Acquitaine till Feb. 2, 1363. William, having once inserted this in the earliest version of his poem, does not seem to have thought it worth while to alter it, as he retains the expression *his sone* even in his latest version (C-text). Cf. note to l. 173.

47. *Put forth a bille;* in the Vernon MS., *put up a bille*, which is the more usual expression, as in Fabyan's Chronicles [1410–11] :—'The commons of this lande *put vp a bylle* vnto the kyng,' &c.

48. *Wronge* is a representative of the oppressive tribe known as *the king's purveyors.* The peasantry often complained of them bitterly, accusing them of taking things by violence; see note to l. 58. In the poem of King Edward and the Shepherd (printed by Hartshorne in his Ancient Metrical Tales) is the following :—

'I hade catell, now have I non;
    Thay take my bestis, and don thaim slon,
        And payen but a *stick of tre* . . . .
    Thai take geese, capons and henne,
    And alle that ever thei may with renne,
        And reves us our catell . . . .
    Thei toke my hennes and my geese,
    And my schepe with all the fleese,
        And ladde them forth away.'

So in Political Songs (Camd. Soc. 1839), p. 186—
        'Est vitii signum pro victu solvere *lignum.*'

So in God spede the Plough, printed at the end of Pierce the Ploughman's Crede, ed. Skeat, 1867, p. 70 :—

> 'The kingis puruiours also they come,
>> To haue whete and otys at the kyngis nede ;
>> And over that befe and Mutton,
>>> And butter and pulleyn [*poultry*], so God me spede !
>> And to the kyngis court we moste it lede,
>>> And our payment shalbe a *styk of A bough;*
>>> And yet we moste speke faire for drede—
>> I praye to God, spede wele the plough !'

55. To *maintain* was the legal term for to aid and abet in wrongdoing; cf. Pass. iii. 90, 149.

56. 'Forestalls my (sales at) fairs.' See *Forstalleth* in the Glossary.

58. *And taketh me,* &c. ; and gives me a tally (and nothing else) for ten quarters of oats; cf. note to iii. 45. The statements in the note to l. 48 were often true in *two* senses ; the peasants were paid (1) by a wooden tally, and (2) by a beating, as William says in the next line. An exchequer tally was an account of a sum lent to the Government. The tally itself was a rod of hazel (one of a pair that *tallied*), with notches on it to indicate the sum lent. It was not easy to realise this sum afterwards. Cf. Chaucer, Prol. 570.

72. *But if Mede,* &c.; unless Meed arrange matters for you, thy misfortune is aloft. *Myschief* means, in Middle English, mishap, ill-luck. *Vppe* is here an adverb, on high, aloft, in the ascendent.

73. *Lyth in his grace.* Offenders convicted of great crimes were put *in the king's grace,* who could hang them and confiscate their property, unless he were pleased to shew mercy. Sometimes he was satisfied with exacting a heavy fine ; see ll. 88, 89.

86. *Seuene ȝere,* seven years; a proverbial expression for a long period. So also in Pass. v. 208.

109. *But lownesse hym borwe,* unless submission go bail for him.

112. *Moste be,* might be. *Meynpernour;* see note to l. 196 of Pass. ii. Cf.

> 'And to prison he goth, he gette[th] no bettir,
> Till his *maynpernour* his areste unfettir,' &c.

Occleve, de Regim. Princip. ed. Wright, p. 86.

115. *Harlotrye,* ribaldry, buffoonery, jester's tales.

116. *Pernelle* or *Peronelle* (from Petronilla) was a proverbial name for a gaily dressed bold-faced woman; it would be long before she put away her finery in a box. May 31 was dedicated to S. Petronilla the Virgin. She was supposed to be able to cure the quartan ague; Chambers' Book of Days, ii. 389. *Hucche,* a clothes-box; see Our English Home, p. 101.

117. *And childryn,* &c.; and the cherishing of children be, that they be chastised with rods. To *cherish* is to cocker spoil. *Childryn* is the genitive plural, like *clerken* in l. 119.

118. *Harlotes*, ribalds, jesters, buffoons ; it is applied to both sexes, but much more commonly to *males* in Early English. *Be holden for an hyne*, be considered of small value, i. e. be no longer rare ; see *Hyne* in the Glossary. The Harleian MS. 875 reads—*be preised ful highe.*

120. *And religious romares*, &c. ; and pilgrims stay at home and sing *recordare* in their cloisters. *Recordare* is the first word of a mass for avoiding sudden death, appointed by Pope Clement at Avignon, the recital of which secured to the hearers 260 days' indulgence. This is best shewn by the following rubric from the Sarum Missal, 1532 ; fol. lij. 'Missa pro mortalitate evitanda, quam dominus papa clemens fecit et constituit in collegio, cum omnibus cardinalibus ; et concessit omnibus penitentibus vere contritis et confessis sequentem missam audientibus .cclx. dies indulgentie. Et omnes audientes sequentem missam debent portare in manu vnam candelam ardentem dum missam audiunt per quinque dies sequentes ; et tenere eam in manu per totam missam genibus flexis : et eis mors subitanea nocere non poterit ; et hoc est certum et approbatum in auinione et in partibus circumuicinis.' Then follows—'*Officium.* Recordare, domine, testamenti tui, et dic angelo percutienti, cesset jam manus tua : vt non desoletur terra : et ne perdas omnem animam viuam :' &c.

By Clement must be meant Clement V, who removed the papal see to Avignon in 1309, and died in 1314. It was he who first made public sale of indulgences in 1313, and whose decretals and constitutions, known as the *Clementines*, were collected and published in 1308.

121. Saint Benedict, founder of the Benedictine order of monks, was born about A.D. 480, and died about A.D. 542. Saint Bernard, of Cistercium or Citeaux, near Chalons, better known as S. Bernard of Clairvaux, founded the order of Cistercians or Bernardines ; he was born A.D. 1091, died 1153. St. Francis of Assisi, founder of the Franciscan order of friars or Friars Minorites, was born 1182, died 1226.

124. 'Till bishops' horses be turned into beggars' chambers ;' i. e. till the money spent by bishops on horses go to furnish rooms for beggars.

126. *There I shal assigne*, where I (Reason) shall ordain. There is no need to go to Gallicia, where is the shrine of St. James of Compostella. See note to Prol. l. 47, and compare—

'But, bi *seint Jame of Galice*, that many man hath souht,
The pilory and the cucking-stol beth i-mad for nouht.'
                                         Political Songs (Camden Soc.), p. 345.

In the C-text, Reason does assign places to find S. James in ; viz. *prisons*, *poor cottages*, and *sick-rooms*.

128. *Rome-renneres*, runners to Rome. 'And all Rome-runners bear no silver over sea that bears the image of the king, for the sake of enriching robbers that dwell beyond sea.' Part of the procurator's oath to the English king was—' that he would not send money out of the kingdom without the royal license.'—Lingard, iv. 205. In 1376, the commons presented a

petition to the king, stating that the taxes paid yearly by them to the pope amounted to five times the royal revenue. 'In the reign of Henry III, the Italians who were beneficed here, drew from England more than thrice the amount of the king's revenues, fleecing, by means of priests, who were aliens also, the flock which they never fed.'—Southey; Book of the Church, p. 187 (6th ed., 1848). Fabyan says that in 1365, Peter's pence were commanded to be no more gathered, but he adds—'neuerthelesse at this present tyme [Henry VII.] they be gaderyd in sondry shyres of Englande;' p. 477.

143. 'For the man named *nullum malum* met with one called *impunitum*,' &c. This is merely a way of introducing the words in italics. The original passage is 'Ipse est iudex iustus ... qui nullum malum praeterit impunitum, nullum bonum irremuneratum'; Pope Innocent, De Contemptu Mundi, lib. iii. c. 15.

145. *Construe this vnglosed*, interpret this without a commentary.

149-156. Not in the earliest version.

156. *I falle in*, I fall amongst, I meet with. Warin Wisdom used to meet with a florin (of course by accident), and suddenly find himself unable to plead.

173-182. Not in the earliest version. Observe that in l. 177 is the phrase—*if I reign any while*. This phrase is a little difficult. It does not seem to imply that the king had just come to the throne, but that his reign was nearly at an end. It is thus equivalent to 'if I reign much longer.' The allusion is to Edward III, weakened by old age and expecting death. This suits with l. 195, which in the A-text took the vaguer form—'As long as I live.'

189. *Be my conseille comen*, when my council is come. The Trinity MS. (printed by Mr. Wright) has *By my counseil commune*, by my common council; which is certainly a corrupt reading.

PASSUS V.

3. *Then waked I.* Here the *first* vision ends, viz. that of the Field Full of Folk, Holy Church, and Lady Meed. In l. 8, the *second* vision begins and may be called the Vision of the Seven Deadly Sins, and of Piers the Plowman. This vision begins with a view of the field before spoken of, whilst Reason preaches a sermon to the folk there collected.

13. *Thise pestilences.* There were three (some reckon four) terrible pestilences at this period, which were long remembered, and which proved such scourges that the land was left partly untilled, so that severe famine ensued. They took place in 1348 and 1349, 1361 and 1362, and 1369; a fourth was in 1375 and 1376. The *two first* are here alluded to. The first of these is computed to have begun at various dates. Mr. Wright gives an extract from one of the Cotton MSS., and says that it began May 31, 1348. Lingard says that it reached Dorchester in August, and London in September, 1348. Fabyan says it began in August, 1348. Sir H. Nicolas, in

The Chronology of History, p. 345, says May 31, 1349, which is surely the wrong year. It terminated on the 29th September, 1349. This was the plague called the *black death*, which occasioned Boccaccio's Decamerone. The *second* pestilence is the one to which William more immediately alludes. It lasted from August 15, 1361, to May 3, 1362. Some records are dated from the times of these plagues. Allusions to them as God's punishments for sin are common in the writers of the period.

14. *Southwest wynde.* Tyrwhitt first pointed out that this is an allusion to the violent tempest of wind on Jan. 15, 1362, which was a *Saturday.* He refers to the mention of it by Thorn, Decem Script. col. 2122 ; by Walsingham (see Riley's edition, vol. i. p. 296) ; and by the Continuator of Adam Murimuth, p. 115. The last notice is the most exact. 'A.D. m.ccc.lxii, xv die Januarii, *circa horam vesperarum*, ventus vehemens *notus Australis Africus* tantâ rabie erupit,' &c. Walsingham calls it *nothus Auster Africus.* It is alluded to by many other chroniclers also. Fabyan says, p. 475—'In this xxxvii yere, vpon the daye of seynt Mauryce, or the xv daye of Januarii, blewe so excedynge a wynde that the lyke therof was nat seen many years passed. This began *about euynsong tyme* in the *South*,' &c. He says it lasted for five days. We find the same notice again in A Chronicle of London, p. 65, where it is said to have taken place, in the year 1361, on 'seynt Maurys day.' This means the same year (viz. 1361-2), which was called 1361 during the months of January and February, and 1362 afterwards; according to the old reckoning. Fabyan wrongly calls it the day of St. Maurice ; the 15th of January is the day of St. *Maur*, a disciple of St. Bennet. It is noticed again in Hardyng's Chronicles, ed. Ellis, 1812, p. 330. Blomefield tells us that it blew down the spire of Norwich Cathedral. It will be observed that the second great pestilence was prevailing at the time.

24, 25. Cf. Prol. 22, and the latter part of Pass. vi.

26, 27. Cf. note to Pass. iv. 116, and see l. 63 below.

28. *Thomme Stowue,* &c. A difficult passage. Whitaker has *Stone* and *wynen*, and explains it—'He taught Thom. Stone to take two sticks, and fetch home Felice, his spouse, from drinking wine.' This does not explain *pyne.* The MSS. have *Stowue, stouue, Stowe, of stowue;* in the unprinted Trinity MS. the other word is clearly *wyuene.* Like *kyngene, clerken,* it is a genitive plural, and as *pyne* invariably means punishment, *wyuene pyne* is only one more allusion to the *women's punishment,* the *cucking-stool.* I suppose the sentence to mean that *Tom Stowe,* who had neglected his wife and let her get into bad ways, or who had allowed her to be punished as a scold, had much better fetch her home than leave her exposed to public derision. Such an errand would require a strong arm, and two staves would be very useful in dispersing the crowd. I do not think it is meant that he is to beat *her,* for then *one* would have sufficed ; nor would Reason give such bad advice.

30. *Watt,* the contraction of *Water,* which was another form of *Walter,* and by no means uncommon. 'Nout Willam ne *Water;*' Ancren Riwle, p. 340.

31. *Hire hed.* Nothing so invited satire as the head-dresses of the females. Chaucer makes the wife of Bath's to have weighed *ten pounds!* The hair was generally enveloped in a caul of network of gold, which fitted close to both sides of the face. Thus, in the *Crede,* we read of 'great-headed queans, *with gold by the eyes,*' l. 84.

32. *Bette,* a male name, as in ii. 109. It is the same as *Bat,* i. e. Bartholomew.

33. *Betoun,* evidently Bette's daughter. Cf. l. 306.

35, 36. 'Let no anxiety for gain cause your children a moral loss, nor unreasonably indulge them because you fear the power of the pestilence.' *For-weny* means to spoil, lit. to *for-wean,* i. e. to wean amiss. Hence the A.S. *forwened* means proud, i. e. spoilt, over-humoured; and in his poem of Richard the Redeles, Pass. i. l. 27, our author says of King Richard's courtiers that they 'walwed in her willis ' *forweyned* in here youthe.' The phrase *forwened child* = a spoilt child, occurs also in O. Eng. Homilies, ed. Morris, 2nd Ser. p. 41, where it is opposed to *wel-þeaud child,* or well-behaved child. Lines 36–41 are not in the A-text. At the time when they were added, both the third and fourth pestilences, viz. of 1369 and 1375, had taken place. Hence there was additional reason to fear that the anxiety to rear children would lead to excessive indulgence to them.

38. *The leuere childe,* &c.; to the dearer child, the more teaching is necessary. This was a common proverb, as pointed out by Mr. Wright, and is found in the proverbs of Hendyng, written about 1300—'*Luef child lore byhoueth,* Quoth Hendyng.' See Specimens of Early English, ed. Morris and Skeat, pt. ii. p. 36 ; or Reliq. Antiq. i. p. 110. So in the poem called How the Goodwife Taught her Daughter—

'And ʒif thou loue thin childryn, loke thou holde hem lowe ;
ʒif any of hem do amys, curse hem nought ne blowe,
But take a smerte rodde, and bete hem alle by rowe,
Til thei crye mercy, and be here gylte aknowe.'

Hazlitt's Early Pop. Poetry, vol. i. p. 191.

The original source is Prov. xiii. 24—'Qui parcit virgæ, odit filium suum ; qui autem diliget illum, instanter erudit.'

43. *That ye prechen,* that which ye preach. Cf. Pass. iv. 122.

49–56. Not in the A-text. Added, probably, in 1377, as a hint to the new king. In the latest version (C-text), he further adds some advice to the commons, not to quarrel amongst themselves. He also, in that version, lengthens out his advice to the pope ; but the advice to the judges he omits.

56. Quoted from Matt. xxv. 12.

58. *Seynt treuthe,* i.e. the Truth of the Divine Nature, formerly spoken of

as being God the Father, but here spoken of as being the Holy Ghost. MS.
Harl. 3954 makes Piers Plowman equivalent to Christ, and its last Passus
ends thus—' Explicit tractus de perys plowman . . . *qui cum patre et spiritu
sancto vivit et regnat per omnia sæcula sæculorum. Amen.*' If for *spiritu
sancto* we substitute *filio,* we have the true Latin ending of Reason's sermon
in full. To it, however, the preacher adds a pious wish for the welfare of
those who follow his advice. Compare—

> ' And whan this frere had sayd al his entent,
>   With *qui cum patre* forth his way he went.'
>
> Chaucer, Somp. Tale, 25.

61. ' Then ran Repentance, and repeated Reason's theme, and made Will
weep water with his eyes.' *Will* means the author himself, who calls himself *Will* in many other places, in the same off-hand manner.

62. *Superbia.* One of the commonest of subjects in old authors is a
description of the Seven Deadly Sins. See Chaucer's Persones Tale, *passim;*
an anonymous poem called ' Gyf me lysens to lyue in Ease,' and a poem of
The Mirror of the Periods of Man's Life, both edited for the Early English
Text Society by Mr. Furnivall, the first in Political, Religious, and Love
Poems, p. 215; the second in Hymns to the Virgin and Christ, p. 58. In
these, the *opposites* of the sins are given, as here enumerated. (1) *Superbia,*
Pride; opposed to *Humilitas,* Humility. (2) *Luxuria,* Lechery; *Castitas,*
Chastity. (3) *Invidia,* Envy; *Caritas,* Love. (4) *Ira,* Anger; *Patientia,*
Patience. (5) *Avaritia,* Coveitise or Covetousness; *Eleemosyna,* Largeness
or Bounty. (6) *Gula,* Gluttony; *Abstinentia,* Abstinence, Measure, or
Moderation. (7) *Accidia,* Sloth; *Vigilantia,* Business. Our author him-
self supplies names for the *opposites,* in Pass. v. ll. 629–632; but he puts
Pees for the opposite of *Anger,* and *Patience* for that of *Sloth.* Of all the
Seven Sins, Pride is the chief, and the root and spring of the rest. It is
expressed in Shakespeare by *ambition :*—

> ' Cromwell, I charge thee, fling away *ambition;*
>   By that sin fell the angels.'
>
> Henry VIII, iii. 2, 441.

Cf. note to Pass. i. 105. It is singular that it is the only vice which William
personifies by a female. He doubtless does so with particular reference to
extravagance in dress, to repress which a special Statute was passed in 1363.
See Lingard, iv. 91 (*note*). In the C-text, however, is a long additional
passage, in which the confession of Peronel Proud-heart is supplemented by
that of a male example of Pride. In Pass. xix. Pride is made leader of the
Vices, who attack the Church of Unity.

66. *An heyre,* a hair shirt. ' She made grete abstynence, and wered *the
hayre* upon the wednesday and upon the fryday'; Knight de la Tour, ed.
Wright, p. 193.

72. *Luxuria.* In *all* the versions of his poem, William purposely curtails
his description of this vice. His chief warning is against getting drunk upon

a Saturday, when work was over sooner than on other days, as it was the eve of Sunday. *To drink with the duck* (l. 75) is to drink water, as a duck does when she is thirsty.

76. *Invidia.* The reader should compare the descriptions in William with those in Dunbar's Dance of the Seven Deadly Sins, and in Spenser's Faerie Queene, bk. i. canto iv. stanzas 8–35.

77. *Mea culpa.* The form of confession contained the words—' Peccavi nimis cogitatione, locutione, et opere : *mea culpa.*' See Procter on the Common Prayer, p. 193.

78. *A pelet,* a pellet, ball used as a war-missile, commonly made of *stone.* whence the present simile.

89. *Bakbitynge.* ' *Bacbitares,* þe biteð oðre men bihinden,' backbiters that bite other men behind, i. e. defame them ; Ancren Riwle, p. 86. In the Rolls of Parliament, at the opening of the Parliament of 2 Richard II, in the year 1378, we find—' Qi sont appellez *Bacbyters,* sont auxi come chiens qi mangeont les chars crues,' &c. See Jesse's Anecdotes of the British Dog, v. 2. p. 94.

92. *Gybbe,* short for *Gilbert;* whence *Gibbs* and *Gibson.* A *Gib-cat* means a male-cat ; we now say a Tom-cat. See *Gib-cat* in Nares.

94. *Ennuyed,* annoyed ; the Trinity MS. has *anoyed.* It is not *enuyed,* envied, for this would spoil the alliteration.

101. ' I salute him courteously, as if I were his friend.'

108. *Bolle.* The ' bowl ' and the ' broken (i. e. torn or ragged) sheet ' were things of no value, but Envy could not refrain from cursing the thief. The bowl was probably a large wooden one, used to contain scraps of broken victuals. It was sometimes large enough to contain a baby.

> ' And at the londes ende laye · a litell *crom-bolle,*
> And thereon lay a little childe · lapped in cloutes.'
>
> Crede, l. 437.

110. The early version has—

> ' How Heyne haþ a new cote · and his wyf anotþer.'

The coat was an article of female as well as of male attire, but the word is much more often used in the latter sense, to which it is now restricted. Cf. Solomon's Song, v. 3.

111. *Al þe webbe after,* and (I wish that) the whole piece of cloth (from which the coat was cut) were mine too.

112. *Of,* at. *That liketh,* that pleases.

114. *And deme,* &c. ' And judge that they do ill, where I do far worse.'

121. *Is yuel to defye,* are difficult to digest.

122–124. ' Cannot any sugar or sweet thing (be found to) assuage my swelling, nor any expectorant drive it out of my heart, nor any kind of penance or shame (relieve me), except some one were (actually) to scrape my maw ? ' A forcible way of expressing the question—' can none but the most violent measures relieve my moral sickness ? ' *Diapenidion* answers almost exactly to the modern barley-sugar, being a kind of sweet stuff twisted into a thread, and used to relieve coughs, &c. The prefix *Dia* is explained by Cotgrave as 'a tearme set before medicinall confections, or electuaries, that were devised by the Greeks.' Hence our author says elsewhere (B. xx. 173) that Life strove to drive Death away 'with *dias* and drugs.' The termination *penidion* means a little twist (of thread, originally), being a diminutive of the Greek πήνη, thread. This *penidion* became *pénide* in French, and *pennet* in English, according to Cotgrave's explanation, who says—'*Penide*, f. a Pennet; the little wreath of sugar taken in a cold.' This puzzling word is thus completely explained; it only remains to add that I am indebted for the explanation of it to Professor Morley.

127. '*I am* sorry; I am but seldom otherwise.' Surely a most clever rejoinder.

129-187. *Not* in the earliest version. Observe that William *now* introduces the words *dwelling in London*.

130. *And gert*, 'And caused detraction to be made by means of a broker, to find fault with other men's ware.' That is, he employed brokers to depreciate his neighbours' goods. *Be* is the preposition *by*. The oath of the brokers, given at p. 273 of the Liber Albus, obliged them not to be themselves dealers in the merchandize in which they were brokers, nor to make any bargain unless they bring buyer and seller together, and lawfully witness the sale.

134. *Ira*. Curiously enough, William entirely omitted this vice in his earliest version. Seeing his mistake, he elaborated the character with great care. He makes Wrath to have been a *friar*, the nephew of an abbess; he was first employed as gardener to the convent, and afterwards as cook in the kitchen. William doubtless refers to the terrible wrath then displayed by the secular clergy against the friars, and by the friars against them, and even by one order of friars against another. Compare the description of *Ire* in Chaucer, Somp. Tale, 299.

138-150. A slightly difficult, but important passage. It means—'I (continually) grafted lying tales upon *limitors* and *lectors*, till they bare leaves of servile speech, to flatter lords with, and afterwards they blossomed abroad in (my lady's) bower, to hear confessions. And now there is fallen therefrom a fruit, that folk have much rather shew their schrifts to *them* than shrive themselves to their own parsons. And now that the parsons have found out that friars share (the profits of confession) with them, these *possessioners* preach (to the people) and calumniate the friars; and the friars (on the other hand) find *them* to be in fault, as people bear witness, (and say) that when they preach to the people, in many places about (it will be found), that I, i.e. Wrath, go with them, and teach them out of my books. Thus both parties talk about spiritual power, so that each despises the other, till either they are both beggars, and live by the spiritual authority which I give them, or else they are all rich, and ride about (like rich people).

I Wrath never rest from following about this wicked folk—for such is my grace.' Wrath here insinuates that the quarrel generally terminates in one of two ways : either the secular clergy turn beggars like the friars, or the friars obtain wealth enough to buy horses like the secular clergy. The quarrel was, as to which should hear confessions.

138. *Limitours* were members of a convent to whom a certain limited district was assigned to beg in, in order that, each mendicant having a certain round to make, no family might be left unsolicited. Bread, bacon, cheese, logs of wood, &c., were often ready for the limitour when he called. See Massingberd's Eng. Reformation, p. 110; and Chaucer, Prol., l. 209; and Somp. Tale, l. 3. *Listres* are *lectors*. This is ascertained by the following entry in the Promptorium Parvulorum, A.D. 1440. '*Lyysterre* [*various readings* lystyr, lystore, listyr] *Lector.*' The editor, Mr. Way, says this is ' the *reader*, who occupied the second place in the holy orders of the Church. By *second* place is meant second in ascending order. The seven orders, excluding the bishop, were the ostiary (door-keeper), lector, exorcist, acolyth, sub-deacon, deacon, and presbyter. Some MSS. have *legistres*, but this would mean *lawyers* and would be out of place; cf. Pass. vii. 14. In this passage, however, it is best to take *lector* in the more important sense of ' preacher' or ' lecturer.' O. F. *listre* or *litre* = Lat. *lector*. *Lister* as a proper name is quite a different word, being corrupted from *litster*, a dyer.

144. *Possessioners;* see Chaucer's Sompnoures Tale, l. 14. Tyrwhitt says—' An invidious name for such religious communities as were endowed with lands. The Mendicant orders professed to live entirely upon alms.' Mr. Wright says—' the regular orders of monks, who possessed landed property and enjoyed rich revenues,' &c. Wycliffe remarks that ' some receauen dymes and dotations, as don these *possessioners*, but some forsaken al such tythes and possessions, as Friers mendicants'; Two Treatises, ed. James, p. 6. But it is probable that, in the present passage, a *possessioner* means one of the *beneficed clergy*, as the word *persones* is used as an equivalent. And it is worth remarking, that this same explanation will suit the context in Chaucer's Sompnoures Tale just as well as if we suppose *monks* to be intended. Observe, for instance, l. 19 :—

> ' Nought for to hold a *prest* jolif and gay;'

and, farther on, the friar says,—

> ' These curates ben ful negligent and slowe;'

> ' This every lewed *vicory* or *parsoun*
> Can say, how ire engendreth homicide,' &c.

Nothing can give us so clear an idea of a friar as the commencement of this tale of Chaucer's.

154. *Hir were leuere*, &c. ' She had rather swoon or die,' &c. Lit. ' it were liefer to her.'

162. *I-made* is the past tense, which is sometimes, but not often, found

with this prefix. Two MSS. read *made*. Cf. l. 507. The sense of the line is—I fed them with wicked words; lit. I prepared their vegetables with wicked words. There is a sort of play upon *words* and *worts*, as in Shak., Merry Wives, i. 1. 124.

163. *Thow lixte*, thou liest. Cf. Crede, 542.

165. *Her eyther*, each of them. *Other*, the other.

166. *Seynt Gregorie.* 'It appears that some Abbesses did at one time attempt to hear the confessions of their Nuns, and to exercise some other smaller parts of the clerical function; but this practice, I apprehend, was soon stopped by Gregory IX, who has forbidden it in the strongest terms.—Decretal. l. v. tit. 38. c. x.;' Tyrwhitt, Introd. Discourse to Cant. Tales, note 7. Tyrwhitt gives the Latin text of the Decretal.

167. *Were prest*, should be a priest; i. e. should hear confessions.

168. *Infamis;* so in the MSS. It is put for the nom. plural. *Thei can*, &c., 'They can so ill conceal counsel,' 'they can so badly keep their own counsel.'

172. *Thei taken*, &c., 'They take counsel together;' they combine to devise a punishment.

177. *Fieble*, weak, poor, thin, watery. So in Havelok, l. 323, a maiden is ill-treated, and clothed ' in *feble* wede,' i. e. in poor or miserable clothing.

184. ' Nor too deeply neither.' This use of *neither* is still common.

186, 187. *Esto sobrius;* cf. 'sobrii estote,' 1 Pet. v. 8. *Me* and *my* are evident blunders; but they seem to have emanated from William himself, as the six best MSS. all have this reading. It would seem also that William afterwards himself perceived and corrected the blunder, for in the C-text or latest version, vii. 168, we find *hym* instead of *me*, in both places, and *hus* (= his) instead of *my*.

189. Skelton has the same name for a covetous man.

'And *Haruy* Hafter, that well coude picke a male.

Skelton (ed. Dyce), i. 35.

194. *Of* = by. ' His beard was beslobbered, as a bondman's is by bacon.'

196. *Tabard;* see Chaucer's Prol. 20, 541 ; and cf. note above, to ii. 185.

198. *Haue lopen þe bettere*, could have been (i. e. were) a particularly good jumper. Hazlitt, in his Book of Proverbs, p. 216, has—' If a louse miss its footing on his coat, 'twill be sure to break its neck.'

203. *A leef other tweyne*, a leaf or two. Avarice talks of his first *lesson* in the next line, and of learning his *Donet* in l. 209. So here, still keeping up the metaphor of reading a book, he learns to lie for a leaf or two, as much, that is, as would fill a couple of leaves. All ambiguity is removed by a passage in Richard the Redeles, where the poet [William himself, as I have elsewhere shewn] says that his poem will do the king good if he will look over a leaf or two of it:—' ȝif him list to loke · *a leef other tweyne;*' Prol. l. 37.

205. *Wy*, Weyhill near Andover in Hampshire, as conjectured by Warton,

in a note too long to quote entire; see Hist. Eng. Poetry, ii. 55, ed. 1840. Weyhill fair is still a most famous one to this day, and lasts eight days. The fair for horses and sheep is on Oct. 10; that for cheese, hops, and general wares, on Oct. 11, and the six days following. 'The tolls derived from the sheepfair form part of the stipend of the rector of Weyhill'; *Standard* newspaper, Oct. 11, 1870. Warton says—'One of the chief of them [the fairs] seems to have been that of St. Giles's hill or down, near Winchester, to which our poet here refers . . . . In the fair, several streets were formed, assigned to the sale of different commodities; and called the Drapery, the Pottery, the Spicery,' &c. Fairs long continued to be the principal marts for purchasing necessaries in large quantities. Winchester fair is mentioned temp. Edw. I; see Liber Albus, p. 201.

207. 'The grace (or favour) of guile' is a satirical expression. We speak rather of 'the grace of God.'

209. *Donet*, primer. 'Properly a Grammar, from *Ælius Donatus*, the Grammarian . . . . Among the books written by bishop Pecock, there is the *Donat* into Christian religion, and the Folower to the Donat.'—Warton's Hist. Eng. Poet. ii. 56. See also the note in Dyce's ed. of Skelton, ii. 343.

210. In 1353, statutes were passed regulating the length and breadth of cloth. Thom. Walsingham, ed. Riley, i. 277.

211. *Rayes*, striped cloths. *Ray* means properly a *ray, streak, stripe;* but it was commonly used in the above sense. It was enacted—' that cloths of *ray* shall be 28 ells in length, measured by the list [*edge*], and 5 quarters in width.'—Liber Albus, p. 631. 'A long gown of *raye*' occurs in Lydgate's London Lyckpeny; Spec. of Eng., ed Skeat, p. 25.

212. *To broche*, &c.;—'To pierce them with a packing-needle, and fasten them together; and then I put them in a press, and penned them fast in it,' &c.

215. *Webbe*, properly a male weaver, *webster* being the feminine; but the rule is not always observed. Observe *spynnestres*, i.e. female spinners, in the next line.

217. *Ac the pounde*, &c. She paid the people whom she employed by the pound, and used too heavy a weight; thus cheating them of their dues.

218. *Auncere*, a kind of steelyard; see the Glossary. In A.D. 1356, we find 'one balance, called an *auncere*,' valued at 12*d.*; and '2 balances, called *aunceres*,' valued at 6*s.* See Riley's Memorials of London, p. 283.

220. *Peny-ale* is common ale, thin ale, as is certain from its being spoken of as a most meagre drink, suitable for strict-living friars, in Pass. xv. *Podyng-ale* (*puddynge-ale* in Trin. MS.) was probably named from its being thick like *pudding*. Thus in Pass. xix., a fraudulent brewer boasts of drawing *thick ale* and *thin ale* out of one hole in a cask. The penny-ale was sold at *a penny a gallon*, but the best ale at 4*d.* See l. 224.

221. *Hymselue* (not *hemselue*, observe) may refer to the *ale;* observe the next line, and note that the use of *hym* for *it* was common. The MS.

from which Crowley printed actually had *itselfe*. Still, the C-text has *hemselue*.

225. *In cupmel*, by cups at a time. She knew better than to measure it in a gallon measure.

227. *Hokkerye*, i.e. the retail trade. A *huckster* was one who retailed ale, &c. from door to door. ' Item, that no *brewer* or *brewster* sell any manner of *ale* unto any *huckster*,' &c.—Liber Albus, p. 312.

228. *So the ik*, so may I thrive, as I hope to prosper.

230. *Walsyngham*. See note to Prol., l. 54.

231. *Rode of Bromeholme*, cross of Bromholm in Norfolk. In A Chronicle of London, p. 10, we find that in 1224 [rather 1223 or 1222], ' the emperour Baldewyn, which whanne he went to bataile to fyghte with Godes enemyes, he hadde a croos boren before hym, whiche crosse seynt Eleyne made of the crosse that Cryst deyde upon ; and there was an Englyssh prest that tyme with hym that was called Sir Hughe, and he was borne in Norfolke, the whiche prest broughte the same crosse to Bromholm in Norfolke.' Mr. Wright refers to Matthew Paris (p. 268). He adds—' In the MS. Chronicle of Barthol. de Cotton, it is recorded at the date 1223—Eo tempore Peregrinatio de Bromholm incepit.' Hence Avarice could visit Our Lady of Walsyngham and the piece of the true cross at Bromholm in one journey, and pray to be brought out of debt by having his cheating tricks forgiven him. The story of the finding of the True Cross by Helen, mother of Constantine, is well known. There is a drama on the subject by Metastasio, called *Sant' Elena*. Cf. Chaucer, Reves Tale, 366 ; Pardoneres Tale, 489.

232-303. Not in the A-text, and considerably varied in the C-text.

238. He pretends that he thought *restitution* was the French for *robbery*. Norfolk is evidently considered as one of the least refined parts of the island, being in an out-of-the-way corner. The common proverb—*Jack would be a gentleman if he could speak French*—shews that the common people had much difficulty in learning it. Trevisa fixes the date 1385 as the year, *just before* which children began to learn to translate Latin into *English* instead of *French*, as formerly. See Warton. Hist. Eng. Poetry, i. 5.

240. *Vsure*, usury. 'All usury was prohibited as a sin by the Canon Law.'—Southey ; Book of the Church, p. 187.

242. *Lumbardes and Jewes*. 'A set of *Lombards* established themselves here, in connexion with the legates, to advance money upon all sums due to the Pope, for which they exacted the most exorbitant usury,' &c.—Southey, *as above*. Cf. Chaucer, Schipm. Tale, l. 367. The Jews were constantly accused of being the offenders, whenever clipped coin was found, which was very often. Thus in the seventh year of Edward I, ' the viii day of seynt Martyn, alle the Jewes of Engelond were taken for clippyng of money.'—A Chron. of London, p. 28.

244. *And lene it*, &c. ; 'and to lend it for love of the cross, to appoint a pledge and get rid of the light coin,' in which case *it* refers to the coin ; or

else, ' and to lend it for love of the cross, (for the borrower) to give me a
pledge and lose it,' where *it* is the pledge. I think the latter is the meaning,
though the change of the subject of the sentence is awkward. Sir John
Maundevile says that a King of France bought the crown of thorns, spear,
and one of the nails used at the Crucifixion, from the Jews, ' to whom the
Emperour had *leyde hem to wedde*, for a great summe of sylvre.' *For love of
the cross* is a clever pun, as *cross* refers frequently to the cross on the back
of old coins, and was a slang name for a coin, as in Shakespeare. *Cross-
and-pile* is the old name for *heads and tails*. It is clear enough what
Avarice did: he first clipped coins and then lent them, taking a pledge
which he hoped would not be redeemed. The reading of the C-text helps
us out ; it is—

> ' And lente for loue of the wed · þe whiche ich let betere
> And more worth þan þe moneye,' &c.   C. vii. 243.

I let betere = I set more store by.

246. Compare—' Jucundus homo, qui *miseretur et commodat*, disponet
sermones suos in judicio.' Ps. cxii. 5 (cxi. 5, Vulgate). Avarice obtained
more manors through his customers being in arrears of payment, than he
could have obtained by practising liberality. *Maneres* is spelt *manoirs* in
the Trinity MS.

249. In an ordinance against usurers (38 Edw. III) we find that certain
persons exerted themselves to maintain usury—' which kind of contract, the
more subtly to deceive the people, they call *exchange* or *chevisance*, whereas
it might more truly be called *mescheaunce* (wickedness).'—Liber Albus,
p. 319.

261. ' As courteous as a dog in a kitchen.' This alludes to an old ironical
proverb, which appears in French in the form—' Chen en cosyn [*cuisine*]
compaignie ne desire ;' in Latin in the form—' Dum canis os rodit, sociari
pluribus odit ;' and in Middle English—' Wil the hund gnaȝh bon, i-fere neld
he non ;' i. e. While the hound gnaws a bone, companions would he none.
See Wright's Essays, i. 149.

263. *Lene . . . the grace*, lend thee grace. The word is here *lene*, not
leue, as it is transitive.

272. *And*, it. Line 273 is from the Cambridge MS.

279. ' Nec dimittitur peccatum, nisi restituatur ablatum ;' Peter Cantor,
cap. 153 (ed. Migne). Migne adds the reference—' Reg. 4, jur. in 6, ex
Aug. ;' which I do not understand. I find, however—' Si enim res aliena,
propter quam peccatum est, cum reddi potest, non redditur, non agitur
poenitentia, sed fingitur ; si autem ueraciter agitur, *non remittetur peccatum,
nisi restituatur ablatum ;* sed, ut dixi, cum restitui potest ;' S. August. Epist.
cliii. sect. 20 ; Opera, ed. Migne, ii. 662.

283. Ps. li. (l. in Vulgate) is called *Miserere mei Deus* from the first
words in it. In verse 6 (8 in Vulgate) we find—' Ecce enim veritatem
dilexisti : incerta et occulta sapientiæ tuæ manifestasti mihi.'

286. Ps. xviii. 25 (xvii. 26, Vulgate). 'Cum sancto sanctus eris, et cum viro innocente innocens eris.'

289. The Latin quotation is omitted in some MSS. It is not quite exact, 'Suavis Dominus universis : et miserationes ejus super omnia opera ejus.' Ps. cxliv. 9, Vulgate.

291. There is a parallel passage in Hampole's Pricke of Conscience, l. 6311–6319 :—

> 'For the mercy of God es swa mykel here,
> And reches over alle, bathe far and nere,
> That alle the syn that a man may do,
> It myght sleken, and mare thar-to.
> And thar-for says *Saynt Austyn* thus,
> A gude worde that may comfort us :
> *Sicut scintilla ignis in medio maris.*
> *ita omnis impietas viri ad misericordiam Dei.*
> " Als a litel spark of fire," says he,
> " In mydward the mykel se,
> Right swa alle a mans wykkednes
> Un-to the mercy of God es." '   (Ed. Morris, p. 171.)

The nearest passage to this which I have yet found is the following :—

> 'Tanquam unda misericordiæ peccati ignis exstinguitur.'

S. August. in Ps. cxliv. 8 (Vulgate).

293. *To gete the with a wastel,* to get thee a cake with. See note to ii. 31 ; and observe Chaucer's use of *wastel*, Prol. 147.

303. *Lent yow of owre lordes good,* lent you, of our Lord's *wealth;* i. e. spiritual strength to resist temptation.

312. *Piones,* seeds of the pæony. They were used as a medicine, but sometimes also as a spice, as here. See note in Liber Albus, p. 197.

313. *Fastyng dayes.* We learn from l. 367 that the circumstances here described took place on a *Friday,* a fitting day for Glutton to go to church and confess. Cf. also ll. 381, 384, 389, 416. The scene here described with such vivid dramatic power took place, it is evident, in some large ale-house in London, not very far from Cock Lane, Smithfield (l. 319), from Cheapside (l. 322), and from Garlickhithe (l. 324). It was also probably very near a *church* (l. 319). It is a very curious fact, that there is absolutely no reason why the 'Boar's Head,' in Eastcheap, immortalized by Shakespeare, should not have been the very tavern here meant. The Boar's Head is mentioned in a will of the date of Richard II, it boasted to be the 'chief tavern in London,' and (which is very curious) its back-windows looked out on to the burial ground of St. Michael's, a church which is now pulled down, but has given its name to St. Michael's Lane. The will above mentioned further shews that 'the tenement called the Boar's Head,' was given to a college of priests, founded by Sir William Walworth in St. Michael's Church. This is, possibly, the true reason for the name of 'the church' not being given. More than this, William lived at one time in *Cornhill*, which is close by. Glutton may be considered as the Sir John Falstaff of the scene. See Larwood, Hist. of Signboards, p. 378.

315. *Cesse*, i. e. Cis or Cicely, short for Cecilia.

319. Women of ill repute might be put in the pillory; and if so, they were afterwards to be led 'through Chepe and Newgate, to *Cokkeslane*, there to take up their abode.'—Liber Albus, p. 395. Cock Lane, West Smithfield, has, I believe, been part rebuilt. The church may have been St. Michael's; see note above. If not, it may have been St. Peter's in Cornhill; see note to l. 328. In the C-text, William adds to the company some pick-purses, and the hangman of Tyburn.

320. *Dawe* or *Davie* is for David. Cf. 'When *Dauie Diker* diggs and dallies not;' Gascoigne's Steel Glass, 1078; in Specimens of English, p. 322. Cf. the names *Dawson, Dawkes, Dawkins, Dakin* (for *Dawkin*), &c.

321. *Flaundres*. There were many Flemish women, mostly residing in Cock Lane, as they were forbidden to lodge in the city; Memorials of London, ed. Riley; i. 535.

322. *Rakyer of Chepe*, a scavenger of West Cheap, or Cheapside. The word *rakyer*, evidently meaning a raker or street-sweeper, occurs in a Proclamation made in the thirty-first year of Edw. III. See Riley's Memorials of London, p. 299, and Liber Albus, p. 289; also p. 23.

324. *Garlekhithe* is near Vintry Ward. Stow says—'There is the parish church of St. James, called at Garlick hithe, or Garlick hive; for that of old time, on the bank of the river Thames, near to this church, garlick was usually sold.'—Survey of London, ed. 1842, p. 93. The next landing-place, westward, is Queen Hithe.

324. It has been suggested that *Griffin* is an allusion to the Griffin (Griffin to the vulgar eye, though Cockatrice in the Heralds' office), which was emblazoned on the ancient shield of the principality of Wales.—Notes and Queries, 3rd S. xii. 513. The Harleian MS. 875 has *Gruffith*, i. e. Griffith, a common Welsh name.

328. *Atte newe faire*, at the new fair. I am told there is a reference here to an old game called handicapping. It seems that Hikke chose Bette to be his deputy. Then Bette and one appointed by Clement tried to make a bargain, but could not settle it till Robyn was called in as umpire; by whose decision Clement and Hikke had to abide. This handicapping or game of public barter is precisely the same thing as what was called *Freimarkt* in Germany; see an article on this subject by Prof. E. Kölbing in Englische Studien, vol. v. p. 150. In the present case it was settled that Clement should fill up his cup (at Hikke's expense), and be content with the hood, the less valuable article. Whichever of them demurred was to pay a fine to Sir Glutton, the president.

353. Gleemen were frequently blind formerly, as now, and were led by a dog.

355. ' Like one who lays nets, to catch birds with.'

370. *Wif;* many MSS. read *wit.* Either will do ; for in the C-text
(vii. 421) the line is—

' Hus wyf and hys inwit [*conscience*] · edwited hym of hus synne.'

402. *Robyn Hood.* This seems to be the earliest mention of Robin
Hood. The next earliest is in Wyntoun's Scottish Chronicle, written about
A.D. 1420, where Little John is also mentioned. But Mr. Wright thinks
that one of the extant Robin-Hood ballads is really of the date of Edward II.
See his Essays on England in the Middle Ages, ii. 174. *Randolf erle of
Chestre* is either the Randulph or Randle, earl of Chester, who lived in
Stephen's time, and was earl from A.D. 1128 to 1153; or else his grandson
of the same name, who married no less exalted a personage than Constance,
widow of Geoffrey Plantagenet, and mother of Prince Arthur ; and who was
earl from 1181 to 1232. Both were celebrated men, but the latter is the
more likely to be meant, both as being more famous and later in date; besides which, he was once released from prison *by a rabble of minstrels;*
Ritson's Ancient Songs, vol. i. pp. vii, xlvi. The lives of these earls are
detailed in an exhaustive manner by Mr. Hales, in the edition of the Percy
Folio MS., 1867. See vol. i. p. 258. Concerning Robin Hood, see also
Chambers' Book of Days, ii. 606, and i. 580. The 'Robin-Hood games'
were held on May 1.

409. *And other,* and otherwise ; cf. *an elles,* Prol. 91.

413. *Somer game of souteres,* a summer game played by shoemakers.
A *summer game* is probably the same as *summering,* a rural sport at Mid-
summer ; *somer-game* occurs in Chaucer, C. T. 6230. See Nares, who
refers to Brand's Pop. Antiq., i. 240 (4to. ed.) ; Strutt's Sports and Pastimes,
p. xxvi, and Mr. Markland's Essay on the Chester Mysteries, in the 3rd vol.
of Malone's Shakespeare, p. 525, ed. Boswell. The great day was on
St. John the Baptist's eve, i. e. June 23, or Mid-summer eve. Nares quotes
an extract about ' May games, wakes, *summerings,* and rush-bearings.'
Large bonfires were always part of the sport. The following passage also
throws some light upon the matter. ' Why, quoth I, could they caste the
barre and sledge well ? I wyll tell you, syr, quoth hee, you knowe there
hath bene *manye games this sommer.* I thinke verely, that if some of these
lubbars had bene there, and practysed amongest others, I beleue they woulde
have carryed awaye the beste games. For they were so stronge and sturdye,
that I was not able to stande in their handes.' Harman's Caveat, ed.
Furnivall, p. 47. See too the description of the Cotswold games at Whit-
suntide in Chambers' Book of Days, i. 714. The modern name for *games*
is ' athletic sports.'

416. *Late I passe,* I let pass, I pay no heed to. Cf. Chaucer, Prol. 175.

419. *Ite. missa est;* the concluding words of the service of the mass.
From this form of words *Missa* and *Missal* are said to be derived.

420. *But-if,* except ; 'except sickness cause it.' See l. 458.

421. *Vp gesse*, upon guess, by guess. A fine touch.

423. *Solfe, sol-fa*. To *sol-fa* is to practise singing the scale of notes. Some MSS. read *solue*. The C-text has *solfye ;* viii. 31.

425. *Beatus vir*, Ps. i, or cxii. *Beati omnes*, Ps. cxxxviii.

429. *But-ʒif*, except; 'except it be scored on a tally.'

439. I. e. unless something eatable is held in the hand.

448. A Leonine hexameter; I do not know from whom it is quoted.

452. *Wolde*, who would. This omission of the relative is not uncommon in Langland.

454. In Hampole's Prick of Conscience, ii. 3398-3411, the ten things that destroy venial sins are holy water, almsdeeds, fasting, the sacrament, the Pater Noster, shrift, the bishop's blessing, the priest's blessing, *knocking upon the breast as practised by a meek man*, and extreme unction. *Bidde hym of grace*, pray to Him for His grace.

458. *But sykenesse it lette*, unless sickness prevent it.

467. *The rode of Chestre*, the cross or rood at Chester. Mr. Wright quotes from Pennant's Tour in Wales (edit. 1778, p. 191), to shew that a famous cross once stood in a spot formerly known as the *Rood-eye*, i. e. Rood-island, but now known only by the corrupted name of *Roodee*, and used as a race-course. There was also at Chester a college of the Holy Cross. See Chambers' Book of Days, i. 428.

469. *Robert*. The similarity of the words *robber* and *Robert* early gave rise to a pun, whereby *Robert* was a common name for a *thief*. Mr. Wright quotes from the Political Songs, p. 49, the expression—'per *Robert, robbur* designatur.' See the note to Prol. l. 44. *Reddite ;* i. e. the text—' Reddite ergo omnibus debita ;' Rom. xiii. 7.

470. *For ther was nouʒte wher-of*, because there was nothing wherewith to do so; i. e. to make restitution. *Of* often has the force of *with* or *by*.

473. In the apocryphal Gospel of Nicodemus, the name of the penitent thief is *Dimas* or *Dismas*, and that of the other thief, *Gestas*. Other names for them are Titus and Dumachus—

> 'Then on my right and my left side
> These thieves shall both be crucified,
> And *Titus* thenceforth shall abide
>   In Paradise with me.'—Longfellow's Golden Legend.

474. *Memento*. An allusion to the words of the thief—' Domine, *memento* mei, cum veneris in regnum tuum.' Luke xxiii. 42.

475. *Reddere ne haue*, have no money to make restitution with.

476. *With crafte, that I owe*, by any handicraft, that which I owe. *Crafte* is here used in a good sense. *Owe* is, in Middle English, both *to possess* and *to owe* in the modern sense To obviate confusion, the scribe of the Laudian MS. has written *debeo* over this word, as a gloss.

482. *That penitencia, &c.*, that he would polish his pike, called *penitencia*, afresh, and by help of it leap over the land (be a pilgrim) all his life-time.

A pilgrim always carried a staff, generally with a spike at the end, whence it was called a *pike-staff*. A *land-leper* or *land-loper* was a vulgar name for a pilgrim. Thus we find in Cotgrave's French Dictionary—'*Villotier*, m. : A vagabond, *land-loper*, earth-planet, continuall gadder from towne to towne.' The word *hym* refers to the pike-staff. Cf. l. 542.

491. *Ade*, written for *Adæ*, i. e. of Adam. Professor Stubbs has kindly pointed out to me that this is taken from a passage in the Sarum Missal, viz. from the Canticle 'Exultet' sung upon Holy Saturday at the blessing of the Paschal candle :—'O certe necessarium Ade peccatum et nostrum; quod Christi morte deletum est. O felix culpa, que talem ac tantum meruit habere redemptorem.' See Wyclif's Works, ed. Arnold, i. 321, note.

494. 'And madest Thyself, together with Thy Son, and us sinful men alike.' The sense is clearer than the construction. Cf. l. 495. The two Latin quotations are from Gen. i. 26 and 1 St. John iv. 16.

495. *Thi self sone*, Thy Son Himself. *In owre sute*; here *sute* is the reading of most MSS., and so also in l. 504, whilst in l. 498, the word is written *secte*. It makes no difference, since *secta* (from Lat. *sequi*) meant, in mediæval Latin, either the right of prosecuting an action at law or the *suit* or action itself; where *suit* is from the Fr. *suivre*, the equivalent of *sequi*. And again, *secta* meant a *suit* of clothes, which is the meaning here. We should now say—'in our *flesh*.' Cf. l. 508. See 'Sect' in Wedgwood's Etymological Dictionary, which makes it clear that *sect* is from *sequi*, not *secare*. *Secta* even means a *suite* or set of people; cf. 'and thereupon he produced his *suit*'—Liber Albus, p. 342; where the Latin has *sectam*, i. e. his set of witnesses.

498. *It ladde*, led it (i. e. the sorrow) captive. See Eph. iv. 8, Ps. lxviii. 18.

500. *Mele-tyme of seintes*, meal-time of saints. This seems to refer to the sacrifice of the mass, when the saints feed upon Christ's body, literally, according to the Romish belief, spiritually, according to ours. Mass could be said only between dawn and midday. Midday was, however, not the usual time for celebration; it was generally much earlier. See Rock, Church of our Fathers, iii. pt. 2. 23. The expression must therefore directly refer to the time of the crucifixion, when Christ's blood was shed upon the cross. The quotation from Isaiah ix. 2 is explained in the apocryphal Gospel of Nicodemus with reference to the 'Harrowing of Hell,' i.e. the descent of Christ into hell to fetch out the souls of the patriarchs. Isaiah is there introduced as explaining that the moment of fulfilment of this prophecy has arrived. See the whole account, as there narrated.

504. *In owre sute*, in our *suit*, i. e. in a human body; see note to l. 495, and cf. l. 508.

506. *Non veni*, &c.; Matt. ix. 13. In MSS. of this date, *sed* is commonly spelt *set*, as here.

507. *Ymade*, composed, narrated. To *make* is to compose, especially in verse; but here it is applied to prose writings.

508. *In owre armes*, in our armour, or in arms marked with our device : a phrase taken from the terms of a tournament. The quotation is from John i. 14.

512. *Ribaudes*, ribalds. See a long note in Political Songs, ed Wright, 1839, p. 369. It was chiefly applied to the lowest class of retainers, who could be relied on to do the lord's dirty work. ' In the household of the King of France there was a *Rex ribaldorum*, whose office was to judge disputes, &c., which might arise among retainers of this class.' And see Du Cange, s.v. *ribaldus* and *goliardia*. Cf. Pass. vi. 75.

514. *Hent*, seized. In Ps. lxxi. 20, we find ' thou shalt quicken me again,' but the Vulgate has the past tense instead of the future—' conversus vivificasti me.'

515. Ps. xxxii. (xxxi. in the Vulgate) begins with—' Beati quorum remissæ sunt iniquitates, et quorum tecta sunt peccata.'

516. See Ps. xxxvi. 7 ; in the Vulgate, xxxv. 7.

520. In the A-text, or earliest version of the poem, a new Passus—Passus vi.—begins here. By this simple test, the MSS. of the A-text may be at once recognised.

523. This excellent description of a Palmer should be noted. Mr. Wright aptly draws attention to a similar description in Sir Walter Scott's Marmion, canto i. st. 23, 27. Instead of quoting these familiar lines, I give Sir Walter Scott's note—' A *Palmer*, opposed to a *pilgrim*, was one who made it his sole business to visit different holy shrines ; travelling incessantly, and subsisting by charity : whereas the Pilgrim retired to his usual home and occupations when he had paid his devotions at the particular spot which was the object of his pilgrimage.' Bell (in his notes to Chaucer) says that this is a fanciful notion, copied by Scott from Speght ; the fact being that a *palmer* meant a pilgrim to the *Holy Land*, which was, doubtless, the *original* meaning. But see the Palmer's speech in the Four P's, by John Heywood ; also the romance of Sir Isumbras, who went about *as a palmer ;* and cf. Chaucer, Prol., l. 13.

526. The *bowl* and *bag* were invariably carried ; the former to drink out of, the latter to hold scraps of meat and bread.

527. The *ampullæ* were little phials, containing holy water or oil. They were generally made of metal, nearly flat, and stamped with a device denoting the shrine whence they were brought. See a drawing of one in Cults, Scenes and Characters of the Middle Ages, p. 171. On pilgrims' *signs*, see Chambers' Book of Days, i. 338 ; see also the Introduction to the Tale of Beryn, ed. Furnivall, 171, 175, 191.

528. *Galice*, Gallicia. This refers to the famous shrine of Santiago (St. James) at Compostella in Gallicia. Cf. Prol., l. 47.

529. *Cruche*, cross. Hence the term Crouched Friars or Crutched Friars.

530. The alliteration is not apparent, but William sometimes makes *f* alliterative with *v*. Cf. Chaucer's Prol., l. 685, and see Chambers' Book of Days, i. 100. 'Inter has feminas una fuit Bernice, sive Veronice, vulgo Veronica, qui sudarium Christo exhibens, ut faciem sudore et sanguine madentem abstergeret, ab eo illud recepit, cum impressa in illo ejusdem Christi effigie, ut habet Christiana traditio.' Cornelius a Lapide, in S. Matt. xxvii, 32.

535. *Ermonye*, Armenia. *Alisaundre*, Alexandria.

544. *Peter!* i. e. by St. Peter. This is a very common exclamation, of which there are several instances. See e. g. Chaucer's House of Fame, ii. 526, in Morris's edition, where Tyrwhitt's edition has *Parde;* also the Cant. Tales, l. 13144. It possibly originated with the popes, as Innocent III used to swear by St. Peter; see Southey's Book of the Church, p. 156. As to the duties of a ploughman, here described in ll. 548–556, we should compare the poem of How the Plowman lerned his Paternoster, printed in Hazlitt's Early Popular Poetry, vol. i. We there read—

> 'He coude eke sowe and holde a plowe,
> Bothe dyke, hedge, and mylke a cowe,' &c.

See also Chambers' Book of Days, i. 96. The character of PIERS THE PLOWMAN is here introduced for the first time. When all the penitents and searchers after Truth are at fault, when even a palmer declares he never heard of any saint of that name, the homely ploughman steps forward, declaring that he knows Truth well. It was his own conscience and his native common sense that led him to this knowledge. We may *here* take Piers as the type of Honesty, not without remembering that William *afterwards* identifies him with the truest of all Teachers of men, our Lord Christ Jesus.

556. *To paye*, lit. to pleasure, i.e. to His satisfaction. By Truth is meant God the Father. *Paye* is not here equivalent to *pay* in the modern sense, notwithstanding the occurrence of *huire* (hire) in the next line.

566. *For seynt Thomas shryne*, for all the wealth on St. Thomas' shrine at Canterbury. No shrine could boast more wealth than this of Beket, the object of the journey of Chaucer's Canterbury pilgrims.

572. The way to Truth lies through the ten commandments, most of which are named below, viz. the fifth in l. 576, the third in l. 579, the tenth in l. 582, the eighth and sixth in l. 586, the ninth in l. 589.

578. *Lightloker*, lightlier, more lightly. These comparatives in *-loker* are not uncommon in Middle English.

579. *Swere-noughte*, &c.; swear not unless it be necessary, and, in particular, (swear not) idly by the name of God Almighty. The whole phrase forms, in William's allegorical language, the name of a place.

589, 590. *Bergh*, a hill. *Frithed in*, enclosed by a wood, wooded thickly round.

594. The description of the way to Truth (ll. 570–593) is partly imitated from a poem called La Voie de Paradis, by Rutebuef, a French trouvère; see the edition by Jubinal, ii. 24–55. Rutebuef, in his turn, imitated an earlier poet, named Raoul de Houdaing. The description of Truth's abode

may have been partly imitated from the French poem Le Chastel d'Amour, by Bishop Grosteste, translated under the title of the Castle of Love. In some particulars, it resembles the old English prose treatise known as the 'Abbaye of Saynte Spirite,' or the Abbey of the Holy Ghost ; see Religious Pieces in Prose and Verse, ed. Perry, 1867 (E. E. T. S.). William's originality is most surprising ; this is one of the few places where there are traces of his borrowing from others. See 'Castel off Loue,' ed. Weymouth, pp. 31, 39.

604. 'The doorkeeper is called Grace.'

612. This Latin quotation is thus Englished in MS. Harl. 7322, fol. 143 :—

 'Þe ȝates of parais · þoruth eue weren iloken,
  And þoruth oure swete ladi · Aȝein hui beoþ nouþe open.'
      Political, Rel. and Love Poems, ed. Furnivall, p. 230.

And in Morris's edition of Chaucer, vol. vi. p. 310, will be found the line—

   'Paradise yettis all opin be throu the,'

where the person addressed is the Virgin Mary. The idea seems to have been taken from St. Jerome ; see Migne's edition, vol. xi. coll. 127, 141.

625. *To late wel by thiselue,* to think much of thyself ; cf. l. 620.

627. *Seuene sustren,* seven sisters. To counteract the seven deadly sins, seven Christian virtues were enumerated by early theologians. Thus, in the Ayenbite of Inwyt (ed. Morris, p. 159) we find this list. ' Boȝsamnesse, a-ye [*against*] Prede. Loue, a-ye Enuye. Mildenesse, a-ye Felhede. Prouesse, a-ye Slacnesse. Largesse, a-ye Scarsnesse. Chastete, a-ye Lecherie. Sobrete, a-ye Glotounye.' See note to l. 62 above, where all the 'seven sisters' are mentioned except 'Peace,' who takes the place of Business.

638. *But grace be the more,* unless mercy be extended.

639. *Cutpurs,* thief. On cut-purses, see Chambers' Book of Days, ii. 669.

641. *Wite God,* God defend us, God protect us, an old oath ; quite distinct from the expression *God wot,* God knows. See *Witen* in the Glossary.

644. *Mercy* is identified here with the Virgin Mary, as in the quotation at l. 612.

651. *Where thei bicome.* The modern equivalent phrase is—' where they are gone to,' or ' what has become of them.' Cf. the first line of the next Passus.

PASSUS VI.

2. *Eche a fote,* each foot of the way, every step of the way.

4. *Erye,* to plough. Cf. Chaucer, Knightes Tale, l. 28—

   ' I have, God wot, a large feeld to *ere.*'

9. *For shedyng,* to prevent spilling. Cf. note to l. 62.

19. *For the lordes loue of heuene* ; for love of the Lord of heaven. Observe the difference of arrangement. So, in Chaucer, Sq. Tale, l. 209, *the Grekes hors Sinon,* is *the hors of Sinon the Greek.* Cf. l. 223 below.

28. Lord Cobham, speaking of the duties of knights, said—' They ought also to preserve God's people from oppressors, tyrants, and thieves ; and to

see the Clergy supported, so long as they teach purely, pray rightly, and minister the sacraments freely.'—Southey's Book of the Church, p. 204. Cf. Gower, Conf. Amant. iii. 380 (ed. Pauli); Wyclif's Works, ed. Arnold, iii. 206.

40. 'And if you fine any man, let mercy assess the fine;' i. e. let it be a light one.

50. *Yuel*, difficult, hard; so *yuel to defye*=hard to digest, in Pass. v. l. 121. All are equal in the grave.

54. *Harlotes*, ribalds; a term generally applied to tellers of loose stories, whence our author calls them 'the devil's *diseurs*,' i. e. the devil's story-tellers. They held forth in the hall 'atte mete,' whilst their employers were eating. They were *men*, as said in l. 55. See Warton's Hist. of Eng. Poet. i. 68 (ed. 1840).

62. *For colde*, as a remedy *against* cold. *For* very often has this sense of *against*. Cf. i. 24, and Chaucer's Sir Thopas, B. 2052.

69. *Maugre*, &c., 'in spite of any one who grumbles about it.'

72. *Iogeloure*, juggler; Lat. *joculator*. See Tyrwhitt's note to Chaucer, C. T. l. 11453. 'The name of *Jogelour* was, in a manner, appropriated to those, who, by sleight of hand and machines, produced such illusions of the senses as are usually supposed to be effected by enchantment. This species of *jogelour* is [also] called a *Tregetour*.' Cf. Chaucer's House of Fame, iii. 169—

> 'There saugh I pleyen *jugelours*,
> Magiciens, and *tregetours*,' &c.

Tyrwhitt's note is long and full. Se also Ritson, Metrical Romances, i. p. ccv. of Preface, where he insists that *jougleour* ought never to be misspelt *jongleur*, as is often done. This, however, is a question of date; *jongleur* occurs frequently in later French than that in which we find *jougleur*; the *n* was inserted, as in *langouste* from *locustum*, *concombre* from *cucumerem*. And compare—

> 'There myghtist thou se these flowtours,
> Mynstrales, and eke *jogelours*,
> That wel to synge dide her peyne.'
>
> Romaunt of the Rose, 763.

Jack Juggler is the name of a play, in Dodsley's Old Plays, ed. Hazlitt, vol. ii.

77. 'Deleantur de libro viventium, et cum iustis non scribantur,' Ps. lxviii. 29 (Vulgate). The last part of the quotation William interprets to mean that churchmen ought not to receive tithes from such people.

79. *They ben ascaped*, &c. Dr. Whitaker paraphrases this by—'they have escaped payment by good luck'—which is probably right. For *auenture* the Vernon MS. reads *thrift*, success.

84. Here Piers again begins speaking. *Late god yworth*, may God be.

88. Lines 88—101 contain Piers' *biqueste*, i. e. his will. It begins with a common formula—*In dei nomine*. He bequeaths his soul to his Maker, his body to the church to which he paid tithes, his money to his wife and chil-

dren. Whitaker remarks upon this passage—'To commit the soul to Him who made it, was, in the course of a century and a half after this time, accounted so heretical, that the church would not have kept the testator's bones. For this very offence, and for omitting the names of the Virgin Mary and other saints, as joint legatees, the body of a Mr. Tracy was dug up out of his grave.' See Tracie's will, in Massingberd, Eng. Ref. p. 165; also in Chambers' Book of Days, ii. 429.

94. *He*, i. e. the *persona ecclesiae*, the parson.

97. *Memorye*, commemoration of benefactors.

102. For *Lukes*, MSS. of the A-type have *Chestre*; cf. Pass. v. 467. *Lukes* is Lucca, formerly also spelt *Luca*, where there was a famous cross.

105. The definition of *plough-foot*, as given in Fitzherbert's Boke of Husbandry, fol. 2 back, is as follows:—'The *plough-fote* is a lyttell pece of wodde, with a croked ende set before in a morteys in the ploughe-beame, sette fast with wedges, to dryue vppe and downe, and it is a staye to order of what depenes the ploughe shall go.' In a modern plough, small wheels take the place of it. I am indebted for this reference to Dr. Morris, who has kindly contributed many useful hints, much to the improvement of the present edition of this work.

107. *Perkyn*, little Piers or Peter ; the same as Peterkin. It is merely a familiar term for Piers in this passage.

114. *High prime.* This expression is copied in a poem by Lydgate, which is better known, perhaps, than any other of his, named 'The London Lick-peny :'

> 'Then to Westmynster gate I presently went,
>   When the sonn was at *hyghe pryme.*'
>   Specimens of English, ed. Skeat, p. 25.

It seems to mean, when *prime was ended*, and it certainly marks the first break in the day's work. *Prime* is commonly explained to mean six in the morning, but Cotgrave explains it as the first hour of the artificial day (or day according to the sun) which begins at about 8 in winter, 4 in summer, and at 6 only at the equinoxes. Again, some explain *prime* to be the *fourth part* of the natural day, viz. from 6 to 9 A.M. always; see Tyrwhitt's note, Cant. Tales, l. 3904. But putting together the various passages where Chaucer uses the word *prime*, I have shewn, in my edition of Chaucer's Astrolabe, p. lxii, that the term was commonly used in the sense suggested by Tyrwhitt, viz. as meaning the period from 6 to 9 A.M.; but, when restricted to a particular moment, it meant the *end* of that period, or 9 A.M. only. It was probably to obviate the vagueness in the use of the word that *high prime* is the term employed here; it doubtless signifies that the period of prime was ended, or that it was nine o'clock. Perhaps the same thing is expressed by the term *fully prime*, in Chaucer's Sir Thopas (Group B, 2015); whilst a little past the hour of nine is denoted by *prime large* in the Squyeres Tale, l. 360. Mr. Dyce says—'concerning this word see Du Cange's Gloss. in

Prima and Horæ Canonicæ, Tyrwhitt's Gloss. to Canterbury Tales, Sibbald's Gloss. to Chron. of Scot. Poetry, and Sir F. Madden's Gloss. to Syr Gawayne.' See also Timbs, Nooks and Corners of English Life, p. 222. It is clear from ll. 115 and 116, that Piers was a 'head harvest-man.' See Knight's Pictorial Hist. of England, i. 840; and a good article on the duties of a ploughman in Chambers' Book of Days, i. 96.

117. *Atte nale* = *atten ale* or *at then ale*, i. e. at the ale. In the same way *atten ende* (at the end) was afterwards corrupted into *at the nende*. See Warton, Hist. E. P., vol. ii. p. 79, note.

118. 'How! trollilolli' is the burden of a song, answering nearly to the modern *tol de rol*. In Ritson's Ancient Songs, vol. ii. p. 7, is a song, with a burden of *trolly loley* occurring at every third line. In the Chester Plays (ed. Wright, p. 136) when the shepherds sing, we find the direction—'Singe *troly loly, troly loe*.' Here is meant, that all which some of the men did towards ploughing the half acre was to sit and sing choruses over their cups.

122. *Haue that reccheth*, take him who cares. *Reccheth* = recketh.

123. *Feyned hem blynde*. Compare—'Also Fryers saien, that it is meedful to leaue the commandement of Christ, of giving of alms to poore feble men, to poore crooked men, to poore blinde men, and to bedredden men, and giue this almes to Hypocrits, that fainen hem holie and needie.'— Wycliffe; Two Treatises against Friers, p. 25.

147. 'The day's work was supposed to be completed at the ninth hour— three in the afternoon according to our reckoning. This hour was called *high noon*, and the meal then taken was called a noonshun or nuncheon.' —Timbs; Nooks and Corners, &c., p. 222. It is certain that *nones* originally meant about three o'clock in the afternoon at the equinoxes, but it was afterwards shifted so as to mean midday, our modern *noon* See Wedgwood, s. v. *Noon*. There seem to have been two principal mealtimes, viz. dinner at about nine or ten A.M., and supper at about five or six P.M.; cf. ll. 262, 265. See Wright's Hist. of Domestic Manners, p. 155. But there is here reference to the *one* meal at twelve o'clock, to which anchorites and hermits restricted themselves. In this they adopted the rule for *fasting-days*, viz. to have dinner at twelve instead of nine, and no supper.

151. *Posteles*, apostles, i. e. preachers, probably preaching friars. Not to be confused with *postills*, i. e. commentaries, which were things preached.

163. *Wolveskynnes*, of the kind or nature of a wolf. Cf.
    'Thei ben wilde werwolves · that wiln the folk robben.'
                                        P. Ploughman's Crede, l. 459.

164. *That ilke while worth*, &c., in the meanwhile there will be no abundance, &c. *Worth*, lit. becomes; but it is often used as a future. *Liggeth*, lies idle.

171. 'And accounted Piers at the value of a pea;' i. e. set him at naught

191. 'And cut their copes, and made them into jackets.' 'They had also,' says Camden (Remains, p. 234, or p. 196, ed. 1657), 'a gowne called

a *git*, a jacket without sleeves called a *haketon*, a loose jacket like a *tabard*, a short gabbardin called a *courtpie*, a gorget called a *chevesail*, for as yet they used no bandes about their necke; a pouche called a *gipser*,' &c. Strutt, Manners and Customs, ii. 85. It was easier to work in jackets.

196. *Bayarde*, a common name for a horse, and used by Chaucer. The passage refers to the custom of giving horses *bread* to eat, as is still common on the continent. Cf. l. 217. A statute of Edward III orders—that horse-bread be made only of beans and peas, without other mixture. The making of horsebread was formerly a regular part of a baker's business. See Toulmin Smith's English Gilds, p. 366.

203. *Owne erde*, native place or country. Cf. A.S. ' on þínum *earde*,' in thine own country; Luke iv. 23. Not the same word as *erthe* (earth).

214. *Make hem to worche.* After the pestilence of 1349, there was a want of labourers. Edward published a proclamation, compelling men and women, in good health, and under sixty years of age, to work at stated wages. But it was evaded, and, in harvest-time especially, exorbitant wages were both demanded and given. See Lingard, Hist. Eng. (3rd ed.) iv. 89, and Liber Albus, pp. 584, 634.

218. *Abate*, keep them thin. *For bollyng*, to prevent swelling; as in l. 62.

224. *Lene hem*, give to them; lit. lend to them. *Alter alterius*, &c.: Gal. vi. 2.

226. *Naughty*, having naught—

> 'She had an idea from the very sound
> That people *with naught* were *naughty*.'

> Hood; Miss Kilmansegg.

228. *Late god yworthe*, let God alone; cf. Prol. 187. *Michi vindicta*, &c.: Rom. xii. 19. *Vindictam* is the reading of the MSS.; the reading of the Vulgate is *vindicta*. But the passage is often quoted with the reading *vindictam*. See Ancren Riwle, pp. 184, 286.

230. Cf. Luke xvi. 9.

238. 'Propter frigus piger arare noluit; mendicabit ergo æstate, et non dabitur illi;' Prov. xx. 4. *Sapience* means the book of Wisdom; William frequently refers to the wrong book of the Bible for his quotations.

240. *With mannes face.* An allusion to a common representation of the evangelists, which likens Matthew to a *man* (sometimes represented by a *man's face only*), Mark to a *lion*, Luke to a *bull*, and John to an *eagle*; Rev. iv. 7. Sometimes the arrangement varied; see the Ormulum, ed. White, vol. i. p. 201.

241. *Nam*, a mina. It is glossed in the Laud MS. by the words—' a besaunt,' which is the word used in Wyclif's version; Luke xix. 16. The parable occurs both in Matt. xxv. and Luke xix.; but the use of the word *nam* shews that our author was thinking rather of St. Luke's account, where

the word μνᾶ is used. In l. 243 we have the better spelling *mnam*. For the value of a *besant*, see Ormulum, ed. White, ii. 390.

251. Richard Rolle de Hampole, amongst others, carefully distinguishes between *active life*, or *bodily* service of God, and *contemplative life* or *ghostly* (i.e. spiritual) service. See his prose treatises, ed. Perry (E. E. T. S. 1866), p. 19 ; and see p. xi. of Mr. Perry's preface.

252. 'Beati omnes, qui timent Dominum, qui ambulant in viis eius. Labores manuum tuarum quia manducabis : beatus es, et bene tibi erit.' Ps. cxxvii. 1, 2 (Vulgate).

269. *Afyngred*, greatly hungry. It is corrupted from the A.S. *of-hingrian*, to be very hungry. The word occurs in the Vox and Wolf, in Hazlitt's Early Popular Poetry, vol. i. p. 58 (also printed in Reliquiæ Antiquæ, ii. 272, from MS. Digby 86), where the fox is described as *afingret*.

272. Cf.

> 'And ȝit ther is another craft that toucheth the clergie,
> That ben thise false fisiciens that helpen men to die,' &c.
>
> Polit. Songs (Camd. Soc.), p. 333.

See Chaucer's Prologue, ll. 411-444, where the Doctour of Phisik is described. A 'cloke of calabre' means a cloke trimmed with Calabrian fur. In the Coventry Mysteries, p. 242, we read—'Here colere splayed, and furryd with ermyn, *calabere*, or satan.' A person who wore an amice trimmed with calabere was *himself* called a 'calaber amyse,' as appears from an extract from a Chapter Minute of Christ Church, Dublin, quoted in Todd's introduction to The Book of Obits, &c. of Christ Church, p. xcii. Cf. Notes and Queries, 3rd S. vol. xi. It appears that calabre was a *grey* fur, the belly of which was *black*.—Riley, Memorials of London, p. 329.

282. 'In the parish of Hawsted, Suffolk, the allowance of food to the labourer in harvest was, two herrings per day, milk from the manor dairy to make cheese, and a loaf of bread, of which fifteen were made from a bushel of wheat. Messes of potage made their frequent appearance at the rustic board.'—Knight, Pict. Hist. of England, i. 839.

287. We find mention of 'colopys of venyson' and 'colypes of the wyld dere' in Hazlitt's Early Pop. Poetry, vol. i. pp. 24, 28. Brand says, 'Slices of this kind of meat (i.e. salted and dried) are to this day termed *collops* in the north, whereas they are called *steaks* when cut off from fresh or unsalted flesh.'—Pop. Antiq. vol. i. p. 62.

291. *Lammasse*, i.e. Loaf-mass, Aug. 1. In Anglo-Saxon times, a *loaf* was offered on this day, as an offering of first-fruits. See Chambers' Book of Days, ii. 154.

306. 'Panis de *coket*' is mentioned in a MS. of Jesus Coll. Oxford, 1 Arch. i. 29, fol. 268, as being slightly inferior to *wastel* bread. The fine kinds of white bread were called simnel bread or *pain demaigne* (Chaucer's Sir Thopas, l. 14), wastel bread, coket, clere matyn, and manchet bread. The common kinds of brown bread were tourte, trete, and bis.

Cf. Riley, Memorials of London, p. 644; Chambers' Book of Days, i. 119; Andrew Boorde's Introduction of Knowledge, ed. Furnivall, pp. 258-282; and see *Coket* in the Glossary.

307. *Halpeny ale.* See note to Pass. v. 220, and cf. l. 311 below.

314. As to the high wages of labourers, see note to l. 214 above. The statutes concerning them are alluded to in l. 318 below.

316. Dionysius Cato is the name commonly assigned to the author of a Latin work in four books, entitled Dionysii Catonis Disticha de Moribus ad Filium. The real author is unknown, but the work may perhaps be referred to the fourth century. It was very popular, both in Latin, and in English and French versions. William here quotes part of the 21st distich of the first book, which runs thus :—

> 'Infantem nudum quum te natura crearit,
> Paupertatis onus patienter ferre memento.'

324. *Water,* i. e. floods ; cf. l. 326.

327. Great disasters were often attributed to the malign influence of the planet Saturn. Besides this, great foresight was attributed to the god Saturn. This is very well illustrated by Chaucer's Knightes Tale, ll. 1585-1620. In the A-text (earliest version), the Passus ends with this line. Ll. 328-332 were added afterwards; in them William imitates, not perhaps without ridicule, the mysterious prophecies which were then popular ; such as, for instance, the prophecies of John of Bridlington. Lines 328, 329, are, of course, inexplicable, but the rest is clear enough. By *deth* is meant such a great pestilence as that which earned the name of the Black Death. The pestilence shall withdraw, Famine shall then be the judge, and Dawe the ditcher (cf. Pass. v. 320) shall die for hunger, unless God grant us a truce. As regards famines and dearths, cf. Polit. Songs (Camd. Soc.), p. 399.

PASSUS VII.

1. This Passus is called *Passus Octavus* in MSS. of the earliest version.

3. *A pœna et culpa.* On this expression see Milman, Hist. of Lat. Christianity, vi. 254 (note), 2nd edit. ; and the note to Wyclif's Works, ed. Arnold, i. 136. See l. 19 below, where it means *plenary* remission.

14. *Bothe the lawes;* referring (perhaps) to the civil and canon laws.

17. ' To sit at the high daïs,' i. e. in a seat of honour.

18. *Many yeres,* i. e. many years' remission of purgatory.

23. *Treuthe,* i. e. God the Father, as before. See l. 33.

26. *Mesondieux,* put for *maisons de dieu,* houses of God. A hospital was called a *maison-dieu* or *masondewe.* Halliwell remarks that, till within the last few years, there was an ancient hospital at Newcastle so called. There was another, I believe, at Ospringe, Kent.

27. *Wikked wayes,* bad roads. See Pass. vi. 1.

31. *Sette scoleres to scole.* To pay for the education of poor scholars, especially at Oxford, was justly esteemed an excellent form of charity. Cf. Chaucer, Prol. 301, 302. In later times, the demand of poor scholars for money was a tax that fell rather heavily upon the poorer class of farmers.

'Than commeth clerkys of Oxford and make their mone,
To her scole hire they most haue money.'

God Spede the Plough, 75.

33. It was thought that 'unto Michael alone belonged the office of leading each soul from earth to the judgment-seat of Christ;' Rock, Church of our Fathers, iii. 149, and 210.

41. 'Qui pecuniam suam non dedit ad usuram, et munera super innocentem non accepit.' Ps. xiv. 5 (Vulgate). The first verse of the same Psalm, which in English Bibles is Ps. xv., is quoted below, at l. 51.

43. I do not know the source of this quotation. It somewhat resembles Ecclus. xxxviii. 2—'A Deo est enim omnis medela, et a rege accipiet donationem.'

44. *Johan* is apparently some unscrupulous fellow of middle rank, not John of Gaunt. In Pass. xxii. 288, it is the name of a cook.

50. 'No devil, at his death-day, shall harm him a mite, so that he may not be safe, and his soul too.' *Worth* is here a verb; the construction is awkward to express. It was believed that dying men beheld devils all around them. Cf. Hampole's Prick of Conscience. ll. 2220–2233.

52. 'But to buy water, nor wind, nor wit, nor fire (which is the fourth thing) *is a thing which Holy Writ never permitted.*' The words italicised must be understood; they occur in the A-text. For *ne*, i. e. nor, we should now write *or*. *Wit* here takes the place of *earth*, along with three of the four elements.

56. *Thei*, i. e. they who take fees from the poor; see l. 58.

61. See Matt. vii. 12; cf. Luke vi. 31.

62. *With*, i. e. by means of.

68. *Bit;* a contracted form of *biddeth*, i. e. begs.

73. *Catoun*, Cato. See note to Pass. vi. 316. Prefixed to Cato's Distiches are some 'Breves sententiæ,' of which the twenty-third consists only of the words—*Cui des, videto*. Mr. Wright says that by *the clerk of the stories* is meant Peter Comestor (died about 1198), to whom Lydgate, in his Minor Poems (p. 102, ed. Halliwell) gives the title of *maister of storyes*. The title *clerk of stories* refers to the Historia Scholastica, of which Peter Comestor was the author. The passage referred to is one in which Peter Comestor abridges the passage in the book of Tobit, iv. 7–11. There are remarks on almsgiving, very similar to this, in the Compendium by Peter Cantor, who was bishop of Tournay, A.D. 1191 : they may be found at p. 150, vol. 205, of Migne's Patrologiæ Cursus Completus. Peter Cantor also quotes the sentence—*cui des, videto*. Cf. 'Circumstantiæ eleemosynarum hæ sunt—quis, quid, quantum, cui, ubi, quando, quare;' Alani de Insulis

Apertly, *adv.* openly, in an open manner, evidently, 3. 256. Lat. *apertus*, open.

Apewarde, *sb.* S. a keeper of apes, 5. 640.

Apeyre, *v.* to injure, 6. 173 ; 2 *p. pl. subj.* Apeyre, 5. 573. Cf. F. *empirer*, to impair, make worse, from Lat. *peius*, worse.

Apoysounde, *pp.* F. poisoned, 3. 127. MS. T. has *enpoisoned;* MS. Bodley 814 has *apoisoned.* *Enpoysened* occurs in Allit. Poems, ed. Morris, B. 242.

Apparaille, *v.* F. to apparel, 2. 170, 6. 59 ; *pt. pl.* Apparailed, pr. 23 ; *pp.* Apparailled, 5. 523. O.F. *aparailler*, to make to suit, from *pareil*, equal, which from Low Lat. *pariculus*, a diminutive of *par.*

Appayre, 3 *p. pl. pr. subj.* injure, 5. 47. See **Apeyre.**

Appeireth, *pr. s.* injures, 7. 47; *pt. pl.* Appeyred, 6. 134 ; *pp.* 6. 221. See **Apeyre.**

Appendeth, *pr. s.* belongs, 1. 45. From Lat. *pendeo.*

Appertly, *adv.* openly, evidently, 1. 98. See **Apertly.**

Appiere, *v.* F. to appear, 3. 113.

Appose, *v.* F. to put questions to, 3. 5 ; *pt. s.* or *pl.* Apposed, 1. 47 ; *pt. pl.* Apposeden, disputed, *as in* Apposeden eyther other, disputed one against the other, 7. 138.

Ar, *adv.* S. ere, before, 1. 73, 3. 120, &c. A.S. *ǽr*, G. *eher*, Mœso-Goth. *air*, which agrees with the root of *early.* Though generally called an adverb, it is frequently a conjunction.

Ar, cont. form of Aren, are, 6. 100. See **Aren.**

Arches, *sb. pl.* used to mean the Court of Arches, 2. 60. 'The Court of Arches is an ancient court of appeal, belonging to the Archbishop of Canterbury, where-

of the judge is called the Dean of *Arches*, because he anciently held his court in the church of St. Mary-le-Bow (*Sancta Maria de Arcubus*) ; though all the spiritual courts are now holden at Doctors' Commons.' (Hook's Church Dict.)

Aredy, *adj.* S. ready, 4. 192. Cf. A.S. *geràd*, ready, which is a fuller form of *ràd*, a form not used.

Aren, 3. *p. pl. pr.* are, pr. 164, 3. 80, 4. 33, 5. 626. See **Be.**

Arest, at rest ; lit. *on* rest, 5. 234. See **A,** and cf. **Aslepe.**

Armes, *pl. sb.* F. coat-armour, 5. 508. *In owre armes* = with our device upon His coat of arms.

Armure, *sb.* F. armour, 1. 156.

Arne, 3. *p. pl. pr.* are, 1. 21. See **Aren** and **Be.**

Arraye, *sb.* F. array, dress, 2. 17.

Arraye, *v.* F. to set in order; hence, Arraye me, prepare myself, 4. 15 ; Arrayen hym, prepare himself, 5. 11. O. Fr. *arroier*, from sb. *roi*, order, which is from the same root as A.S. *geràd*, ready, and M.H.G. *reiten*, Mœso-Goth. *raidjan*, to set in order.

Arrere, *adv.* F. backwards, 5. 354. Lat. *retro.*

Arst, *adv. superl.* S. erst, first, soonest, 4. 105, 5. 468. See **Ar.**

Artow, art thou, 5. 260.

Arwes, *sb. pl.* S. arrows, 3. 323. A.S. *arwe*, an arrow.

Ascapen, *v.* F. to escape, 2. 202; *pp.* Ascaped, 6. 79. O.F. *eschapper*, Picard *escaper.* See *échapper* in Brachet.

Askes, *sb. pl.* S. ashes, 3. 97. A.S. *asce*, *pl. ascan.*

Askeþ, *pr. s.* S. asks, requires, pr. 19, 120. See **Axe.**

Aslepe, asleep, lit. *on* sleep, 2. 51, 5. 8.

Aspye, *v.* F. to espy, to spy out, 5. 170. Derived from a Teutonic source; cf. O.H.G. *spehon*, G. *spähen*, to spy, Lat. *specere*.

Assaye, *v.* F. to try, examine, 3. 5, 5. 310; to try, endeavour, 6. 24. From Lat. *exagium*, a proof; which from *exigere*, to examine.

Assele, *1 p. s. pr.* F. I seal, 2. 112. O.F. *seel*, Lat. *sigillum*.

Assemble, *sb.* F. assembly, pr. 217. Lat. *assimulare*, from *simul*, together; cf. A.S. *sam*, *samod*, together, whence *samnian*, to collect.

Assoile, *v.* F. to absolve, 3. 40; Assoilen, pr. 70; Assoille, 5. 276; *pt. s.* Assoiled, 3. 47; Assoilled, 5. 186; *pp.* Assoiled, 3. 142; *pr. s.* Assoileth, 3. 236. O.F. *assoiler*, *absoiller*, Lat. *absoluere*.

Asspye, *v.* F. to espy, see, 6. 131, 225. See **Aspye**.

Asswage, *v.* F. to assuage, soothe, subdue, 5. 122. From O.F. *assouager*, formed from O.F. *soef*, Lat. *suauis*, sweet, soft (Burguy).

At, *prep.* S. (used where we should now use *of*), 3. 25; (used for *in*) 7. 128. At ones, at once, together, 5. 163.

Attache, *v.* F. to arrest, apprehend, 2. 199; *pp.* Attached, 2. 236. Low G. *tacke*, Bret. *tach*, a nail; cf. Bret. *tacha*, to fasten with a nail; It. *attaccare*, to fasten, E. *tack* (a small nail).

Atte, at the; *as in* Atte mele, 1. 24; Atte dore, 2. 205; Atte stile, 5. 201, &c. Cf. note to 6. 117.

Atweyne, in twain, lit. on twain, 7. 116. The A.S. for *two* is *twegen* in the masc., *twá* in the feminine. (So G. *zween* masc., *zwei* fem.) Hence E. *twain* and *two*.

Atwo, in two, 6. 105. See the preceding word.

Auarousere, *pl. adj.* F. more avaricious, 1. 189. Lat. *auarus*.

Auaunced, *pp.* F. advanced, 1. 189, 3. 33. F. *avancer*, It. *avanzare*,

from Lat. *ab ante*, which gives the It. *avanti* or *avante*, before.

Auenture, *sb.* F. adventure, chance; hence good auenture = by good luck, 6. 79. An auenture, in case, 3. 72, 279; 6. 43; *better written* On auenture, 3. 66.

Auncere, *sb.* a kind of weighing machine, 5. 218. It is spelt *auncere*, *auncer*, *aunser*, *auncel*, and *aunsel* in the MSS. From the descriptions by Cowell (in Halliwell) and Phillips, it may be the steelyard commonly known as the 'Danish steelyard,' which has a fixed weight and a moveable fulcrum. Probably from *lanx*; whence *launcere = l'auncere*.

Auoutrie, *sb.* F. adultery, 2. 175. Lat. *adulterium*, whence O.F. *avulterie*, *avouterie*.

Auowe, *sb.* F. vow, 5. 457. Not derived from F. sb. *veu*, but from the vb. *avouer*. See next word.

Avowe, *v.* to make oath concerning, 3. 255; *pt. s.* Avowed, made a vow, 5. 388. From Low Lat. *aduoare*, which from Low Lat. *uotare*, to vow; which from Lat. *uouere*.

Auter, *sb.* F. altar, 5. 109.

Au3te, *sb.* S. *put for* something, 5. 439; everything, 5. 489. Used adverbially, in the sense of *at all*, 5. 311, 540. A.S. *áwiht*, from *á*, ever, and *wiht*, a whit; cf. O.H.G. *eowiht*, from *eo* or *io*, ever, and *wiht*. See **Nau3te**.

Au3te, *1 p. s. pt.* I ought, 2. 28. A.S. *ic áhte*, I owned, possessed, from *ágan*, to own. Cf. Mœso-Goth. *aigan*, to own. pr. t. *ik aih*, I own, pt. t. *ik aihta*, I owned. Note that M.E. *owe*, to possess, is the mod. E. *own*. To *owe* a debt is to *have* to pay it. See **Owe**, **Owen**.

Awreke, *imp. s.* S. revenge, take vengeance on, 6. 175; *pp.* Awroke,

avenged, 6. 204. A.S. *áwrecan*, to avenge ; cf. Mœso-Goth. *wrikan*, *wrakjan*, to persecute, Du. *wreken*, G. *rächen*, E. *wreak*.

Axe, *v.* S. to ask, 4. 102 ; Axen, *v.* 5. 543 ; *pr. pl. subj.* Axe, 5. 430 ; *pr. s.* Axeth, 2. 27 ; *pt. s.* Axed, 1. 49, 5. 307, 6. 298. A.S. *ácsian*, *áxian*, *áhsian*, *áscian*, to ask.

Ay, *adv.* S. aye, ever, 6. 212. A.S. *á*, *aa*, O.H.G. *eo*, G. *je*, ever.

Aȝein, *prep.* S. against, 3. 155, 291 ; in a direction opposite to ; *hence*, come aȝein = came to meet, 4. 44 ; in return for, 5. 437. *Spelt* Ayein, 3. 291. See Aȝeines.

Aȝein, *adv.* S. again, 6. 44, 7. 25.

Aȝeines, *prep.* against, 4. 48, 6. 316, 7. 70 ; Aȝeins, 3. 92. A.S. *ongeán*, is both *adv.* (*again*) and *prep.* (*against*). We do not find *ongeánes*, but we find *togeánes*, *prep.* against. Cf. Su. Goth. *gen*, against, *gena*, to go to meet, G. *gegen*, against.

B.

Babeled, 1 *p. s. pt.* I babbled, said my prayers in a mumbling manner, 5. 8. Du. *babbelen*, to chatter ; Fr. *babiller*. A word formed from the repetition of the syllables *ba*, *ba*, by a child. Cf. **Mamely**.

Baberlipped, *adj.* having full, large, thick lips, 5. 190. Cf. Fr. *babines*, the lips, Du. *babbel*, the mouth. Formed from the sound *ba*, made by the lips. See word above.

Bachelers, *sb. pl.* F. novices in the church, pr. 87. A *bacheler* is a novice, generally in arms or arts. From Low Lat. *baccalarius*, a cowherd, or man attached to a *baccalaria*, or grazing-farm, so named from Low Lat. *bacca*, a cow = Lat. *uacca* (Brachet). In like manner the French *berger*, a

shepherd, is the Low Lat. *berbecarius*, from *berbex = ueruex*, a sheep.

Bad. See Bidde.

Baiardes, *sb. pl.* F. horses, 4. 124. *Bayard* was a favourite name for horses, and originally meant a *bay*-horse, from Lat. *badius*, brown, whence Fr. *bai*.

Bailliues, *sb. pl.* F. bailiffs, 2. 59. Lat. *baiulus*, a tutor, O. F. *baillir*, to take charge of.

Bakbite, *v.* S. to backbite, slander, 2. 80. *Back* frequently means in the wrong direction, as in M.E. *back-friend*, a secret enemy, *back-slide*, to slide into error. Cf. Icel. *bakborði*, the left side of a ship.

Bakbitynge, *sb.* S. slander, 5. 89.

Bake, *pp.* S. baked, 6. 196 ; Baken, *pp.* 6. 295.

Bakesteres. See Baxteres.

Balder, *adj. comp.* S. bolder, 4. 107 ; 7. 183. A.S. *beald*, bold, Mœso-Goth. *balthaba*, boldly, O. H. G *balt*, bold.

Bale, *sb.* S. evil, injury, wrong, 4. 89, 92. A.S. *bealo*, torment, wickedness, Mœso-Goth. *balwjan*, to torment.

Balkes, *sb. pl.* S. balks, 6. 109. ' *Balk*, a ridge of greensward left by the plough in ploughing, or by design, between different occupancies in a common field.' (Halliwell). Cf. A.S. *balca*, (1) a heap, ridge ; (2) a beam. Icel. *bálkr*, a wooden division.

Banne, *v.* S. to curse, 1. 62 ; *pr. s.* Banneth, forbids, prohibits severely, 7. 88. Cf. G. *bann*, a ban.

Bar, *pt. s.* bore. See Bere.

Barne, *sb.* S. a child, 2. 3 ; *pl.* Barnes, 3. 151, 7. 92. A. S. *bearn*, Mœso-Goth. *barn*, Sw. *barn*, Sc. *bairn*. Cf. E. *bear*.

Barste, *pt. s.* S. burst, 6. 180. A.S. *berstan*, to burst, break ; pt. t. *ic bærst*, I burst.

Baslarde, *sb.* F. 3. 303. 'The *Baselard* was a kind of long dagger, which was suspended to the girdle . . . Knighton tells us that Sir Wm. Walworth put Jack Straw [? Wat Tyler] to death with a *bassilard*.'—Way, in note to Promptorium Parvulorum. It was also called a *badelaire*, which is perhaps connected with Low Lat. *balteus*, a belt, which is also the root of E. *bauldric*, *bawdric*, or *baldrick*. See also the note.

Batailles, *sb. pl.* F. battles, 3. 321.

Batered, 1 *p. s. pt.* I battered, I patted, 3. 198. It is the frequentative of *beat*, which is represented both by A.S. *beátan* and F. *battre*.

Baudy, *adj.* dirty, 5. 197. W. *baw*, dirt, *bawaidd*, dirty.

Baxteres, *sb. pl.* S. bakers (properly *female* bakers), pr. 218; Bakesteres, 3. 79. A.S. *bæcere*, a man who bakes; *bæcestre*, a woman who bakes.

Bayarde, *sb.* F. a horse, 6. 196; Bayard, 4. 53. See Baiardes.

Bayllyues, *sb. pl.* F. bailiffs, 3. 2. See Bailliues.

Be, *v.* S. to be, pr. 79, &c.; 1 *p. pl. pr.* we Beth, 3. 27; 2 *p.* 3e Ben, 6. 132; 3 *p.* they Ben, 6. 79; Aren, 3. 80; 2 *p. s. pr.* (*in future sense*) Beest, shalt be, 5. 598; 3 *p. pl.* Beth, shall be, 7. 66; *imp. pl.* 1 *p.* Be we, pr. 188; 2 *p.* Be 3e, 7. 183; *imp. pl.* (*without ye*) Beth, 2. 137; *pr. s. subj.* Be = if (my council) be, 4. 189; 2 *p.* Be þow = if thou be, 6. 207; *pt. s. subj.* Were, pr. 165; *pp.* Be, 5. 129, 155. Other parts of the verb present no forms worth notice. See Were. With A.S. *beón*, to be, cf. G. *ich bin*, I am, Lat. *fui*, I was, Gk. φῦναι, to be. With *I was*, cf. A.S. *ic wæs*, G. *ic war*, from A.S.

wesan, G. *wesen*, to be. With *we are*, cf. Icel. *vér erum*, and Lat. *esse*. The three Sanskrit roots are (1) *bhû*, (2) *vas*, (3) *as*; which seem to be distinct.

Be, *prep.* S. by, 5. 130.

Beau filtz, = fair son, 7. 162. Fr. *beau fils*.

Beches, *sb. pl.* S. beech-trees, 5. 18. The A.S. has both *béce* and *bóc*.

Bedel, *sb.* a beadle, apparitor, or summoner, 2. 109; *pl.* Bedelles, beadles, officers, 2. 59; Bedellus, 3. 2. O.F. *bedel*, a beadle, F. *bedeau*.

Bedeman, *sb.* S. one who prays for another, 3. 41, 46. Edie Ochiltree, in the 'Antiquary,' was a King's *Bedesman*. A.S. *gebed*, a prayer, Du. *bede*.

Bedered, S. bedridden, 7. 101. MS. T. has *bedreden*; MS. O. has *bedrede*. The latter is nearest to the A.S. *bedredda* or *bedrida*, one who is bedridden, from *bed* and *rida*, a rider; so that *bedridden* is an early corruption of *bedride*, having the sense of *bedrider*. We also find the spelling Bedreden, 6. 194.

Bedes, *sb. pl.* S. prayers, 5. 8, 407. To *bid one's beads* is, properly speaking, *to pray one's prayers*; but the name *beads* was afterwards transferred to the balls strung upon a string, by which the prayers were counted off. See Bedeman.

Beest, 2 *p. s. pr.* shalt be, 5. 598. The A.S. *beón*, to be, was most commonly used in a *future* sense; thus *þu eart* = thou art; *þu býst* = thou shalt be.

Behote, 1 *p. s. pr.* S. I promise, vow, 5. 462. A.S. *behátan*, to vow; cf. G. *heissen*, Du. *heeten*, Mœso-Goth. *haitan*, to name, call.

Beire, *gen. pl.* of both, 2. 66. It is a corruption of *begra*, the *gen. pl.* of A.S. *bá*, both.

Beiȝ, *sb.* S. an ornament for the neck, neck-ring, a sort of collar of bright metal, pr. 165, 176; *pl.* Biȝes, pr. 161. A.S. *beáh,* a neck-ring, a crown, any circular ornament; prob. from *búgan,* to bend, pt. t. *ic beáh.*

Belsabubbes, *gen. case,* Beelzebub's, 2. 130.

Bely, *sb.* S. belly, pr. **41.** MS. T. has the pl. *belies.*

Bely-ioye, *sb.* appetite, delight in food, lit. belly-joy, 7. 118.

Belye, *v.* S. to lie against, slander, 5. 414.

Bemeneth, *pr. s.* S. means, signifies, pr. 208. A.S. *mǽnan,* to intend, G. *meinen,* Du. *meenen,* Lat. *me-minisse,* Sanskrit *man,* to think, deem. Cf. Lat. *mens,* E. *mind.*

Ben, 3 *p. pl. pr.* they are, 6. 79. Observe the curious construction *it ben* = they are, 6. 56. So in the A.S. Gospels, *ic hit eom,* I it am (It is I), S. John vi, 20.

Benefys, *sb.* F. benefice, 3. 312.

Benes, *sb. pl.* S. beans, 6. 184.

Benfait, *sb.* F. a benefit, kind deed, 5. 436. F. *bien fait,* a thing well done.

Berde, *sb.* S. beard, 5. 194.

Bere, *imp. s.* S. bear, carry, 3. 268; *pt. s.* Bar, bare, 2. 3; Bare, 5. 524; **2** *p. s.* Bere, didst bear, 3. 195; *pt. pl.* Baren, 5. 108, 365; Bere, *pt. pl. subj.* 5. 139. A.S. *beran,* pt. t. *ic bær,* pl. *we bǽron,* pp. *boren.*

Berghe, *sb.* S. a hill, 5. 589. A.S. *beorg* or *beorh,* G. and Du. *berg.* Cf. Mœso-Goth. *bairgan,* to hide, A.S. *beorgan,* G. and Du. *bergen.*

Bernes, *sb. pl.* S. barns, 6. 186. A.S. *bærn* or *bern.* The derivation from *bere,* barley, and *ern,* a place, looks fanciful, but is sustained by the fact that the full forms *bere-ern,* and *ber-ern* are found in the Northumbrian glosses to Luke xii. 24.

Bernes, *gen. sing.* barn's, 4. 57 See the above.

Bestes, *sb. pl.* F. beasts. 6. 142 O. Fr. *beste,* whence F. *bête.*

Bete, *v.* S. to beat, 5. 33; Bet, *pr. s.* (contracted form of *beteth*) beats, 4. 59; *pt. s.* Bette, beat, 6. 180 A.S. *beátan,* to beat, pr. s. *bet,* he beats, pt. t. *ic beót.* This is a clear instance of a *strong* verb becoming a *weak* one at the date of the Laud MS., for the Vernon MS. has *he beot* in this very place.

Bete, *v.* S. to amend, satisfy, remedy, 6. 239. A.S. *bétan,* to make *better,* Du. *baten,* to avail, profit; from the root of *boot, better;* cf. Mœso-Goth. *batizo,* better, *batista,* best; also Sc. *beet,* used by Burns.

Beth, (1) we will be, 3. 27; (2) they shall be, 7. 66; (3) be ye, **2.** 137. See Be, Beest.

Beton, *proper name, dim.* of Bette, little Bat, 5. 306; spelt Betoun, 5. 33. Cf. *Kitoun, Ratoun.*

Bette, *adv.* S. better, 5. 601, 6. 49. A.S. *bet.*

Bette, *proper name,* Bat, 5. 330.

Bi, *prep.* S. by, 4. 134; in accordance with, 4. 70; with reference to, 4. 71, 5. 180 (cf. 1 Cor. iv. 4); By myself, as far as I am concerned, 4. 137; Bi my lyue, throughout my lifetime, 6. 103; Bi so, provided that, 5. 647; By þat, by that time, 6. 292, 301; according to that which, 7. 122. By þe bischop (pr. 80) may mean either with reference to the bishop, or by the bishop's permission. Mr. Aldis Wright takes the former view (Bible Word-book, p. 83); but the latter seems better. See the note.

Bicche, *sb.* S. bitch, 5. 353. A.S. *bicce.*

Bicome, *pt. pl.* 5. 651; where þei bicome = where they have gone to. It is also used as a past tense in

Joseph of Arimathie, ed. Skeat (E. E. T. S.) l. 607, in the phrase 'wher the white kniht *bicom*,' i. e. where the white knight had got to. Cf. A. S. *bicuman*, Du. *bijkomen*, to happen, G. *beikommen*, to reach to.

Bicometh to, *pr. s.* is suitable for, becomes, 3. 208. See the preceding word.

Bidde, *v.* S. to pray, 5. 231; to beg, 6. 239; 1 *p. s. pr.* Bidde, pray (see *Bedes*), 5. 407; *pr. s.* Biddeth, begs, 7. 81; Bit (contracted form of *biddeth*), begs, 7. 68; bids, commands. 3. 75; Bidden, *pr. pl.* beg, solicit, 3. 218; Bidde, *imp. s.* pray, 5. 454; Biddeth, *imp. pl.* beg ye, ask ye, pray ye, 5. 610, 7. 84; *pt. s.* Bad, commanded, 7. 5. A. S. *biddan*, to beg, to pray, Du. *bidden*, G. *bitten*, to beseech.

Bidders, *sb. pl.* S. beggars, pr. 40; *spelt* Bidderes, 6. 206; 7. 66. See Bidde.

Biddynge, *sb.* S. praying (to God), prayers, 3. 218. See Bidde.

Bidráueled, *pp.* S. slobbered, covered with grease, 5. 194. Cf. A. S. *drabbe*, dregs; Low G. *drabbelen*, to slobber, *drabbelbart*, one who dirties his beard in eating.

Bienfetes, *sb. pl.* F. (lit. benefits) good deeds, 5. 621. The phrase means 'presumption arising from trusting to your own good actions.'

Biennales, *sb. pl.* F. biennials, 7. 170. As *trentals* means a series of masses said daily for thirty days, so I suppose *biennales* to mean masses said for a space of two years, and *triennales* masses said for three years. They must have been expensive luxuries. Cf. the term *annuellere* in Chaucer.

Biernes, *sb. pl.* S. men, 3. 265. A. S. *beorn*, a chief, a man.

Bifalle, 3 *p. s. pr. subj.* S. it may befall, it may happen (*feire* being an adv. = well), 5. 59; *pr. s.* Bifalleth, belongs, 1. 52; *pt. s.* Bifel, happened, 5. 479, 7. 164.

Bifor, **Biforn**, *prep.* S. pr. 183, 7. 188. A. S. *biforan*.

Bigge, **Biggen**, *v.* S. to buy, 4. 89, 6. 282; 1 *p. s. pr.* Bigge, I buy, 5. 429. A. S. *bycgan*, to buy.

Bigileth, *pr. s.* beguiles, cheats, 7. 70. O. F. *guile*, from a Teutonic source; cf. A. S. *wile*, wiliness.

Bigruccheth, *pr. s.* begrudges, repines at, murmurs at, 6. 69. O. Fr. *grocer*, *groucher*, to murmur; cf. G. *grunzen*, to grunt.

Bihelde, 1 *p. s. pt.* S. I beheld, 7. 109.

Biheste, *sb.* S. promise, 3. 126. A. S. *behǽs*, a promise. Cf. next word.

Bihight, *pt. s.* S. promised, 3. 29. A. S. *behátan*, to vow, promise. See Behote.

Bihote, 1 *p. s. pr.* S. I promise, 6. 233. See Behote, Bihight.

Bihoueth, *pr. s.* S. needs, requires, (*not* impersonal) 5. 38. A. S. *behófian*, to need.

Bikenne, 1 *p. s. pr.* S. I commit (thee to Christ), 2. 49. See Kenne.

Biknowen, *v.* S. to acknowledge, confess, pr. 204; 1 *p. s. pr.* Biknowe, 5. 200; *pp.* Biknowen, acknowledged, well known, favourably received, 3. 33.

Bileue, *sb.* S. belief, creed, 5. 7, 7. 175. Cf. A. S. *geleáfa*, creed.

Bille, *sb.* F. a bill, petition, 4. 47. Mr. Wedgwood rightly connects it with *bull*, a *sealed* document, from Lat. *bulla*, Low Lat. *billa*, a leaden seal. The diminutive of it is the F. and E. *billet*.

Biloue (þe), *imp. s.* S. makes thyself beloved, 6. 230; *pp.* Biloued, beloved, 3. 211.

Bilowen, *pp.* S. told lies about, be-lied, 2. 22. A.S. *leógan,* to lie, pt. t. *ic leág,* pp. *logen.*

Binam, *pt. s.* S. took away from, 6. 243. A.S. *beniman,* to deprive. See **Nam.**

Biqueste, *sb.* S. bequest, will, 6. 87. A.S. *becweðan,* to bequeath ; from *cweðan,* to say. Cf. **Quod.**

Birde, *sb.* S. lady, 3. 14. Apparently the same as *bride,* A.S. *brýd ;* see *Burde* in Allit. Poems, ed. Morris, B. 653. Cf. M. E. *brid* for the modern word *bird.*

Bireue, *v.* S. bereave, take it away by force, 6. 248. A. S. *bereáfian,* from *reáfian,* to reave, rob. Cf. Du. *bercoven,* from *rooven,* to rob ; O. F. *rober,* Sp. *robar,* It. *rubare,* Dan. *röve,* to rob, Icel. *raufa.* Connected also with *robe.*

Bisette, *v.* S. to bestow, 5. 264, 299. A.S. *settan,* to set, place. Cf. O. Fries. *bisetta,* and see Chaucer, C. T. 3299, 7534.

Bishetten, *pt.pl.* S. shut up, 2. 213. A.S. *scyttan,* to shut up, *scyttels,* a bar, bolt.

Bisitte, *v.* S. to sit close to, beset, oppress, 2. 140. A.S. *bisittan,* to sit near, besiege.

Bisi, Bisy, *adj.* S. busy, 7. 118, 125.

Bislabered, *pp.* beslobbered, be-dabbled, dirty, 5. 392. G. *schlab-bern,* E. *slabber, slobber, slubber ;* cf. *slop.*

Bismer, *sb.* S. calumny, 5. 89. A.S. *bismer,* reproach ; from *bismerian,* to besmear (lit. to cover with fat, from A. S. *smero,* fat).

Biswynke, *v.* S. to obtain by work, to earn by labour, 6. 216. A.S. *swincan,* to toil.

Bit, short for Biddeth. See **Bidde.**

Bitelbrowed, *adj.* S. with beetling brows, having prominent brows, 5. 190. The A.S. *bitel* means the insect called a *beetle,* lit. the *biter ;* the M.E. adj. *bitel* means biting,

sharp ; hence perhaps the meaning of toothlike, projecting.

Bitter, *sb.* S. bitterness, 5. 119.

Bittere, *adv.* S. bitterly, 3. 249.

Bitwixen, *prep.* S. betwixt, amongst, 5. 338. A. S. *betwix, betwux,* be-tween; from *twá,* two, *twy,* double.

Bityme, *adv.* S. betimes, soon, 5. 647.

Bi3es. See **Bei3.**

Bi3ete, *sb.* S. offspring, 2. 40. From *bigitan,* to obtain; cf. modern E. *beget.*

Bi3unde, *adv.* S. beyond, 3. 109.

Blame, to, *gerund,* to blame, 7. 60.

Blenche, *v.* S. to blink, blench; hence, to flinch at, turn from, glance or turn aside, 5. 589. Cf. Du. *blinken,* to glitter, A.S. *blican,* to glitter, Sc. *blent,* a glance.

Blent, *pp.* S. blinded, 5. 502. A.S. *blendan,* to blind.

Blered, *pt. s.* made dim, blurred ; blered here eyes = cast a mist over their eyes, i. e. deceived them, pr. 74. Cf. Bavarian *plerren,* a blotch, *plerr,* a mist before the eyes. Probably only another spelling of *blurred.*

Blered, *pp.* bleared, sore, inflamed, 5. 191. Perhaps *blurred ;* but Mr. Wedgwood makes a difference be-tween this word and the preceding one. Cf. Low G. *bleeroged,* with red wet eyes.

Blisful, *adj.* S. full of happiness (which He bestows on others), 2.3.

Blissed, *pp.* S. rendered happy, filled with bliss, 5. 503. A.S. *blissian,* to make happy, which is distinct from *blétsian,* to bless.

Blo, *adj.* S. blue, livid, 3. 97.

Blody, related by blood, near akin, 6. 210.

Blosmed, *pt. pl.* S. blossomed, 5. 140. A.S. *blóstmian,* from *blóstma,* a blossom, bloom.

Blowen, *pp.* S. blown, 5. 18.

Blustreden, *pt. pl.* wandered blindly about, 5. 521. Very rare—but '*blustreden* as blynde,' = 'wandered about like blind people,' occurs in Alliterative Poems, B. 886; ed. Morris, 1864.

Bochere, *sb.* F. a butcher, 5. 330; *pl.* Bocheres, pr. 218, 3. 79.

Boden, *pp.* S, bidden, invited, 2. 54. See Bidde.

Boke, *sb.* S. book, 7. 85, 88.

Bolded, 1 *p. s. pt.* S. I emboldened, 3. 198.

Bolle, *sb.* S. bowl, wooden platter, 5. 108, 369, 526. A.S. *bolla.*

Bollyng, *sb.* S. swelling, 6. 218. For bollyng of her wombe = to prevent swelling of their bellies, to prevent their growing too fat. Cf. Dan. *bulne,* to swell, *bullen,* swollen. See next word.

Bolneth, *pr. s.* swells, 5. 119. See the preceding word.

Bolted, *pp.* S. supported by iron bands, 6. 138. A.S. *bolt,* an arrow; hence, a bar.

Bonched, *pt. s.* struck, lit. banged, pushed, knocked about, pr. 74. ' Bunchon, *tundo, trudo.*' Prompt. Parv. ' To bounche or pusshe one; he buncheth me and beateth me, *il me pousse.*' Palsgrave. Dan. *banke,* Du. *bonken,* to knock, rap.

Bondman, *sb.* S. peasant, 5. 194. A.S. *bónda,* a husbandman, Suio-Goth. and Dan. *bonde,* a peasant; from A.S. *búan,* Icel. *búa,* G. *bauen,* Du. *bouwen,* to till, of which Icel. *búandi, bóndi* was originally the present participle. Hence E. *boor* (from Du. *boer*), a tiller, peasant, *husband,* the manager of the house. No connection with *to bind.*

Bondemen, *pl.* of Bondman, q. v.; pr. 216, 6. 46.

Borde, *sb.* S. board, table, 6. 267.

Bores, *sb. pl.* S. boars, 6. 31.

Borghe, *sb.* S. borough, town, 2. 87, 6. 308.

Borghe, *sb.* S. pledge, security, 7. 82; Borwgh, surety, bail, 4. 89; *pl.* Borwes, 1. 77. A.S. *borh,* Du. *borg,* a pledge. Both this word and the preceding are from A.S. *beorgan,* to secure. See **Borwe.**

Bornes, *gen. s.* of Borne, *sb.* S. a brook, bourn, pr. 8. A.S. *burne,* Du. *borne,* a stream, spring, G. *brunnen.* Often confused with F. *borne,* a bound, limit, from a quite different root.

Borwe, *v.* S. to borrow, 5. 257; 1 *p. s. pr.* I borrow, or rather, I promise to pay, 5. 429; *pr. s.* Borweth, 7. 81; *pr. pl.* Borwen, 7. 82; 1 *p. s. pt.* Borwed, 6. 101; *pt. s.* Borwed, 4. 53; *pr. s. subj.* Borwe, give security for, 4. 109. See **Borghe,** a pledge.

Bote, *sb.* S. boot, remedy, restoration, amendment, 4. 89, 6. 196, 7. 28. From the root of *better.*

Bote, *pt. s.* bit, 5. 84. A.S. *bítan,* pt. t. *ic bát.*

Botened, *pp.* S. restored, assisted, bettered, 6. 194. See **Bote,** *sb.*

Boterased, *pp.* F. buttressed, furnished with buttresses, 5. 598. F. *bouter,* to thrust, *but.*

Boure, *sb.* S. bower, lady's chamber, 2. 64, 3. 14, 5. 222; Bowre, 3. 102. A.S. *búr.*

Bouȝte, *pt. s. and pl.* bought, 2. 3, 3. 86, 6. 210. See **Bigge.**

Bow, *sb.* S. bough, 5. 32; *pl.* Bowes, 5. 584.

Boweth, *imp. pl.* S. bend, turn, 5. 575.

Bown, *adj.* ready, 2. 159. Icel. *búinn,* pp. of vb. *búa,* to prepare. Now corrupted into *bound,* as in ' *bound* for New York.'

Boxome. See **Buxome.**

Bras, *sb.* brass, 3. 195; i. e. money, as in Matt. x. 9.

Bredcorne, bread-corn, 6. 64. *Breadcorn* is corn to be ground into *breadmeal,* for brown bread.

Farmers allow their bailiffs *bread-corn* in Lincolnshire, at 40*s*. per quarter (Peacock's Linc. Glossary). In this case, Piers uses some of it for sowing.

Brede, *sb*. S. breadth, 3. 202.

Breke, *v*. S. to break, 7. 183; *pr. pl.* Breketh, 6. 31; 2 *p. pl. pr. subj.* Breke, 5. 584; *pt. s. subj.* Breke, should break, miss, 5. 245.

Bren, *sb*. F. bran, 6. 184, 285. F. *bran*, *bren*, W. *bran*, a husk.

Brenne, *v*. S. to burn, 3. 97; *imp. s.* Brenne, 3. 265; *pp.* Brent, burnt, i. e. very bright, 5. 271.

Breuet, *sb*. F. a letter of indulgence, pr. 74; *pl.* Breuettes, 5. 649. O. F. *brievet*, a little letter, from Lat. *breuis*. Cf. F. *brevet*, a commission, indenture.

Brewestere, *sb*. S. a female brewer, 5. 306; *pl.* Brewesteres, pr. 218, 3. 79.

Bridale, *sb*. S. bride-ale (wedding-feast) now corrupted into *bridal*, 2. 54; Bruydale, 2. 43.

Britoner, *sb*. an inhabitant of Brittany, a Frenchman (a term of reproach), 6. 178.

Brockes, *sb. pl.* S. badgers, 6. 31. A.S. *broc*, Dan. *brok*; cf. Dan. *broget*, pie-bald; W. *broc*, grizzled. The *badger* had two other names, viz. *bausin* and *grey*; Juliana Berners, Book of St. Alban's, sig. D vi.

Brocour, *sb*. broker, 5. 130, 248; Brokour, 2. 65, 3. 46.

Brokages, *sb. pl.* F. brocages, commissions, 2. 87.

Broke, *sb*. S. brook, 6. 137. Cf. A.S. *bryce*, a fracture.

Broke, *pp.* S. broken, torn, 5. 108.

Brolle, *sb*. a child, brat, 3. 204. It occurs in P. Ploughman's Crede, 745.

Brugge, *sb*. S. a bridge, 5. 601; *pl.* Brugges, 7. 28.

Bruydale. See **Bridale**.

Brytonere, 6. 156. See **Britoner**.

Bugge, *v*. S. to buy, pr. 168, 7. 24; Buggen, 7. 85; *pr. pl.* Buggen, 3. 81.

Bulle, *sb*. F. a bull, papal rescript, pr. 69, 7. 107; *pl.* Bulles, 3. 147 Lat. *bulla*, a boss, a name given to the lump of metal which formed the seal of a bull.

Bummed, *pt. s.* tasted, 5. 223. Probably from the sound made by the lips; W. *bwmp*, a hollow sound, Du. *bommen*, to sound hollow, *bom*, a drum; and E. *boom*.

Burdoun, *sb*. F. a staff, 5. 524. Fr. *bourdon*, It. *bordone*.

Burgages, *sb. pl.* F. lands or tenements in towns, held by a particular tenure, 3. 86. From F. *bourg*, town.

Burgeis, **Burgeys**, *sb. pl.* F. burgesses, pr. 216, 3. 162; less frequently spelt Burgeyses, 5. 129.

Busked hem, *pt. pl.* prepared themselves, got ready to go; hence, repaired, went, 3. 14. Icel. *búask*, to prepare oneself, reflexive form of *búa*, to prepare. See Phil. Soc. Trans. 1866, p. 83.

But, *conj*. S. except, 3. 112, 6. 120; But if, except, 3. 305, 5. 420. A.S. *búte*, *bútan*. See *But* in my Etym. Dict.

Buxome, *adj*. S. obedient, humble, 1. 110, 6. 197; Boxome, 3. 263. A.S. *búhsom*, obedient, from *búgan*, to bow.

Buxomnes, *sb*. S. obedience, 4. 187; Buxumnesse, 1. 112.

By, By þat. See **Bi**.

Bydde, 5. 510. See **Bidde**.

Byfel me, happened to me, pr. 6. See **Bifalle**.

Byhiȝte, *pt. s.* vowed, 5. 65. See **Bihight**.

Byhote god, I vow to God, 6. 280. See **Behote**.

Bymeneth, 1. 1. See **Bemeneth**.

Bynome, *pp.* taken away; worth

bynome hym, shaň be taken away from him, 3. 312. See **Binam.**

Byschrewed, *pt. s.* cursed, 4. 168. A mere derivative from the sb. *shrew.* From A. S. *screáwa,* a shrew-mouse, once thought to be venomous.

C.

Cacche, *v.* F. to catch, pr. 206, 4.192. O. F. *cachier,* F. *chasser,* It. *cacciare.* Only a variation of E. *chase.*

Caityue, *sb.* F. a wretch, a caitiff, 5. 200. From Lat. *captiuus,* whence It. *cattivo,* a captive, F. *chétif,* wretched. poor.

Cake, *sb.* a loaf (lit. a cake), 6. 284. In prov. Eng. *cake* is a loaf.

Calabre, 6. 272. See note.

Caleys, *pr. name,* Calais, 3. 195.

Cam, *pt. s.* came, pr. 114. See **Comen.**

Can, 1 *p. s. pr.* I know, 3. 3, 329, 5. 239. 401; Can. *pr.s.* can, is able to, pr. 199. A. S. *cunnan,* to know, pr. s. *can.*

Canoun, *sb.* 5. 428. As this is mentioned with the *decretals,* it probably means the *canon-law,* with special reference to that part of it which had received the assent of our kings ; see *Canon* in Hook's Church Dictionary. Otherwise, it must mean the most solemn part of the service of the mass, called *Canon Missæ,* or the Canon of the Mass. See Burguy, and Proctor on the Common Prayer, p. 319. A. S. *canon,* a rule, from Lat. *canon,* Gk. κανών.

Canonistres, *sb. pl.* professors of the canon-law, men skilled in ecclesiastical law, 7. 149.

Caple, *sb.* a horse, 4. 23 ; *pl.* Caples, 2. 161. O. Icel. *kapall,* W. *ceffyl,* Lat. *caballus,* a horse.

Cardinales, *pl. adj.* F. pr. 104. In M. E. pl. adjectives from the French sometimes take a final *s.*

Cared, *pt. pl.* S. were anxious about, 2. 161.

Carefullich, *adv.* S. anxiously, sorrowfully, 5. 77. A. S. *cearu,* M.-Goth. *kara,* anxiety.

Caroigne, *sb.* F. carcase, body, 6. 93. Caroyne, pr. 193. F. *charogne,* O. Fr. *caroigne,* from Lat. *caro,* flesh ; now spelt *carrion.*

Carped, *pt. s.* said, told, 2. 191. ' Carpyn or talkyn. *Fabulor.*' Prompt. Parv.

Carpyng, *sb.* talking, discussion, pr. 203. It means—nor should there be any talk about, &c.

Cartesadel, *imp. s.* harness, 2. 179. Lit. saddle for the cart.

Cas, *sb.* F. mishap, misfortune, 7. 48. Lat. *casus.*

Caste, *sb.* contrivance, device ; *conscience caste* = conscience's device, 3. 19. From the verb to *cast.*

Casten, *pt. pl.* contrived, planned, pr. 117. Icel. *kasta,* Dan. *kaste,* to cast.

Catel, *sb.* F. wealth, goods, property, pr. 204, 3. 68, 271, &c. O. F. *catel, chaptal,* Low Lat. *catallum,* from Lat. *capitale,* which is our modern E. *capital.* Thus *chattels* and *capital* were originally identical.

Caurimaury, *sb.* the name of some coarse rough material, 5. 79. In the Ploughman's Crede, the ploughman is miserably clad—' His cote was of a cloute · that *cary* was y-called.' In Skelton's Elynour Rummyng, some slatterns are thus spoken of—' Some loke strawry, Some cawry mawry' ; l. 149 ; i. e. some look as if covered with straws, some appear in coarse gowns. Halliwell also refers to Collier's Memoirs of Alleyn, p. 21. The word is *very* uncommon.

Certis, *adv.* F. certainly, assuredly, 2. 151, 7. 180. O.F. *certes,* from adj. *cert,* Lat. *certus.*

Cesse, *pr. n.* Cis, i. e. Cicely, Cecilia, 5. 315.

Cesse, *v.* F. to cease, 6. 181; Cessen, 7. 117; *imp. pl.* Cesseth, cease ye, leave off, 4. 1.

Chaffare, *sb.* chaffer, merchandise, pr. 31, 2. 59, &c. Put for *chap-fare;* so that the first syllable is the same as in *chapman, Cheapside,* from A.S. *ceáp,* barter. Cf. G. *kaufen,* Du. *koopen,* Icel. *kaupa,* to buy; but the original sense was to barter, i. e. to *chop.*

Chaffare, *v.* to bargain, trade, 6. 241. See above.

Chalangynge, *sb.* accusation, 5. 88.

Chalengen, *pl. pr.* F. to challenge, claim, make a claim for, pr. 93; *pp.* Chalanged, charged with offences, accused, 5. 174. From forensic Lat. *calumniare,* to bring an action, accuse.

Chapitele, *sb.* F. chapter, i. e. an assembly of the governing body belonging to a cathedral, 3. 318; Chapitere, 5. 161. F. *chapitre,* Lat. *capitulum,* from *caput.*

Chapitelhous, *sb.* chapterhouse, 5. 174.

Chapeleynes, *sb. pl.* F. chaplains, 1. 188; Chapelleynes, 6. 12.

Chapman, *sb.* S. merchant, trader, pr. 64; *pl.* Chapmen, tradesmen, hucksters, 5. 34, 233, 331. See Chaffare.

Charnel, *sb.* F. charnel-house, 6. 60. F. *charnier,* from Lat. *caro.*

Chaste, *v.* F. to chastise, chasten, 6. 53, 324; Chasten, 5. 34. F. *châtier,* O.F. *chastier,* Lat. *castigare,* from *castus.*

Chastelet, *sb.* F. little castle, 2. 84. O.F. *chastelet,* dimin. of *chasteau* or *chastel* (now *château*), from Lat. *castellum,* dimin. of *castrum.*

Chastyng, *sb.* chastisement, 4. 117.

Chateryng, *sb.* chattering, idle talking, 2. 84.

Chaude, *adj.* F. hot; *plus chaud,* more hot, hotter, 6. 313.

Cheker, *sb.* exchequer, pr. 93, 4. 28. ' To *check* an account, in the sense of ascertaining its correctness, is an expression derived from the practice of the King's Court of Exchequer, where accounts were taken by means of counters upon a *checked* cloth.' Wedgwood.

Chele, *sb.* S. coldness, chilliness, 1. 23. A.S. *céle,* cold (sb.)

Chepe, *sb.* Cheap, i. e. Cheapside or West Cheap, London, 5. 322.

Chepynge, *sb.* S. market, 4. 56, 6. 301. See Chaffare.

Cherissyng, *sb.* cherishing, over great indulgence, 4. 117. F. *chérir,* from Lat. *carus.*

Cherles, *sb. pl.* churls, boors, peasants, 6. 50. A.S. *ceorl,* a man, a *churl;* Du. *karel,* a fellow.

Cheruelles, *sb. pl.* S. chervils, 6. 296. A.S. *cerfille,* a contraction of Lat. *chœrophyllum.*

Chesibles, *sb. pl.* F. chasubles, 6. 12. O.F. *chaisuble, casule.*

Chest, *sb.* S. dissension, strife, contention, enmity, 2. 84. A.S. *ceást,* strife.

Chetes, *sb. pl.* F. escheats, property reverting to the king. 4. 175. O.F. *escheoir,* mod. F. *échoir,* to fall to; from Lat. *cadere,* to fall. The mod. E. *cheat* is corrupted from *escheat.*

Cheuen, *pr. pl.* F. succeed, thrive, lit. achieve, pr. 31. F. *chevir,* to compass, manage, from *chef,* Lat. *caput.*

Cheuesances, *sb. pl.* F. agreements about the loan of money, negociations, 5. 249. F. *chevir.* See Cheuen, and the note.

Chibolles, *sb. pl.* F. cibols, 6. 296. A *cibol* is a sort of small onion; F. *ciboule,* Lat. *cœpulla,* from *cœpe,* an onion.

Childryn, *gen. pl.* children's, 4

117; *childryn cherissyng* = pampering of children.

Chillyng, *sb.* S. chilling, 6. 313; *for chilling* = against chilling, i. e. to prevent chilling.

Chiries, *sb. pl.* cherries, 6. 296. Lat. *cerasus.*

Chirityme, *sb.* cherry-time, time of gathering cherries, 5. 161.

Chiueled, *pt. pl.* trembled, 5. 193. MS. Bodley 814 has *cheuerid;* and certainly to *chiuel* is only another form of M. E. *chiuer* or *chever,* our modern *shiver.* 'Chyue-ryng as one dothe for colde;' Palsgrave. Another spelling is *chymer.* 'Chymerynge, or chy-uerynge, or dyderynge. *Frigutus.*' Prompt. Parv.

Clameþ, *pr. pl.* F. proclaim, publish, cry aloud, 1. 93. Lat. *cla-mare.*

Clarice, *pr. name,* Clarissa, 5. 159, 319.

Clerematyn, *sb.* a kind of fine white bread, 6. 306. O.F. *cler,* clear, Lat. *clarus;* the latter part of the word points to F. *matin,* morning, when perhaps it was most used; cf. O.F. *matinel,* breakfast.

Clergealy, *adv.* in a clerkly manner, pr. 124.

Clergye, *sb.* F. the clergy, a body of clerks, men of letters, pr. 116, 3. 164; *gen. s.* Clergise, 3. 15. It has reference rather to scholarly attainments than to holy orders.

Clerke, *sb.* F. a man of learning, student of letters, 3. 3, 7. 73; *pl.* Clerkes, Clerkis, pr. 114, 7. 153; *gen. pl.* Clerken, 4. 119. O.F. *clerc,* Gk. κληρικός, from κλῆρος.

Cleue, *v.* S. to cleave, divide, 7. 155.

Cliket, *sb.* a latchkey, 5. 613. In Shropshire, to *clicket* is to fasten as with a link over a staple. and Hartshorne well points out that it

properly means a *latch,* although Chaucer and Langland use it to mean a latchkey; see Merchant's Tale, C. T. 9990. The etymology is given in the New E. Dictionary. It is from O. F. *cliket,* F. *cliquet,* a latch; of Germanic origin. Named from the *clicking* sound. Cf. O. Swed. *klinka,* a door-bolt.

Cliketed, *pp.* fastened with a latch, or catch, 5. 623. W. *cliciedu,* to fasten with a latch, from the *click-ing* sound. Cf. Du. *klikklakken,* to clash.

Cloches, *sb. pl.* clutches, pr. 154. Allied to *claw.*

Cloke, *sb.* a cloak, 6. 272.

Clokke, *v.* F. to limp along lamely, to hobble, to lag, to be left in the lurch, 3. 34. F. *clocher,* to limp (see Brachet), Picard *cloquer.*

Cloutes, *sb. pl.* S. clouts, patched clothes, 2. 220. A.S. *clút,* a clout.

Clowe, *v.* S. to claw, clutch, pr. 154. A.S. *clawian.*

Cnowe, *v.* S. to know, 6. 222.

Cobelere, *sb.* cobbler, 5. 327. O.F. *cobler, coubler,* to join, bind to-gether; from Lat. *copulare,* to join together.

Coffes, *sb. pl.* cuffs, 6. 62.

Cofre. *sb.* F. coffer, chest, 5. 27. O.F. *cofre,* from Gk. κόφινος, a basket.

Cokeres, *sb. pl.* S. short woollen socks or stockings without feet, perhaps worn as gaiters, 6. 62. A.S. *cocer,* a sheath, Du. *koker,* a sheath, case, quiver.

Coket, *sb.* a kind of fine white bread, 6. 306. The finest kind was *simnel* bread, *paindemaigne,* or sacramental bread; the next, wastel bread; 'nearly resembling this in price and quality, though at times somewhat cheaper, was *light bread* or *puffe,* also known as *French bread* or *cocket . . . it* seems far from improbable that it was so called from the word *cocket*, as meaning a seal, it being a strict regulation . . . that each loaf (at all events each loaf below a certain quality) should bear the impress of its baker's seal.'—Chambers. (See note.) The word *cocket*, a seal, occurs in Liber Albus, p. 40.

Cokkeslane, i.e. Cock Lane, Smith-field, 5. 319.

Colers, *sb. pl.* F. collars, pr. 162. Lat. *collum*, the neck.

Coloppes, *sb. pl.* collops, 6. 287. Suio-Goth. *kollops*. Ihre says—'*Kollops*, edulii genus, confectum ex carnis segmentis, tudite lignea probe contusis et maceratis.' But *collops* are fried ham and eggs.

Comen, *v.* S. to come, 7. 188; *pt. s.* Come, pr. 112, 5. 532, &c.; *pt. pl.* Comen, 2. 150; *pp.* Comen, 4. 189; *pt. s. subj.* Come, should come, 6. 116.

Comeres, *sb. pl.* S. chance-comers, strangers, 2. 230. Cf. A.S. *cuma*, a comer, guest, stranger.

Comissarie, *sb.* F. 2. 179, 3. 142. '*Commissary*, an officer of the bishop, who exercises spiritual jurisdiction in places of the diocese so far distant from the episcopal see, that the chancellor cannot call the people to the bishop's principal consistory court, without putting them to inconvenience.'—Imp. Dict.

Comseth, *pr. s.* F. commences, begins, 1. 161, &c.; *pt. s.* Comsed, 3. 103, &c. Corrupted from F. *commencer*.

Comune, *sb.* F. the commonalty, 3. 77; *pl.* Comunes, the commons, pr. 113. In 5. 47, Mr. Wright suggests the meaning commons, i.e. allowances of provision; which suits the context.

Comune, *adj.* F. common, general, p. 148.

Conforte, *v.* F. to comfort, 1. 201, 2. 150, &c.; *imp. s.* Conforte, 6. 223. O.F. *conforter*, to invigorate, from *fortis*. Perhaps it seems better explained by *comfort* than by *strengthen*.

Congey, *v.* to bid farewell to, dismiss, 3. 173; *imp. s.* Congeye me, say farewell to me, 4. 4. O.F. *congier*. It. *congedare*, to dismiss.

Conne, *pr. pl.* they can, 6. 151. See **Can**.

Conneth, *pr. pl.* they know how to, pr. 33, 6. 124. See **Can**.

Conscience, *gen.* conscience's, 3. 19.

Conseille, *sb.* F. council, pr. 148, 3. 114; counsel, pr. 202.

Conseille, 1 *p. s. pr.* F. I counsel, pr. 187, 7. 195; 2 *p. s. pt.* Conseil'dest, 3. 205.

Consistorie, *sb.* F. consistory, i.e. the ecclesiastical court of an archbishop, bishop, or commissary, pr. 99, 2. 177, 3. 141, 318. See **Comissarie**.

Construe, *v.* F. to translate, explain, pr. 144, 5. 426, &c.

Contenaunce, *sb.* F. outward show, display, pr. 24; favour (as opposed to *right*), 5. 183.

Contrarieth, *pr. s.* F. acts or speaks contrary to, 5. 55.

Contreued, *pt. s.* F. contrived, devised, pr. 118. F. *trouver*.

Conynges, *sb.* conies, rabbits, pr. 193. W. *cwnyng*; cf. also Du. *konijn*, G. *kaninchen*. But the word is really from the O.F. *connil*, It. *coniglio*, Lat. *cuniculus*.

Cope, *v.* F. to provide a cope for, 5. 296; *pr. s.* Copeth, 3. 142; *pt. pl.* Coped, 2. 230; *pp.* Coped, 3. 35. In the two last passages it refers to the dress of a friar in particular. E. *cope*, *cape*.

Copes, Copis, *sb. pl.* F. copes (with reference to *hermits*), pr. 56, 6. 191; (with reference to *friars*) pr. 61. Not short, like our modern *cape*, but a large cloak reaching down to the feet. F. *chappe*, It. *cappa*. Cf. *coping-stone*, *cope* or vault of heaven. Du. *kap*, coping, cap. Allied to E. *cape*, *cap*.

Coppis, *sb. pl.* L. cups, 3. 22. A. S. *coppa*, Low Lat. *cuppa*.

Corps, *sb.* F. body, 1. 137. Lat. *corpus*.

Corseint, *sb.* F. a saint, lit. a holy body, but applied here to a living saint, 5. 539. Cf. Chaucer's Dream, l. 942; Morte Arthure, ed. Brock, 1164.

Coste, *sb.* F. cost, expense, expenditure, 3. 68. O.F. *couster*, Lat. *constare*.

Costed, *pt. s.* F. cost, pr. 203; *pp.* Costed, pr. 204.

Costes, *sb. pl.* F. coasts, regions, 2. 85. Lat. *costa*.

Coteth, *pr. s.* F. provides with a coat, 3. 142. O.F. *cote*, a tunic.

Coude, *pt. pl.* S. could, pr. 129. See **Couthe**.

Coudestow, 2 *p. s. pt.* (= coudest þou) couldst thou, 5. 540.

Coueitise, *sb.* F. covetousness, avarice, pr. 61, 3. 68, &c. Provençal *cobeitos*, Lat. *cupidus*, covetous. The O.F. sometimes wrongly inserts an *n*, as in *convoitise*, covetousness.

Couent, *sb.* F. convent, 5. 155; *gen.* Couentes, convent's, 5. 137. O.F. *covent* (as in *Covent* Garden), Lat. *conventus*.

Countè, *sb.* F. county, 2. 85. F. *comté*, from Lat. *comes*, a count, lit. a companion.

Coupe, *sb.* F. fault, sin, 5. 305. Lat. *culpa*, whence F. *coupable*, E. *culpable*.

Coupes, *sb. pl.* goblets, bowls (distinguished from cups), 3. 22. See the note.

Coupleth, *pr. s.* F. couples, links, fastens, 3. 164; *pt. pl.* Coupled hem, joined themselves, 4. 149; *pp.* Coupled, fastened, held in with a leash; *coupled and vncoupled*, whether held in or free, pr. 206. From Lat. *copula*.

Courbed, 1 *p. s. pt.* F. I bent, bowed, knelt, 1. 79, 2. 1. Lat. *curvare*.

Courte, *sb.* F. courtyard, 5. 594. Lat. *cohors*, O.F. *cort*, It. *corte*.

Courtpies, *sb. pl.* pea-jackets, short coats, 6. 191. Du. *kort*, short, and *pije*, coat of a coarse woollen stuff; also the material itself; whence *pea*-jacket. Cf. Mœso-Goth. *ga-paidon*, to clothe, *paida*, a coat.

Couth, 1 *p. s. pr.* I make known, I proclaim, 5. 181. A.S. *cýðan*, to make known.

Couthe, *pt. s.* knew, pr. 182, 5. 520; could, 1. 115; 2 *p. pl.* Couthe, ye could, pr. 200, 3. 340. A.S. *cunnan*, to know, whence *ic can*, I know, can, *ic cuðe*, I knew, M.E. 1 *coude*, now misspelt *could*. Cf. Mœso-Goth. *kunnan*, to know, *ik kan*, I can, *ik kuntha*, I could.

Cracche, **Cracchy**, *v.* to scratch, pr. 154, 186. Cf. Du. *krassen*, to scratch.

Craft, **Crafte**, *sb.* craft, contrivance, 1. 137, 2. 4, 3. 19; handicraft, trade, 5. 554; *pl.* Craftes, employments, trades, pr. 221, 7. 31. A.S. *cræft*, skill, faculty, G. *kraft*, strength.

Crafty, *adj.* S. skilful, cunning, well-executed, pr. 162: *alkynnes crafty men*, skilled men (*craftsmen*) of every kind, 3. 224, 6. 70.

Credo, *sb.* the creed, 6. 91; from the first word in Latin—*credo*.

Cristene, *adj.* F. Christian, 3. 287; *pl.* Cristene, 1. 190, 7. 195.

Croft, **Crofte**, *sb.* croft, small enclosed field, 5. 581, 6. 33. A. S. *croft*.

Crope, 2 *p. s. pt.* S. didst creep, 3. 190; 1 *p. pl. subj.* we crept, pr.

186. A.S. *creópan*, pt. t. *ic creáp*, þu *crupe*, 1 p. pl. *crupon*.

Crosse, *sb.* F. cross, 5. 472. See the note.

Crounyng, *sb.* the tonsure, lit. crowning, pr. 88. Lat. *corona*.

Cruche, *sb.* F. cross, mark of a cross, 5. 529. Lat. acc. *crucem*, whence O.F. *crois*, *cruix*, and E. *Crutched* Friars.

Cruddes, *sb. pl.* curds, 6. 284. W. *crwd*, a round lump.

Culled, 1 *p. pl. subj.* killed, pr. 185. Allied to A.S. *cwelan*, to die.

Culorum, *sb.* ending, conclusion, 3. 278. Evidently a corruption of *sæculorum*, the last word of the *Gloria Patri*. It only occurs, I believe, in 'Piers Plowman' and in the 'Deposition of Rich. II.' It has, besides, a stronger force than *conclusion* merely, as it signifies the conclusion *which gives the key-note to the whole*. In the Sarum Psalter, the first word or words of the Anthem (with music) and the music of the *seculorum Amen* are given. The latter is denoted only by its *vowels*; so that under the final musical phrase we find *e. u. o. u. a. e.*

Culter, *sb.* Lat. coulter, 6. 106. Lat. *culter*, from *colere*.

Cupmel, *sb.* S. 5. 225. *In cupmel* = in portions such as a cup will hold, in cupfuls. A.S. *mǽlum*, in parts, dat. pl. of *mǽl*, a fixed time, a fixed portion. So *flocmeel*, by flocks, *gobetmele*, by pieces at a time, &c. in Wycliffe's Bible. See *Parcelmele*. Cf. E. *piecemeal*.

Curatoures, *sb. pl.* F. guardians, men who are entrusted with their wards' money, 1. 193. 'Curatier, Curatour: curateur, tuteur, courtier.'—Roquefort.

Cure, *sb.* F. a cure of souls, pr. 88. Lat. *cura*.

Curteise, *adj.* F. courteous, 4. 16.

Curteisye, *sb.* F. courtesy, kindness, 1. 20, 5. 437.

Curteisliche, *adj.* courteously, 3. 103, 4. 44, &c.

Cutpurs, *sb.* a cutpurse, thief, 5. 639.

D.

Daffe, *sb.* a stupid, a dolt, 1. 138. Really allied to *deft*; cf. A.S. *gedæfte*, mild, gentle, meek; hence innocent, silly.

Dampne, *imp. s.* F. condemn, damn 5. 478; *pp.* Dampned, 2. 102. Lat. *damnare*, *dampnare*.

Dar, 1 *p. s. pr.* I dare, pr. 209, 6. 270; 1 *p. s. pt.* Durst, 3. 201; *pt. s.* Dorst, pr. 178. A.S. *ic dear*, I dare, *ic dorste*, I durst; Mœso-Goth. *ik dars*, I dare, *ik daursta*, I durst, inf. *daursan*.

Daunten, *v.* to daunt. tame, subdue, 3. 286. F. *dompter*; cf. Lat. *domare*.

Dawe, contr. form of Davy or David, 5. 320, 6. 331.

Debate, *sb.* F. strife, discussion, 5. 98, 337. F. *débattre*, to contend, from the same root as *beat*.

Decretals, *sb. pl.* 5. 428. A collection of popes' edicts and decrees of councils, forming a part of the canon law. Five books of them were collected by Gregory IX. in 1227; a sixth by Boniface VIII, in 1297.

Ded, *sb.* S. death, 3. 265. Mœso-Goth. *dauthus*, A.S. *deáð*, Sw. *döc*, Du. *dood*, G. *tod*.

Ded-day, *sb.* S. death-day, 7. 50, 115.

Dede, did. See **Do**.

Dede, *adj. pl.* the dead, 7. 187.

Defaute, *sb.* F. default; *in defaute*, in fault, 2. 139, 5. 145; *for defaute*, for want, for lack, for need, 5. 6, 6. 209, 7. 162.

Defendeth, *pr. s.* F. forbids, 3. 64.

Defien, *v.* to be digested, 5. 389; **Defye,** 5. 121; to digest, pr. 229.

O.F. *deffier*, to distrust, Lat. *fides*. Hence M.E. *defy*, to reject, renounce; also to withstand, digest; see the last passage cited.

Dele, *v.* to distribute, divide, share, 6. 99; to share money or other things with others, to give away, 1. 197; 2 *p. pl. pr.* Delen, 3. 71; *v.* to have dealings, 6. 77; 2 *p. pl. pr.* Delen, 7. 90. A.S. *dǽlan*, to divide, from *dǽl*, a portion, deal, Du. *deel*, G. *theil*.

Dele, *sb.* S. a part; *some dele*, partly, 5. 438.

Delitable, *adj.* F. delightful, pleasant, nice, 1. 34.

Deluen, *v.* to dig, 6. 143; 1 *p. s. pr.* Delue, 5. 552. A.S. *delfan*, Du. *delven*.

Delueres, *sb. pl.* S. diggers, ditchers, pr. 223, 6. 109.

Deluynge, *sb.* S. digging, 6. 250.

Deme, *v.* to deem, think, judge, 1. 86, 4. 178; 1 *p. s. pr.* Deme, 5. 114; 3 *p. pl. pr.* Demen, pronounce judgment, pr. 96; *imp. s.* Deme, 6. 83, 182; *pt. s.* Demed, decided, 7. 169; *pp.* Demed, condemned, 4. 181. A.S. *déman*, to judge, *dóm*, judgment, doom.

Denote, *a proper name*, 6. 73.

Departed, *pp.* F. divided, parted, 7. 156. O.F. *despartir*, Lat. *dispartiri*, from *pars*.

Depraue, *v.* F. to depreciate, revile, 3. 178; *pr. pl.* 5. 144.

Dere, *adv.* S. dearly, 6. 293; *me dere liketh*, it dearly pleases me, I like best.

Dere, *v.* to injure, harm, 7. 34; Deren, 7. 50. A.S. *derian*, to injure, Du. *deren*.

Derke, *adj.* S. dark, pr. 16.

Derne, *adj.* S. secret, 2. 175.

Derrest, *adj.* S. dearest, i. e. most valuable, 2. 13.

Derthe, *sb.* S. a dearth, 6. 330.

Derworth, *adj.* precious, 1. 87. A.S. *deórwurðe*, precious, of dear worth.

Descryue, *v.* to describe, 5. 188; Discreue, 5. 79. O. F. *descriure*, from Lat. *scribere*.

Despended, *pp.* spent, 5. 267. O. F. *despendre*, Lat. *dispendere*.

Destruye, *v.* to destroy, pr. 197; 2 *p. s. pr. subj.* 3. 269; *pr. pl.* Destruyeth, waste, pr. 22. O.F. *destruire*.

Deth-day, 7. 199. See Ded-day.

Deuine ȝe, *imp. pl.* explain ye, pr. 209; *pt. s.* Deuyned, 7. 152. O. F. *deviner*, Lat. *diuinare*.

Deuynour, *sb.* F. expounder, teacher, 7. 135.

Deuorses, *sb. pl.* F. divorces, 2. 175.

Deye, Dey, *v.* to die, 1. 142, 3. 261, &c.; 2 *p. pl. pr. subj.* Deye, 6. 122; 2 *p. s. pt.* Deydest, 5. 472. Suio-Goth. *dö*, Icel. *deyja*, Sw. *dö*, Dan. *döe*, to die.

Deyinge, *sb.* dying, death-hour, 7. 34.

Deyned, *pt. pl.* F. deigned, 6. 310. From Lat. *dignus*.

Deyse, *sb.* daïs, high table at the end of the dining-hall, 7. 17. O.F. *dais*, *deis*, *dois*, originally a table, from Lat. *discus*; it afterwards meant a seat of state, a canopy, or an elevated platform.

Diademed, *pp.* crowned, 3. 286. Gr. διάδημα, a fillet, from δέειν, to bind.

Diamantz, *sb. pl.* diamonds, 2. 13.

Diapenidion, *sb.* an emollient, expectorant, 5. 123. The meaning and derivation are given in the note to the present edition, which see.

Did. See Do.

Diete þe, 2 *p. s. subj.* diet thyself, 6. 270. Gk. δίαιτα, mode of life.

Dignelich, *adv.* worthily, honourably, 7. 171. Lat. *dignus*.

Diken, *v.* to make ditches or dykes, 6. 143; 1 *p. s. pr.* Dyke, 5. 552; *pt. pl.* Dykeden, 6. 193.

Dikeres, *sb. pl.* ditchers, 6. 109. See Dykere.

Dismas. 5. 473. See note.

Discreue. See Descryue.

Disgised, *pp.* tricked out, pr. 24. See note. O. F. *desguiser,* to change one's clothes; Span. *guisar,* to dress meat, from a Teutonic source; O. H. G. *wisa, wise,* G. *weise,* A. S. *wise,* Du. *wijs,* E. *wise, guise.*

Disoures, *sb. pl.* story-tellers, romance-reciters, 6. 56. O.F. *diseor,* a taleteller; cf. F. *dire,* Lat. *dicere.*

Dissheres, *sb.* a female maker, or retailer, of metal dishes, 5. 323. 'John le Disshere' is mentioned (A.D. 1304) in Memorials of London, ed. Riley, p. 54.

Diȝte, *v.* S. dight, prepare, make ready, 6. 293. A.S. *dihtan,* to arrange, from Lat. *dictare.*

Do, *v.* to do, to cause, *2 p. s. pr.* Doste, 6. 83; *2 p. pl. pr.* Done, 1. 53; *pr. pl.* Don, 6. 66; *pp.* Do, ended, 5. 418. When followed by another verb, the latter is always in the infin. mood, and, *if transitive,* apparently receives a *passive* signification. Thus, *do maken,* I cause to be made, 3. 60; *do peynten,* cause to be painted, 3. 62; *don saue,* cause to be saved, 7. 177. Yet it must be remembered that the second verb is not really passive, but we have lost the idiom which enables a German to say *bauen lassen,* to cause to be built, and the like. Hence we rightly translate *don hym lese* by *cause him to lose,* 5. 95, &c.; *do men deye,* cause men to die, 6. 276; *I do it on,* I refer it to, I make it depend on, 1. 86, 3. 187. *To done* (gerund), to transact business, 4. 27; to work, 6. 112; to be done, 6. 206. *Doth hym to go,* prepares himself to go off, 2. 211. *Do me,* make

my way, 5. 459. *Doth,* imp. pl. do ye, 5. 44. *Dede,* pt. s. did, 3. 140. *Dedest,* didst, 7. 190. *Dede, Deden,* pt. pl. 7. 122, 5. 547. *Did,* caused, 5. 245.

Doel, *sb.* mourning, lamentation, 5. 386. O.F. *doel, duil,* F. *deuil,* Lat. *dolium* in the comp. *cordolium.* Cf. Lat. *dolor.*

Doke, *sb.* duck, 5. 75. Cf. Du. *duiker,* a diver.

Dole, *sb.* sorrow, grief, 6. 122. See Doel.

Doluen, *pt. pl.* delved, dug, 6. 193; *pp.* Doluen, buried, 6. 182. See Deluen.

Dome, *sb.* doom, sentence, 2. 205; judgment, 3. 316, &c. A.S. *dóm,* judgment, Gk. θέμις.

Domesday, *sb.* doom's-day, judgment-day, 5. 20, 478.

Donet, 5. 209. See note.

Dongeon, Dongeoun, *sb.* donjon, pr. 15, 1. 59. The 'donjon' or keep-tower is the principal tower in a castle; in it prisoners often were confined, whence our *dungeon.* From Low Lat. *domnio* a strong tower, which from Lat. *dominio,* rather than from the Celtic (Gaelic and Irish) *dùn,* a fortified place. O.F. *donjon, dungon, doignon,* a keep-tower.

Dore-tre, *sb.* S. side post of a door, or wooden bar of a door, 1. 185.

Dorst. See Dar.

Doted, *adj.* or *pp.* simple, foolish, 1. 138. Cf. F. *radoter,* to dote, Du. *dut,* sleep, dotage.

Douere, *pr. name,* Dover, 4. 131.

Doute, *sb.* fear, pr. 152. O.F. *dute, doute,* fear; from Lat. *dubitare.*

Douȝter, *sb.* S. daughter, 2. 30; *pl.* Douȝtres, 6. 99.

Draddest, *2 p. s. pt.* S. didst dread, didst fear, 3. 192.

Dremeles, *sb.* a dream, 7. 154. The usual form is *dreme* (cf. 7.

152), but the form *dremeles* is imitated from *meteles* or *metels*; that it is in the singular number is clear from the passage—'A meruellouse meteles'—in Pass. xi. 5, Text B. of the poem. A.S. *dréman*, which usually meant *to rejoice, to make a loud sound like a musical instrument*. Cf. Du. *droom*, a dream.

Drewery, *sb.* a favourite, darling, object of affection, 1. 87. O.F. *druerie*, affection, love, from *drut*, a lover, which from O.H.G. *triuten*, to love, cf. G. *traut*, dear. See Romaunt of the Rose, l. 5067.

Drowe, 1 *p. s. pt.* drew (myself), went (amongst), 5. 209; *pt. s.* Drowgh, drew near, 5. 356. A.S. *dragan*, to drag, draw, pt. t. *ic dróg, ic dróh*.

Dryest, art dry, art thirsty, 1. 25.

Dryuen forth, i. e. pass, spend, pr. 220.

Dureth, *pr. s.* F. endures, lasts, 1. 78, 6. 58. Lat. *durare*. Cf. S. Matt. xiii. 21.

Durst. See Dar.

Dyke, Dykeden. See Diken.

Dykere, *sb.* S. a ditcher, 5. 320; Dyker, 6. 331; *pl.* Dykers, pr. 223. A.S. *dic*, a dyke, either a mound or a ditch.

Dyngen, *v.* to strike violently, as with a flail, 6. 143; to keep pounding away at, 3. 310. Sw. *dänga*, Dan. *dænge*, to bang, hit violently. Cf. Sc. *ding*.

Dys-playere, *sb.* diceplayer, 6. 73.

E.

Eche a, every, 3. 310, 6. 249. Cf. Sc. *ilka*.

Edwite, *v.* to rebuke, reprove, 5. 370. A.S. *edwitan*, to reproach; cf. *ætwitan*, to twit. The prefix *ed-* means over again, and has just the force of Lat. *re-* or *red-*.

Eet, *v.* S. to eat, 5. 120; *pt. s.* Eet, ate, 6. 298.

Eft, *adv.* again, 3. 344, 5. 624. A.S. *eft*, again.

Efte, *adv.* afterwards, 4. 107, 5. 626. A.S. *æftan*, afterwards.

Eftsones, *adv.* S. soon afterwards, 5. 481; Eft sone, 6. 172.

Egged, *pt. s.* egged on, incited, 1. 65. A.S. *eggian*, to incite; Icel. *eggja*, to sharpen, incite, from *egg*, an *edge*. Cf. Chaucer, C. T. 5262.

Eighen, *sb. pl.* eyne, eyes, 5. 356, 392; Eyghen, 5. 191; Eyen, 5. 62. A.S. *eáge*, pl. *eágan*.

Ek, *conj.* eke, moreover, 2. 236; Eke, besides, 2. 92. A.S. *eác*, G. *auch*, Du. *ook*.

Elde, *sb.* old age, 5. 193. A.S. *eldo, yldo*, Mœso-Goth. *alds*, old age.

Eldres, *sb. pl.* S. ancestors, 3. 261.

Eleyne, *pr. n.* 5. 110.

Eller, *sb.* an elder tree, 1. 68. A.S. *ellen*, the elder. See note.

Elles, Ellis, *adv.* S. else, otherwise, pr. 91, 6. 233, &c. Cf. Lat. *ali-ter*.

Elyng, *adj.* tedious; hence, miserable, wretched, pr. 190. Cf. A.S. *ǽlenge*, protracted; and hence, tedious. 'His labour to him is the *elengere*,' i. e. more miserable; Occleve, De Regimine Principum, ed. Wright, p. 37.

Enfourmeth, *pr. s.* instructs, teaches, 3. 240. O.F. *enformer*, to instruct (Roquefort).

Engreyned, *pp.* dyed in grain, i. e. of a *fast* colour, 2. 15.

Enioyned, *pt. s.* F. enjoined, appointed, imposed, 5. 607; Enioigned, *pp.* joined, 2. 65. Lat. *iniungere*.

Ennuyed, *pp.* F. annoyed, 5. 94. F. *ennui*, Span. *enojo*, from Lat. *in odio* (Brachet).

Ensample, *sb.* F. example, 5. 17 ; *pl.* Ensamples, Ensaumples, 1. 170, 4. 136. Lat. *exemplum.*

Enuenymes, *sb. pl.* F. poisons, 2. 14. Lat. *uenenum.*

Eny, *adj.* any, 2. 203.

Enykynnes, of any kind, 2. 200.

Er, *conj.* ere, 5. 352. *See* **Ar.**

Erchdekenes, *sb. pl.* archdeacons, 2. 173.

Erde, *sb.* habitation, native place, home, 6. 202. A.S. *eard,* native soil.

Ere, *adv.* S. formerly, 1. 129.

Erie, *v.* to plough, 6. 67, 7. 6 ; *pp.* Eried, 6. 5. Mœso-Goth. *arjan,* A.S. *erian,* Icel. *erja ;* cf. Lat. *arare.* See *ear* in the Bible, Deut. xxi. 4 ; 1 Sam. viii. 12 ; Is. xxx. 24.

Erldome, *sb.* earldom, 2. 83. A.S. *eorl,* Dan. *jarl,* an earl.

Ermonye, *sb.* F. Armenia, 5. 533.

Erye, Eryen, 6. 4, 7. 5. See **Erie.**

Eschaunges, *sb. pl.* F. exchanges, 5. 249.

Eschue, *imp. s.* avoid, shun, 6. 55. F. *esquiver,* M.H.G. *schiuhen,* G. *scheuen,* to be shy of, evade.

Ese, *sb.* F. ease, 1. 19, 6. 152.

Eten, *pr. pl.* they eat, 6. 147 ; *pt. s.* Ete, 7. 121 ; *pp.* Eten, 5. 381, 6. 266 ; see also **Eet.** A.S. *etan,* pt. t. *ic æt,* pp. *eten.*

Euen, *sb.* evening, 6. 187. A.S. *éfen.*

Euene-cristene, *sb.* fellow-Christian, 2. 94, 5. 440. Sw. *jämn-christen,* fellow-Christian. Sw. *jämn,* Dan. *jæmn,* is our E. *even,* Shropshire *eme.*

Euensonge, *sb.* S. evensong, the *vespers* or evening service, 5. 345, 462. The M.E. name for *vespers.*

Euermo, *adv.* S. euermore, 7. 82. See **Mo.**

Eury (i.e. evry), every, 3. 63.

Ewages, *sb. pl.* F. beryls, 2. 14. O. F. *ewe,* water, has a derivative *ewage* also *evage, aigage* = Lat. *aquatica,* of the colour of water (Godefroy). Here it is the same as *aqua-marina,* a name given by the jewellers to the green beryl, with reference to its colour.

Eyen, *sb. pl.* eyne, eyes, 5. 480. &c.; Eyghen, 5. 109. See **Eighen.**

Eyleth, *pr. s.* troubles, vexes, ails, 6. 130, 259. A.S. *eglan,* to prick, to torment, *egl,* a prick.

Eyre, *sb.* F. air, pr. 128, 1. 123.

Eyres, *sb. pl.* heirs, 2. 101, 3. 277. O. F. *eir, hoir,* Lat. *hæres.*

Eyther . . . other, each . . . the other, 5. 148, 164, 7. 138.

F.

Fader, *sb.* father, 1. 14 ; Fadre, 3. 126. A.S. *fæder.*

Faire, *adv.* S. fairly, well, 1. 2, 6. 25.

Faire, *sb.* fair, 5. 205, 328. O.F. *foire, feire,* Lat. *feriæ.*

Fairy, *sb.* enchantment, pr. 6. O.F *faerie,* enchantment, *fae,* a fay, from Lat. *fatum,* destiny.

Faite, *sb.* F. deed, action, 1. 184. Lat. *factum.*

Faiten, *v.* F. to use false pretences, to beg under false pretence, 7. 94. See next word.

Faitoures, *sb. pl.* lying vagabonds, who begged money under false pretences, canting rogues, 6. 123, 186; Faitours, 2. 182. O. F. *faiteor* (Lat. *factor*), a maker; hence, a pretender, swindler.

Falle, 1 *p. s. pr.* S. I fall (amongst), I light (upon), 4. 156 ; 3 *p. s. subj.* happen, come to pass, 3. 323 ; *pr. s.* Falleth, belongs, appertains, 1. 164 ; *pp.* Fallen, happened, come to pass, pr. 65.

Fals, *adj.* F. *used as a proper name,* False, the false one, impersonation of falsehood, 2. 25, 123 ; *pl.* Fals, false men, 3. 138.

Falshed, Falshede, *sb.* falsehood, pr. 71, 1. 64; 5. 295.

Famed, *pp.* F. defamed, slandered, 3. 185. Cf. Lat. *fama,* often used to mean *scandal.*

Fange, *v.* to take, receive, 5. 566. A.S. *fón,* pt. t. *ic féng,* pp. *fangen, fongen,* G. *fahen,* Du. *vangen,* to take, catch. Cf. E. *fang.*

Fantasies, *sb. pl.* F. fancies, tricks, silly inventions, pr. 36. Gk. φαν-τασία, display, from φαίνω, I shew, φάω, I shine. M.E. *fantasy,* now corrupted into *fancy.*

Fare, *v.* to go, depart, 7. 98; *pr. pl.* Fareth, go, travel, fare, 2. 183; *pp.* Faren, gone, 5. 5. A.S. *faran,* to go, G. *fahren,* Du. *varen,* to travel.

Faucones, *sb. pl.* F. falcons, 6. 32.

Fauel, *sb.* the impersonation of Flattery, Cajolery, or Deceit, 2. 6. O.F. *favele,* Lat. *fabella,* idle discourse, from Lat. *fabula.* Quite distinct from *favel* or *fauvel,* which means of a yellow colour (G. *falb*), and was sometimes used as a name for a horse, as in the Romance of Richard Cœur de Lion.

Fauntes, *sb. pl.* F. children, lit. infants, of which it is a shortened form, 7. 94; Fauntis, 6. 285.

Fayne, *adj.* fain, glad, 4. 12, 6. 273. A.S. *fægen,* glad, Mœso-Goth. *faginon,* to rejoice.

Fayteden, *pt. pl.* F. begged in a dissembling or lying manner, pr. 42. See **Faitoures.**

Faytoure, *sb.* 6. 74. See **Faitoures.**

Fecche, Fecchen, *v.* to fetch, take, 2. 180, 5. 29; *pr. pl.* Feccheth, steal, 4. 51. A.S. *feccan, fetian,* G. *fassen,* Du. *vatten,* to fetch, seize.

Feffe, *v.* to fee, retain by means of fees, 2. 146; *pr. s.* Feffeth, infeoffs, endows with property, 2. 78. O.F. *fiefer,* from the *sb. fief,* which is

from a Teutonic source. Mœso-Goth. *faihu,* A. S. *feoh,* Sw. *fä,* Icel. *fé,* G. *vieh,* Du. *fooi,* cattle, property, fee. Cf. Lat. *pecus.*

Feffement, *sb.* F. enfeoffment, deed of gift or endowment, 2. 72.

Feire, *adv.* 5. 59. See **Faire.**

Fel, *sb.* skin, 1. 15. A.S. and G. *fell,* Du. *vel.*

Felawes, *sb. pl.* S. associates, companions, 2. 209, 7. 12. Icel. *félagi,* from *fé,* cattle, property, and *lag,* law, society; so also Suio-Goth. *fælage,* from *fæ* (Sw. *fä*) and *laga;* it thus implies one who possesses property in partnership with others. See **Feffe.**

Felawship, *sb.* S. fellowship, society, companionship, 1. 113, 3. 118; crew, 2. 207.

Felde, *sb.* S. field, 1. 2, 6. 142. A.S. *feld.*

Fele, *adj. pl.* many, numerous, 3. 338. A.S. *fela,* G. *viel,* Du. *veel.*

Feledest, 2 *p. s. pt.* S. didst feel, 5. 497.

Felice, *pr. name,* F. Felicia, 5. 29.

Felle, *adj. pl.* fell, cruel, severe, 5. 170. A.S. *fell.*

Felle, (*rather read* Fel), S. *pt. s.* happened, 7. 157; *pt. pl.* Fellen, fell, 1. 119.

Felled, *pt. s.* S. felled, i.e. caused to fall, 3. 126.

Fende, *sb.* a fiend, 1. 40; *gen. sing.* Fendes, 2. 40. The Mœso-Goth. *fijan,* to hate, has a pres. part. *fijands* used as a sb. and meaning *an enemy:* so A.S. *feón,* to hate, *feônd,* a fiend.

Fenel-seed, *sb.* fennel-seed, 5. 313. 'The fruit or, in *common language,* the seeds, are carminative, and frequently employed in medicine.'— Imp. Dict. They were used to put into drinks, as a spice. Some MSS. have *fenkel,* which is nearer to the Lat. *fœniculum.*

Ferde, 2 *p. pl. pt. subj.* ye would

have fared, ye would fare, 3. 340. See **Fare.**

Fere, *sb.* comrade, companion, 4. 26; *pl.* Feres, 2. 6, 5. 170. A.S. *féra, geféra,* one who *fares* with one, a travelling companion.

Fere, *v.* S. to frighten, terrify, 7. 34. So used by Shakespeare.

Ferly, *sb.* a wonder, marvel, pr. 6; *pl.* Ferlis, pr. 65. A.S. *fǽrlic,* sudden, from *fǽr,* fear, sudden danger; Du. *vaarlijk,* quickly; G. *gefährlich,* dangerous.

Fernyere, *adv.* in former years, formerly, 5. 440. A.S. *fyrn,* old, former; O.H.G. *firni,* old.

Ferthynge. *sb.* S. a farthing, 4. 54, 5. 566. Lit. a *fourth-ing,* fourth part; hence it was used for a quarter of a noble or other gold coin, but commonly for a quarter of a penny, as here.

Ferthyngworth, *sb.* farthing's worth, small quantity, 5. 313.

Fest, *pp.* S. fastened, joined, 2. 123. [The readings vary; the A-text MSS. have *feffed, festnyd, fastnid;* the B-text MSS. have *fest* and *fast;* the best form would be *festned.*]

Fet, *pr. s.* S. feeds (a contr. form of *fedeth*), pr. 194.

Fetislich, *adv.* featly, handsomely, 2. 11, 165. Lat. *factitius,* artificial, O.F. *faictis,* well made, handsome, E. *feat.*

Fette, *pt. s.* fetched, produced, 2. 162, 5. 450; *pt. pl.* Fetten, 2. 229, 6. 294. A.S. *fetian,* pt. t. *ic fette.*

Fettren, *v.* S. to fetter, 2. 207; *imp. pl.* Fettereth, 2. 200. A.S. *fetor,* a fetter.

Fewe, *adj. pl.* S. few, 6. 284.

Feyned hem, *pt. s.* F. feigned themselves, pretended to be, 6. 123; *pr. pl.* Feynen hem, feign for themselves, invent, imagine for themselves, pr. 36.

Feyntise, *sb.* F. a faintness, weakness, 5. 5. The O.F. *faintise*

properly means falseness, and secondarily cowardice, sluggishness. Lat. *fingere.* See Wedgwood.

Feyres, *sb. pl.* F. fairs, markets, 4. 56. See **Faire.**

Fieble, *adj.* F. feeble, weak, 5. 177, 412; Feble, pr. 180.

Fierthe, *adj.* S. fourth, 7. 52.

Fikel, *adj.* treacherous (*rather that* changeable), 2. 129; Fykel, 3. 121.

File, *sb.* F. girl, wench, 5. 160. Lat. *filia.*

Filtz, *sb.* F. son, 7. 162. Lat. *filius.*

Flapten, *pt. pl.* flapped, flogged, slapped, worked at threshing, 6. 187. Du. *flap,* a flap, blow, stroke.

Flatte, *pt. s.* slapped, dashed, 5. 451. Cf. O.F. *flat, flac,* a slap, *flatir, flaccer,* to dash.

Flaundres, Flanders, 5. 321.

Flayles, *sb. pl.* 6. 187. O.F. *flael,* from Lat. *flagellum.*

Fleiჳ, *pt. s.* fled, 2. 210. A.S. *fleón,* pt. t. *ic fleáh.*

Flex, *sb.* flax, 6. 13. A.S. *flex, fleax,* Du. *vlas.*

Floreines, *sb. pl.* florins, 2. 143, 3. 156, 4. 156, 5. 590. So named from the town of Florence.

Flowen, *pt. pl.* S. fled, flew, 2. 233, 6. 186. See **Fleiჳ.**

Folde, *sb.* S. fold, earth, world, 7. 53.

Foles, *sb. pl.* F. fools, pr. 26. F. *fou,* O.F. *fol,* W. *ffol,* foolish.

Folus, *sb. pl.* S. foals, 2. 162. A.S. *fola,* a colt.

Folwar, *sb.* S. follower, 5. 549.

Folwen, *v.* S. to follow, 6. 2.

Fonde, *imp. s.* endeavour, 6. 222. A.S. *fandian,* to try to find, seek.

Fonde, 1 *p. s. pt.* S. I found, pr. 17, 58.

Foon, *sb. pl.* foes, 5. 96. A.S. *fáh,* pl. *fá;* but A.S. *gefáh* has the pl.

gefáhen. The Chaucer MSS. have *fone, foon,* and *foos.*

For, *conj.* S. because, for the reason that, **2.** 166, 3. 271, 7. 20; *prep.* against, as a preventive against, 1. 24, 3. 190, 6. 9.

For-, in composition, has the senses (1) *fore-,* G. *vor-,* Du. *voor-,* A.S. *fore-,* (2) *for-,* (in forbid, &c.) A.S. *for-,* G. and Du. *ver-.* The first implies precedence, the second abstraction, or completeness; in Mœso-Goth. there is some confusion, *faur-* being used for both, but *fra-* only in the latter sense; cf. E. *from.* *Fore* and *From* are the nearest intelligible English equivalents. The ' fore ' words in Piers Plowman are *Forfadres, Forgoer, Forsleues, Forstalleth, Forward,* and *Forwit.* The rest are ' from ' words.

Forbare, *pt. s.* suffered to live, spared, 3. 272. A.S. *forberan,* to forbear, allow.

Forbede, *pr. s. subj.* forbid, 3. 111, 119; *pp.* Forbode, lit. forbidden, but *forbode lawes* is incorrectly used to mean laws *that forbid it;* 3. 151. A.S. *forbeódan,* to forbid, restrain, Mœso-Goth. *faurbiudan,* G. *verbieten,* Du. *verbieden.*

Forebode, *sb.* a forbidding, used in the phrase *goddes forbode* or *lordes forbode* = it is God's (or the Lord's) prohibition, 4. 194, 7. 176. A.S. *forbod,* a forbidding.

Fordon, *v.* to ' do for,' undo, destroy, 5. 20. A.S. *fordón,* G. *verthun,* Du. *verdoen.*

Forfadres, *sb. pl.* S. forefathers, 5. 501.

Forfeture, *sb.* F. forfeiture, 4. 131. From Fr. *forfaire,* to do amiss, Low Latin *forisfacere.*

Forgoer, *sb.* S. foregoer, guide, **2.** 187; *pl.* Forgoeres, well explained by Mr. Wright—' people whose business it was to go before the great lords in their progresses, and buy up provisions for them '—avant-couriers, 2. 60.

Forpyned, *pp.* pined or wasted to death, miserable, wretched, 6. 157.

Forsake, 1 *p. s. pr.* I deny, 5. 431. A.S. *forsacan.*

Forsleues, *sb. pl.* short sleeves covering the fore-arm, 5. 81.

Forsleuthed, *pp.* wasted idly, spoilt for want of use, 5. 445.

Forstalleth, *pr. s.* forestalls, 4. 56. To *forestall* is to buy or bargain for corn or other provisions, before they arrive at the *stall* or market, with intent to sell them at higher prices.

Forth, *sb.* course, 3. 156; cf. the phrase—*course* of justice. Cf. W. *ffordd,* a way, passage, Sw. *fürd,* G. *fahrt,* a way, journey, Du. *vaard,* a canal. From the same root as *fare.*

Forth, *sb.* a ford, 5. 576. A.S. *ford,* G. *furt,* a ford.

Forþi, *conj.* on that account, therefore, pr. 111, 3. 69, &c.; Forthy, 6. 96: *-thy* is the ablative or instrumental case of the def. article; cf. Mœso-Goth. *the.*

Forwandred, *pp.* wearied out with wandering, pr. 7. Cf. G. *wandern.*

Forward, *sb.* S. agreement, compact, 6. 36; Forwarde, 4. 12. A.S. *foreweard,* from *fore* and *weard,* ward, guard.

Forweny, *v.* spoil, 5. 35. A.S. *wenian,* to wean. See note.

Forwes, *sb. pl.* furrows, 6. 106. A.S. *furh,* Du. *voor.*

Forwit, *sb.* S. forewit, foreknowledge, forethought, 5. 166.

Forȝelde, *pr. s. subj.* repay, requite, 6. 279. A.S. *geldan, gyldan,* to pay.

Forȝete, *pp.* forgotten, 5. 404 A.S. *forgitan,* pt. t. *ic forgeat,* pp. *forgeten.*

Foule, *adv.* S. foully, 3. 185.

Foules, *pl.* birds, 5. 355, 6. 32, 7. 128. A.S. *fugel,* a bird, fowl.

Fouleth, *pr. s.* S. fouls, runs foul of, 3. 153.

Fourlonge, *sb.* S. furlong, furrow, 5. 5, 424.

Fourmed, *pt. s.* F. formed, 1. 14.

Fou3ten, *pt. pl.* S. fought, pr. 42.

Frained, 1 *p. s. pt.* asked, 1. 58. A. S. *fregnan,* G. *fragen,* Du. *vragen,* to ask ; cf. Lat. *precari.*

Fram, *prep.* S. from, 6. 162.

Frayned, *pt. s.* asked, 5. 532. See **Frained.**

Freke, *sb.* a man, 4. 12, 156 ; *pl.* Frekis, 5. 170. A.S. *freca,* one who is bold, a hero ; cf. G. *frech.*

Frele, *adj.* F. frail, 3. 121.

Frelete, *sb.* F. frailty, 3. 55.

Frere, *sb.* F. friar, 3. 55 ; *gen. sing.* Freres, 5. 81 ; *pl.* Freres, 2. 182 ; Freris, pr. 58. Lat. *frater.*

Frete, *v.* to eat, 2. 95. A.S. *fretan,* to fret, devour (Mœso-Goth. *fra-itan,* to eat up, from *itan,* to eat). Cf. G. *fressen.*

Fretted, *pp.* adorned, 2. 11. A.S. *fretwian,* to adorn, *fraetu,* an ornament.

Frithed, *pp.* surrounded by a forest, hemmed in with trees, 5. 590. W. *ffridd,* a forest (of E. origin).

Fro, *prep.* S. from, 3. 109, 6. 90. A.S. *frá, fram.*

Frutes, *sb. pl.* F. fruits, 6. 326.

Ful, *adv.* S. full, very, pr. 20, 6. 45.

Fulle, *sb.* S. fill, 6. 266.

Furst, *adj.* S. first, 3. 243.

Fynden, *v.* S. to find, 7. 30 : *pr. s.* Fynt (contr. from *fyndeth*), 4. 131, 7. 128 ; *pp.* Founden, 3. 338.

G.

Gabbe, *v.* to lie, 3. 179. A.S. *gabban,* to delude. Icel. *gabba,* O.F. *gaber,* It. *gabbare,* to cheat.

Gable, *sb.* gable-end of a church,

3. 49. Sw. *gafvel,* G. *giebel,* Du. *gevel ;* cf. Mœso-Goth. *gibla,* a pinnacle.

Gadelynges, *sb. pl.* associates, fellows, 4. 51. A.S. *gaedeling,* a companion. In Mœso-Goth. *ga-diliggs* means a sister's son, a nephew (Col. iv. 10).

Gaf, *pt. s.* gave, 3. 21. See **Gyue.**

Galice, Gallicia, 5. 528 ; Galis, 4. 127.

Galle, *sb.* gall, bile, 5. 119. A.S. *gealla ;* cf. Gk. χολή.

Galoun, *sb.* F. a gallon, 5. 224 ; (used without *of* following), 5. 343.

Gamen, *sb. sing.* game, play, pr. 153. A.S. *gamen,* a game.

Gan, *pt. s.* lit. began ; but commonly used as an auxiliary = did, pr. 143, 1. 112, &c. A.S. *ginnan,* to begin.

Gange, *v.* to go, travel, 2. 167. A.S. *gangan,* Mœso-Goth. *gaggan* (pronounced *gangan*), to go.

Garlekehithe, Garlickhithe, 5. 324.

Garlike, *sb.* S. garlic, 5. 312. A.S. *gár-leác,* from *gár,* a spear, and *leác,* a leek.

Garte, *pt. s.* caused, made, 1. 121 : Gerte, 6. 303 ; *pp.* Gert. 5. 130. Icel. *gjöra,* Sw. *göra,* Sc. *gar.*

Gascoigne, Gascony, pr. 228.

Gate, *sb.* way, road, 1. 203 ; 3. 155 ; hei3e gate = high road, 4. 42. Sw. *gata,* street, G. *gasse.*

Gateward, *sb.* S. gatekeeper, porter, 5. 604.

Gees. See **Gose.**

Gernere, *sb.* F. granary, garner, 7. 129. F. *grenier,* from Lat. *granum,* a grain.

Gert. See **Garte.**

Gerthes, *sb. pl.* girths; witty wordes gerthes = the girths of wise speech, 4. 20. G. *gurt.*

Gete, *v.* S. to get, 4. 141 ; 1 *p. s. pt.* Gat. 4. 79.

Geuen. See **Gyue.**

Gilte, *sb.* guilt, offence, 4. 101. A.S. *gylt.*

Girt, 1 *p. s. pt.* cast, threw, 5. 379; Probably part of vb. *gurde*, to strike (q. v.), which is related to A.S. *gyrd*, G. *gerte*, a rod, switch.

Glade, *v.* S. to gladden, 6. 121.

Glasen, *v.* S. to glaze, 3. 61; Glase, 3. 49. A.S. *glæs*, glass.

Glede, *sb.* a burning coal, a glowing ember, a spark, 2. 12, 5. 291. A.S. *gléd*, a hot coal.

Glewmannes, *gen. sing.* gleeman's, 5. 353. A.S. *gleó, gliw*, glee, music.

Glose, *sb.* F. a gloss, comment, 5. 282. F. *glose;* cf. A.S. *glésan*, to gloss, explain; from Lat. *glossa*, Gk. γλῶσσα, γλώσσημα; cf. *glossary.*

Glosed, *pt. pl.* commented on, explained, made glosses on, pr. 60. Cf. Glose.

Glotoun, *sb.* glutton, 6. 303; Glotown, 5. 310, *pl.* Glotones, pr. 76. F. *glouton*, Low Lat. *glotonus*, Lat. *gluto*, from *glutus*, the throat.

Go slepe = go and sleep, 6. 303; Go swynke = go and work, 6. 219. *Slepe* and *swynke* are verbs in the infin. mood.

Gode, *sb.* S. property, wealth, 2. 131, 3. 168; *to gode* = to good objects, to good conduct, 3. 222, 5. 643; Goed, wealth, 1. 180; *pl.* Godis, goods, wealth, 4. 163.

Godelich, *adv.* in a good manner, kindly, liberally, 1. 180. A.S. *gódlic*, kind.

Goliardeys, *sb.* F. a buffoon, pr. 139. See the note.

Gome, *sb.* a man, 5. 541, *pl.* Gomes, 2. 73, 6. 219. A.S. *guma*, Mœso-Goth. *guma;* cf. G. *braütigam*, Du. *bruidegom*, E. *bridegroom.* *Gome* and *groom* are unrelated forms. Cf. Lat. *homo.*

Gommes, *sb. pl.* F. gums (used generally for spices), 2. 226. Gk. κόμμι.

Gon, *v.* S. to go, 2. 154; *pr. pl.* pr. 43, 7. 94; Gone, 1 *and* 3 *p. pl.* pr. 7. 197, 3. 244.

Gonne, 2 *p. pt. s.* begannest, didst begin, 5. 488. A.S. *ginnan*, pt. t. *ic gan*, 2 p. *þú gunne.*

Good, 6. 231. See Gode.

Gose, *sb. gen. sing.* goose's, 4. 36; *pl.* Gees, 6. 283. A.S. *gós*, gen. *góse*, pl. *gés.*

Gossib, *sb.* gossip, friend, 5. 310. A.S. *godsib*, one related in God, a sponsor in baptism.

Goste, *sb.* S. the spirit, soul, 1. 36.

Goth, *pr. s.* goes, 5. 314.

Gowe, i.e. Go we, let us go, pr. 226.

Graciouse, *adj.* F. pleasing, acceptable, 6. 229.

Graffe, *v.* F. to graft, 5. 137. F. *greffer*, from Lat. *graphium.*

Graith, *adj.* direct, straight, 1. 203; *graith gate*, direct road. Icel. *greiðr*, ready; cf. G. *gerade*, direct.

Graue, *v.* S. to engrave, write, viz. on a brass beneath the window, 3. 49; *pp.* Graue, engraved, 4. 130. Cf. Gk. γράφειν.

Grauynge, *sb.* S. engraving, writing, 3. 64.

Greden, *v.* to cry, cry aloud, 2. 73; *to greden after* = to cry out for, send for, 3. 71. A.S. *grǽdan*, to call.

Grete, *v.* to weep, 5. 386. A.S. *grǽtan*, Sc. *greit.*

Greue, *v.* F. to grieve, vex, pr. 153, 6. 316; *pr. s.* Greueth hym, vexes himself, becomes angry, 6. 317; *pt. s.* Greued hym, grew angry, pr. 139.

Gripeth, *pr. s.* clutches, grips, 3. 248; *pp.* Griped, clutched, 3. 181. A.S. *grípan*, to gripe, grip, grasp, G. *greifen*, Du. *grijpen.*

Gris, *sb. pl.* little pigs, pr. 226.

Icel. *griss,* **grislingr,** Sw. *gris,* a pig. Cf. E. *griskin.*

Grote, *sb.* a groat, 5. 31; *pl.* Grotes, 3. 137. Du. *groot,* large.

Gruccheth, *pr. s.* grudges, murmurs, 6. 317; 1 *p. pl. pr. subj.* Grucche, pr. 153; *pr. pl. subj.* 6. 219. O.F. *grocer, grochier, grousser,* to grumble. Cf. Gk. γρύζειν.

Grys, 4. 51, 6. 283. See **Gris.**

Gult, *sb.* S. guilt, 5. 455, 481. See **Gilte.**

Gurdeth of, *imp. pl.* strike off, 2. 201. Cf. A.S. *gyrd,* a rod.

Gyaunt, *sb.* F. giant, 6. 234.

Gybbe, *short for* Gilbert, 5. 92.

Gyed, *pt. s.* F. guided, 2. 187.

Gyf, *pr. s. subj.* give, 2. 120.

Gyle, *sb.* guile, 2. 187, 5. 207. (Used as a proper name.)

Gyloure, *sb.* beguiler, deceiver, 2. 120.

Gynnynge, *sb.* S. beginning, 2. 30.

Gyue, *pr. s. subj.* give, 7. 197; Gyf, 2. 120; *pr. pl.* Geuen, pr. 76, 5. 326; Geueth of, give heed to, regard, 4. 36; *pp.* Gyue, 2. 148. A.S. *gifan,* G. *geben,* Du. *geven.* See **Ʒiue.**

Gyuere, *sb.* S. giver, donor, 7. 70.

H.

Hadde, *pt. s.* had; *used nearly in the sense* of experienced, 3. 284.

Hagge, *sb.* a hag, 5. 191. A.S. *hægesse, hægtesse,* a witch, fury.

Hailse, 1 *p. s. pr.* I salute, greet, 5. 101; *pt. pl.* Hailsed, made obeisance to, 7. 160. Sw. *helsa,* to salute, hail; cf. Sw. *helsa,* health. Not to be confused with A.S. *healsian,* to embrace, from *heals,* the neck.

Hakeneyman, *sb.* one who lets out horses for hire, 5. 318. F. *haquenée,* Sp. *hacanea,* a hackney; cf. Du. *hakkenei,* an ambling horse.

Half, *sb.* S. side (lit. half), 2. 5, 3. 73, 180.

Haliday, *sb.* S. holiday, 5. 588; *pl.* Halidayes, 7. 20.

Halidom, *sb.* 5. 376. Cognate with Icel. *helgir dómar,* sacred relics, relics of saints. The primary meaning of *dómr* is *doom.*

Halpe. See **Holpyn.**

Hals, *sb.* S. the neck, pr. 170, 2. 195, 6. 63. G. and Du. *hals.*

Halt, *pr. s.* holds (contr. from *holdeth*), 3. 241.

Halue, *adj.* S. half, 5. 31, 6. 108.

Han, have. See **Haue.**

Handidandi, *sb.* forfeit, 4. 75. *Handydandy* is a children's game, played with the *hands,* one of which conceals a marble. If another child guesses which hand contains the marble, he wins it; if he fails, he pays forfeit. See Halliwell's Dict., and cf. King Lear, Act iv. Sc. 6.

Hanged, *pp.* hung, pr. 176, 3. 180.

Hansel, *sb.* a bribe, 5. 326. It properly means an earnest. A.S. *handsylen,* a giving into the hands; see my Etym. Dict. *To hansel* for a bribe or treat.

Happe, *v.* to happen, 3. 284, 6. 47. O.F. *happer,* to snatch; cf. Icel. *happ,* W. *hap,* luck; Icel. *heppinn,* fortunate, *happy.*

Happes, *sb. pl.* successes, 5. 97. Icel. *happ,* W. *hap,* fortune.

Happily, *adv.* perhaps, 5. 624; Happiliche, 5. 626.

Hardiliche, *adv.* boldly, 6. 30,

Harlotes, *sb. pl.* buffoons, tellers of ribald stories (by no means used in the modern sense), 4. 118, 6. 54. W. *herlod,* a stripling, lad.

Harlotrie, *sb.* tale-telling, jesting talk, buffoonery, 5. 413; Harlotrye, 4. 115.

Hastow, hast thou, 3. 105.

Hat, *pr. s.* is named, is called, 5. 582, 629; Hatte, 5. 604, 6. 45;

pl. Hatte, 5. 586. A.S. *hátan*,
O. Fris. *heta*, G. *heissen*, to call,
name ; also, to have for a name,
be called. Properly, however, it
was a *passive* form of the verb, as
shewn by Mœso-Goth. *haitith*, he
calls, *haitada*, he is called ; as in—
Thomas, saei haitada Didimus,
Thomas, who is called Didymus,
John xi. 16.

Hatie, 2 *p. s. subj.* thou hate, 6.
52.

Hatte, *sb.* S. a hat, 5. 536 ; Hatt,
5. 527.

Haukes, *gen. sing.* hawk's, 5. 438 ;
pl. Haukes, 4. 125.

Haukynge, *sb.* hawking, 3. 311.

Haue, *v.* S. to have ; *pr. s. subj.*
Haue, 7. 68 ; 1 *p. pr. pl.* Han, 3.
48 ; 2 *p.* 3. 72, 6. 260 ; 3 *p.* 7.
11 ; *pr. pl.* Haueth, 7. 65 ; *pt. s.*
Hadde (experienced), 3. 284 ;
Haued, 3. 39 ; *pt. pl.* Haued, 2.
166, 219 ; *imp. pl.* Haueth, 1.
173.

Hauer, *adj.* (*or part of compound
sb.*) oaten, made of oats, 6. 284. G.
hafer, Du. *haver ;* whence Du.
haverzak, a bag of oats, *haver-
sack.*

He, *pron.* used indefinitely, in the
sense *one of you*, 6. 138, 7. 93.

He, *pron. fem.* she, 1. 140. A.S.
heó, hió. Not uncommon. See
Heo.

Hedes. *pl.* S. heads, 6. 328.

Hegges, *sb. pl.* S. hedges, 6. 31.

Heighe, *adj.* S. high, 6. 4, 114 ;
Heiȝ, 1. 162 ; *adv.* Heighe, 5.
588 ; Heiȝe, 4. 162 ; Heighlich (at
a high price), 6. 314 ; Heiȝ, loudly,
2. 73. Heiȝe gate, high road,
4. 42.

Hele, *n.*S. health, 5270. See
Soule.

Hele, *sb.* 7. 194. See note.

Hele, *v.* S. to conceal, 5. 168. A.S.
helan, Du. *helen*, G. *hüllen*, Lat.
celare. Cf. E. *hell, hole.*

Helpith, *imp. pl.* help ye, 6. 21.

Hem, *dat. pl.* to them, 3. 345, 6.
16 ; *acc. pl.* 7. 27, &c. A.S.
him, heom.

Hem-seluen, themselves, pr. 59,
3. 215.

Hende, *adj.* courteous, 5. 261.
Dan. and Sw. *händig*, dexterous,
E. *handy.*

Hendeliche, *adv.* courteously, 3.
29, 5. 101.

Hennes, *adv.* hence, 3. 108, 244,
&c.

Hente, *v.* S. to catch, seize, take
possession of, 5. 68 ; *pt. s.* Hente,
5. 5 ; Hent, 6. 176 ; *pt. pl.* Henten, 6. 190. A.S. *hentan*, to
clutch in the hand, grasp, *hunt*
after.

Heo, *pron. fem.* she, 1. 73, 3. 29,
5. 632. See He.

Hep, *sb.* a heap, a large number, 5.
233 ; Heep, pr. 53. A.S. *heáp*,
G. *haufe*, Du. *hoop.*

Her, their. See Here.

Herberwed, *pp.* S. harboured,
lodged, 5. 233. A.S. *here*, an
army, and *beorgan*, to hide.

Herde, *pt. s.* S. heard, 2. 205.

Here, *pr.* S. their, pr. 28, 7. 105 ;
Her, 7. 105. In the same line also
here = here, *adv.*

Heremites, *sb. pl.* Gk. hermits, pr.
28, 6. 190 ; Heremytes, 6. 147.

Hernes, *sb. pl.* corners, nooks,
hiding-places, 2. 233. A.S. *hirne ;*
cf. E. *horn*, Gaelic *cearn*, a corner.
E. *corner* is from Lat. *cornu.*

Herre, *adj.* S. higher, 2. 28.

Hertis, *sb. pl.* S. hearts, 6. 217.

Heruest, *sb.* S. harvest, a crop, 6.
292.

Heste, *sb.* behest, commandment,
3. 112 ; *pl.* Hestes, 7. 183. A.S.
hǽs, a command. See Hote.

Heuede, *sb.* S. head, 1.162 ; Heued,
5. 637. A.S. *heáfod*, Goth. *haubith.*
The Goth. diphthong shews that
the L. *caput* is unrelated.

Heuene, *gen. sing.* of heaven, pr. 106.

Heueneriche, *sb.* the kingdom of heaven, pr. 27. A.S. *heofon-rice.*

Hewe, *sb.* a servant, 5. 559; *pl.* Hewen, 4. 55. A.S. *hiwan, sb. pl.* domestics.

Heyre, *sb.* S. hair (i. e. a hair-shirt), 5. 66.

Hiderward, *adv.* hitherward, 6. 323.

Hiedest, 2 *p. s. pt.* didst hie, didst hasten, 3. 193. A.S. *higan.*

Hight, *pt. s.* commanded, pr. 102, 3. 9. A.S. *hátan,* pt. t. *ic hét* or *ic héht.* See **Hote.**

Hij, *pron. pl.* they, pr. 43, 5. 114, &c. A.S. *hi, hig,* they.

Hiled, *pp.* S. covered, roofed, 5. 599. See **Hele.**

Hitte, *pt. s.* lit. hit; hence, cast down hastily, 5. 329.

Hiȝte, *pt. s.* bade, commanded, 5. 206, 7. 200; *pp.* bidden, 6. 133. See **Hight.**

Hiȝte, *pt. s.* was named, 6. 80, 81, 82. See **Hat.**

Hode, *sb.* S. a hood, 5. 31, 195; *pl.* Hodes, 6. 271.

Hoked, *pp.* S. provided with a hook at the upper end, pr. 53.

Hokes, *sb. pl.* S. hooks, hinges, 5. 603.

Hokkerye, *sb.* hucksterry, retail dealing, 5. 227. G. *höker,* a *hawker,* Sw. *hökare,* a cheese-monger, retail-seller. I doubt the connection with Icel. *okr,* G. *wucher,* usury; Lat. *augere,* to *eke,* increase; Low Lat. *auxiatrix,* a huckster, *auxionarius,* (lit. a seller by auction) a retail-dealer.

Holde, 1 *p. s. pr.* I hold, esteem, consider, 5. 419; *pr. pl.* Holde, 1. 9; *inf.* Holde hym, to stay, 7. 5; Holden hym, 6. 202; *pp.* Holden, 4. 118, 5. 261; *imp. pl.* Holdeth, 7. 59. A.S. *healdan.*

Hole, *adj.* full of holes, 6. 61. Some MSS. read *Ihole.* Cf. A.S.

holian, to make a hole, *geholed,* pierced.

Holely, *adv.* S. wholly, 3. 112.

Holicherche, *sb.* holy church, 1. 75, &c.; Holikirke, 6. 28.

Holpyn, *pt. pl.* S. helped, 6. 108; Halpe, 7. 6; *pp.* Holpe, 4. 169. See **Hulpen.**

Hondes, *sb. pl.* S. hands, 5. 294.

Hondreth, *sb.* S. a hundred, pr. 210.

Honged hym, *pt. s.* S. hung himself, 1. 68; *pl.* Hongen, hung, crucified, 1. 172. A.S. *hón,* to hang, crucify.

Hoper, *sb.* a seed-basket, 6. 63. In the Oriel MS. it is glossed by *seed-leep.* It may be quite unconnected with the *hopper* of a mill, and may be named from the *hoops* it is made of; cf. A.S. *hóp,* a hoop, a twig.

Hore, *adj.* hoary, 6. 85, 7. 99. A.S. *hár,* hoar, grey-haired.

Ho-so, whoso, pr. 144.

Hostellere, *sb.* an innkeeper, keeper of a hostelry or hotel, 5. 339. From l. 329 it appears that the same man kept horses for hire. From Lat. *hospitale,* a hostel, *hospes,* a guest. It is now *ostler,* with a lower meaning.

Hote, 1 *p. s. pr.* I command, bid, 2. 199, 6. 261; *pr. s.* Hoteth, 3. 262, 5. 555; *pt. s.* Hiȝte, 5. 206; Hight, pr. 102; *pp.* Hote, 6. 78. A.S. *hátan,* to bid.

Hoten, *pp.* named, 2. 21. See **Hat.**

Houeth, *pr. s.* hovers; *ouer houeth* = hovers over, floats over (said of rain-clouds) 3. 207; *pt. s.* Houed, hovered about, rocked about (implying slight undulating movement whilst keeping in one place) pr. 210. W. *hofio, hofian,* to hang, hover. Cf. our phrase *to hang about.* (W. *hofio* is of E. origin).

Houped, *pt. s.* whooped, shouted after, called loudly, 6. 174. O.F.

houper, 'to hoop unto, or call a-far off'; Cotgrave. Hence Mod. E. *whoop*, to call out.

Houres, *sb. pl.* 'hours,' or services for particular times of the day, 1. 181. There were seven, viz. matins, prime, tierce, sext, nones, vespers, and compline.

Housbonderye, *sb.* husbandry, economy, frugality, 1. 57. Icel. *búa*, to till, *bú*, a farm, *bóndi*, a farmer. A *husband* means a master of a house, male house-keeper. See Bondman.

Houues, *sb. pl.* coifs, pr. 210. A.S. *húfe*, a mitre, tiara, &c.

How, *interj.* ho ! 6. 118.

Howue, *sb.* S. a coif, 3. 293. See Houues.

Hucche, *sb.* a hutch, an iron-bound clothes-box once common in bed rooms, 4. 116. O.F. *huche*.

Hulles, *sb. pl.* S. hills, pr. 5, 214, 7. 141.

Hulpen, *pt. pl.* S. helped, 6. 118; *pp.* Hulpe, 5. 633, 7. 72. See Holpyn.

Hundreth, a hundred, 5. 527.

Huyre, *sb.* hire, 6. 141; Huire, 5. 557. A.S. *hýre*, G. *heuer*, Du. *huur*.

Huyred, *pp.* hired, 6. 314.

Hyed, 1 *p. pt. s.* I hied, hastened, 5. 384. See Hiedest.

Hym-self, *used for modern* itself, 1. 151; Hymselue, 5. 221. A.S. *him*, acc. and dat. (neuter) of *hit*.

Hyne, *sb.* S. hind, servant, pr. 39, 6. 133; *for an hyne*=as a thing of small value, 4. 118.

Hyȝte, 1. 17, 6. 236. See Hiȝte.

I, J.

J is written like I in the MSS.; hence *Iakke* is for *Jakke* (Jack), &c.

Iangelers, *sb. pl.* tattlers, chatter-boxes, babblers, pr. 35. 'Jange-lyng is whan a man spekith to moche bifor folk, and clappith as

a mille, and taketh no keep [heed] to what he saith ;' Chaucer, Pers. Tale, De Superbia. O. Fr. *jan-gleur*, a tattler, liar, from *jangler*, to lie, jest ; but the root is doubt-less Teutonic ; cf. Du. *janken*, to howl. The O. Fr. *jangleur* (from the root of *jangle*) has been hope-lessly confused with *jougleur* (Lat. *joculator*) owing to both being names given to buffoons. See Iogeloure.

Iangle, *v.* to chatter, prate, talk fast, pr. 130, 2. 94, 6. 316; *pr. s.* Iangleth, 4. 155.

Ianglyng, *sb.* prattle, talk, 4. 180.

Iape, *vb.* to jape, jest, 2. 94; *pt. s.* Iaped, befooled, deceived, 1. 67. F. *japper*, to yelp, chatter. Cf. E. *gab, gabble, jabber*.

Iapers, *sb. pl.* jesters, fools, pr. 35.

Ich, *pron.* I, 5. 262. See Ik.

Iille, *sb.* a gill, now used to mean a quarter of a pint, 5. 346. 'Gylle, lytylle pot. *Gilla, vel gillus, vel gillungulus.*' Prompt. Parv. O.F. *gelle* (Roquefort).

Ik, *pron.* I, 5. 228. A.S. *ic*.

Ilke, *adj.* S. same, 1. 83, 6. 164.

Ilyke, *adj.* like, 1. 50. A.S. *gelic*.

I-made, 1 *p. s. pt.* made, 5. 162. A.S. *gemacian*, to make. [The prefix is the A.S. *ge-*, often found before past participles, less often before preterites and infinitives.]

Infamis, old Lat. pl. for *infames*, but probably employed instead of it by mere mistake, 5. 168.

Ingonge, *sb.* S. ingoing, ingress, 5. 638. Cf. Sc. *gang*.

Inne, *adv.* within, 6. 305. A.S. *innan*, adv.

Innocentz, *sb. pl.* innocent people, prob. children, 7. 41.

Inpugnen, *v.* F. to impugn, pr. 109; *pt. s.* Impugned, 7. 147.

Iogeloure, *sb.* F. a buffoon, juggler, 6. 72. Lat. *joculator*, O. Fr. *jougleur*, often written *jongleur*, and confused with O. Fr. *jangleur*, a tattler. See Iangelers.

Ioutes, *sb. pl.* pottage, 5. 158. 'Iowtys, potage. *Brassica, juta.*' Prompt. Parv. See Way's note. Low Lat. *juta, jutta;* see Ducange.

It ben, i.e. it is, or, they are, 6. 56.

Iugge, *v.* F. to judge, pr. 130, 2. 94; *pt. s.* Iugged, 7. 161.

Iugges, *sb. pl.* F. judges, 7. 184.

Iustice, *sb.* F. a justice, magistrate, 3. 319, 7. 44.

Iuwen, *gen. pl.* of the Jews, 1. 67.

K.

Kairen, *v.* S. to go up and down, wander (lit. to turn), pr. 29; *pr. s.* Kaireth, goes, travels, 4. 23; Kaires hym, turns, betakes himself, 5. 305; cf. Kairen hem, to carry themselves, 2. 161. In all these passages some MSS. read *karien*, and there seems to be some confusion of A.S. *cerran*, O. Fris. *kera*, G. *kehren*, Du. *keeren*, to turn, with F. *charier*, E. *carry*.

Kayed, *pp.* fastened with a key, 5. 623.

Kenne, *v.* to make known, 1. 92; to explain, 5. 426, 7. 107; to teach, 1. 81; *pr. s.* Kenneth, teaches, 6. 22, 7. 73; *pt. s.* Kenned, guided, 4. 43; taught, 7. 133; *pt. pl.* Kenned, guided, 5. 546; *imp. s.* Kenne, teach, 2. 4, 6. 24; *imp. pl.* Kenneth, teach, 6. 14. Icel. *kenna*, to teach, to know; the Mœso-Goth. has *kannjan*, to make known, *kunnan*, to know.

Kepe, 1 *p. s. pr.* I care, care for, desire, 3. 278, 4. 193.

Kerneled, *pp.* F. furnished with battlements, embattled, 5. 597. F. *crénelé*, from *créneau*, a battlement; Lat. *crena*, a notch.

Kerue, *v.* S. to carve, cut, 6. 106.

Ketten, *pt. pl.* S. cut, 6. 191.

Keure, *v.* F. to cover, 3. 60.

Kidde, *pt. s.* exhibited towards, shewed, 5. 440. A.S. *cýðan*, to make known, tell, pt. t. *ic cýðde*.

Kingene, *gen. pl.* of kings, 1. 105.

Kirke, *sb.* church, 5. 1, 6. 93.

Kirtel, *sb.* a kind of under-jacket, worn beneath the jacket or *kourteby*, 5. 80. A *full kirtle* was a jacket and petticoat, a *half-kirtle* was either one or the other; and the word *kirtle* alone meant any of the three, according to the context. A.S. *cyrtel*, Sw. *kjortel*.

Kitoun, *sb.* a kitten, pr. 190, 202.

Kitthe, *sb.* region, country, 3. 203. A.S. *cýð*, a region.

Knappes, *sb. pl.* knops, knobs, 6. 272. A.S. *cnæp*, a knop, button.

Knaue, *sb.* S. a boy, lad, servant, 4. 16, 5. 116; *pl.* Knaues, pr. 44, 225.

Knowe, *pp.* S. known, 5. 648.

Knowes, *sb. pl.* S. knees, 5. 359.

Knowing, *sb.* S. knowledge, 1. 136.

Knowleched, *pt. s.* acknowledged, confessed, 5. 481. In Swedish, some abstract nouns end in *-lek*, and *lek* means *sport*; in Icel. the termination is *-leikr*, also meaning *sport;* in A.S. it is *-lác*, which means (1) a gift, (2) sport. Hence we must connect *-leche* with Mœso-Goth. *laikan*, to sport, play, and consider it distinct from the endings *-ly* and *-like*.

Kokeney, *sb.* small egg, inferior egg, or (simply) egg, 6. 287. The meaning and etymology of this difficult word have been fully investigated; and the results are given in the New E. Dictionary, s. v. *Cockney*, which is the same word. The literal sense is 'egg of cocks'; where *coken* is the M. E. gen. pl. of *cok*, a cock, just as *Iuwen* is the gen. pl. of *Jew*; see Iuwen above; and *ey* is the common M. E. word for 'egg'; from A. S. *ǽg*, an egg. There was an old popular belief that some small and inferior eggs were laid by cocks; even in Mod. G. we have, in dialect speech, the word *hahneneier*, lit. cocks' eggs. 'The constituents of a *collop* were precisely bacon and an egg.'

Kokewolde, *sb.* a cuckold, 4. 164, 5. 159.

Koleplantes, *sb. pl.* coleworts, cauliflowers, cabbages, &c., 6. 288. A.S. *cawl*, Lat. *caulis*, G. *kohl*.

Konne, *pr. pl.* S. can, know how to, 6. 70; 2 *p. pl. subj.* Kunne, know, 6. 255; *pr. pl.* Kunneth, know, 7. 41.

Konning, *adj.* S. cunning, clever, 3. 34.

Kourteby, *sb.* 5. 80. See Courtpies.

Kullen, *v.* S. to kill, 1. 66; *pt. s.* 1 *p.* Kulled, 3. 186. See Culled.

Kulter, *sb.* coulter, 3. 306. The A.S. *culter*, E. *coulter* are simply borrowed from the Latin.

Kynde, *adj.* S. natural, innate; *kynde witte* = natural intelligence, pr. 118; common sense, 1. 55.

Kynde, *sb.* S. kind, pr. 186; nature, natural disposition, 2. 27.

Kyndely, *adv.* intimately, 1. 81, 161, 5. 545; kindly, 3. 15.

Kyne, *sb. pl.* kine, cows, 6. 142.

Kyngriche, *sb.* S. kingdom, pr. 125. Cf. G. *königreich.*

Kynne. *sb.* S. kin, kindred, 2. 130.

Kynnes, *gen. sing.* in phr. *any kynnes*, of any kind, 5. 273. See Alkin.

Kyrke, *sb.* S. church, 5. 269.

L.

Lacche, *v.* to catch, 5. 355; to get, acquire, 6. 230; 2 *p. s. subj.* Lacche, catch, 2. 202; *pt. s.*

Lauȝte, pr. 150; *pt. pl.* Lauȝte leue, took leave, 3. 25. A.S. *lǽccan, gelǽccan*, to seize; cf. E. latch.

Lacchyng, *sb.* S. clutching, receiving, 1. 101.

Ladde, led. See Lede.

Lafte, left. See Leue (3).

Lafte, 1. *p. s. pt.* remained, stayed behind (*some MSS. have* lefte), 3. 196. See Wright's P. Plowman, p. 440, l. 14426, but especially William of Palerne, ed. Skeat, ll. 1588, 1858.

Laike, *v.* to play, sport, pr. 172. Icel. *leika*, Sw. *leka*, Goth. *laikan*, to sport.

Lakke, *v.* to blame, find fault with, 5. 132; *pr. pl.* 2 *p.* Lakkeþ, 3. 54; *imp. s.* Lakke, 2. 47, 6. 227. A.S. *leahan*, O. Fris. *lakia*, Du. *laken*, to blame.

Lammasse, Lammas, 6. 291.

Lappe, *sb.* a portion, 2. 35; *pl.* Lappes, laps, 6. 295. A.S. *lǽppa*, a flap or loose border of a garment, also the lap; G. *lappen*, a flap, rag, lobe; cf. E. *lappet, lobe, flap, flabby, lip.* See Leef.

Largenesse, *sb.* bounty, largesse, 5. 632.

Lasse, *adj. and adv.* S. less, 2. 45, 3. 201, &c.

Lat, Late, let. See Lete.

Late, *adv.* late, 3. 73; *comp.* Latter, later, less readily, 1. 197.

Laughen, *v.* S. to laugh, rejoice, 4. 106.

Lauȝte, caught, took. See Lacche.

Lawȝe of, *v.* to laugh at, 4. 18; *pres. part.* Lawghyng, 4. 153. See Laughen.

Leche, *sb.* a leech or physician, 1. 202; *pl.* Leches, 6. 275. A.S. *lǽce*, Mœso-Goth. *lekeis.*

Lechecraft, *sb.* medicinal art, 6. 256.

Lede, *sb.* lead, 5. 600. A.S. *leád*, Du. *lood.*

Lede, *sb.* man, 1. 139, 5. 522; *pl.*
Ledes, 3. 96. A.S. *leóda*, G.
leute, Du. *lieden*, people, folks.
Perhaps cf. also Low Lat. *litus*,
ledus, a sort of peasant-farmer.

Lede, *v.* S. to lead, guide, govern,
4. 148; to draw (a cart), 2. 179;
pt. s. 1 *p.* Ladde, led, took, carried,
5. 251; 2 *p.* Laddest, didst lead,
7. 189; *pt. s.* Ladde, led (captive),
5. 498; *imp. pl.* Ledeth, conduct,
2. 134.

Leder, *sb.* S. leader, governor, 1.
157; Ledere, 1. 159.

Ledyng, *sb.* S. leading, guidance,
2. 42.

Leef, *sb.* a bit, piece, small portion,
6. 256, 7. 110; cf. 5. 203; Lef,
a leaf (of a book), 3. 337; *gen.
case,* Leues, 3. 336. The idea of
a small flat, flapping substance is
expressed by *lap, lappet, leaf;* if
the substance is rounded, by *lobe,
lip.* See **Lappe,** and note that
another reading for *lappe* (2. 35)
is *lippe.* From signifying *leaf* it
also means a *part* of a leaf, as in
5. 203, &c. See **Lyppe.**

Legge, *v.* S. to lay, 2. 34, 6. 270.

Legistres, *sb. pl.* legists, advocates,
men skilled in the law, 7. 14, 59.
O.F. *legistre.*

Lelli, Lelly, *adv.* F. loyally, faith-
fully, verily, 1. 78, 3. 30; Lelliche,
1. 179.

Lemman, *sb.* sweetheart, mistress,
lover (used of both sexes), 2. 21;
pl. Lemmannes, 3. 150. Contr.
from *leof man* or *lef man;* A.S.
leóf, dear.

Lene, *v.* to lend, give, 5. 244, 6. 17;
1 *p. s. pr.* 5. 250; 2 *p. pl. pr. subj.*
1. 179. A.S. *lǽnan.*

Lenge, *v.* to dwell, linger, tarry, 1.
207. A.S. *lengian,* to prolong;
from *lang,* long.

Lenger, *adv.* S. longer, 1. 207; *adj.
comp.* 3. 336, 5. 210.

Lent, *pt. s.* gave, 5. 303; Lente-

stow, 2 *p.* didst thou lend, 5. 253.
See **Lene.**

Lenten, *sb.* the season of Lent, pr.
91. A.S. *lencten,* the spring of the
year.

Leode, *sb.* S. man, 3. 32; *pl.*
Leodes, 4. 148. See **Lede.**

Lepe, *pt. s.* leapt, 2. 68, 5. 502.
A.S. *hleápan,* pt. t. *ic hleóp.*

Lere, *sb.* face, countenance, 1. 3.
A.S. *hleór,* the face, a cheek.

Lere, *v.* to teach, 1. 144; 1 *p. s. pr.*
3. 69; *pr. s.* Lereth, 3. 125; 2 *p.
pr. pl.* Leren, 5. 45; *pt. s.* Lered,
1. 149; *imp. pl.* Lereth, 1. 134;
pp. as adj. Lered, instructed,
learned, 4. 11. A.S. *lǽran,* G.
lehren, Du. *leeren.*

Lerned, (1) 1 *p. s. pt.* I learnt, 5.
203; 2 *p.* Lernedest, 1. 139; (2)
2 *p. s. pr.* Lernest, teachest, 4. 11;
pt. s. Lerned, taught, 5. 302, 7.
131. The latter meaning is more
common in Langland. A.S. *leorn-
ian.*

Lese, *v.* to lose, 2. 35, 3. 135, &c.;
Lesen, *v.* to lose, 5. 625; *pt. s.*
Lese, 7. 158; *better spelt* Les, 5.
499. A.S. *leósan,* Mœso-Goth.
fraliusan, G. *verlieren,* Du. *ver-
liezen.*

Lese, *v.* to glean, 6. 68. Still in
common use in Shropshire.

Leste, *adj.* least, 3. 204.

Lesyng, *sb.* leasing, lying, telling of
idle tales, 4. 18; *pl.* Lesynges, 2.
124. A.S. *leásung,* lying, from
leás, false, loose, vain.

Lesynge, *sb.* S. losing, loss, 5.
112.

Lete, (1) *v.* to let, permit, allow;
Lat worþe, to let be, let alone, pr.
187; *pr. s.* Leteth, 3. 136; *pt. s.*
Lete, 1. 165; *pr. s. subj.* Lete, pr.
155; *imp. s.* Lat, 2. 47; Late, 4.
86, 6. 227; *imp. pl.* Late, 5. 53;
(2) to leave, forego, 4. 191, 5. 26,
6. 273; Leten, leave off, cease,
5. 465; (3) to cause; *pt. pl.*

Leten, **2.** 158; *imp. s.* Lat, 3. 112; Lete, 4. 20; (4) to hold, consider, esteem; Late wel by, to think well of, set store by, 5. 625; *pt. s.* Lete, 4. 161, 6. 170; *pt. pl.* Leten, pr. 181, 4. 160. A.S. *lǽtan*, G. *lassen*, Du. *laten*.

Lette, *v.* to hinder, prevent, 1. 156, 3. 32; to restrain, 5. 303; *pr. s.* Letteth, 3. 155, 4. 176; *pr. s. subj.* Lette, 5. 458; 1 *p. s. pt.* Lette, put a stop to, 3. 197; where the Oriel MS. has *letted*; cf. Chauc. C. T. 8265. A.S. *lettan*, Du. *letten*, to hinder.

Letter, *sb.* S. an impeder, preventer, hinderer, 1. 69.

Letterure, *sb.* knowledge of letters, learning, pr. 110.

Lettred, *pp. as adj.* lettered, learned, 1. 134, 7. 131.

Lettynge, *sb.* S. hindrance, 6. 7.

Leue, *pr. s. subj.* permit, grant, pr. 126, 5. 263; 1 *p. s. pr.* Leue, I allow, 3. 333. A.S. *lýfan*, G. *erlauben*.

Leue, *v.* to believe, 5. 45; 1 *p. s. pr.* Leue, 6. 92; *pr. s.* Leueth, **2.** 101; *pt. pl.* Leueden, 1. 117; *imp. s.* Leue, 5. 302; *imp. pl.* Leueth, 3. 174. Mœso-Goth. *laubjan*, G. *glauben* (for *ge-lauben*); radically the same as the preceding.

Leue, *v.* to leave, to let alone, 1. 101, 7. 149; *imp. s.* Leue, 5. 292; *imp. pl.* Leueþ, 3. 69; *pt. pl.* Lafte, left, 4. 153. A.S. *lǽfan*, to leave; cf. G. *b-leiben*, to remain.

Leue, *sb.* S. leave, permission, pr. 85, 3. 15.

Leue, *adj.* (*voc. case*) lief, dear, 5. 563; *pl.* 4. 39. The nom. case is *lef*; cf. A.S. *leóf*.

Leue, *adv.* dearly, pr. 163, 3. 18; *compar.* Leuer, 1. 141; Leuere, 5. 413; *superl.* Leuest, 5. 572.

Leute, *sb.* F. loyalty, pr. 126; Lewte. pr. 122, **2.** 21.

Lewdnesse, *sb.* S. ignorance, 3. 32.

Lewed, Lewde, *adj.* S. lay, unlearned, 7. 136; useless, 1. 187; Lewede, 4. 11. E. *lewd*, but not used in the modern sense.

Lewte. See Leute.

Leyde, *pt. s.* S. laid, 5. 359, 6. 124; *pp.* Leyde, 3. 201.

Leyes, *sb. pl.* leas, fallow lands, 7. 5. A.S. *leág*.

Libbe, *v.* to live, 3. 226; *pr. pl.* Libben, 5. 149; Libbeth, 2. 186; *pres. part.* Libbyng, pr. 222; Lybbyng, 7. 62. A.S. *lybban*.

Liche, *adj.* S. like, 5. 353, 489.

Lief, *adv.* dearly; þe *lief likeþ* = it dearly pleases thee, i. e. you like best, 4. 148. Cf. Leue, *adv.*

Liflode, *sb.* means of life, food, livelihood, diet, pr. 30, 1. 37. A.S. *líf-lád*; from *lád*, a way, modern E. *lode*. The modern *livelihood* has gradually replaced the old word *liflode*. See Prompt. Parv.

Lige, *adj.* F. liege, 4. 184.

Ligge, 1 *p. s. pres.* I lie (*iaceo*), 5. 417; *pr. s.* Liggeth, 3. 175; *pr. pl.* Liggen, pr. 91; Liggeth, 6. 15; *pr. s. subj.* Ligge, 5. 439; *pr. pl. subj.* Ligge, **2.** 135; *pres. part.* Liggyng, **2.** 51. A.S. *licgan*, Du. *liggen*.

Likam, *sb.* body, 1. 37; Lykam, pr. 30. A.S. *líc-hama*, from *líc*, the body, and *hama*, covering or skin. Cf. E. *lich-gate* and G. *leichnam*.

Likerous, *adj.* lickerish, delicate, dainty, pr. 30, 6. 268. G. *lecker*, Du. *lekker*, dainty; cf. A.S. *liccera*. a glutton.

Liketh, *pr. s. impers.* it pleases, 1. 43, **2.** 231. 5. 112, &c.; *pt. s.* Lyked, pr. 60, 149. Mœso-Goth. *leikan*, to please.

Limitoures, *sb. pl.* friars licensed to ask alms within a limited district, 5. 138.

List, *pr. s. impers.* it pleases, pr. 172, 3. 157; *pt. s.* Liste, 1. 148; *pt. s. subj.* Liste, it would please, 5. 400. A.S. *lystan,* to please; cf. E. *list, lust.*

Listres, *sb. pl.* lectors, 5. 138. See the note.

Lith, *pr. s.* lies (*iacet*), 1. 124.

Lith, *pr. s.* lies (*mentitur*), 3. 155.

Lither, *adj.* defective, vicious, 5. 387; Luther, ill-tempered, 5. 118. A.S. *lyðre,* bad; Sw. *lyte,* a defect, fault.

Lixte, *? p. s. pr.* liest, tellest lies, 5. 163.

Liзte, *adv.* S. lightly, 4. 161; *comp.* Liзtloker, 5. 578.

Lobyes, *sb. pl.* loobies, lubbers, pr. 55.

Loke, *v.* (1) to look, see, find out, pr. 172, 2. 155; to look up, look about, 4. 60; *? p. s. pr.* Lokestow, lookest thou, 7. 136; *imp. s.* Loke, 3. 269; *pt. s.* Loked, 6. 321; Lokyd hym, appeared (?), 5. 189; (2) Loken, *v.* to look after, guard, 7. 165; Loke, *v.* to enforce, 6. 319; *pr. s. subj.* Loke, protect, 1. 207; (3) Loke, *v.* to look upon, allow, 2. 135. A.S. *lócian.*

Lokke, *sb.* S. lock (of a door), 1. 200; cf. 5. 604.

Lolled, *pt. s.* lolled about, 5. 192.

Lombe, *sb.* S. a lamb, 5. 560.

Londe, *sb.* S. land, 3. 135.

Longe, *adj.* S. tall, pr. 55.

Longeth, *pr. pl.* belong, 2. 45, 5. 628. Cf. G. *gelangen.*

Lope, *pt. pl.* leapt, ran, 4. 153; Lopen, 1. 116, 5. 163; *pp.* Lopen, 5. 198. See Lepe.

Lorel, *sb.* good-for-nothing fellow, 7. 136. Also spelt *losel.*

Lorkynge, *pres. part.* lurking, 2. 216.

Loseles, *sb. pl.* good-for-nothing fellows, 6. 124. See Lorel.

Losengerye, *sb.* flattery, lying, 6. 145. O.F. *losanger,* to flatter, lie.

Lotebies, *sb. pl.* concubines, 3. 150. Probably from the root of E. *lot.*

Lothelich, *adj.* S. loathsome, 1. 116.

Lotheth, *pr. s. impers.* it irks, causes (us) to loathe, pr. 155.

Louedayes, *sb. pl.* love-days, days for the settlement of differences by arbitration, 3. 157, 5. 427.

Loues, *sb. pl.* S. loaves, 6. 285.

Loupe, *pt. s.* leapt away, escaped, 4. 106. See Lope.

Loure, *v.* to look frowningly, 5. 132; *pres. part.* Lourynge, 5. 83 Du. *loeren;* cf. Sc. *glowre.*

Louryng, *sb.* frowning, scowling, 5. 344.

Louted, *pt. s.* bowed, made obeisance, 3. 115. A.S. *hlútan.*

Louye, *v.* to love, 5. 49, 6. 211; *pres. s. subj.* Louye, pr. 126. A.S. *lufian.*

Lowed, *pt. s.* stooped, pr. 129.

Lowen, *pp.* lied, told lies, 5. 95. A.S. *leógan,* to lie, pp. *logen.*

Luft, *sb.* a light, worthless fellow, 4. 62. Spelt *lift* in Oriel MS. Cf. A.S. *lyft,* Du. *lucht,* air; Du. *luchtig,* airy, light, merry, careless; also Old Du. *lucht,* O.E. *lufte, lifte, left* (in sense *left* hand).

Lumbardes, *sb. pl.* Lombards, 5. 242.

Luther. See Lither.

Lybbyng, 7. 62. See Libbe.

Lyf, *sb.* (1) life, 1. 202; (2) a living person, man, 3. 292. Very rare in the latter sense, except in Langland, who has it frequently, in the *Vita de Dowel,* &c. The Icel. *lif* has the same double usage.

Lyflode, *sb.* 5. 88, 6. 17. See Liflode.

Lykam. See Likam.

Lyked. See Liketh.

Lyme, *sb.* S. limb, 5. 99; *pl.* Lymes, 6. 126.

Lynde, *sb.* S. linden-tree, 1. 154.

Lynnen, *sb.* linen, pr. 219, 1. 18.

Lyppe, *sb.* a portion, part, 5. 250. See Lappe.

Lyser, *sb.* list, selvage, 5. 210. F. *lisière.*

M.

Maceres, *sb. pl.* mace-bearers, officers of the courts of justice, 3. 76.

Made. See Make.

Maire, *sb.* F. a mayor, 3. 87; *pl.* Maires, 3. 94.

Maistre, *sb.* F. master, 3. 217; *pl.* Maistres, 7. 184.

Maistrie, *sb.* F. mastery, dominion, sway, 6. 329; Maistrye, 3. 228, 4. 135; *pl.* Maistries, 4. 25.

Make, *sb.* S. mate, 3. 118. A.S. *maca*, a mate.

Make, *v.* S. (1) to compose poetry, write, 7. 61; *pp.* Made, composed, 5. 403; *pt. s.* Made, wrote, 5. 415; (2) to cause, bring about; *pr. s. subj.* Make it, cause it (to be otherwise), 4. 72, 5. 420; Maketh it, causes it (to be so), 6. 208; *pp.* Maked, made, 7. 143.

Males, *sb. pl.* bags, wallets, 5. 234. F. *malle*, E. *mail-bag.*

Mamely, *v.* to mumble, prate, 5. 21. Cf. Momme.

Manaced, *pt. s.* F. menaced, 6. 172.

Manere, *sb.* F. manor, 5. 595; *pl.* Maneres. 5. 246.

Maner, Manere, *sb.* F. manner, sort, 5. 25, 7. 96. The word *of* is generally suppressed after it.

Manered, *adj.* conditioned, like in character, 2. 27.

Manliche, *adj.* S. manly, humane, charitable, 5. 260.

Mansed, *pp.* cursed, 2. 39, 4. 160. A.S. *ámánsumian*, to curse. Very

corruptly used; properly *mǽnsumian* is to join; *ámánsumian,* to disjoin, excommunicate; so that *mansed* is short for *amansed* or *amansumed;* the corruption was readily brought about by confusion with A.S. *mán*, wicked.

Marchen, *pr. pl.* F. march, go, pr. 63.

Mase, *sb.* a confused throng, 1. 6; *þe mase,* a state of confusion, pr. 196, 3. 159. Cf. E. *maze.*

Masse-pans, *sb. pl.* pence for saying masses, 3. 223. See Pens.

Maugre, F. in spite of, 2. 204, 6. 69; *sb.* ill will, 6. 242. F. *mal gré;* from Lat. *male gratum.*

Maunged, *pp.* F. eaten, 6. 260.

Mawe, *sb.* maw, stomach, 5. 124. A.S. *maga*, G. *magen.*

Mayntenaunce, *sb.* F. support, protection, 5. 253.

Mayntene, *v.* F. to abet, 3. 90, 184, 6. 37.

Mede, *sb.* S. (in a good sense) reward, pay, 3. 217, &c.; (in a bad sense) bribery, 2. 131, &c. See 3. 230.

Medeth, *pr. pl.* pays, 3. 215.

Meke, *v.* S. to humble, 5. 70.

Melke, *sb.* milk, 5. 444, 6. 185. A.S. *meolc,* Du. *melk.*

Mellere, *sb.* S. miller, 2. 111.

Melleth, *pr. s.* speaks, 3. 104; *pt. s.* Mellud, 3. 36. A.S. *mǽlan,* *maðelian,* Icel. *mæla*, to speak.

Mene, *sb.* F. go-between, mediator, 1. 158. 7. 196; *pl.* Menes, 3. 76. F. *moyen,* Lat. *medius.*

Mene, *adj.* mean, common, 3. 596; *pl.* pr. 18, 2. 55; *meneale,* common ale, 6. 185. A.S. *mǽne,* mean, false, *mán,* bad; Mœso-Goth. *gamains,* unclean.

Mene, 1 *p. s. pr.* I speak, tell, 5. 283; *gerund,* To mene, to signify, 1. 11, 60. A.S. *mǽnan,* to have in mind, tell. E. *mean, mind;* cf. Lat. *mens.* See Mengen.

Mened hire, *pr. s.* bemoaned herself, complained. 3. 169; Mened hem, complained, 6. 2. A.S. *mænan,* to moan, lament.

Mengen, *v.* to keep in mind, remember, 6. 97. See Mene, *v.*

Mengen here, *v.* to remember herself, reflect, 4. 94. A.S. *myngian.*

Mennes, *gen. pl.* men's, pr. 198, 5. 112.

Menske, v. to make a man of, to honour, 3. 183. Icel. *menska,* humanity, virtue, honour. Sc. *mense,* good manners; G. and Du. *mensch,* a man.

Merciable, *adj.* F. merciful, 5. 511.

Merciment, *sb.* F. amercement, fine, 1. 160.

Mercy, *sb.* F. (your) pardon, 1. 11, 43, 2. 2.

Mercyed, *pt. s.* F. thanked, 3. 20.

Merke, *adj.* S. dark, murky, 1. 1.

Meschaunce, *sb.* F. mischance, ill luck, 3. 166, 5. 92.

Meseles, *sb. pl.* lepers, 7. 102. O. F. *mesel,* a leper, from Lat. *misellus,* dimin. of *miser;* distinct from G. *masern,* the measles.

Mesondieux, *pl. sb.* hospitals, 7. 26. O. F. *maison dieu* (for *maison de dieu*).

Messageres, *pl. sb.* F. messengers, 2. 27. From Lat. *mitto.*

Messe, *sb.* F. the mass, pr. 97 ; *pl.* Messes, 3. 251.

Messie, the Messiah, 3. 301.

Mesurable, *adj.* F. moderate, fair, 1. 19, 3. 254.

Mete, *v.* to mete, measure, pr. 214 ; 2 *p. pr. pl.* 1. 175. A.S. *metan.*

Metelees, *adj.* meatless, 7. 141.

Meteles, *sb.* (commonly in sing. signification), a dream, 2. 52, 7. 143. See Meten and Dremeles.

Meten, *v.* to dream, pr. 11 ; *pt. s.* Mette, 7. 159. A.S. *mǣtan.*

Mette, *pt. pl.* S. met, 5. 522, 6. 172.

Meyne. *sb.* F. retinue, household, 1. 108, 3. 24. O. F. *magnie,*

mainie (spelt 38 ways), Low Lat. *maisnada,* a family ; from Low Lat. *mansionata,* a household ; Lat. *manere,* to dwell.

Meynpernour, *sb.* F. lit. a taker by the hand, bail, surety, 4. 112. Used by Occleve, De Regimine Principum, ed. Wright, p. 86.

Meynprise, *sb.* F. lit. a taking by the hand, bail, security, 2. 196, 4. 88.

Meyntene, *v.* F. to support, abet, aid in doing wrong, 3. 246 ; *pr. s. and pl.* Meynteneth, 3. 149, 166.

Miȝtful, *adj.* S. mighty, 1. 171.

Mnam, *sb.* Gk. a 'mina,' talent, 6. 243 ; *pl.* Mnames, 6. 244.

Mo, *adj.* more, 1. 115, 5. 246; Moo, 2. 111. A.S. *má.*

Moder, *sb.* S. mother, 7. 196.

Modilich, *adv.* angrily, 4. 173. A.S. *mód,* mood, passion.

Moebles, *sb. pl.* F. moveables, goods, 3. 267.

Molde, *sb.* S. mould, the earth, 2. 186, 7. 96.

Momme, *sb.* the least sound that can be made, a *mum* or mumbling with closed lips, pr. 215. Cf. Gk. μῦ.

Mone, *sb.* S. moon, 7. 159 ; a lunation, 3. 325.

Mone, *sb.* S. moan, 6. 125.

Monelees, *adj.* moneyless, 7. 141.

Moot-halle, *sb.* a hall of meeting, court, 4. 135. E. *mote.*

Morther, *v.* to murder, 4. 55. Mœso-Goth. *maurthrjan;* cf. E. *mar* and Lat. *mort-em.*

Morthereres, *sb. pl.* murderers, 6. 275.

Morwe, *sb.* S. morning, 5. 325, 6. 187.

Most, must. See Mot.

Moste, *adj.* greatest, pr. 67, 1. 7.

Mot, 1 *p. pl. pr.* (we) must, 6. 291 ; 2 *p.* Mote, 1. 136, 5. 570 ; 3 *p.* Mote, 5. 257 ; 1 *p. s. pt.* Most, 7. 106 ; Moste, 5. 151 ; *pt. s. subj.*

Moste, might, 4. 112. A.S. *ic mót* (pres. t.), *ic móste* (pt. t.), I must.

Mote, *sb.* F. a moat, 5. 595. O.F. *mote.*

Mote, *v.* to cite to a law-court, summon, plead, 1. 174. A.S. *mótan,* to cite; cf. E. a moot point.

Motoun, *sb.* F. a 'mutton,' gold coin, 3. 24. See note.

Motyng, *sb.* S. pleading, 7. 58. See Mote.

Mouthen, *v.* to utter, talk about, 4. 115; *pt. s.* Mouthed, 6. 240.

Mowe, Mowen, 1 *p. pl. pr.* (we) may, pr. 172. 5. 509; 2 *p.* Mowe, 6. 40; 3 *p.* Mowe, 3. 217; 2 *p. s. pt.* My3te, 3. 28, 6. 225; My3tow (mightest thou), 1. 170.

Moylere, *sb.* a woman, a lady, 2. 118, 131. O.F. *moilier,* Lat. *mulier.*

Muryer, *adv.* merrier, pleasanter, 1. 107.

Myd, *prep.* with, 4. 77, 5. 75. A.S. *mid,* G. *mit,* Du. *med.*

Myddes, *adj. as sb.* midst, 2. 184. A.S. *middes,* gen. case of *midde,* adj. mid.

Mykel, *adj.* great, 5. 477; much, pr. 201. A.S. *mycel.*

Mys, *sb. pl.* S. mice, pr. 147.

Mysbede, *imp. s.* injure, misgovern, 6. 46. A.S. *misbeódan,* to bid amiss.

Myschief, *sb.* F. ill success, mishap, ruin, pr. 67, 4. 72.

Mysdo, *v.* S. (*neut.*) to do amiss, transgress, 3. 122; *pt. s.* (*act.*) Mysdid, injured, 4. 99; *pp.* Mysdo, 4. 90.

Myseise, *sb.* ill ease, discomfort, 1. 24.

Myseyse, *pl. adj.* ill at ease, wretched, 7. 26.

Myshappe, *v.* to meet with misfortune, 3. 327.

Myssayde, *pp.* evil spoken of, slandered, 5. 69.

Mysshape, *pp. as adj.* mis-shapen, 7. 95.

Myster, *sb.* F. employment, occupation, 7. 7. O.F. *mestier,* Lat. *ministerium,* F. *métier.*

My3te, My3tow. See Mowe.

My3tful, *adj.* powerful, 1. 174.

N.

Na, S. no, 1. 181; *na mo,* no more, 3. 1.

Nale; *in phr.* atte nale = atten ale (at þen ale), at the ale, 6. 117.

Nam (*for* ne am), am not, 5. 420.

Nam, 6. 241. See Mnam.

Namelich, *adv.* S. especially, 7. 41, 184. Cf. G. *namentlich.*

Namore (na more), no more, 3. 108. See Na.

Nau3t, *adv.* not, pr. 80; Nou3t, pr. 79.

Nau3te, *sb.* naught, nothing, 5. 489. A.S. *ná wiht,* no whit.

Nau3ty, *adj.* S. having nothing, very poor, 6. 226.

Ne, *conj.* nor, pr. 129, &c. A.S. *ne.*

Nedeler, *sb.* needle-seller, 5. 318.

Nedes, *adv.* necessarily, 5. 257; Nede, 3. 225. A.S. *neádes, neáde,* gen. of *neád,* need.

Nedle, *sb.* S. a needle, 1. 155. Cf. Du. *naad,* a seam, Lat. *nere,* to spin.

Neighed, *pt. s.* S. nighed, drew near, 6. 301.

Nei3e, *adv.* S. nigh, nearly, 3. 144

Nel (*for* ne wil), will not, 1 *p. s. pr.* pr. 38; Nelle, pr. 109, 4. 191; 2 *p.* Neltow, thou wilt not, 6. 158. A.S. *nyllan* (Lat. *nolle*), pt. t. 1 *p. ic nelle,* 2 *p. þú nelt.*

Nempne, *v.* to name, 1. 21; *pt. s.* Nempned, 5. 328; *pp.* Nempned, 2. 178, 7. 153. A.S. *nemnan.*

Nere (*for* ne were), were not, pr. 199, 3. 134. Cf. Nam.

Newe, *adv.* S. anew, 5. 482.

Ney3e, *prep.* nigh, 5. 94.

Noble, *sb.* F. a gold coin, **worth** 6s. 8d., 3. 45, 5. 250.

Noither, *conj.* S. nor, 1. 130. See **Noyther.**

Noither, *adj.* S. neither, 4. 32; *of her noither* = of neither of them.

Nolde (*for* ne wolde), would not, 1 *p. s. pt.* 5. 566; *pt. s.* 6. 238. See **Nel.**

Nones, *sb. pl.* 'nones,' the dinner-hour, 5. 378, 6. 147. The 'nones,' originally at about 3 p.m., were advanced to about 2 p.m., and afterwards to *noon.* Haydn (Dict. of Dates) says 2 p.m.; and see note to 6. 147.

Nonnes, *sb. pl.* F. nuns, 7. 29.

Nought, not, pr. 29.

Noumpere, *sb.* umpire, 5. 337. '*N*(o)*wmpere,* or *ownpere.* Arbiter, sequester.'—Prompt. Parv. O. F. *nonper,* without equal (Roquefort). See Tyrwhitt's note on *nompere* in Chaucer.

Nouthe, *adv.* now, 3. 288, 6. 208. A.S. *nú þá,* just now; cf. Prov. E. *now then.*

Nou3t, *adv.* not, 7. 180; Nou3te, 6. 130.

Now, *adv.* now that, 5. 143.

Noyen, *v.* to annoy, injure, harm, 5. 583; *pr. pl.* Noyeth, 2. 126; *pp.* Noyed, 3. 188. O.F. *nuire, noire,* Lat. *nocere.*

Noyther, *conj.* neither, 4. 130; *adv.* 5. 184.

Nym, *imp. s.* take, 6. 43; *imp. pl.* Nymmeth, 6. 15. A.S. *niman,* G. *nehmen,* Du. *nemen.* Hence E. *numb.*

Nyuelynge, *pres. part.* sniveling, 5. 135. Cf. *neese* for *sneeze.*

Nys, (*for* ne is), is not, 5. 455. See **Nam.**

Ny3t-olde, *adj. pl.* a night old, not freshly gathered, 6. 310.

O

O, *adj.* one, 2. 30, 3. 237; On, 3. 237.

Obrode (lit. on broad), abroad, 5. 140. A.S. *brád,* broad.

Of, *prep.* for, 2. 1, 3. 21, 5. 126, 473, 486; by, 7. 153; some of, 6. 98; in return for, 6. 129; *of more,* besides, 6. 38.

Ofsent, *pt. s.* sent for, 3. 101. Cf. La3amon, vol. ii. p. 235.

On, *prep.* in, 7. 107; *on auenture* in case, 3. 66.

One, *adv.* only, 1. 170. A.S. *ána,* only.

Ones, *adv.* once, 2. 227, 6. 76; Onis, pr. 213; *at ones,* at once, 5. 516. A.S. *ánes,* gen. of *án,* one.

Or, *adv.* ere, pr. 155, 6. 87. See **Ar.**

Ordeigned, *pt. s.* F. ordained, 5. 167; Ordeygned, pr. 119.

Ordre, *sb.* F. order, rank, 1. 104, 6. 168; *pl.* Ordres (foure), pr. 58.

Orientales, *sb. pl.* sapphires, 2. 14. 'The precious stones called by lapidaries *Oriental Ruby, Oriental Topaz, Oriental Amethyst,* and *Oriental Emerald,* are red, yellow, violet, and green sapphires, distinguishable from the other gems of the same name which have not the prefix *Oriental,* by their greatly superior hardness, and greater specific gravity.'—*English Cycl.* s.v. Adamantine Spar.

Otes, *sb. pl.* oats, 4. 38. A.S. *áta,* an oat.

Other, *conj.* S. or, 3. 304, &c.

Otherwhiles, *adv.* sometimes, 5. 557; Otherwhile, pr. 164.

Ouerlede, *v.* S. to domineer over, 3. 314.

Ouerlepe, *v.* S. to outrun, catch, seize, pr. 199; *pt. s.* Ouerlepe, pr. 150. Cf. Lat. *insultare,* from *salere.*

Ouermaistrieth, *pr. s.* overmasters, 4. 176.

Ouersen, *v.* to oversee, 6. 115; *pp.* Ouerseye (me), overseen, i. e. forgot myself, 5. 378. Halliwell quotes from Cotgrave—'almost drunke, somewhat *overseene.*'

Oures, *sb. pl.* F. 'hours' of the breviary, pr. 97.

Owe, 1 *p. s. pr.* I owe (glossed in the MS. by *debeo*), 5. 476; *pt. s.* Ouȝte, ought, 5. 120. A.S. *ágan,* to own, pt. t. *ic áhte; Mœso-*Goth. *aigan,* to have, own. E. *owe, own,* are two forms of the same infin., and *ought, owed,* of the same pt. t.

P.

Paknedle, *sb.* a strong needle, such as is used for sewing up packages, 5. 212.

Paleys, *sb.* F. palace, 2. 23.

Palfrey, *sb.* a palfrey, horse, 2. 189. Low Lat. *paraveredus,* from *vere-dus,* a postnorse; which has also given rise to G. *pferd.* See Diez and Ducange.

Palmere, *sb.* F. a palmer, 5. 542; *pl.* Palmers, pr. 46, 6. 66.

Panel, *sb.* F. 3. 315. 'The *pannel* of a jury is the slip of parchment on which the names of the jurors are written.' (Wedgwood.)

Panne, *sb.* S. the brain-pan, skull, 4. 78.

Parcel-mele, *adv.* by parcels at a time, retail, 3. 81. The M. E. ending -*mele,* by parts, is the A.S. ending -*mélum,* which is the dat. pl. of *mél,* a part. Cf. M. E. *flok-mele,* by flocks, *poundmele,* by pounds. See Poundmel.

Pardonere, *sb.* F. a seller of pardons, 2. 108; *pl.* Pardoneres, 2. 219.

Pare, *v.* F. to pare, cut down, 5. 243. F. *parer,* to trim.

Parfourned, 1 *p. s. pt.* F. performed, 5. 405, 607.

Paroschienes, *sb. pl.* F. parishioners, pr. 89; Parochienes, 5. 426.

Partie, *sb.* F. part, 1. 7.

Passynge, i.e. over, above, 5. 422.

Patentes, *sb. pl.* F. letters of privilege (so called because open to the inspection of all men), 7. 194.

Paye, *sb.* pleasure; *to paye =* to his pleasure, so as to please him, 5. 556. (A common phrase.) F. *paye,* from Lat. *pacare,* to satisfy, It. *pagare.*

Paye, *v.* F. to please, satisfy, 6. 311. See above.

Payn, *sb.* F. bread, 7. 121; Payne, 6. 152.

Paynym, *sb.* a pagan, Saracen, 5. 523. Low Lat. *paganismus,* whence O.F. *paiennisme,* the land of pagans. Lat. *pagus,* a village,

Peces, *sb. pl.* F. cups (lit. pieces). 3. 89. 'Pece, cuppe. *Crater.*' (Prompt. Parv.)

Pedlere, *sb.* a pedlar, 5. 258. Also spelt *peddare, peddere,* one who goes about with a *ped.* i.e. a basket. See *Ped* in Halliwell, and 'Pedde, *idem quod* pannere,' in Prompt. Parv.

Pees, *sb.* F. peace, 1. 150, 3. 220.

Pees, *sb.* a pea (*sing.*) 6. 171: *pl.* Pesen, 6. 198; Peses, 6. 189. A.S. *piss,* F. *pois,* W. *pys,* Lat. *pisum.* The A.S. sing. is *pise,* the pl. *pisan;* the modern form is corrupt.

Peired, *pp.* F. impaired, injured, 3. 127. See Apeyre.

Pelet, *sb.* a pellet, a stone ball, 5. 78. *Pellets,* used for the old war-missiles, were large balls of stone, of course frequently of a pale-white colour. See Prompt. Parv., and Ch. Ho. Fame, iii. 553.

Pelure, *sb.* fur, 2. 9, 3. 294. O.F. *pelure,* fur; Lat. *pellis.*

Penaunt, *sb.* F. penitent, 4. 133.

Pens, *sb. pl.* pence, 2. 222, 3. 161.

Peny, *sb.* a penny, 1. 47, 6. 282 ; *pl.* Penyes, pr. 212 ; Pens, 2. 222.

Peny-ale, *sb.* ale sold at a penny a gallon, small beer, 5. 220. Stow's Chron. p. 218.

Percil, *sb.* parsley, 6. 288. F. *persil,* Gk. πετροσέλινον.

Pere, *sb.* F. a peer, equal, 3. 204 ; *pl.* Peres, 7. 16. Lat. *par.*

Peren, *v.* to appear, pr. 173. O.F. *parer,* Lat. *parere.*

Perkyn, *sb.* Peterkin, little or dear Piers, 6. 25.

Peronelle, *a name,* 5. 26 ; *gen.* Pernelles, 4. 16. Lat. *Petronilla.* St. Petronilla's day was May 31.

Persones, *sb. pl.* parsons, 3. 149, 5. 142. Mid. Lat. *persona ecclesiæ,* the person of the church in a parish ; an etymology of which there is no doubt, though often needlessly denied.

Pertly, *adv.* openly, evidently, 5. 23 ; Pertliche, 5. 15. See **Apertly.**

Pesecoddes, *sb. pl.* peashells, with the peas in them (peas were often boiled in the shells), 6. 294. See **Pees.** A.S. *codd,* a bag.

Pese-lof, *sb.* loaf made from peas, 6. 181.

Pesen, Peses. See **Pees.**

Peter, *interj.* by Saint Peter, 5. 544, 7. 112, 130.

Pétit, *adj.* F. small, 7. 57.

Peynen hem, *v.* give themselves trouble, take pains, 7. 42.

Peynten, *v.* F. to paint, 3. 62.

Peys, *sb.* weight, 5. 243. O.F. *peis,* F. *poids,* Lat. *pensum.*

Picche, *v.* to pierce, peck, pick, divide with a sharp point, 6. 105. A.S. and F. *pic,* a point ; E. *peak, pike, pick-axe, peck.*

Pies, 7. 194. See the note.

Piked, *pt. pl.* picked with a sharp instrument, hoed (as we should now say), 6. 113. See **Picche.**

Piloure, *sb.* F. pillager, robber, 3. 194. O.F. *piller,* to rob, to *peel.*

Piones, *sb. pl.* F. seeds of the peony 5. 312. Gk. παιωνία.

Piries, *sb. pl.* F. pear-trees, 5. 16. Lat. *pyrus.* (Chaucer.)

Pitaunce, *sb.* F. pittance, 5. 270.

Platte hire, *pt. s.* threw herself flat, 5. 63. F. *plat,* Sw. and G. *platt,* flat.

Plede, *v.* F. to plead, 7. 42 ; *pt. pl.* Plededen, pr. 212 ; Pleteden, 7. 39.

Pleyne hem, *v.* F. to complain, 3. 167 ; *pt. s.* Pleyned hym, 6. 161 ; *pt. pl.* Pleyned hem, pr. 83.

Pleyne, *adj.* F. full, 7. 103.

Pleyntes, *sb. pl.* F. complaints, pleas, 2. 177.

Pliȝted, *pr. pl.* ; pliȝted hem = joined (pledged) themselves, pr. 46.

Plomtrees, *sb. pl.* S. plum-trees. 5. 16.

Plowfote, plough-foot, *sb.* 6. 105. The *plough-foot* is part of a plough, formed like a staff, propping up the beam so as to regulate the depth of the furrows. In a modern plough, small wheels are used instead. See the note.

Podyng-ale, *sb.* a kind of ale, 5. 220. See the note.

Poeple, *sb. pl.* E. people, 1. 5, 2. 214.

Poised, *pt. s.* weighed, 5. 217. See **Peys.**

Poke, *sb.* a bag, 7. 191. A.S. *pocca,* a pouch.

Poletes, *sb. pl.* pullets, 6. 282. F. *poulet,* from Lat *pullus.*

Polsche, *v.* F. to polish, 5. 482.

Ponfolde, *sb.* a pinfold, 5. 663. A.S. *pund,* a pound, a fold.

Poraille, *sb.* the poor people, pr. 82. O. F. *pouraille* (Roquefort).

Pore, *adj.* poor, pr. 84, 3. 81.

Poret, *sb.* a kind of leek, 6. 300 ; *pl.* Porettes, 6. 288. O.F. *poret,* F. *porreau.*

Portatyf, *adj.* portable, hence quick, light, 1. 155.

Possed, *pt. s.* pushed, pr. 151. F. *pousser,* Lat. *pulsare.*

Possessioneres, *sb. pl.* 5. 144. See the note.

Posteles, *sb. pl.* apostles, 6. 151. [Other passages shew that *postles* = apostles; but the reason for its use here is not clear.]

Potagere, *sb.* F. a maker of pottage, 5. 157.

Pouere, *adj.* F. poor, 1. 173.

Poundmel, *adv.* by pounds at a time, 2. 222. Cf. **Parcelmele.**

Pouste, *sb.* power, 5. 36. O.F. *poeste,* Lat. *potestas.*

Preise, *v.* F. to appraise, value, 5. 331 ; *pt.s.* Preysed, praised, 6. 110; *pt. pl.* Preyseden, 7. 38.

Prentis, *sb.* an apprentice, 5. 202 ; *pl.* Prentis, 3. 224, 5. 317. F. *apprentis,* a learner, from Lat. *prehendere.*

Prentishode, *sb.* apprenticeship, 5. 256.

Prest, *sb.* a priest, 7. 112.

Prest, *adj.* ready, 6. 199. O.F. *prest,* F. *prêt.*

Prestest, *adj.* readiest, 5. 558.

Prestly, *adv.* quickly, 6. 95.

Preue, *v.* F. to prove, 5. 43 ; *pt. s.* Preued, 7. 168; *pp.* Preued, 4. 122.

Pris, *sb.* F. price, value, 2. 13.

Prisounes, *sb. pl.* F. prisoners, 7. 30 ; Prisoneres, 3. 136. O.F. *prison,* a prisoner.

Prouendreth, *pr. s.* provides for, provides with prebends, 3. 149. ' *Provendre.* Bénéfice ecclésiastique.' (Roquefort.)

Prouinciales, *adj. pl.* provincial, 7. 191.

Prouisoures, *sb. pl.* provisors, persons nominated by the Pope to livings not vacant, 2. 170, 3. 146.

Pruyde, *sb.* S. pride, pr. 23.

Pryue, *adj.* familiar, 2. 23; *pl.*

intimate, 2. 63 ; Pryues, *pl. adj. as sb.* secret friends, 2. 177.

Pukketh, *pr. s.* pokes, pushes, 5. 620; *pt. s.* Pukked, incited, 5. 643. Du. *poken,* to poke.

Pult, *pt. s.* put, 1. 125. *Pult* for *put* is not uncommon.

Purfil, *sb.* the embroidered or furred trimming of a dress, 4. 116; Purfyle, 5. 26. F. *pourfiler,* to work on an edge, embroider with thread; It. *filo,* a line, edge. Hence our *profile.*

Purfiled, *pp.* trimmed (with fur), 2. 9.

Purs, *sb.* a purse, bag, 5. 192, 311. F. *bourse,* Gk. βυρσα.

Purtenaunces, *sb. pl.* F. appurtenances, 2. 103.

Purtraye, *v.* to portray, draw, 3. 62. F. *pourtraire,* from Lat. *trahere.*

Puttes, *sb. pl.* lit. pits ; hence, dungeons, 5. 412. Du. *put,* Lat. *puteus.*

Pyke, *sb.* a staff with a spike, 5. 482. See **Picche.**

Pykoys, *sb.* a pickaxe, 3. 307. O.F. *piquois,* from *pic,* a pike.

Pyk-staf, *sb.* a staff with a spike, 6. 105. See **Pyke.**

Pyne, *sb.* pain, 2. 103. A.S. *pín* pain.

Pynned, 1 *p. s. pt.* fastened, 5. 213. A S. *pyndan,* to shut in, *pen* in.

Pynynge-stoles, *sb. pl.* stools of punishment, 3. 78. See **Pyne.**

Q.

Quarteroun, *sb.* a quarter, 5. 217. See Halliwell.

Quat3, (*for* Quath), *pt. s.* quoth, said, 6. 3 ; Quod, 3. 111, &c. A.S. *cweðan,* to speak; *pr. t. ic cweðe,* pt. t. *ic cwæð.*

R.

Radde. See Rede.

Ragman, *sb.* a papal bull, with many

seals of bishops attached, pr. 75.
A *ragman* or *ragman-roll* means
a document with a long list of
names, or with numerous seals.
See Halliwell, for a long note upon
it; and Dyce's Skelton, ii. 335.
Hence E. *rigmarole*, which see in
Wedgwood.

Rakyer, *sb.* a raker, a scavenger,
5. 322. A.S. *racian*, to rake.
See Liber Albus, p. 34.

Rape þe, *imp. s.* make haste, 4. 7,
5. 399; 2 *p. pl. pr. subj.* Rape 30w,
6. 120. Icel. *hrapa*, to rush.

Rappe, *v.* to strike, beat (down),
1. 95. Sw. *rappa*, to beat.

Rathe, *adv.* S. early, soon, 3. 73;
comp. Rather, 4. 5, 5. 263; *sup.*
Rathest, soonest, 5. 342. A.S.
hraðe, soon.

Ratonere, *sb.* a rat-catcher, 5. 322.

Ratoun, *sb.* a small rat, pr. 167;
Raton, pr. 158; *pl.* Ratones, pr.
146. F. *raton*. The F. -*on* is often
a *diminutive* ending, though the
It. -*one* is commonly *augmentative*.
Cf. Span. *raton, ratona*.

Rau3te, *pt. s.* raught, reached, got,
pr. 75: extended himself, *in pass.
sense*, was extended, 4. 185. A.S.
ræcan, to reach, extend, pt. t. *ic
ræhte*. Cf. Sc. *rax*.

Rayes, *sb. pl.* striped cloths, also
called *cloths of raye*, 5. 211. F.
raie, a stripe, streak, Lat. *radius*.

Recche, *v.* S. to reck, care, 4. 65;
pr. s. Reccheth, 6. 122.

Reconforted, *pp.* F. comforted
again. 5. 287.

Recorded, *pt. pl.* gave opinion, 4.
157.

Recrayed, *pp.* recreant, craven, 3.
257. O.F. *recroire*, to give up
one's faith, to be beaten, whence
O.F. *recreu*, O. It. *ricreduto*, pp.
beaten, O.F. *recréant*, O. It. *ricre-
dente*, pr. p. a recreant. See *Recreant* in Wedgwood. *Recrayed*
occurs in Skelton, i. 189.

Rede, *v.* (1) to advise, 4. 9, 29;
1 *p. s. pr.* Rede, 1. 173, 7. 181;
imp. s. 4. 113; *pt. s.* Radde, 5. 46,
125; Redde, instructed, bade, 5.
485: (2) to read, 7. 106; 2 *p. s. pt.*
Reddestow, readest thou, 3. 257;
pt. s. Redde, 3. 334. A.S. *rædan*,
to counsel, read; G. *reden.* Cf.
A.S. *ræd*, advice, G. *rath.*

Redyngkyng, *sb.* one of a class of
feudal retainers, who held their
land by serving their lord on
horseback, 5. 323. They were
also called *Rodknightes.* A.S.
ridend, one who rides, a chevalier,
rád-cniht, a riding youth, soldier.

Regne, *v.* F. to reign, 3. 283.

Regratere, *sb.* one who sells by
retail, 5. 226; *pl.* Regrateres, 3.
90. F. *regrattier*, It. *rigattiere*,
a huckster; cf. Span. *regatear*, to
wriggle; also to haggle, sell by
retail.

Regraterye, *sb.* F. selling by retail,
3. 83.

Regystreres, *sb.* F. registrars, 2. 173.

Reherce, *v.* to repeat, declare, 7.
190; *imp. s.* 5. 182; *pt. s.* Reherced,
repeated, pr. 184, 5. 61. O.F.
rehercer, to repeat (Roquefort).

Rekne, *v.* to reckon up, 1. 22; 2 *p.
s. pr. subj.* 5. 277. A.S. *reccan*,
to order, direct.

Releue, *v.* F. to relieve, 7. 32.

Religioun, *sb.* F. religious orders,
5. 46, 6. 153, 7. 32.

Renable, *adj.* loquacious, pr. 158.
Some MSS. have *resonable*, which
also has the same meaning; from
F. *raison*, M. E. *reson*, which often
means *talk.* But the Norfolk word
is *runnable*, evidently (falsely) connected with the verb to *run.*

Renke, *sb.* a man, pr. 192, 5. 399;
pl. Renkes, 7. 181. A.S. *rinc*, a
warrior.

Renne, *v.* to run, pr. 166, 3. 213;
pr. pl. Rennen, 2. 182. A.S. *ren-
nan*, G. *rennen.*

Renne-aboute, *sb.* Run-about, 6. 150.

Rental, *sb.* 6. 92. Properly, a schedule or roll containing an account of the rents of an estate. *A remissioun on that rental* = a release from rent as recorded in the rental.

Renten, *v.* to provide with rents, endow, 7. 32. Cf. F. *rendre*, Lat. *reddere*.

Repentedestow, 2 *p. s. pt.* repentedst thou, 5. 232.

Repentestow þe, 2 *p. s. pr.* repentest thou, 5. 449.

Rerages, *sb. pl.* arrears of debt, 5. 246. Also spelt *arerages*.

Rest, *pr. s.* (contr. from *resteth*), pr. 171.

Restitue, *v.* F. to make restitution, restore, 5. 281.

Retenauns, *sb. sing.* retinue, 2. 53. Also spelt *retenaunce*.

Reue, *sb.* a reeve, steward, bailiff, 2. 110; *gen.* Reues, 5. 427. A. S. *geréfa*.

Reulen, *pr. pl.* F. rule, 7. 10. Lat. *regula*, a rule.

Reumes, *sb. pl.* realms, 7. 10. O.F. *reaume*, F. *royaume*, formed as if from a Lat. *regalimen*.

Reuthe, *sb.* ruth, pity, 1. 173, 4. 108, 5. 434. A.S. *hreáw*, sorrow, *hreówan*, to grieve; Icel. *hrygð*, ruth, sorrow.

Rewarde, *v.* to recompense (whether good or evil), 3. 316. O.F. *rewarder*, from the Teutonic root of *ward* or *guard*.

Rewe, *imp. s.* have pity, 5. 475. See **Reuthe**.

Rewlyng, *sb.* ruling, pr. 127.

Rewme, *sb.* realm, pr. 177. See **Reumes**.

Reyne, *sb.* rain, 3. 207. 'Reyne. *Pluvia.*' (Prompt. Parv.) A.S., G. and Du. *regen*, Mœso-Goth. *rign*.

Ribanes, *sb. pl.* rows forming a band, either of gold lace or of precious stones, 2. 16. Cf. Du. *rijgen*, to lace *rijgliif*, stays, *rijgsnoer*, lace; from Du. *rij*, G. *reih*, a row, and *band*. (So Wedgwood; but very doubtful.)

Ribaudes, *sb. pl.* F. profligate men, sinners, 5. 512. See *Ribald* in Wedgwood, and note to the line.

Ribaudye, *sb.* F. ribaldry, sin, pr. 44.

Ribibour, *sb.* a player on the *ribibe* or *rebeck*, a kind of fiddle; from the Arab. *rabáb*; 5. 322. It is said to have had three strings, to have been played with a bow, and to have been introduced into Spain by the Moors.

Ricchesse, *sb. sing.* F. riches, wealth, 2. 17, 3. 90; *pl.* Ricchesses, 3. 23.

Ritt, *pr. s.* (contr. from *rideth*), rides, 4. 13; is moving about, running about, pr. 171; in 4. 24, we must also read *rit*, not *ritte*; see Critical Note.

Riȝtful, *adj.* S. just, pr. 127, 1. 54; *pl.* righteous, 4. 157, 3. 241.

Riȝtfullich, *adv.* justly, 4. 172.

Robyn hood, 5. 402.

Rode, *sb.* the rood, crucifix, 2. 3, 4. 134, &c. A.S. *ród*, a crucifix.

Rolle, *pr. s. subj.* to enrol, register, 5. 278.

Romares, *sb. pl.* pilgrims to Rome, 4. 120. O. Fr. *romier*, It. *romeo*, a pilgrim to Rome.

Rome-renneres, *sb. pl.* runners to Rome, 4. 128. See last word.

Roos, 1 *p. s. pt.* S. rose, 5. 234.

Ropere, *sb.* a rope-maker, 5. 323.

Roste, *sb.* roast meat, pr. 229.

Rotes, *sb. pl.* S. roots, 6. 105.

Rotland, i. e. Rutland, 2. 110.

Rouned, *pt. pl.* whispered, 5. 333; *pr. s.* Rowneth, 4. 13; *pres. part.* Rownynge, 4. 24. A.S. *rúnian*, from *rún*, a rune, a mystery.

Route, *sb.* a troop, company, pr.

146. 4. 168. O. F. *route*, G. *rotte*, a troop; cf. Provençal *rota*, tumult.

Rusty, *adj.* filthy, foul, 6. 75.

Rybaudoure, *sb.* a teller of loose tales, 6. 75. See Ribaudes.

Rychen, *pr. pl.* grow rich, 3. 83.

Ryflynge, *sb.* plunder, 5. 238. Cf. E. *rifle*, *raffle*, Du. *rijf*, G. *raffel*, a rake, G. *raffen*, to seize, sweep off, O. F. *riffler*, to snatch.

Rymes, *sb. pl.* rimes, 5. 402. F. *rime*, It. *rima*, A. S. *rim*, E. *rime* (now misspelt *rhyme*, through confusion with *rhythm*).

Ryne, i. e. the Rhine, pr. 229.

S.

Sadder, *adv.* more soundly (with reference to sleep), 5. 4. Cf. W. *sad*, firm; from A. S. *sæd*.

Sadnesse, *sb.* firm faith, confidence, 7. 150. See above.

Safferes, *sb. pl.* sapphires, 2. 13.

Safte, *sb.* F. safety, 7. 36.

Salamon, i. e. Solomon, 3. 330; *gen.* Salamones, 7. 137. The Lat. form is *Salomo*.

Salmes, *gen. sing.* psalm's, 3. 247.

Sapience, the apocryphal book of Wisdom, 3. 330.

Saracenes, *sb. pl.* Arabians, 3. 325. Derived from Arab. *sharkeyn*, i. e. 'Eastern people.' The name *Saraceni* occurs in Pliny (vi. 7).—*Eng. Cycl.*

Sarmoun, *sb.* F. sermon, 3. 93.

Sauacioun, *sb.* F. salvation, 5. 126.

Sauf, *adj.* F. safe, 7. 51.

Sauoure, *sb.* delight, pleasure, 7. 148. O. F. *savour*, *savor*, Lat. *sapor*. Mr. Wright explains it by 'knowledge,' as if from F. *savoir*, but this is not borne out by other passages in Mid. E., whereas the meaning given is so. See 6. 264 —*to sauoure with thi lippes*, to please thy lips with (by its nice taste).

Sauter, *sb.* psalter, 2. 37, 7. 40; *gen.* Sauter, 5. 282.

Saujtne, *v.* become reconciled, 4.2. Cf. A.S. *sahtlian*, to reconcile, from *saht*, peace. The ending *-ne* (Mœso-Goth. *-nan*) gives it a passive signification.

Sawes, *sb. pl.* sayings, 7. 137. A. S. *sagu*, a tale.

Say, *pt. s.* 1 *p.* I saw, 5. 10; spelt *saw* in preceding line. See Seigh.

Schendeth, *pr. pl.* harm, injure, disgrace, 6. 175; Schenden, 2.125. A. S. *scendan*, to disgrace.

Schete, *sb.* a loose bit of cloth, such as a skirt of a garment or a sheet, 5.108. Mœso-Goth. *skauts*, the hem of a garment, A.S. *sceát*, the skirt of a garment, a sheet.

Schrape, *pr. s. subj.* S. scrape, 5. 124.

Schrewe, *sb.* a shrew, a cursed or depraved one, a sinner, pr. 196, 4. 110. Cf. M. E. *schrewe*, to beshrew, to curse.

Schyreue, *sb.* a sheriff, 2. 163. A.S. *scir-geréfa*, a *shire-reeve*, sheriff.

Seche, *v.* S. to seek, 7. 163; *pt. pl.* Soujte, 7. 166. See Seketh.

Secte, *sb.* a suit, applied both to a suit of clothes and to a sect or following of people (like our *suite*), 5. 498. See the note.

Seel, *sb.* F. a seal, pr. 78, 3. 145; *pl.* Seles, pr. 69.

Seem, *sb.* S. a horse-load, 4. 38. 'A sack of eight bushels is now called a *seam*, which was a horseload; hence, generally, a load, a burden.' (Bosworth's A.S. Dict.) Cf. G. *saum*, a burden, F. *sommier*, a *sumpter* or pack-horse.

Segge, *sb.* a man, 3. 63, 5. 127. A.S. *secg*, a man, Icel. *seggr*, a man.

Segge, *v.* to say, 5. 617. A.S. *secgan*.

Sei, *v.* to say, 2. 67; 2 *p. s. pr.*

Seist, 6. 232; *pt. pl.* Seiden, 2. 151.

Seigh, *pt. s.* 1 *p.* I saw, pr. 50, 6. 237; Seighe, 7. 140; Sei3, pr. 230; *pt. s.* Sei3, 2. 188; Seighe, 5. 505; *infin.* Seen, 4. 86.

Seketh, *imp. pl.* seek ye, 5. 58. See **Seche.**

Selde, *adv.* seldom, pr. 20, 5. 127; Selden, 7. 137. A. S. *seld, seldan.*

Seleth, *pr. pl.* seal, 3. 147.

Selke, *sb.* silk, pr. 210. Lat. *sericum,* Gk. σηρικόν, belonging to the *Seres* (Chinese).

Selles, *sb. pl.* F. cells, pr. 28.

Selue, *pron.* himself, 1. 202. Cf. G. *selbst.*

Seme, *sb.* 3. 40. See **Seem.**

Sendal, *sb.* a kind of thin rich silk, 6. 11. F. *sendal,* It. *cendalo,* Low Lat. *cendalum.*

Seriaunt, *sb.* F. serjeant, 3. 293; *pl.* Seriauntz, pr. 211. Lat. *seruiens* (*ad legem*).

Serke, *sb.* a sark, shirt, shift, 5. 66. A. S. *serce, syrce,* Dan. *særk.*

Sestow, seest thou, 1. 5.

Seten, *pt. pl.* S. sat, 6. 117, 195.

Seth, 1 *p. pl. pr.* (we) see, 3. 216.

Sette, 1 *p. s. pr.* I set, place, reckon, 7. 194; *pt. s.* Sette, 6. 171; *infin.* Sette, to plant, 7. 6; *pp.* Sette, placed, 6. 48. A. S. *settan.*

Seweth, *pr. pl.* follow, pursue, pr. 45; Suweth, 5. 60. O. F. *suire, sevre,* Lat. *sequi.* Cf. E. *sue.*

Sey, 1 *p. s. pr.* I say, 6. 286. See **Segge,** *v.*

Seygh, 1 *p. s. pt.* I saw, 5. 542. See **Seigh.**

Seyn, *v.* to say, pr. 189; 2 *p. pl. pr.* Seyne, 6. 131.

Seyned hym, *pt. s.* blessed himself, 5. 456. O. F. *seigner, signer,* to make the sign of the cross, Lat. *signare,* from *signum.*

Shaltow, i. e. shalt thou, 5. 579.

Shamedest, 2 *p. s. pt.* didst bring shame upon, 3. 189.

Shapeth, *pr. s.* causes, disposes, 7. 67; determines, 1. 159; 1 *p. s. pt.* Shope me, arrayed myself, pr. 2; *pt. pl.* Shope, disposed, ordered, pr. 122; Shopen hem, arrayed themselves as, made themselves, pr. 57. A. S. *scapan,* to shape, form.

Shedyng, *sb.* dispersion, scattering; *for shedyng* = to prevent scattering, 6. 9. A. S. *sceadan,* to disperse.

Shenfullich, *adv.* shamefully, 3. 275. The full form is *shendfullich,* as written in other MSS A. S. *scendan,* to reproach.

Shendeth, *pr. s.* corrupts, brings reproach on, ruins, 3. 154; *pp.* Shent, ruined, 3. 134, 4. 174. See last word.

Shepe, *sb.* a shepherd, pr. 2. See the note.

Shette, *pt. s.* shut, 5. 611. A. S. *scyttan,* to shoot a bolt, to lock.

Shireues, *sb. pl.* 2. 58. See **Schyreue.**

Shodde, *pp.* shod, 2. 163.

Sholdest, Sholde. See **Shul.**

Shonye, *v.* to shun, avoid, pr. 174; 1 *p. s. pr.* I get out of the way, 5. 169. A. S. *scunian,* to shun.

Shope, Shopen. See **Shapeth.**

Shrewe, *sb.* the cursed one, Satan, 1. 127; a sinner, 5. 471. See **Schrewe.**

Shrewednesse, *sb.* sin, 3. 44.

Shroudes, *sb. pl.* garments, rough outer clothes, pr. 2. A. S. *scrúd,* a garment, shroud.

Shryue, *v.* to shrive, confess, pr. 64; Shryuen, pr. 89; *pt. s.* Shroue, 3. 44; *pp.* Shryuen, 5. 309. A. S. *scrifan,* Sw. *skrifta.*

Shull, Shulle, Shullen, 1, 2, *and* 3 *p. pl. pr.* shall, 3. 34, 5. 578, 7. 162; 2 *p. s. pt. subj.* Shulde, shouldest, oughtest, 6. 49; *pt. pl.* Shulden, should, ought to be, 7. 13. A. S. *ic sceal,* pl. *we sculon,* pt. t. *ic sceolde.*

Sibbe, *adj.* akin, related to, 5. 634. A.S. *sib,* peace, relationship; Mœso-Goth. *sibja,* relationship; G. *sippe,* kindred.

Siker, *adj.* certain, sure, 1. 130, 3. 50. A.S. *sicor,* from Lat. *secūrus,* variant of *secūrus.*

Sikerere, *adv.* more securely, 5. 509.

Sikerly, *adv.* with certainty, surely, 5. 547.

Sikul, *sb.* a sickle, 3. 306. A.S. *sicel, sicol.*

Silke, *sb.* silk, 6. 11. See Selke.

Sire, *sb.* F. father, pr. 189. O.F. *sire, seigneur,* from Lat. *senior.*

Sisoure, *sb.* a person deputed to hold assizes, 2. 164; *pl.* Sisoures, 2. 62, 3. 133. Low Lat. *assisarii,* from *ad* and *sedere,* to sit.

Sith, Sitthe, Sithen, *adv. and conj.* since, pr. 64, 4. 14, 7. 94. A.S. *siðða, siðδan,* afterwards, after that, since; *síð, adv.* late; *síð, sb.* a turn, a time. Cf. G. *seit,* since. See **Sithes.**

Sithe, *sb.* a scythe, 3. 306. A.S. *síðe.*

Sithenes, *adv.* afterwards, 7. 25; Sitthenes, 6. 65. See Sith.

Sithes, *sb. pl.* times, 5. 431; Sythes, 5. 441. A.S. *síð,* a turn, time, journey, Mœso-Goth. *sinth,* a time, a journey.

Sitten, *v.* to cost (lit. to sit), 3. 48. Cf. our phrase, to *stand* one in a large sum.

Sklayre, *sb.* a veil, 6. 7. Cf. G. *schleier,* Du. *sluijer,* Sw. *slöja.*

Sleen, *v.* to slay, 3. 285; *imp. s.* Slee, 3. 264. A.S. *sleán, slagan,* G. *schlagen,* to strike.

Slepe, 1 *p. s. pt.* I slept, 5. 382; 2 *p. s. pr.* Slepestow, 1. 5; *pp.* Sleped, 5. 4. A.S. *slǽpan,* pt. t. *ic slép.*

Sleuth, *sb.* S. sloth, 2. 98; Sleuthe, pr. 45.

Slombred, 1 *p. s. pt.* S. I slumbered, pr. 10.

Slyken, *pr. pl.* render sleek 2. 98. Halldórsson gives Icel. *slikja,* to polish; cf. Icel. *sleikja,* to lick, E. *slick, sleek.*

Smerte, *pr. pl. subj.* smart, suffer, 3. 167. Cf. G. *schmerz.*

Smythye, *v.* to forge, 3. 305; *pr. s.* Smytheth, 3. 322. A.S. *smiðian,* to forge.

Soffre, *imp. s.* suffer, permit, 3. 92.

Soft, *adj.* S. mild, warm, pr. 1.

Sokene, *sb.* explained by Mr. Wright as 'a district held by tenure of *socage,'* 2. 110. Bosworth explains the Law-Latin word *soca* as a 'lordship enfranchised by the king, with the liberty of holding or keeping a court of his *socmen* or *socagers,* that is, of his tenants, whose tenure is hence called *soca-gium,* in Eng. *socage.'* See A.S. *sóc* in Bosworth.

Solfe, *v.* to *sol-fa,* i. e. sing by note, to call over the notes by their names, viz. ut, re, mi, *sol, fa,* &c., 5. 423. Dyce's Skelton, ii. 94.

Some dele, partly, 5. 438. See Dele, *sb.*

Somer-game, *sb.* a summer-game, 5. 413. See the note.

Somme, *adj. pl.* some, pr. 31, 222; *dat. pl.* to some, 3. 284. In 3. 13 it means 'some of them;' see note. Connected with *same,* and A.S. *sam,* together. *Sam* is the Greek ἅμα, Lat. *simul;* the base of G. *sammeln,* Eng. *assemble.*

Sompne, *v.* F. to summon, 2. 158, 3. 314. Lat. *summoneo.*

Sompnoure, *sb.* F. a summoner or *somner* (an officer who summons delinquents to appear in an ecclesiastical court; now called an *apparitor*), 4. 167; *pl.* Sompnoures, 3. 133. See Chaucer's Prologue.

Sonde, *sb.* 3. 349. Explained as 'a mission, sending,' by Mr. Wright; but I feel sure that the true sense is—that which is sent, viz. a present; cf. Dan. *sending*, a gift, a present, from *sende* (A.S. *sendan*) to send. In Mid. Eng. *sonde* also means a portion of food sent in a dish, a present of viands. Observe the context.

Songen, *pt. pl.* S. sang, 5. 345, 6. 117.

Songewarie, *sb.* the interpretation of dreams, or more properly, observation of dreams, 7. 148, 150. O.F. *songe*, Lat. *somnium*, and O.F. *warir*, *garir*, A.S. *warian*, to guard, ward, keep.

Sonne, *sb.* S. the sun, pr. 1, 6. 328.

Sonnest, *adv.* soonest, 1. 70, 3. 281.

Sori, *adj.* sorry, miserable, pr. 45.

Soth. *adj.* S. true, 5. 282, 6. 131, 7. 67.

Sothe, *sb.* S. truth, sooth, 4. 2, 5. 569; *pl.* Sothes, 3. 281. A.S. *sóð*, truth.

Sothly, *adv.* S. truly, 5. 241; Sothely, 3. 189; Sothelich, 3. 5.

Sothnesse, *sb.* S. truth (used as a proper name), 2. 24, 188.

Souereygne, *adj.* F. excellent, pr. 159. O.F. *sovrain*, from O.F. *sovre*, Lat. *supra*, above.

Souereynes, *sb. pl.* superiors, lords, 6. 82.

Soule, *gen. sing.* soul's; hence *soule hele* = soul's health, 5. 270.

Soupen, *v.* to sup, 2. 96; Soupe, 6. 220. F. *souper*, G. *saufen*, to sup, sip. Cf. Icel. *saup*, soup.

Soure, *adv.* bitterly, 2. 140. Icel. *súrr*, W. *sur*, G. *sauer*, Du. *zuur*.

Souteres, *sb. pl.* cobblers, shoe-makers, 5. 413. A.S. *sútere*, a shoemaker (Lye), probably borrowed from Lat. *sutor*. This seems more likely than Mr. Wedgwood's derivation from F. *savetier*.

Souteresse, *sb.* a female shoe-maker or shoe-seller, 5. 315.

Souȝte, sought. See **Seche.**

Sowe, *v.* S. to sow (seed), 7, 6; *pp.* Sowen, 6. 5.

Spede, *v.* to speed, i. e. succeed, thrive, prosper, 3. 270, 5. 601.

Sperhauke, *sb.* a sparrow-hawk, 6. 199. A.S. *sperhafoc*.

Spiceres, *sb. pl.* sellers of spices, grocers, 2. 225.

Spices, *sb. pl.* spices, 5. 311. F. *épice*, O.F. *espisce*, *espece*, from Lat. *species*.

Spille, *v.* to destroy, ruin, 3. 308; Spilleth, *pr. s.* spoils, 5. 41; Spille, *imp. s.* destroy, 3. 270. A.S. *spillan*, Du. *spillen*, Sw. *spilla*, E. *spill*, to waste.

Spiritualte, *sb.* F. spirituality, spiritual authority or influence, 5. 148, 149.

Sprynge, *sb.* a switch, springy rod, 5. 41.

Spynnesteres, *sb. pl.* S. women engaged in spinning, 5. 216.

Stable, *v.* to render firm or stable, to cause to rest, 1. 120.

Stede, *sb.* stead, place, pr. 96, 6. 63; *pl.* Stedes, places, 5. 48. A.S. *stede.*

Stekye, *v.* to stick fast, remain closed, 1. 121. A.S. *stician*, to pierce, also to *stick*, adhere; G. *stecken*, Sc. *steik*.

Sterres, *sb. pl.* S. stars, 7. 160.

Stile, *sb.* a stile, 5. 201.

Stokkes, *sb. pl.* S. the stocks, 4. 108, 5. 585.

Stole, *sb.* S. a stool, 5. 394.

Stonden, Stonde, *v.* to stand, 1. 121, 6. 114.

Stories, *sb. pl.* F. histories, 7. 73.

Streyte, *adv.* straitly, strictly, pr. 26. O.F. *estroit*, Lat. *strictus.*

Streyues, *sb. pl.* estrays, pr. 94. Explained by Mr. Wright—'beasts which have gone astray'—in accordance with the *present* usual meaning. But the old meaning is different, viz. goods which a stranger leaves behind him **at** death, and which go to the king or lord for default of heirs. See *estrahere* in Roquefort. O. F. *estrahere, estreyere,* &c., from Lat. *extra.*

Stroke, *pt. s.* moved rapidly, brushed quickly past the rest and advanced, pr. 183. A. S. *strícan,* to go, G. *streichen,* Du. *strijken,* to sweep rapidly over a surface, to graze, *stroke.* See **Stryke.**

Struyeth, *pr. pl.* destroy, 6. 29. O. F. *destruire;* cf. It. *struggere,* to destroy, waste.

Stryke, *imp. s.* go quickly, pass quickly, 5. 586. See **Stroke.**

Studye, *v.* F. to study, muse, 7. 143.

Stues, *sb. pl.* F. stews, 6. 72.

Stuwardes, *sb. pl.* stewards, pr. 96, 5. 48. A. S. *stiward,* Icel. *stívardr,* one whose business it is to look to the daily work of a farm; cf. Icel. *stjá,* domestic occupation, especially foddering the cattle; Icel. *stía,* a sheep-house, E. *sty;* cf. Sw. *stia,* a pen for geese. Thus *steward* is for *sty-ward.* See Wedgwood.

Stynte, *v.* to cease, rest, pause, 1. 120; *imp. pl.* Stynte, stop, rest, 5. 585. A. S. *stintan,* to be blunt, *stunt,* blunt. Cf. E. *stint, stunted.*

Suddenes, *sb. pl.* subdeans, 2. 172. F. *sou,* under, and M. E. *dene,* a dean, F. *doyen,* Lat. *decanus,* from *decem.*

Sueth, *pr. s.* follows, pursues, persecutes, tempts, 1. 41; *pp.* Sued, followed, driven, 5. 550. F. *suivre,* Lat. *sequi.*

Suffrance, *sb.* F. long-suffering of God, 6. 146.

Suffre, *v.* to suffer, permit, allow to exist, 2. 174.

Suggestioun, *sb.* F. reason, occasion, 7. 67.

Supprioure, *sb.* subprior, 5. 171.

Suren, *v.* to plight one's troth to, give security to, 5. 547.

Surfait, *sb.* surfeit, excess, 6. 267. F. *surfaire,* to exceed, to do too much.

Sustre, *sb.* S. sister, 3. 63; *pl.* Sustren, 5. 627.

Sute, *sb.* F. suit, clothing of human flesh, 5. 495, 504. See the note.

Suweth, *pr. pl.* pursue, follow, 5. 60. See **Sueth.**

Swelte, *v.* to die, 5. 154. A. S. *sweltan,* Mœso-Goth. *swiltan,* to die.

Swete, *v.* S. to sweat, 6. 26, 130.

Sweuene, *sb.* a dream, pr. 11, 7. 161. A. S. *swefen.*

Sweyued, *pt. s.* sounded, pr. 10. A. S. *swégan,* to sound, *swég,* a sound, sound of music; Mœso-Goth. *swigljon,* to play upon **a** pipe. Cf. Sc. *sough.*

Swithe, *adv.* very, exceedingly, 5. 456, 470. A. S. *swið,* strong, great.

Swonken. See **Swynke.**

Swowe, *v.* to swoon, 5. 154. Probably connected with Mœso-Goth. *gaswogjan,* to sigh, A. S. *swógan,* to make a sighing noise. See **Sweyued.**

Swynke, *v.* to toil, 6. 26; *pt. pl.* Swonken, pr. 21. A. S. *swincan.*

Swynke, *sb.* S. toil, 6. 235.

Syb, *adj.* S. akin, 5. 636. See **Sibbe.**

Sydder, *adj.* wider; *wel sydder* = even lower, 5. 193. A. S. *sid,* ample, broad, wide.

Sykenesse, *sb.* sickness, 6. 259.

Syker, *adj.* safe, secure, 7. 180. G. *sicher.* See **Siker.**

Symonye, *sb.* simony, pr. 86, 2. 62.

Synful, *adj.* sinful (men), 7. 15.

Synnelees, *adj.* sinless, 6. 232.

Sysoure, 4. 167. See **Sisoure.**

Sythes, pr. 230. See **Sithes.**

Syȝt, *sb.* S. sight, pr. 32.

T.

Tabarde, *sb.* F. a loose over-coat, sometimes sleeveless, sometimes with loose wide sleeves, open at the sides, 5. 196. F. *tabarre,* Sp. *tabardo.*

Taile, *sb.* a tally, a stick (one of a pair) on which the amount of money is notched or scored, 4. 58. F. *tailler,* to cut, *taille,* a tally.

Taille, *sb.* a tally, 5. 252. See preceding word. Skelton, ii. 176.

Taille, *sb.* S. a tail, end, conclusion, 3. 347 ; tail of followers, train, 2. 185; *pl.* Tailles, roots of trees, 5. 19.

Take, *v.* S. (1) to take; (2) to give, 1. 56 ; Taketh, *pr. s.* gives, 4. 58 ; Toke, *pt. s.* gave, 3. 45. The latter meaning is common, and occurs in Chaucer.

Tale, *sb.* (1) account (*holde þei no tale* = take no account), 1. 9; (2) a tale, esp. a lying tale, 2. 114, 3. 45. The former is the original meaning; cf. A. S. *talu,* a number, reckoning, G. *zahl,* a number.

Tauerners, *sb. pl.* F. keepers of taverns, pr. **227.**

Tauny, *adj.* tawny, of a dull yellow colour, 5. 196. F. *tanné,* tawny, tanned. Roquefort gives the O.F. *tané,* enfumé, de couleur rousse.

Tauȝte, *pt. s.* S. taught, 3. 282, 6. 211 ; *pp.* Tauȝte, 6. 23.

Taxoure, *sb.* an imposer of taxes, 6. 40.

Tellen, *pr. pl.* count over, reckon up, pr. 92 ; Tolde, *pt. s.* told, 3. 45. See **Tale.**

Teme, (1) *sb.* a team, 6. 136, 7. 2. A.S. *teám,* a succession of children, a row, a team.

Teme, (2) *sb.* a theme, statement, 3. 95, 5. 61 ; a subject, 6. 23. Gk. θέμα, a proposition or **case** for discussion.

Tempred, *pp.* accommodated, **pr.** 51. Lat. *temperare.*

Tene, *sb.* vexation, anger, 6. 119, 7. 116; trouble, worry, 6. 135. See next word.

Tene, 1 *p. s. pr.* I vex, worry, injure, 5. 432; *pt. s.* injured, 3. 320; *tened hym* = was vexed, 2. 114. A.S. *týnan,* to vex, *teón,* injury.

Teneful, *adj.* harmful, 3. 345.

Þanne, *adv.* then, 6. 34.

Þat, *put for* that which, pr. 38, **3** 84, &c.

Þat þat, that which, 3. 347.

Þat ilke, that very, 6. 164.

The, 1 *p. s. pr. subj.* may I thrive, prosper, 5. 228. A.S. *þeón,* to thrive, G. *ge-deihen,* Du. *gedijen.*

Þeiȝ, *conj.* though, 1. 10; þeiȝe, 3. 148, &c.

Þen, than, pr. 147.

Þennes, *adv.* thence, 1. 73, 2. 229. A.S. *þanon.*

Þerafter, *adv.* accordingly, 6. 116.

Þer, Þere, *adv.* where, 1. 131, 3. 14, &c.; There as, there where, 4. 34.

Þere-inne, *adv.* therein, 1. 61.

Þeremyde, *adv.* therewith, 7. 26; þermyde, 6. 160 ; þeremydde, 6. 69. A.S. *mid,* with.

Þerfore, *adv.* for it, on account of it, 4. 54, 5. 236.

Þer-while, *adv.* whilst that, pr. 173, 6. 165; þere-whiles, in the meantime, 6. 8.

Þider, *adv.* S. thither, 2. 161.

Þikke, *adv.* S. thickly, often, **3.** 156.

Þinge, *used as pl.* things, 6. 212.

Þirled, *pt. pl.* pierced, 1. 172. A.S. *þirlian,* to pierce, drill ; *þirl,* a hole. Cf. E. *drill, thrill.*

Þis, *pl.* these, pr. 62, 2. 170, 5. 634; þise, 1. 132.

Þo, when, pr. 176, 1. 47. A. S. *þá.*

Þo, *pl.* the, those, 1. 21, 4. 40, &c.

A.S. þá, pl. of the article, *se, seó,* þæt.

Þolye, *v.* to suffer, 4. 84. A.S. *þolian,* to endure; cf. G. and Du. *dulden.*

Þonkynge, *sb.* S. thanking, thanksgiving, 2. 148.

Þorw, *prep.* S. through, by, 2. 41, 6. 20; Thorwgh, 6. 326.

Thouȝte, *pt. s.* it seemed; *me thouȝte* = it seemed to me, pr. 6, 182; *hem þouȝte* = it seemed to them, 1. 107.

Þowgh, þowȝ, *conj.* though, 6. 36, 40. A.S. *þeáh.*

Thresche, 1 *p. s. pr.* I thresh, 5. 553. A.S. *þerscan,* G. *dreschen.*

Thresshewolde, *sb.* threshold, 5. 357. As if the piece of wood beaten by the feet, from A.S. *wald,* wood, and *þerscan,* to thresh, to beat.

Threttene, thirteen, 5. 214. A.S. þreótyne.

Thretti, thirty, 5. 422. A.S. þrittig.

Threwe, *pt. s.* threw himself, fell, 5. 357.

Thridde, third, pr. 121. A.S. þridda.

Þrungen, *pt. pl.* thronged, pressed closely together, 5. 517. A.S. þringan, to press, G. and Du. *dringen.*

Thynketh, *pr. s. impers.* seems; *me thynketh* = it seems to me, pr. 165, 3. 182, 227; 1 *p. s. pers.* Thynke, I intend, 3. 95. Cf. A.S. þyncan, G. *dünken,* and A.S. þencan, G. *denken.*

Tidy, *adj.* (lit. timely) orderly, careful, 3. 320. Du. *tijdig,* seasonable, G. *zeitig,* early, ripe.

Til, *prep.* to, 5. 610. Icel. and Dan. *til,* Sw. *till.*

Tilie, *v.* to till, cultivate, pr. 120; Tilye, 6. 238; to earn by tilling, procure, 6. 235. A.S. *tilian,* Du. *telen.*

Tixt, *sb.* a text, 2. 121; Tixte, 3. 342.

To, *prep.* to; but often used in very different senses, as in *to body* = so as to have a body, 1. 62; *to man* = so as to become a man, 1. 82; after, 6. 30; upon, 5. 173; *to nonne* = as a nun, who is a nun, 5. 153; for, 7. 135. A.S. *tó,* to, for, at.

To, *adv.* too, 6. 265. A.S. *tó.*

To-, *prefix,* (1) apart; answering to G. *zer-,* O. Fris, *to-, te-,* O. H. Germ. *za-, ze-,* Mœso-Goth. *dis-,* Lat. *dis-,* with the force of in twain, asunder; examples, *to-broke, to-lugged, to-torne,* which see: (2) exceedingly, a modification of the former; example, *to-bolle:* (3) the prep. *to-* in composition, as in A.S. *tó-gang,* approach. Of this third use there is no example in Piers the Plowman, except *tofore,* but it is common in German, as in *zugang,* approach.

To-bolle, *pp.* swelled exceedingly, swelled so as to be ready to split, 5. 84. Dan. *bulne,* Sw. *bulna,* to swell; Dan. *bullen,* swollen, etymologically connected with *boil, ball, bole, bowl, belly, billow;* cf. Lat. *bulla,* G. *bolle. Bolled* occurs in Exod. ix. 31. See To-, *prefix.*

To-broke, *pp.* broken apart, broken in pieces, 7. 28. G. *zerbrechen,* to break in pieces. See To-, *prefix.*

To-fore, *prep.* S. before, in presence of. 5. 457. A.S. *tóforan.*

Toft, pr. 14, 1. 12. Here, a slightly elevated, exposed site; properly, the Su.-Goth. *tomt* is a cleared space, area, or site; cf. Dan. *tomt,* a site, toft, Dan. *toft,* an enclosed field near a farmhouse, Icel. *topt,* a farm, area. See Tome.

Togideres, together, 1. 195, 2. 83.

Toke, *pt. s.* gave, 3. 45; *toke þei on* = if they added to their wealth, 3. 85. See Take.

Tokenynge, *sb.* S. token, 5. 19.

To-kirke-ward, i.e. towards kirk or church, 5. 305.

Tolde, 1 *p. s. pr.* I counted out, reckoned, 5. 252.

Tolled, *pp.* 5. 214. Either this means *counted*, in which case it should be spelt *told* (which is not in the MSS.), or rather it is an example of the somewhat rare M.E. verb *tolle, tille, tulle,* to fondle, coax, also to draw; thus *tolled out* = drew out, were drawn out into by coaxing. That this last is the right explanation is rendered probable by the fact that some MSS. read *tilled. Tulle* occurs in Chaucer. See *Tillen, Tollen, Tullen,* in Stratmann's Dictionary.

Tolleres, *sb. pl.* collectors of tolls or dues, pr. 220.

To-lugged of, *pp.* pulled about in various directions by, 2. 216. See **To-,** *prefix.*

Tome, *sb.* leisure, 2. 185. Icel. *tóm,* leisure, *tómr,* vacant, empty, Sw. *tom,* Sc. *toom.* See **Toft.**

Toppe, *sb.* top, properly, a tuft of hair on the top of the head, 3. 139. A.S. *top,* a tuft at the top of anything; cf. G. *zopf,* a pigtail.

Torne, *v.* F. to turn, i.e. to deprave, 3. 42; to be converted, 3. 325; **Torned,** *pt. pl.* 5. 19; *pp.* 3. 337.

Totorne, *pp.* torn apart, 5. 197. See **To-,** *prefix.*

Toure, *sb.* F. tower, pr. 14, 1. 12. Lat. *turris,* W. *twr;* Devonshire *tor,* a peaked hill.

Trauaille, *sb.* F. work, toil, 7. 43.

Trauaille, *v.* F. to toil, 6. 141.

Treieth, *pr. s.* betrays, 3. 123. O.F. *trair,* Lat. *tradere.*

Tresore, *sb.* F. treasure, 1. 45; *pl.* **Tresores,** 7. 54. It. *tesoro,* Gk. θησαυρός, from τίθημι.

Trewlich, *adv.* S. truly, 7. 63.

Triacle, *sb.* a remedy, healing medicine, 1. 146, 5. 50. Lat. *theriacum,* whence O.F. *triacle,* E. *treacle*

(like *trésor,* from *thesaurus*), Gk. θηριακὰ φάρμακα, antidotes against the bite of poisonous animals, from θήρ.

Trielich, *adv.* choicely, pr. 14. F. *trier,* to pick, select.

Triennales, *sb. pl.* 7. 170, 179. See **Biennales.**

Triest, *adj.* choicest, 1. 135. F. *trier,* to select.

Trolli-lolli, 6. 118. See the note.

Troneth, *pr. s.* enthrones, places upon thrones, 1. 131.

Trowe, 1 *p. s. pr.* I trow, believe, think to be true, 1. 143, 3. 19. A.S. *treów,* true, *treówan,* to think to be true.

Trusse, *v.* to pack off, 2. 218. Sc. *turss,* to take oneself off, F. *trousser,* to pack, O.F. *torser,* to pack up, from Lat. *torquere.*

Tulyen, *v.* to till, 7. 2. See **Tilie.**

Tutour, *sb.* warden, keeper, 1. 56. Lat. *tueor,* I keep.

Tweye, *adv.* twice, 4. 22. A.S. *twýwa.*

Tweyne, *adj.* twain, two, 5. 32, 203, 317. A.S. *twegen,* which is the masculine form, as *twá* is the feminine and neuter; G. *zween.*

Tymbred, *pt. pl. subj.* would have built, 3. 85. A.S. *timbrian,* to build, A.S. *timber,* wood, Du. *timmeren,* to build.

Tyne, *v.* to lose, 1. 112. Icel. *týna,* to lose.

Tynkares, *gen. sing.* tinker's, 5. 554; **Tynkeres,** *pl.* pr. 220. Cf. W. *tincerdd,* a tinker, from *tincio,* to ring, *tinkle.*

Tythe, *sb.* a tithe, 6. 78, 94. A.S. *teóða,* the tenth.

V.

Vche a, each, pr. 207, 5. 116.

Vchone, each one, 1. 51, 2. 138.

Veille, *sb.* 5. 450. Mr. Wright

explains it by 'an old woman,' but I think it means a watcher, a waker ; just as we confuse the meanings in English, and say 'a watch' for a watcher. O.F. *veile*, Lat. *uigilia*, a vigil, watch. This is confirmed by the Harleian MS. 875, which reads—'Vigilate þe *wakere*.'

Venesoun, *sb.* venison, pr. 194. Properly it means that which is taken in hunting ; cf. F. *venaison*, Lat. *uenatio*, from *uenari*, to hunt.

Venge, *v.* F. to avenge, 5. 128. Lat. *uindicare*.

Veniaunce, *sb.* F. vengeance, 3. 258.

Vernicle, *sb.* the vernicle, 5. 530. A *vernicle* is a copy of the handkerchief of St. Veronica, on which the features of Christ were miraculously impressed. See the note.

Vesture, *sb.* F. clothing, 1. 23.

Vigilies, *sb. pl.* vigils, fasts, 5. 416. Used by Chaucer.

Vitaillers, *sb. pl.* victuallers, 2. 60.

Vitailles, *sb. pl.* victuals, 5. 443. O.F. *vitaille*, It. *vittuaglia*, from Lat. *uiuere*.

Vmwhile, *adv.* for a time, 5. 345. A.S. *ymbe*, G. *um*, about, and *hwil*, a time. Cf. S. *umquhile*.

Vnboxome, *adj.* S. disobedient, 2. 82. See **Buxome**.

Vncoupled, *pp.* unfastened, loose, pr. 162, 206. See **Coupleth**.

Vncristne, *adj. pl.* unchristian men, heathens, 1. 93.

Vnderfonge, 1 *p. s. pt.* I received, 1. 76; Vnderfongen, *pr. pl.* receive, 3. 214; *pp.* Vnderfongen, 7. 171. See **Fange**.

Vndernymeth, *pr. s.* reproves, reprehends, 5. 115. I cannot find that William uses it anywhere in the sense of 'to undertake, take possession of,' given in Mr. Wright's glossary. 'Vnderneme. *Reprehen-*

do, deprehendo, arguo, redarguo.' Prompt. Parv. See **Nym**.

Vneth, *adv.* scarcely, 4. 60. A.S. *eáð*, easy.

Vnglosed, *pp.* without a gloss or comment, 4. 145. See **Glosed**.

Vngraue, *pp.* not engraved, 4. 130.

Vnhardy, *adj.* not hardy, not bold, timid, pr. 180.

Vnkouth, *adj.* strange (lit. unknown), 7. 155. A.S. *cúð*, known.

Vnlese, *pr. pl.* unloose, unclose, pr. 213. A.S. *lýsan*, to loosen, from *léas*, loose.

Vnmoebles, *sb. pl.* immoveable property, 3. 267. See **Moebles**.

Vnsowen, *v.* to unsew, 5. 66.

Vnthende, *adj.* small, half-grown, out-of-season, 5. 177. Cf. A.S. *þeónde*, increasing, growing, powerful, from *þeón*, to flourish, thrive. Mr. Wright explains it 'unserved, without sauce,' which I think lacks proof. Some MSS. have *vnhende*.

Vntil, *prep.* to, pr. 227.

Vokates, *sb. pl.* advocates, 2. 60.

Vp, *prep.* upon, 1. 12 ; *vp gesse* = upon a guess, by guess, 5. 421.

Vpholderes, *sb. pl.* sellers of second-hand clothes and furniture, old-clothes-men, 5. 325. They were also called *upholdsters*, whence our *upholsterer*, i.e. a furniture-broker. Palsgrave has—'Uphol-star, *fripier*,' which was once the nearest French word in signification. From the vb. to *uphold*, to keep up.

Vppe, *adv.* aloft, 4. 72. A.S. *uppe* =aloft, on high.

Vs selue, ourselves, 7. 127.

Vsedestow, didst thou use, 5. 240.

Vsurè, *sb.* F. usury 5. 240, 7. 83 ; Vsurye, 2. 175.

W.

Wafrestre, *sb.* a female maker or seller of wafers, 5. 641.

Wage, v. to wager, engage, give surety, 4. 97; Waged, *pp.* 4. 100. Low Lat. *uadium*, O.F. *gage*, a pledge, connected with Mœso-Goth. *wadi*, A.S. *wed*, a pledge. See **Wedde**.

Waited, 1 *p. s. pt.* looked, 7. 139. O.F. *gaiter*, to *watch*.

Walshe, *sb.* Welshman, 5. 324. Lit. a foreigner; A.S. *wealh*, a foreigner; *wealhas*, foreigners, Welshmen. Cf. G. *wälsch*, foreign, Italian.

Wan, *pt. s.* went, *or perhaps* strove, 4. 67. Some MSS. have *wente;* cf. the Scotch use of *win.*

Wanhope, *sb.* S. despair, 2. 99, 5. 286. *Wan-* is an A.S. prefix, expressing lack, want; from *sb. wana*, deficiency; cf. E. *wane.*

Wanye, v. to wane, 7. 55. A.S. *wanian.*

War, *adj.* S. aware, 2. 8.

Wardemotes, *sb. pl.* meetings of a ward, pr. 94. Cf. *witena gemót*, i.e. meeting of wise men.

Ware þe, *imp. s.* guard thyself, 5. 452. A.S. *warian*, to be cautious.

Wareine, *sb.* a warren, pr. 163. O.F. *garene, warene,* a place for keeping animals, from O.F. *garer*, to keep. Cf. *warrant, guarantee, garrison.*

Warner, *sb.* a warrener, keeper of a warren, 5. 316. See above.

Warpe, *pt. s.* uttered, 5. 87, 369. A.S. *weorpan*, G. *werfen*, to cast.

Warrok, v. to girt, fasten with girths, 4. 20. Cf. M.E. *warlok*, a fetter, in Prompt. Parv.

Wastel, *sb.* a cake of bread of fine flour, 5. 293. O.F. *gasteau, gastel,* F. *gâteau.*

Wastoure, *sb.* F. a waster, wasteful person, 6. 154; Wastoures, *pl.* 6. 29. Cf. Lat. *uastare.*

Watt, Watte, short form of Walter 5. 30, 316.

Wawe, *pr. s. subj.* walk, go about,

7. 79. Many MSS. have *walke.* Cf. A.S. *wagian*, to *wag.*

Wax, Waxen, v. to grow, increase, 7. 55, 3. 300. See **Wex.**

Wayue, v. to lift (up), so as to open, 5. 611. Apparently to put aside, remove. Dr. Stratmann prints *Wayue*, and refers it to O. Fr. *weiver* or *guesver*, which is our word to *waive;* yet the Troybook has *Wayne* six times, meaning to raise, lift, wind up. However, the word should perhaps be printed *wayue* there also.

Wayte, v. F. to watch, look after, serve, 5. 202; Wayted, *pp.* 5. 551. See **Waited.**

Webbe, *sb.* a web, thing woven, 5. 111. See note.

Webbe, *sb.* a female weaver, 5. 215. We find A.S. *webbe*, a female weaver, as well as *webbestre;* and *webbere* for a male weaver.

Wedde, *sb.* S. pledge, gage, wager, 3. 201, 5. 244. See **Wage.**

Wederes, *sb. pl.* weathers, storms, 6. 326. A.S. *weder.*

Wedes, *sb. pl.* weeds, i. e. clothes, 6. 113. A.S. *wǽd*, apparel.

Wehe, *sb.* a word intended to denote by its sound the neighing of a horse, 4. 22. W. *wihi*, with same meaning. Cf. Chaucer, C.T. 4064.

Wel, *adv.* well; used as an adj. 3. 65, 152: (2) very, 3. 161; *wel worse*=much worse, 5. 114.

Welche, *sb.* 5. 199. It is perhaps hardly possible to settle the meaning of this word, respecting which MSS. differ. The Vernon MS. has *walk*, which is intelligible; the Trin. MS. (Mr. Wright's) has *welþe*, which Mr. Wright explains by *weli*, which is not satisfactory. The Rawl. MS. has *welsch;* but the best suggestion is in MS. Trin. R. 3. 15, which has—*þat walsshe scarlet.* i. e. Welsh scarlet, or red flannel. I think that *Welche* means flannel.

Wende, *v.* to wend, go, 6. 60; Wenden, 2. 160; *pr. s.* Wendeth, 4. 105; *pr. pl.* Wenden, pr. 162; *pt. pl.* Wenten, 4. 76; *pp.* Went, gone, 6. 207; turned, changed, 3. 280; *imp. s.* Wende, go, 3. 264. A.S. *wendan*, to go, turn; pt. t. *ic wende*; E. *wend, went*; G. *wen-den*, to turn.

Wende. See **Wene**.

Wene, *v.* to ween, imagine, think, 3. 300; 1 *p. s. pt.* Wende, I thought, 5. 238; 2 *p. s. pt.* Wendest, thou didst ween, 3. 191. A.S. *wénan* (pt. t. *ic wénde*), G. *wähnen*, to think; from A.S. *wén*, thought, Du. *waan.*

Wepe, *v.* S. to weep, 5. 62; *pt. s.* Wepe, 5. 470; Wepte, 5. 480; *pt. pl.* Wepten, 7. 37.

Wepne, *sb.* S. a weapon, 3. 304.

Werche, 7. 198. See **Worche**.

Were, *v.* S. to wear, 3. 293.

Were, *pt. s. and pl. subj.* should be, might be, were, 5. 167, 6. 213, &c. A.S. *wesan*, to be.

Wernard, *sb.* F. a deceiver, liar, 3. 179; *pl.* Wernardes, 2. 128. Roquefort has—'*Guernart*, trompeur;' cf. M.E. *werne*, to deny.

Wesshen, *pt. pl.* S. washed, 2. 220.

Weueres, *sb. pl.* weavers, pr. 219.

Wex, *pt. s.* waxed, grew, 3. 328, 5. 286. A.S. *weaxan*, pt. t. *ic weox*. Cf. G. *wachsen*, Du. *wassen.*

Weye, *v.* to weigh, 5. 204; *pt. s.* Wey3ed, 5. 218; *pp.* Weyen, I. 176. A.S. *wegan*, to move, weigh; cf. E. *wag, waggle.*

Weye, *sb.* a wey, a certain *weight*, 5. 93. A *wey* of butter or cheese varies from 2 to 3 cwt. A wey of *Essex* cheese was 3 cwt., whilst of *Suffolk* cheese it was less, viz. 256 lbs. Arnold's Chron. p. 263. Cf. the preceding word.

Weyues, *sb. pl.* waifs, pr. 94. O. F. *gayver, guever, guesver*, to *waive*, abandon.

Whas, whose, 2. 18.

Whennes, *adv.* whence, 5. 532.

Where, *conj.* whether (a common contraction), pr. 171, 5. 283.

Which a, what sort of a, 7. 146; *pl.* Whiche, what sort of, 4. 25.

Whiles, *adv.* whilst, 6. 320. Gen. case of A.S. *hwil*, a time.

Wiket, *sb.* a wicket-gate, a small gate or shutter made within a large door, 5. 611. F. *guichet*, O. F. *guischet, wiket*; W. *gwiced.*

Wikke, *adj.* wicked, 5. 229. A.S. *wican*, to become weak, decay; G. *weichen*, to yield, *weich*, soft, weak.

Wikked, *adj.* rotten, bad (because too soft and yielding), 6. 1, 7. 27. See **Wikke**.

Wil, *pr. s.* wishes, 5. 40.

Wilne, *v.* to desire, 5. 187; *pr. s.* Wilneth, 4. 163; *pr. pl.* Wilne, 1. 8. A.S. *wilnian.*

Wiltow, wilt thou, 5. 310; *wiltow or neltow* = wilt thou or wilt thou not, 6. 158.

Wissen, *v.* to teach, tell, shew, 5. 540; Wisse, 5. 562; 1 *p. s. pr.* Wisse, 1. 42, 5. 147; *pt. s.* Wissed, 6. 167. A.S. *wissian, wisian*, to guide, shew the way.

Wist, knew. See next word.

Wite, *v.* to know, 4. 139, 5. 561; Wyte, 3. 74; Witen, to learn, ascertain, 6. 213; 1 *p. s. pt.* Wist, pr. 12; Wyst, 5. 272; *pt. s.* Wist, 7. 71; *pr. s. subj.* Wite, 5. 606; *imp. pl.* Witeth, 2. 74. A.S. *witan*, to know, *ic wát*, I wot, I know, *ic wiste*, I knew, *witen*, known; Du. *weten*, G. *wissen*. See **Wote**.

Witen, *v.* to preserve, keep, 7. 35; Wite God, may God defend us, 5. 641. From the same root as the last; so Mœso-Goth. *witan* (pt. t. *ik wissa*), to know, and *witan* (pt. t. *ik witaida*), to keep, both from the sense of *seeing;* cf. Lat. *uidere,* Gk. ἰδεῖν, εἰδέναι.

With, *prep.* S. together with; *also* by, by means of, 3. 2. *With þat,* provided that, 5. 74; withal, moreover, 5. 307. See note to 2. 31.

With-halt, *pr. s.* withholdeth, 5. 559.

Withewyndes, *gen. sing.* of Withe-wynde, i. e. the wild convolvulus or bindweed, 5. 525. A. S. *wiðwinde,* convolvulus or bindweed. 'Woodbinde, binde-weede, or *with-ie-winde,* because it windes about other plantes.'—Minsheu.

Witterly, *adv.* unmistakeably, with certainty, clearly, 3. 175, 5. 562. Cf. Dan. *vitterlig,* publicly known, A. S. *witodlice,* verily.

Wiȝte, *sb.* S. a wight, person, pr. 207, 1. 63; **Wyȝte,** 5. 520.

Wiȝtliche, *adv.* nimbly, actively, 2. 208, 6. 21. Sw. *vig,* agile.

Wo, *used as adj.* woful, 5. 3. Cf. 3. 152.

Woke, *sb.* week, 5. 93. A. S. *wuce,* G. *woche.*

Wol, *pr. s.* will, 5. 250; **Wolde,** I *p. s. pt.* would, 3. 51; *pt. s.* would, has desired, 1. 13, 6. 251. **Woldestow,** if thou wouldst, 3. 49. A. S. *ic will,* Lat. *uolo;* pt. t. *ic wolde;* cf. G. *wollte.*

Wolle, *sb.* S. wool, 6. 13.

Wollen, *adj.* woollen, 5. 215; *used as sb.* 1. 18.

Wollewebsteres, *sb. pl.* wool-weavers, pr. 219.

Wolt, wilt, 2. 44. See **Wol.**

Woltow, wilt thou, 3. 117.

Wolues-kynnes, of the kin or nature of wolves, 6. 163.

Wombe, *sb.* S. the belly, 3. 84, 193. Sc. *wame.*

Wonden, *pt. pl.* S. wound, 2. 220.

Wones, *sb. pl.* habitations, 3. 234. See next word.

Wonye, *v.* to dwell, 2. 106; *pr. s.*

Wonieth, 1. 63; **Woneth,** 2. 232. A. S. *wunian,* G. *wohnen,* Du. *wonen,* to dwell.

Worche, *v.* S. to work, 6. 120; *pr. pl.* Worcheth, 3. 80; **Worchen,** 7. 91; *imp. pl.* Worcheth, 2. 133; *pt. s.* Wrouȝte, 6. 115; *pt. pl.* Wrouȝten, 6. 111; *pp.* Wrouȝt, created, 7. 98.

Worthe, *v.* to be, pr. 187 (see the note); Worth, *pr. s. as future,* shall be, 1. 186, 2. 43, 3. 33, 5. 160, 6. 165, 7. 51; 2 *p.* Worth, mayst be, 1. 26. See **Yworth.**

Wote, 1 *p. s. pr.* I wot, I know, 5. 180, 6. 132; *pr. s.* knows, 2. 77, 5. 181, 6. 132; *pr. pl.* know, 3. 329; Wot god = God knows, 4. 37; god it wote = God knows it, pr. 43. See **Wite.**

Wowed, *pt. s.* S. wooed, coaxed, intreated, 4. 74.

Wowes, *sb. pl.* walls, 3. 61. A. S. *wáh,* a wall.

Wratthe, *v.* S. to enrage, 2. 116; 2 *p. s. pr.* Wratthest þe, makest thyself angry, art angry, 3. 182.

Wreke, *v.* S. to wreak, avenge, 5. 85; *pp.* Wroke, avenged, 2. 194.

Wronge, *pt. s.* wrung, 6. 177; wrung (her hands), 2. 236. A. S. *wringan,* to wring, squeeze, pt. t. *ic wrang.*

Wrouȝt, Wrouȝten. See **Worche.**

Wy, *sb.* a man, 5. 540. A. S. *wiga,* a warrior, *wig,* war.

Wyght, 5. 116. See **Wiȝte.**

Wyke, *sb.* week, 6. 258. See **Woke.**

Wyltow, wilt thou, 3. 110.

Wyn, *sb.* S. wine, pr. 228.

Wynkynge, *sb.* nodding, slumber, 5. 3; Wynkyng, 5. 368. A. S. *wincian,* to nod, *wink.*

Wynneth, *imp. pl.* earn by labour, 6.322. A.S. *winnan,* to labour, *win.*

Wyntre, *sb. pl.* winters, i. e. years, 3. 39; Wynter, 1. 99.

Wyte, Wyst. See **Wite.**

Wytte, *sb.* S. wit, intelligence, pr.114.

Wytterly, 5. 272. See **Witterly**.

Wyuen, *gen. pl.* women's, 5. 29; *nom.* **Wyues**, women, 5. 570.

Wyȝte, 5. 520. See **Wiȝte**.

Y.

Y-, *prefix*, answering to the G. and A.S. *ge-*, Goth. *ga-*, which is etymologically the same with L. *cum, com-, con-*, with. It is usually prefixed to past participles (see below), but also to past tenses (see **Yrifled, Yspilte**), to infinitives (see **Yworth**), and to adjectives (see **Yliche, Ywar**).

Ybake, baked, 6. 312; **Ybaken**, 6. 184.

Ybette, beaten, 4. 93.

Yblamed, blamed, 3. 281.

Yblessed, blessed, 7. 13; **Yblissed**, pr. 77.

Ybore, born, 2. 130.

Ybounde, Ybounden, bound, pr. 178, 5. 524.

Ybouȝt, bought, pr. 176.

Ybroken, broken, pr. 71.

Ychose, chosen, 5. 331.

Yclothed, clothed, l. 3, 2. 8.

Yclouted, patched, 6. 61.

Ycrammed, crammed, pr. 41.

Ycrounede, crowned, 2. 10.

Ydel, in phr. *an ydel* = idly, in vain, 5. 580.

Ydronke, drunk, 6. 281.

Yeten (*y-eten*), eaten, 1. 152.

Yfolwed, followed, 3. 39.

Yfouȝte, fought, 6. 154.

Yglobbed, gulped down, 5. 346. Cf. E. *gulp*, Du. *gulpen*, to swallow eagerly, Sw. *glupsk*, voracious.

Ygo, gone, 5. 207.

Ygraced, thanked, 6. 126. Lat. *gratiæ*, thanks.

Ygraunted, granted, 7. 8.

Yhasped, hasped, fastened as with a hasp, 1. 195.

Yholden, holden, esteemed, 1. 84.

Yhote, named, 1. 63; bidden, 2. 218. See **Hat** and **Hote**.

Yhowted, hooted at, 2. 218.

Ylakked, blamed, 2.21. See **Lakke**.

Yleye, lain, 5. 82.

Yliche, *adj.* like, alike, 5. 494 (see l. 489); **Ylike**, 1. 91. A.S. *gelic*, like, Goth. *galeiks*.

Ymade, made, 2. 43, 5. 255.

Ymaked, made, 2. 72, 6. 189.

Ymaried, married, 2. 39.

Ymped, 1 *p. s. pt.* I grafted, engrafted, 5. 138.

Ympes, *sb. pl.* shoots grafted in, 5. 137. W. *imp*, a shoot, scion; A.S *impan*, to engraft, of Gk. origin.

Ynowe, *adv.* S. enough, 2. 162.

Ypassed, past, pr. 189.

Ypliȝte, pledged, plighted, 5. 202. A.S. *pliht*, a pledge.

Yrens, *sb. pl.* irons, 4. 85; **Yrnes**, 6. 138.

Yrifled, 1 *p. s. pt.* rifled, robbed, 5. 234. O.F. *riffler*, to snatch. Cf. Lat. *rapere*.

Ysein, seen, pr. 160; **Yseiȝen**, 5. 4.

Yserued, (1) served, suited, 5. 341, 419; (2) deserved, 6. 89. 'I haue serued þe deth' = I have deserved death; William of Palerne, 4352.

Yshewed, shewn, declared, 2. 134.

Yshryue, shriven, 5. 91.

Ysouȝt, sought, pr. 50.

Ysowen, sown, 5. 550.

Yspilte, 1 *p. s. pt.* wasted, 5. 380; *pp.* 5. 442. See **Spilte**.

Ysue, *sb.* F. issue, 5. 265.

Ytailled, scored on a tally, 5. 429. See **Taile**.

Ytermyned, decided upon, settled upon determinately, 1. 97. Spelt *determined* in a parallel passage in Dep. of Rich. II, p. 11, l. 18 (Camden Soc.); see P. Plowman, C-text, p. 481, l. 97.

Ytried, tried, tested, 1. 133; **Ytryed**, 1. 205. See **Triest**.

Yuel, *adv.* ill, 5. 168.

Yuel, *adj.* ill ; *also* hard (*both in one line*), 5. 121 ; difficult, 6. 50.

Ywar, *adj.* wary, cautious, pr. 174, 1. 42. A. S. *gewær*, wary.

Ywedded, wedded, 2. 42.

Ywonne, won, 5. 93.

Yworth, *v.* to be, 6. 84 ; Yworþe, 6. 228. G. *werden*, A. S. *weorð-an*, Goth. *wairthan.* See note to pr. 187.

Ywounden, wound, bound round, 5. 525.

Ywrouȝte, wrought, done, 4. 68.

ȝ

ȝaf, *pt. s.* gave, 1. 15, 6. 201.

ȝarketh hym, *pt. s.* prepares himself, gets himself ready, 7. 80. A. S. *gearcian*, to make ready ; M. E. *yare*, ready ; cf. E. *gear.*

ȝatis, *sb. pl.* gates, pr. 104.

ȝe, yea, 3. 111, 5. 254, 563, 6. 38, 233. See ȝus.

ȝe, *pron. pl. nom.* ye, pr. 198 ; *acc.* ȝow, you, pr. 199.

ȝede, 1 *p. s. pt.* went, 7. 142 ; 2 *p.* ȝedest, 5. 504 ; *pl.* ȝede, pr. 40. A. S. *ic éode*, used as pt. t. of *gán*, to go ; cf. Goth. *ik iddja*, pt. t. of *gaggan*, to go ; see note, p. 94.

ȝelde, *v.* to yield, render, 7. 188 ; ȝelden, 7. 83 ; 2 *p. s. pr.* ȝeldest, payest, 5. 296 ; *pr. s. imp. or subj.* ȝelde, repay, 6. 129 ; *pres. part.*

ȝeldyng, paying, 2. 104. A. S. *gildan*, to pay.

ȝeode, *pt. s.* went, 1. 73. See ȝede.

ȝerdes, *sb. pl.* yards, 5. 214 ; rods, 4. 117. A. S. *gyrd*, a staff, rod.

ȝere, *sb. pl.* years, 5. 208, 6. 325 ; ȝeres, 7. 18 ; ȝeris, pr. 65.

ȝeresȝyues, *sb. pl.* year-gifts, annual presents, 3. 99.

ȝerne, 2 *p. s. subj.* yearn for, long for, 1. 35. A. S. *geornian.*

ȝerne, *adv.* eagerly, 4. 74, 6. 299. A. S. *georne*, earnestly.

ȝet, *conj. and adv.* yet, 1. 136 ; besides, 7. 83. A. S. *git, get.*

ȝeue, 2 *p. s. pr.* ye give, 4. 170 ; *pr. s. imp.* ȝif, may he give, 3. 165, 5. 107. See ȝiue.

ȝif, *conj.* if, pr. 37. A. S. *gif.*

ȝiftes, *sb. pl.* gifts, 3. 99 ; ȝiftis, 6. 42. A. S. *gift.*

ȝiue, *v.* to give, 7. 71 ; *pr. s.* ȝiueth, 7. 80 ; *pp.* ȝiue, 5. 390 ; ȝoue, 2. 31. A. S. *gifan*, pt. t. *ic gæf*, pp. *gifen*; G. *geben*, Du. *geven.*

ȝouthe, *sb.* S. youth, 5. 241, 7. 93. A. S. *geóguð.*

ȝow-self, *pron. acc. pl.* yourselves, 2. 38.

ȝus, *adv.* yes, 5. 125, 233, 643. It answers questions that contain or involve a negative, and is thus distinguished from the affirmative particle ȝe; it is also of greater force, and signifies declaration of opinion, whereas ȝe merely assents.

ȝut, *adv.* yet, pr. 185.

ADDENDUM.

It has been kindly suggested that the verb to *clow*, meaning (in the school-slang at Winchester) to box the ears, may explain the verb *clowe* in our author. I would rather identify the former word with the prov. E. to *clout.* Cf. '*Clowe*, to scratch, to beat. "She gev him a *clowin.*"'— Dickinson's Cumberland Glossary.

INDEX

TO THE

PRINCIPAL SUBJECTS EXPLAINED IN THE NOTES.

For explanations of words, see the preceding Glossarial Index. A few words are also more particularly explained in the Notes; these are indicated in the following Index by being printed *in italics*. The references are to the pages of the volume.